Land Tenure and Natural Resource Management

**Other Books Published in Cooperation with
the International Food Policy Research Institute**

IFPRI

*Intrahousehold Resource Allocation in Developing Countries: Models,
Methods, and Policy*
Edited by Lawrence Haddad, John Hoddinott, and Harold Alderman

*Sustainability, Growth, and Poverty Alleviation: A Policy and Agroecological
Perspective*
Edited by Steven A. Vosti and Thomas Reardon

Famine in Africa: Causes, Responses, and Prevention
By Joachim von Braun, Tesfaye Teklu, and Patrick Webb

Paying for Agricultural Productivity
Edited by Julian M. Alston, Philip G. Pardey, and Vincent H. Smith

*Out of the Shadow of Famine: Evolving Food Markets and Food Policy in
Bangladesh*
Edited by Raisuddin Ahmed, Steven Haggblade, and Tawfiq-e-Elahi
Chowdhury

Agricultural Science Policy: Changing Global Agendas
Edited by Julian M. Alston, Philip G. Pardey, and Michael J. Taylor

Land Tenure and Natural Resource Management

A Comparative Study of Agrarian Communities in Asia and Africa

EDITED BY KEIJIRO OTSUKA AND FRANK PLACE

Published for the International Food Policy Research Institute

The Johns Hopkins University Press
Baltimore and London

The Johns Hopkins University Press
2715 North Charles Street
Baltimore, Maryland 21218-4363
www.press.jhu.edu

International Food Policy Research Institute
2033 K Street, NW
Washington, D.C. 20006
(202) 862-5600
www.ifpri.org

LIBRARY OF CONGRESS CATALOGING-IN-PUBLICATION DATA
Land tenure and natural resource management : a comparative study of agrarian communities in
Asia and Africa / edited by Keijiro Otsuka and Frank Place.
    p.   cm.
    "Published for the International Food Policy Research Institute."
    Includes bibliographical references and index.
    ISBN 0-8018-6746-0 (cloth : alk. paper) — ISBN 0-8018-6747-9 (pbk. : alk. paper)
    1. Land tenure—Asia.   2. Land tenure—Africa.   3. Land use, Rural—Environmental
aspects—Asia.   4. Land use, Rural—Environmental aspects—Africa.   5. Forest
management—Asia.   6. Forest management—Africa.   7. Natural resources—Asia—
Management.   8. Natural resources—Africa—Management.   I. Otsuka, Keijiro.   II. Place,
Frank.   III. International Food Policy Research Institute.
HD843.2 .L36   2001
333.7'095—dc21   2001029330

A catalog record for this book is available from the British Library.

To Peter Hazell

Contents

PART IV   Common Property Management

PART V   Conclusion

Figures

Tables

Foreword

When rising populations put pressure on limited land and other natural resources, the result—in the absence of technological and institutional innovations—is poverty and unsustainable use of natural resources. Poor farmers who suffer from food shortages and food insecurity often seek to expand cultivation by cutting down trees. Such deforestation is common in poor regions of developing countries, and it seriously degrades the natural resource base. To achieve sustainable development, policymakers urgently need knowledge on how to prevent excessive use of natural resources, enrich the natural resource base, and reduce food insecurity and rural poverty. The International Food Policy Research Institute (IFPRI) aims to provide such knowledge for the purpose of supporting appropriate policies. We recognize that there is still a huge gap between what we know and what we *need* to know to achieve sustainable management of natural resources and food security.

In 1993 IFPRI initiated research on land tenure and the management of land and trees in a number of countries in Africa and Asia. The research focuses on how land tenure or land rights institutions affect the use and allocation of natural resources. Researchers have collected detailed data from communities and households, because taking practical steps toward achieving sustainable development requires information on how these groups, who ultimately determine the institutions governing the use of natural resources, behave. Study sites were located in seven countries and characterized by different physical, social, and political environments. Generally, however, the sites consist of agriculturally marginal, hilly and mountainous areas, where people are commonly very poor and where tree resources are important components of people's livelihood.

In the summer of 1998, collaborators, representative researchers in the countries covered by the project, and experts in natural resource management gathered at an international workshop at Tokyo Metropolitan University. Preliminary results of the country case studies were reported, and constructive and insightful discussions took place. *Land Tenure and Natural Resource Management* presents the final research findings of the project.

The book makes clear that to reduce poverty and exploitative use of natural resources, it is imperative to manage natural resources more *efficiently*. The fundamental research question, then, is how to identify economic, social, and political forces conducive to an efficient outcome. This book answers the question by means of international collaborative research, and its findings make important contributions to the literature on natural resource management.

Not only does *Land Tenure and Natural Resource Management* add to scientific knowledge, but even more important, it contributes to the formation of sensible development policies. Policymakers who seek to achieve sustainable development have had difficulty devising appropriate policies to reverse unsustainable trends, as they have too little information on the role of land tenure institutions in managing natural resources and on how these institutions are changing. The final chapter summarizes critical policy implications in a way that policymakers and other noneconomists can grasp. We anticipate that this book will stimulate further discussions among a large circle of researchers and policymakers on the most appropriate policies for the sustainable development of agriculturally marginal areas.

Per Pinstrup-Andersen
Director General
International Food Policy Research Institute

Preface

This volume represents a synthesis of the multicountry collaborative research project titled "Land Tenure and the Management of Land and Trees: Community and Household Case Studies from Asia and Africa," organized by the International Food Policy Research Institute (IFPRI). Although there has been considerable recognition of land degradation and deforestation at the global level, we felt that hardly any attention had been given to understanding these changes and their causes at the landscape and household level. Therefore, these undesirable trends were likely to continue unless solid quantitative research was undertaken to identify fundamental causes of natural resource problems and options for their solution. We formed this study around the issue of property rights, a key factor in achieving efficient long-term management of forestland, rangeland, and farmland, as well as tree resources and other minor forest products.

The guiding principle of this project is "generalization through rigorous analysis of quantitative field data." In order to derive generalizable conclusions, this project covers such diverse areas as southwestern Ghana, north-central Uganda, almost the whole of Malawi, western Sumatra (Indonesia), northern Vietnam, both hill and inner Tarai regions of Nepal, and central Japan. Since land tenure is highly complex and elusive, there was a danger that such wide geographical coverage might prevent a sufficiently deep understanding of reality. We therefore sought the most knowledgeable and determined collaborators in each site. The collaborators spent many days at the research sites to grasp the structure of the land tenure institutions and the practice of natural resource management, identify the most critical issues, and ensure the collection of high-quality data. During a series of formal and informal surveys, all the collaborators made every effort to facilitate dialogues on facts, theories, and methodologies. Together they developed appropriate insights, translated the insights into testable hypotheses, and designed appropriate survey methodologies. Added to this, the project coordinator spent more than six months in the field.

A unique feature of this study is the use of primary data sets collected by different survey methodologies and the combined use of secondary data and data based on aerial photographs, wherever these were available (that is, in Japan, Malawi, Nepal, and Uganda). Also unique was the attention paid to dynamics and the measurement of changes in land use and natural resources. In fact, we conducted (1) extensive community surveys, (2) extensive forest surveys, (3) supplementary brief individual household surveys, (4) intensive household surveys in selected communities, and (5) intensive forest user surveys. Justification for each survey methodology is provided in the text. It suffices here to point out that we attempted to apply the most suitable survey methodology for the issues addressed with due consideration of the availability of aerial photographs and other secondary information. We are aware that new high-resolution satellites will greatly enhance the ability to measure changes in the quantity and quality of natural resources in the future. We hope that the survey methodologies developed in this volume will stimulate further quantitative research on why such changes have occurred and how they may be modified through policy and institutional change. We are hopeful that the compilation of quantitative case studies will eventually help resolve the problem of natural resource management in agrarian communities in developing countries.

This volume focuses on the two major land tenure institutions, the customary land tenure institution and the common property system. These institutions are by no means static, rigid, and culturally predetermined; they are subject to change. What are their characteristics? What factors affect the evolution of these institutions? What are the consequences of such evolutionary changes on land use and natural resource management? Are customary land tenure institutions efficient in allocating land and other natural resources? Under what conditions is the common property regime viable and efficient in forest resource management? These are some of the key issues to be addressed in this study.

An originally unexpected but possibly important contribution of this volume may be to elucidate the similarity and the commonality of the land tenure issues and natural resource management across Africa and Asia. In order to draw broad conclusions on institutional changes and their consequences on economic development, we now believe that a comparative study of Africa and Asia is useful. For instance, we found many similarities in the evolution of customary land tenure institutions and its consequences in Ghana and Sumatra. A comparison of common property forest management in Japan, Nepal, and Malawi was useful to identify the effectiveness and the limitation of common property forest management. It seems to us that excessive geographical division of labor exists between African and Asian specialists in our professions.

We have benefited from useful comments and suggestions at various stages of research from numerous researchers, government officials, farmers, and village chiefs. In particular, we would like to acknowledge the support and encouragement we received from Per Pinstrup-Andersen, Pedro Sanchez, Peter Hazell, Yujiro Hayami, and Alain de Janvry. Special thanks are due to participants in the Tokyo workshop held in June 1998: Aulia Aruran, Iwan Azis, George Benneh, Robert T. Deacon, Peter Dewees, Jonna P. Estudillo, Gershon Feder, Nobuhiko Kaho, Michael Kirk, W. Kisamba-Mugerwa, Govind P. Koirala, Masanori Kondo, Takashi Kurosaki, William Magrath, Douglas McGuire, Yasuhiro Mitshui, Motoe Miyamoto, Davies Ng'ong'ola, John Pender, Brent Swallow, Ganesh Thapa, and Dao The Tuan. We have also benefited from comments and suggestions from Robert Allen, John Aluma, Masahiko Aoki, Brad Barham, Hans P. Binswanger, Jutta Breyer, Daniel W. Bromley, Michael Carter, Ian Coxhead, Partha Dasgupta, Gaurav Datt, Robert E. Evenson, Marcel Fafchamps, Bob Green, Merilee S. Grindle, N. S. Jodha, D. Gale Johnson, Ramon Lopez, Ruth Meinzen-Dick, Vincent Mkandawire, Yair Mundlak, Ken Neils, Jeffrey Nugent, Elinor Ostrom, Robert Paarlberg, Jean-Philippe Platteau, Gustav Ranis, Thomas Reardon, Sherman Robinson, Mark Rosegrant, Scott Rozelle, Elizabeth Sadoulet, Sara Scherr, T. Paul Schultz, Tetsushi Sonobe, T. N. Srinivasan, Steve Vosti, Michael Wohlgenant, and Manfred Zeller. Finally, we would like to express our gratitude to Ellen Payongayong for assistance in data collection and processing and Beverly Abreu, Audrey Abernathy, and Heidi Fritschel for editorial assistance.

This project has been supported by a research grant from the Government of Japan to IFPRI and supplementary grants from the Danish International Development Agency (DANIDA), the Department for International Development (UK), the Rockefeller Foundation, and the Sumitomo Foundation.

This research project began in October 1993, when the two coeditors were brought together by Peter Hazell. Peter displayed his unsurpassed wisdom and judgment in helping to formulate and guide this project. Without his support, this project would not have been possible. We dedicate this book to Peter Hazell to express our sincere appreciation and the respect we have for him.

Land Tenure and Natural Resource Management

PART I

Introduction

1 Issues and Theoretical Framework

KEIJIRO OTSUKA AND FRANK PLACE

In much of the developing world, poverty remains as much of a problem in the early twenty-first century as it did several decades ago. Poverty is particularly acute in rural areas, where it is estimated that approximately 80 percent of the poor in developing countries currently reside (World Bank 1990). Annual growth in agriculture value-added in low-income countries (excluding China and India) was 3.0 percent in the 1980s and 2.5 percent in the 1990s, which was on average only slightly above the rural population growth rate (World Bank 2000). High population growth rates coupled with poor performance within nonagricultural employment sectors has created unprecedented pressure on rural natural resources (Cleaver and Schreiber 1994; Hayami 1997), resulting in the conversion of ever more marginal lands into agriculture. Several decades of conversion and lackluster agricultural performance have left the majority of rural areas, particularly those in Sub-Saharan Africa, in states characterized by low-input and low-output agriculture with depleted soil bases and depleted supplies of fuelwood and other tree products.

The conversion and degradation of forests and woodlands continue, though rates have abated somewhat in certain regions. Loss in forestland was estimated at 0.9 percent per year throughout the 1980s and 0.7 percent in the 1990s in Africa (World Resources Institute et al. [hereafter cited as WRI] 1998). It is estimated that between 1960 and 1990, 30 percent (of 1960 levels) of tropical forests were cleared in Asia and 17 percent in Africa (WRI 1998). Pressure on woody land remains strong owing to demand for agricultural land, logging, and energy needs. Little progress has been made in replacing wood as the primary source for energy in Africa (World Bank 1996).

Land use change need not be alarming if the new uses are productive and sustainable. However, there is strong evidence that much land has become degraded. Overgrazing has been the chief culprit of land degradation in Africa,

We are particularly grateful for valuable comments on an earlier version by Michael Carter, Per Pinstrup-Andersen, Partha Dasgupta, Sherman Robinson, N. S. Jodha, Merilee S. Grindle, and Robert Paarlberg.

contributing to more than 200 million hectares of degraded land (WRI 1998). Agricultural land has been subjected to degrading practices as well, and nearly 40 percent of such land worldwide has been estimated to be degraded (WRI 1998). Degraded agricultural land amounts to 120 million hectares in Africa and slightly more than 200 million hectares in Asia. Degradation occurs in the form of erosion, mainly due to rain-induced runoff, and soil quality loss. Stoorvogel, Smaling, and Janssen (1993) estimate large annual nutrient losses from African soils accumulating to 660 kilograms of nitrogen and 75 kilograms of phosphorus per hectare over a 30-year period. This is mainly due to continued cultivation with very limited use of nutrient inputs by farmers.

These gloomy natural resource trends are serious well beyond their environmental implications: they jeopardize the already fragile livelihoods of rural households in the developing world. Poor households in many marginal areas are no longer able to open up new lands because forests and woodlands have disappeared in previous massive conversion into agriculture. Farmers are also no longer able to practice traditional long fallows because of reduced farm sizes. They also have difficulty obtaining drinking water, fuelwood for cooking meals, and other basic forest resources. The result is greater expenditure of labor (or scarce cash) for the acquisition of inferior resource products (for example, lower-quality fuelwood).

Since the attainment of strategies for urban and rural nonfarm development continues to be beyond the short-term reach of many countries, many communities and policymakers are now realizing the vital importance of maintaining the integrity of the rural natural resource base. In most developing countries, policymakers are thus now grappling with creating a policy environment that fosters economic growth and provides opportunities for the poor to escape from poverty while also maintaining or enhancing the natural resource base. The major information gap in achieving this difficult task is a lack of understanding of how policies affect the management of the natural resource base.

In the remainder of this chapter, we first motivate the importance of the study of property rights in the context of natural resource management. Second, we highlight what we feel are the important contributions that this study brings to the base of knowledge on these issues. Next, we specify major research objectives and develop a general theoretical framework, leading to the development of our major hypotheses.

The Critical Role of Property Rights

Getting property rights institutions correct is the most compelling policy to resolve at the outset (Deacon 1994). This is so because property rights affect the way in which other policies will work. In the extreme, if there are no property rights over a resource—that is, if there is a situation of open access—changes in prices and other policies will do little to overturn the strong incentives for mining this resource before others deplete it. Similarly, in areas where property rights over surrounding resources are poorly defined, road construction may lead to massive resource degradation. In contrast, when property rights are well defined, the development of roads can lead to improved management of the resource base, and users can profit from improved access to markets.

The use and allocation of forestlands, woodlands, rangelands, and croplands are governed by property rights institutions or land tenure systems, ranging from communal ownership of land to state ownership, common property, and private ownership.[1] Individual land rights under the communal system are restricted. The usufruct right of individual members of the community is usually established, but the rights to transfer, including sales and leasing, are vested in the extended family, clan, or community. Individual land rights are generally more restricted under state ownership, whereby nobody has clear rights to use the state-owned land, unless the state grants clear property rights to individuals, such as through a leasehold. Likewise, the rights of individuals are restricted by the larger group under a common property regime. It is clear that the incentives to preserve natural resources and to invest in trees and other land improvements for future benefits will be thwarted without well-established property rights, be it individual, family, or group ownership, simply because the future benefits will not otherwise accrue to those who manage them (Mendelsohn 1994). As populations grow and markets penetrate into rural areas, demand for individual property rights over resources grows, and the communal and state ownership systems face serious difficulties.

This does not necessarily imply that a private ownership system with clear land title is socially most desirable. For example, negative externalities, such as soil erosion, may arise under the private ownership system, when forestlands are opened up and newly brought into cultivation. Private ownership may create an inequitable distribution of the benefits from natural resources. Furthermore, farmers may not be able to protect their own properties if it is costly to exclude other users. By definition, this is likely to be the case if resources are common-pool type, that is, those resources for which exclusion of nonowners from use is difficult or costly. In these cases, common property regimes with communal rules and regulations on the use and extraction of natural resources may be socially more desirable (Gardner, Ostrom, and Walker 1990; Ostrom 1990).

The management of nonagricultural natural resources interacts with agriculture in a number of ways. The management of forests, woodland, and rangeland affects the efficiency of crop farming through the supply of animal feeds leading to draft power and manure and through their effects on the production environment (for instance, soil erosion). On the other hand, forests and wood-

---

1. There is no established taxonomy of property rights institutions in the literature. See subsection "Characteristics of Land Tenure Institutions" below.

lands compete with grazing and cropland, as they are alternative ways of using land (for example, Kaimowitz 1995). When the food supply is insecure, poor farmers tend to destroy forests to expand crop area or overuse rangeland to increase livestock production. Forests and woodlands can also harbor pests and rodents that are harmful to livestock and crop production. Thus, there are clear links between property rights on nonagricultural land and the management of agricultural land. The linkage between poverty, intensification of agriculture, and natural resource management is a key issue that needs urgent analytical attention (Pinstrup-Anderson and Pandya-Lorch 1994).

The Contribution of This Study

While the data depicting natural resource problems are profuse and striking, they are often not sufficiently detailed to provide policymakers with useful recommendations. One of the valuable contributions of this study will be to provide clearer indicators of natural resource problems, most especially as they pertain to the management of trees and agricultural land. For instance, national-level deforestation rates, the most widely publicized indicators of forest management, are useful in demonstrating potential problems but, because of highly varying situations within countries, not very useful in developing solutions. Only by determining the conditions under which relatively more excessive deforestation is taking place can one then begin to identify more fundamental causes. This in turn requires a focus at an appropriate scale, certainly below that of a nation and above that of a household.

For the sake of identifying causes of inefficient uses of land and trees, this multicountry comparative study goes well beyond the current state of knowledge, in terms of both statistical rigor and breadth of geographical coverage. The combined use of community and household studies integrating information from remote sensing and surveys is unique. Further, the quantification of the information ensured that rigorous statistical testing of hypotheses could be carried out. Finally, the wide geographical coverage of the study enabled the inclusion of a variety of property rights institutions and dynamics, basic agroecological conditions, and natural resource management strategies. Without such a broad scope it would have been difficult to draw more broadly relevant conclusions given that property rights systems are notoriously subject to differences on a case-by-case basis.

In general, the study provides voluminous and timely information on the likely effects of various types of policies on the way natural resources are managed. The range of analyses covers issues of efficiency, conservation, sustainability, and equity implications of natural resource management under different tenure arrangements. Among the policy variables examined are alternative property rights and collective action institutions, access to infrastructure and markets, migration and population, and the introduction of new technology.

FIGURE 1.1 Country locations of project sites

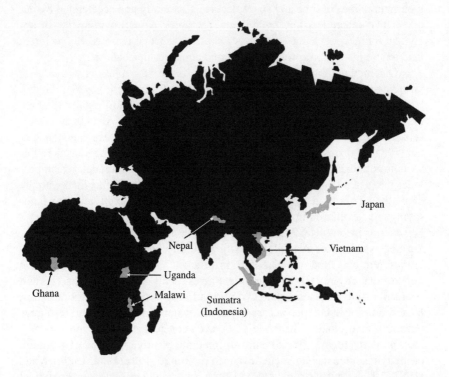

Of these, the study provides most illuminating understanding in the area of the evolution of property rights and consequences of different property rights institutions on the management of land and trees. Specifically, the study provides information on the effectiveness of various national-, local-, and even household-level property rights institutions and arrangements. Because of the diversity of sites across two continents, Asia and Africa, some of the property rights arrangements may be new to the reader and thus stimulate more thought on attempting to analyze and address important property rights issues in their sites of interest.

In short, the purpose of this multicountry study is to explore the causes and consequences of the choice of land tenure institutions and the role of collective action in the management of land and trees with special reference to the interaction with agriculture. As study sites we have selected northern Vietnam, central Uganda, western Sumatra, western Ghana, almost the whole area of Malawi, and the hill and inner Tarai regions of Nepal in view of the diversity of land tenure institutions (see Figure 1.1 for location). In the last phase of the project, we added the case of postwar Japan to supplement the analysis of common property forest management. We attempt to deal with the cases of forest, woodland, rangeland, and cropland management simultaneously because of their interactions in time and space occurring naturally and accelerated by human management decisions over natural resources. After providing a basic analytical framework in this chapter, we explore principal reasons why different land tenure institutions prevail in different countries in Chapter 2.

Our methodology is based on a synthesis of the evolutionary model of farming systems developed by Boserup (1965), Ruthenberg (1980), Pingali, Bigot, and Binswanger (1987), and McIntire, Bourzat, and Pingali (1992); a theory of property rights developed by Demsetz (1967) and Alchian and Demsetz (1973); and a theory of induced innovation developed by Hayami and Ruttan (1985) and Hayami (1997). The former two models can be considered as specific applications of the induced institutional innovation model, which provides the general analytical framework. Boserup's study is concerned with the evolution of farming systems from land-using shifting cultivation to land-saving intensive farming when population increases over time. Her argument, however, is incomplete. Although investment is required to establish intensive farming systems (for example, investment in the construction of irrigation facilities, terracing, and tree planting), insufficient attention is paid to incentive systems that ensure that the appropriate investments are made. Demsetz's and Alchian's study focuses on the evolution of property rights institutions from loosely administered open access to private ownership when natural resources become scarce. None of the models, however, considers the evolution to a common property regime. We attempt to integrate positive theories of common property resource management advanced by Runge (1981, 1984, 1986), Wade (1987, 1988), and Ostrom (1990, 1994), among others, into our analytical framework. Thus, our framework is designed to be general and capable of explaining evolution of property rights institutions, changing roles of collective action, and their consequences on the efficiency of farming and natural resource management.

Research Objectives

This multicountry study has five basic research objectives. The first and primary objective is to explore quantitatively the effects of various land tenure institutions on investments in and the efficiency of forest, woodland, agroforestry, and cropland management. Despite the widely recognized importance of land tenure institutions in the management of natural resources, the extent and ways in which the former affect the latter are not well understood, especially outside agriculture. This study attempts to assess quantitatively the efficiency of natural resource management as much as possible. Note that the term *efficiency* is used broadly throughout this book to encompass technical or production efficiency, the allocative efficiency of variable inputs, and the efficiency of investments, from the viewpoint of local communities and households. We do not explicitly analyze regional, national, or global externalities associated with the natural resource management.

Land tenure systems in many developing countries have been historically shaped by governments through land laws and regulations (Peluso 1992). These include the nationalization of land, restrictions on land sales and leasing, land consolidation, and creation of collective farms. Large absentee landlordism, insecure tenure due to the lack of clear ownership rights, and state ownership, which are potentially detrimental to the conservation of natural resources and agricultural production, are often consequences of these land tenure policies. We pay special attention to the effects of these policies on the efficiency of natural resource management and agriculture, particularly in the context of northern Vietnam, where state ownership of land and collective farming have been replaced by individualized ownership and farming systems, and Uganda, where large private land ownership systems were created by colonial governments in the midst of communal land.

The second objective of this study is to identify major factors affecting the evolution of customary land tenure institutions. Customary or communal land tenure institutions are dynamic. Recent research suggests that the system of communal or family land rights on cultivated agricultural fields tends to evolve toward greater privatization with population growth and greater commercialization in many parts of Sub-Saharan Africa (Bruce and Migot-Adholla 1994). No rigorous statistical analysis, however, has been attempted. Furthermore, to our knowledge, no comparable attempt has been made to quantify the changes in land tenure institutions on forestland, woodland, and rangeland in response to changing external conditions. We address this issue in the light of experience of western Ghana, western Sumatra, and Malawi. On the other hand, fundamental features of land tenure institutions in Vietnam and Uganda have been exogenously imposed by governments.

If degradation of natural resources leading to unsustainable development takes place under customary land tenure systems, such systems may give rise to new property rights systems that are conducive to conserving the use of natural resources and promoting their regeneration (Feder and Noronha 1987). Casual observation suggests that land rights in forest- and grazing lands do evolve toward privatization (Ault and Rutman 1979).[2] This, however, is not always the case; communal land tenure institutions or loosely managed common property systems

---

2. Platteau (1996) criticizes the evolutionary theory of property rights proposed by Demsetz (1967) and Alchian and Demsetz (1973), among others, as applied to Sub-Saharan Africa on the ground that the property rights institutions did not evolve toward complete private property with land titling. Privatization or individualization in this study implies any changes that enhance property rights of individuals (for instance, changes from joint ownership by extended family to that by siblings) without any regard to land titling, which is beyond the control of local communities. In other words, we place more emphasis on customary tenure rights than on statutory rights in view of the former's practical importance.

sometimes evolve toward common property regimes with strict control of natural resource extraction. Such a case is widely observed in the hill region of Nepal.

If land tenure institutions evolve toward their social optimum with population growth and commercialization of agriculture, there will be little need for policy interventions in land rights systems. On the other hand, if inappropriate land rights institutions tend to persist, or if they move in the wrong direction, effective policy options must be sought.

It is important to realize that how smoothly traditional land tenure regimes (such as communal and state ownership) evolve toward new regimes (such as private ownership and common property including user group management systems) often depends on the effectiveness of collective action. In order to protect private or common property, new rules of ownership must be understood, agreed on, and enforced by community members.[3]

Collective action is essential for establishing and enforcing rules of resource access, use, and management under common property regimes; without it, common property systems deteriorate into open-access situations with degradation of the resource a likely outcome (Ostrom 1990; Bardhan 1993a, 1993b; Nugent 1993). Various forms of collective action are also important in coordinating and regulating the use of private property and even play a considerable role in the actual use of state properties. The nature and strength of collective action for natural resource management vary considerably, depending on the structure of incentives and transaction costs governed by community norms, culture, and tradition (Hayami 1997). We undertake case studies in Nepal and Japan to analyze the role of collective action in community forest management.

The third objective of this study is to analyze and quantify the impact of various collective action institutions on the efficiency of natural resource management, particularly under common property systems. Although theoretical literature supporting the idea of common property as an effective social organization abounds (for example, Runge 1981, 1984, 1986; Bromley 1992; McKean and Ostrom 1995; Baland and Platteau 1996), there are relatively few empirical studies on the efficiency of common property resource management.[4] Among these, impact studies that properly control for the effect of other conditions, such as physical infrastructure and market conditions, are rare. Identifying the enabling conditions under which collective action is likely to emerge and be sustained contributes to our understanding of resource man-

---

3. The role of government in formally implementing and enforcing private-property institutions through land titling and the establishment of adjudication systems is emphasized in the literature (Feder and Feeny 1993). But in practice the ability of government in land administration is often limited, and the litigation is costly, so that the community mechanism of enforcing agreements based on collective action must play a role in implementing and enforcing property rights institutions (Atwood 1990).

4. See, however, contributions by Jodha (1986), Wade (1988), Ostrom (1990), Azhar (1993), Wilson and Thompson (1993), and White and Runge (1994).

agement practices. Nepal and Japan are the primary countries in which this objective is tested.

The fourth objective of this study is to examine the effect of land tenure institutions on the distribution of land resources. Because customary tenure institutions have been noted to provide a relatively equitable distribution of land to rural households, changes in these property rights systems raise concerns over land concentration. In fact, however, equitable land distributions can be easily maintained under customary tenure systems only when land is abundant. When land becomes scarce, it is an empirical question as to whether individualization of land rights institutions under communal tenure systems or the establishment of common property promotes or discourages concentration of landholdings or benefits obtained from land and tree resources. Communal tenure systems are not alike, and they will not have uniform effects on the distribution of land. For instance, farm sizes may be reduced faster under inheritance systems prone to encourage more claimants, such as matrilineal systems that may permit daughters and nieces to make legitimate claims to the same piece of land. State intervention in property rights law may also affect land distribution, as is the case when highly influential people are given access to large tracts of land. Thus, we assess the distributional effects of different property rights systems in Ghana and Indonesia.

The fifth objective of this study is to assess the implications of land tenure institutions for equity. At the outset we must point out that most of our study sites lie within marginal, less favored, or low-potential areas, where the incidence of poverty is generally high. The ultimate purpose of this study is to seek effective ways to reduce poverty by increasing the efficiency of land use and management in such areas based on proper understandings of the nature and the role of land tenure institutions. We also analyze how changes in land tenure institutions affect women's status and how women's status, wealth of farm households reflected in farm size, and the gender composition of family labor affect investment in trees and management efficiency of perennial and annual crop farming (in Ghana, Indonesia, and Malawi).

Theoretical Framework

Characteristics of Land Tenure Institutions

In our empirical research, we classify land property rights into bundles of rights encompassing use, investment, exclusion, and transfer rights with and without permission from chief, family head, community organizations, and outside authorities. Our study is designed to explore the perception of these rights by community members as distinct from externally created legal rights. These may then be classified into four major "pure types": (1) communal ownership, (2) state ownership, (3) individual or private ownership, and (4) common property.

The first and the last tenure institutions need explanations, as the difference between the two is not always clear and is often a source of confusion. Under the communal ownership regime, primary forests and uncultivated woodlands are owned communally and controlled by an authority such as a village chief, whereas exclusive use rights of cultivated land are assigned to individual households of the community, and its ownership rights are held traditionally by the extended family. The ownership of cultivated land, however, has evolved toward more individualized ownership over time. This system is alternatively called the customary land tenure institution. Land tenure institutions that are observed in Sumatra, Ghana, Uganda, and Malawi fall in this category. On the other hand, common property is defined by the joint use of resources such as forestland, woodland, or rangeland by a group of community members. Property is usually owned jointly, as in the case of community-owned forests and rangelands, but it may be owned individually and used jointly, as in the case of common grazing land under the open field system in England. The joint ownership and use are justified by the nonexcludable nature of forest resources, which makes it difficult for individual community members to protect properties effectively under private ownership. The distinction between communal ownership and common property is not made in Johnson (1972), Feder and Noronha (1987), and Feder and Feeny (1993). Demsetz (1967) and Alchian and Demsetz (1973) identify communal ownership with open access.

Open access is considered to be a category of land tenure institutions by Feder and Noronha (1987), Bromley (1992), and Feder and Feeny (1993). We consider it more appropriate to regard open access as an extreme outcome of land management, which can theoretically occur under any land tenure regime. In fact, common property can be open access, if the community or a group of users do not manage it or if the resources are truly nonexcludable. There are also cases in which the use of common property forests is strictly regulated by community members, as in the case of selected forests in the hill region of Nepal. Uncultivated portions of communally owned land can also be regarded as common property, as they are owned by a group of people and used jointly for hunting and extraction of trees and minor forest products. In our study sites, however, this area is characterized by open access for the community members almost without exception. While private property is seldom open access (absentee owners are one possible exception), state-owned forests or woodlands are generally open access as a result of the inability of governments to enforce property rights.

Further classifications within each tenure category are useful depending on the cases under examination. For example, under communal ownership, the rights to bequeath may or may not exist, and use rights may be established for joint families rather than individuals. State or public land may be managed by collective farms under the socialist-type regimes, occupied and used by squatters with no effective restrictions, or managed as common property through voluntary action of the community members. Tenure security under private ownership may differ considerably depending on whether land rights are legally established and protected by government or informally recognized and respected by community agreements. We empirically examine the importance of various rights in specific case studies. Nonetheless, as a conceptual guide, the broad classification will be useful.

An Evolutionary Model of Property Rights Institutions

A simplified version of our theoretical framework can be illustrated by assuming that there are only two factors of production, land and labor, following Hayami and Ruttan (1985). Land represents natural resources, and it could be cropland (with or without irrigation), rangeland, woodland, or forestland. The central issue is how the stock of natural resources (both quantity and quality) changes with evolution of farming systems from extensive to intensive systems—or more generally from natural resource using to natural resource saving systems. Although for concreteness we consider the evolution from shifting cultivation to sedentary farming, the basic theoretical framework can be applied to the case of other natural resources management.

Under shifting cultivation, food crops are usually grown for a couple of years after clearing forest, and a fallow period of varying length follows until next cultivation. As Boserup (1965) emphasizes, fallow land is not "unused" land; fallowing is a labor-saving method for restoring soil fertility. Under sedentary farming, either annual food crops or perennial tree crops are grown without long fallow periods.

If initially population is scarce and land is abundant with vast areas of virgin forests, people have little incentive to claim individual property rights in land, and, hence, the use of forest areas is unrestricted except for the exclusion of outsiders. The usufruct rights of individual members of the community are well established for cultivated fields, but the usufruct rights of fallow land is less clear, and the leader of the extended family or chief of the community sometimes determines its allocation to members of the group. Usually, usufruct rights are transferred from one generation to another in accordance with traditional inheritance rules. The individual rights to transfer, including sales and leasing, are restricted.

Since land is abundant, it is cost-effective to practice shifting cultivation with sufficiently long fallow periods, which ensures complete restoration of soil fertility. Curve I_0I_0 in Figure 1.2 portrays the unit isoquant for an individual farmer to produce $1.00 worth of food crops by using land and labor under shifting cultivation in period 0. Here we measure land input in terms of area "used" for cultivation, including fallow land, some of which may be secondary forest or woodlands, but excluding land that has never been cultivated. It is assumed for simplicity that the production function is subject to constant returns to scale, so that each technology or farming system is characterized by a single unit iso-

FIGURE 1.2 A model of induced institutional innovation

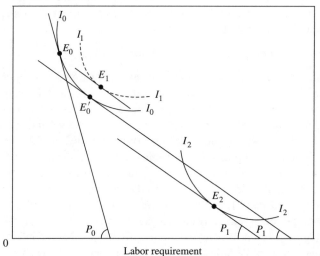

quant. The relative factor scarcity may be indicated by relative factor price line, P_0.[5] Then the optimum production point is given by E_0, where the production is assumed to be sustainable, that is, the production can continue to take place at this point with unchanged soil fertility.

As population increases, however, land becomes scarce relative to labor. This process is accelerated in areas where in-migration is high. Because of inefficient markets or abundant supply, forest products are not traded for required food, and the growing population will require increasing area for agricultural production. Larger areas of forestland are thus opened up, but the rate of area expansion eventually falls short of the growth rate of population. As a result, the scarcity value of land increases relative to labor, which is reflected in changes in relative factor price ratio from P_0 to P_1 in period 1. Accordingly, the optimum production point changes to E_0', so long as shifting cultivation continues to be practiced. Fallow period at E_0' tends to be shorter than at E_0.

As a result of the shorter fallow cycle, soil fertility declines, and farming becomes unsustainable at E_0', resulting in the shift of unit isoquant from $I_0 I_0$ to $I_1 I_1$. Thus, the equilibrium point moves to E_1. If shifting cultivation continues with the shortened fallow periods under increasing population pressure, pro-

---

5. Although a straight factor price line indicates the existence of perfect factor markets, such an assumption is unnecessary for our arguments. A critical assumption is that the slope of factor price curve becomes flatter as population pressure increases.

duction efficiency will further decline over time. Note that a large area of land is under fallow at E_0 and that larger and less fertile land is cultivated at E_1.

Commercialization of agriculture may accelerate the process of change. Since commercialization will increase crop prices at the local level, demand for factors of production will increase, with the greatest increases in the prices of those factors whose supply is less elastic. To the extent that the supply of land is less elastic than labor, which is likely to be the case when virgin forests have been cleared, the relative price of land will increase. Commercialization will also increase the profitability of cultivation compared with fallow, thereby shortening the fallow period and reducing sustainability under shifting cultivation.

During the processes of population expansion and increasing commercialization, deforestation continues to take place, corresponding to an increasing demand for cultivated land. Thus, as is illustrated by Path I in Figure 1.3, in which the horizontal axis measures either time or population density, the stock of natural resources—for example, biomass and timber volume—continues to be depleted in this process.

An alternative to unsustainable farming under shifting cultivation and continued deforestation is to improve land quality by investing in land (for instance, construction of irrigation facilities or terracing) or by investing in trees (for example, commercial trees, such as cocoa, rubber, coffee, and cinnamon). To maintain soil fertility under continuous growing of annual crops, new farming systems may be adopted involving the application of compost made from grasses and leaf litter collected from the forest and woodland, as well as manure.[6] Relative to pure cropping systems, the productivity of tree-farming systems can be sustained for longer periods of time with lower application of organic or inorganic fertilizer primarily owing to their deeper and denser rooting systems and to their perennial ground cover. Because of the increasing use of labor and continuous cropping, new farming systems are labor-using and land-saving. Thus, the unit isoquant corresponding to this farming system is depicted by curve $I_2 I_2$ in Figure 1.2.

Crops grown under the new farming system are likely to be different from crops grown under shifting cultivation. We can directly compare the efficiency of producing different crops in Figure 1.2, because we define the unit isoquant in terms of the combination of inputs necessary to produce $1.00 worth of output regardless of which crops are grown. What types of crops will be grown will depend on, among other things, the natural environment and access to markets. For example, if an area is mountainous and sloping, tree crops are likely to have comparative advantage over food crops. If the area has good access to urban markets, production of fresh vegetables and fruits may have comparative advantage over storable products, such as grain, cocoa, and coffee.

---

6. We can also consider application of commercial fertilizer. To do so, however, requires an extension of our model to the case with more than two inputs, which is straightforward but cumbersome.

FIGURE 1.3 Evolutionary changes in stock of natural resources

Stock of
natural resources

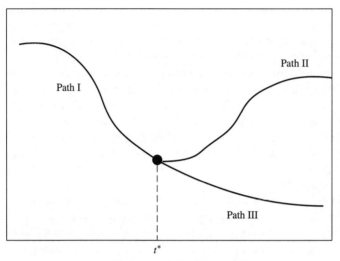

Time or population density

Given a relative factor price of P_1, the optimum is attained at E_2 in Figure 1.2 under the new farming system, at which production is assumed to be more profitable than at E_1 and may be more profitable at $E_0{}'$ as well. There is no technological innovation; it is a matter of the choice of alternative farming systems by farmers. The shift from E_1 to E_2, however, is not costless. As mentioned earlier, physical investment, such as terracing and tree planting, is required to adopt the new farming system. Thus, it does not pay to adopt the new farming system unless the difference in the short-run profitability between the old and new systems warrants the cost of long-term investment.

Furthermore, land tenure institutions must change in order to encourage investments. Since usufruct rights are not totally secure and transfer rights are restricted under traditional land tenure institutions, the expected returns to investment may be depressed: those who plant trees may not be able to reap the benefits because of tenure insecurity or an inability to bequeath the property to desired heirs or to sell the land freely if the need arises (Fortmann and Bruce 1988; Besley 1995). This incentive issue is not considered in the Boserupian model. We hypothesize that in order to provide appropriate incentives to invest in land and trees, land rights institutions in cultivated land are induced to change through a demand-driven process toward greater individualization. As is demonstrated in our empirical studies in Chapters 3 to 6, in practice, efforts to invest in tree planting are rewarded by strong individual land rights, if investment is socially profitable, according to customary land tenure rules. This is a built-in institutional innovation mechanism that makes it possible to arrive at socially more profitable farming systems.

Another possible institutional development is the establishment of common property for those degraded secondary forests and remaining woodlands whose ownership or enforcement of property rights has been unclear. Some of these forests and woodlands might have been common property of the community without any management beyond the exclusion of outsiders, because of the continued and sufficient abundance of forest resources or the relatively low value of woodland products as compared with agricultural products. The new common property regime may be different from the traditional one in that the extraction of forest resources (not to mention the conversion to farmland) by community members is restricted by certain rules and regulations agreed on by themselves.

Resource degradation, however, may continue without accompanying intensification of farming systems. High costs of investment in land improvements, poor returns from the investments, difficulties in organizing collective action, and high transaction costs or legal restrictions on the choice of property rights institutions may all inhibit innovative institutional responses, resulting in the delay of rehabilitation efforts and continued resource degradation. Possible examples are nationalization of forest areas, granting of leasehold and freehold titles to large holders, and suppression of tenancy contracts. These policies may prevent land tenure institutions from evolving, thereby adversely affecting the efficiency of farming systems and natural resource management. The identification of factors affecting continuous degradation of natural resources is a primary goal of this study.

In sum, there are at least four possible pathways responding to increased scarcity of land and natural resources in our model:

1. Privatization of property rights and investment in the improvement of land quality for annual crop farming
2. Privatization of property rights and investment in trees for commercial tree crop or mixed tree/crop farming systems
3. Establishment of common property forests with effective rules of management
4. Continuous degradation of natural resources due to continued shifting cultivation with shorter fallow periods, overexploitation of natural resources without development of effective community organizations, or conversion of forest and woodland to crop farms under extensive farming systems

The first two developments are associated with changes in land tenure institutions toward more individualized systems. Whether individualized land rights develop or a common property system emerges will depend on the extent of market failures under private-property rights systems and the costs and benefits of organizing collective action necessary to manage common property. For example, some types of forests are common-pool resources by nature, which are difficult to protect from theft (Grafton 2000). This would be the case if resources extracted from forests are such minor products as firewood, fodder, grasses, and leaf litter. In this case, even if ownership of forest land is privatized, these minor resources cannot be protected cost-effectively. It may then be managed by a group of resource users under the common property regime, even though the choice of such regime is "second best" because of the cost of collective management. We presume that the common property system is not appropriate for food and tree crop farming, because the cost of protection under private ownership regime is low relative to the benefits and relative to costs of preventing free riding under the common property system. The final pathway is one of failure, and the community is unable to intensify land use.

The implication of these arguments for changes in the stock of natural resources may be explained by using Figure 1.3. Resources will be depleted over time with population growth, so long as community members have free access to the forest areas. But increases in population may induce successful changes in land rights institutions at period t^*, after which the stock of tree and forest resources may increase following Path II (equivalent to pathway 2 or 3 above). Timing of the turning point will depend on the cost of implementing the institutional innovation, as well as the nature of the existing land tenure institutions (Anderson and Hill 1990). If pathway 1 is chosen, tree resources may continue to deplete along Path III, as secondary forest and bushland, which are fallow lands under shifting cultivation, will disappear. Yet investment in land improvement will be conducive not only to the conservation of soil fertility of the cultivated land but also to the preservation of remaining uncultivated forest areas located elsewhere. This is because increased food production from the same unit of land will reduce food prices, thereby reducing incentives to clear uncultivated forestland for the production of food crops. If pathway 4 is chosen, natural resources will continue to deplete along Path III.

Among the factors influencing the choice of property rights institution and its evolution, in-migration seems to have played a significant role. First, by accelerating the rate of population growth, migration has placed more pressure on local institutions to adapt to changing factor scarcities. Second, migrants often bring with them different knowledge of resource management, and this will create the need for local institutions to facilitate or restrict these new practices accordingly. Finally, migrants may often come with their unique property rights institutions, such as inheritance rules, and these must somehow become integrated with local rules. Thus, there is potential for increased conflicts with the influx of migrants. However, there are also great opportunities for institutional change as the migrants bring with them knowledge of alternative institutions.

We hypothesize that new land tenure institutions are induced to develop when the expected benefits of institutional change exceed the costs thereof. The expected benefits are assumed to be determined by efficiency gains associated with the institutional change; hence, they are determined, among other things, by population pressure and commercialization of agriculture. On the other hand, the costs are assumed to consist of reaching and enforcing new agreements among community members. To the extent that the new institutional rules reduce social equity and stability, the cost associated with such institutional transformation needs to be duly taken into account as well.

Modeling the Impact of Property Rights Institutions on Natural Resource Management

In the previous section, the linkage between the evolution of property rights institutions and natural resource management was highlighted. Because of the diversity of tenure institutions and the unique historical development of them, it is extremely difficult to model these dynamic processes in a unified and formal manner. On the other hand, the types of natural resource management decisions made by rural households are remarkably similar across countries, lending themselves more easily to modeling efforts. Thus, we depart from the dynamic interactive conceptualization of the previous section to take a more rigorous modeling approach to the consequences of property rights institutions on natural resource management. This is important, for the additional insight it provides is critical in the formulation of specific hypotheses regarding the anticipated effects of different property rights systems on natural resources.

In this section, we develop a model for analyzing two types of natural resource management decisions undertaken by rural households: (1) long-term tree investments made on agricultural land and (2) conversions of forests and woodlands to agricultural land. We could also construct a more comprehensive model, which also considers the choice of agricultural land for shifting cultivation of food crops and tree crop cultivation. Such a model, however, is unduly complex.

To analyze these two decisions, we use a three-period model in which decisions to convert are made in period 0 and decisions to invest in farms are made in period 1. Farmland is cultivated in periods 1 and 2, and the two production periods allow for trade-offs between short-term production and investment.

Agricultural land accrues a profit of Π_{Ai} ($i = 1, 2$) in periods 1 and 2 following conversion in period 0. We assume that the profit grows or shrinks at the rate of α from period 1 to 2:

$$\Pi_{A2} = \Pi_{A1}(1 + \alpha), \tag{1}$$

where α depends on productivity and price changes and is determined by the profit-maximizing behavior of the cultivator and will reflect investment in or mining of agricultural land resources.

Now we introduce the possibility for investment on the land. For simplicity, we assume that the household may make one type of investment, tree planting. It is assumed that tree planting in period 1 entails a cost of wl_T, where w is the wage rate and l_T is the labor used for tree planting. Further, it is assumed that the planting of trees, designated by T, is a productive investment that leads to a higher growth rate of profits at diminishing rate, that is, $\partial\alpha/\partial T > 0$ and $\partial^2\alpha/\partial T^2 < 0$.

Future benefits are discounted because of time preference and the risk of losing rights over future benefits from farmland, which can happen in several different scenarios across our study sites. Equation (2) allows for the possibility that by investing in tree planting households may reduce the probability of losing rights to the land (p) in periods 1 and 2 (that is, $\partial p/\partial T < 0$).[7] The manner by which p is affected by T depends on land tenure rules. Later, we discuss the types of situations among our study sites in which such possibilities exist. The present value of the profit from agricultural land (Π_{A0}) is:

$$\Pi_{A0} = \Pi_{A1}[(1 - p(T)) / (1 + r) + (1 + \alpha(T)) (1 - p(T))^2 / (1 + r)^2]$$
$$- wl_T/(1 + r), \qquad (2)$$

where r is the discount rate.

First we consider an investment in tree planting. A household will maximize (2) with respect to l_T:

$$\partial\Pi_{A0}/\partial l_T = (\partial\alpha/\partial T)(\partial T/\partial l_T)\Pi_{A1}(1 - p)^2 / (1 + r)^2$$
$$- (\partial p/\partial T)(\partial T/\partial l_T)\Pi_{A1} / (1 + r)$$
$$- (\partial p/\partial T)(\partial T/\partial l_T)2\Pi_{A1}(1 + \alpha)(1 - p) / (1 + r)^2 - w/(1 + r) = 0. \qquad (3)$$

Equation (3) shows that the optimal amount of labor invested in tree planting balances the first three positive terms against the fourth negative term. The first term shows that the larger the tenure security as reflected in smaller p, the greater the expected profit accrued to the cultivator from tree planting. Hence, greater tenure security will lead to greater incidence of tree planting, as is indicated in Besley's (1995) model. Needless to say, these arguments hold only when a profitable long-term investment opportunity exists, which is indicated by the positive sign of $\partial\alpha/\partial T$. If such investment opportunity does not exist, land tenure security does not matter, and profits are determined by short-term production decisions. The next two terms in equation (3) also show that, all else equal, where opportunities for tenure security enhancing investment exist ($\partial p/\partial T < 0$), a greater investment in tree planting will be made. It is important

---

7. Tree planting is the most commonly reported investment used to enhance rights to land (Shepherd 1991), but other types of investments may also lead to the same outcome.

to emphasize that investments depend not only on the initial level of tenure security but also on its expected change following the investment. This is not the case where $\partial p/\partial T = 0$, and then tree planting is clearly positively linked to the initial level of tenure security. Thus, whether long-term investment, especially in tree planting, depends critically on initial level of tenure security is an empirical question. We hypothesize that so far as village communities strive for higher income and greater production efficiency, the institutional rule to grant stronger land rights will emerge in those areas where tree planting brings about significantly large profits. This is how the equilibrium moves from E_1 to E_2 in terms of Figure 1.2.

In order to examine the process of conversion of land from forest or woodland into agriculture, we now formally introduce a second land type, and the present value of the profits derived from this land is labeled Π_{N0} with a growth rate of profits between periods 1 and 2 of β. A household will convert the land if the present value from conversion to agriculture far exceeds that from the alternative use. The net value from converting is:

$$V = \Delta x \, [\Pi_{A0} - \Pi_{N0}], \tag{4}$$

where Δx is the amount of land converted to agriculture. If V is negative, no conversion will take place. If it is positive, some conversion will take place assuming that the costs of conversion are sufficiently low.[8] Whether agriculture is more profitable depends on several factors. First is the difference in short-run (that is, the first-period) profits $\Pi_{A1} - \Pi_{N1}$, which would likely be positive given that newly converted land would be fertile. Second is long-term profits, which depend on the difference $\alpha - \beta$, which in turn depends on sustainability and prices for products in the different land uses. Whether agriculture is sustainable depends on the existence of long-term productivity-enhancing investments as indicated in equation (3). Third, expected profits will depend on the probability of retaining rights to the resources under the different land uses. Generally, conversion to agriculture increases the individual rights of households, thus encouraging conversion. This is because effort to convert forestland into cultivable fields is rewarded by strong individual land rights under communal tenure systems. Perhaps the most striking example is the case of an open-access woodland. Since other households are also unrestricted to convert this land, rights to future forest resources for any given household are highly uncertain, and, owing to the open access, the resources are likely to deplete rapidly. Thus, Π_{N0} is likely to be small. In contrast, conversion to agriculture can greatly enhance expected profits, particularly if strongly individualized land rights are granted. In short, the weaker the individual rights of forestland and

---

8. Costs may rise with scarcity because the last lands to be cleared are often difficult to access or to develop (for example, steep slopes) and because pressures to retain some woodland may increase, raising its value.

the stronger those of agricultural land, the greater will be the incentive to convert (Anderson and Hill 1990). This is, of course, not the case where the woodland or forest is already found on private land.

It is clear from equation (4) that if the profitability of farming is great, a larger area of forestland is converted to farmland, as in the models of Ehui, Hertel, and Preckel (1990) and Barbier and Burgess (1997). This is likely to be the case in areas where land is homogeneous. In the context of Asia, where village land typically consists of flat paddy fields and sloped upland fields (for example, Sumatra and Vietnam), the distinction must be made between increased profitability in lowland and upland farming (Kaimowitz and Angelsen 1998; Angelsen 1999). If the profitability of lowland farming increases, more resources may be allocated to lowland farming, thereby reducing the pace of deforestation (see Appendix in Chapter 7).

A couple of hypotheses can be advanced from the theoretical model. First, the higher the profitability and sustainability of farming, the lower the benefit and sustainability of forest management, and the greater the individual land rights granted to the converted land, the greater will be the conversion of forestland to agricultural land. Second, the greater the initial tenure security *and* the expected increase in tenure security associated with tree planting, the greater will be tree planting. Thus, whether the greater initial tenure security results in more tree planting is an empirical question. If management of trees, such as weeding and pruning, is required subsequently, management efficiency will depend on tenure security achieved after tree planting. If tenure security does not change with investment, it is the level of tenure security in the initial period that affects investment. Needless to say, if profitable investment opportunities do not exist, tenure does not affect the management of farmland. In the next section, we explain how we empirically assess the significance of the tenure rule that grants larger land tenure security after tree planting.

Formulating Regression Models for Empirical Testing

Empirically we would like to assess the effects of land tenure institutions on the incidence of tree planting and management as well as the use of land for fallow. Our basic presumption is that land rights affect investment incentives as they determine the expected returns to investment for those who actually invest (Besley 1995). There are, however, a couple of difficulties in empirical estimation. First, it is difficult to quantify land rights. Strength of land rights cannot be expressed as a continuous cardinal variable by adding up the number of rights, as there is no reason to assume that each right has equal importance. Thus, land rights must be regarded as qualitative. Second, land rights are dynamic and may be influenced by actions of land users. Land rights may weaken if land is put into fallow, and strengthen if trees are planted. In our study sites, households seek to attain and maintain strong land rights mainly to thwart attempts by extended family members to claim their land. Third, it is difficult to measure the extent to which land rights have changed after tree planting or fallow. Partly because of the paucity of exogenous variables that can be used as instruments and partly because of the qualitative and sometimes unobservable nature of the land rights, it is difficult to apply the simultaneous equations estimation methods to the explanation of land rights and tree planting. Thus, we estimate a reduced-form function explaining the incidence of the observed tree planting as a function of the modes of land acquisition, which are related to the initial endowment of land rights and can be considered as predetermined with respect to the tree-planting decision. Below we demonstrate how such reduced-form relationships can be used to test hypotheses about the relationships between land tenure institutions and tree planting.

We assume that tree planting (T) is a linear function of the expected land rights (R^e):

$$T = a_0 + a_1 R^e, \tag{5}$$

where a_0 and a_1 are parameters. We expect that a_1 is positive, as stronger expected land rights increase expected future returns.

The expected value of land rights (R^e) is not directly observable, because it is affected by the land use patterns (for example, tree planting and fallowing), in addition to the manner of land acquisition. For simplicity, we assume that there are two types of land, inherited family land and privately acquired land (for instance, through forest clearance or purchase). It may be assumed that R^e is determined by the following linear relation:

$$R^e = b_0 + b_1 T + b_2 L, \tag{6}$$

where b's are parameters and L is a land tenure dummy representing the privately acquired land. The parameter b_0 refers to land rights on inherited land with no tree planting, b_1 represents the marginal effect of tree planting on land rights, and b_2 measures the difference in land rights between inherited and privately acquired lands. It will be legitimate to assume that b_0 and b_2 are positive. Conventionally, b_1 is assumed to be zero (for example, Johnson 1972). Then it is straightforward to show that land tenure institutions affect tree planting through their effects on land rights. Besley (1995) considers the possibility that tree planting increases land rights, which may imply in the context of our simple linear model that b_1 is positive.

By substituting equation (6) into equation (5) and rearranging terms, we obtain the following reduced-form function:

$$T = (a_0 + a_1 b_0)/(1 - a_1 b_1) + [a_1 b_2/(1 - a_1 b_1)]L. \tag{7}$$

In order to ensure a positive solution, $(1 - a_1 b_1)$ must be positive. In this case, it is clear that tree planting is more active on individually acquired land, since land rights affect tree planting positively ($a_1 > 0$) and land rights are initially stronger on the individually acquired land than on inherited land ($b_2 > 0$). This qualitative conclusion holds regardless of whether tree planting increases land rights or not, or whether b_1 is positive or zero.

We must point out that in the specification formulated above, tree planting is assumed to affect the expected land rights with no regard to the manner of land acquisition. An alternative hypothesis is that tree planting creates sufficiently strong rights when the original land rights are weak, so that the manner of land acquisition does not affect tree planting. To demonstrate this, we now assume that privately acquired land has the locally defined maximum land rights, which are given by $b_0 + b_2$ and are unaffected by tree planting. Thus, equation (6) can be rewritten as

$$R^e = b_0 + b_1 (1 - L)T + b_2 L, \tag{8}$$

where b's are positive parameters. From equations (5) and (8), we obtain the following solutions for T^* and R^{e*}:

$$T^* = (a_0 + a_1 b_0)/[1 - a_1 b_1(1 - L)] + \{a_1 b_2/[1 - a_1 b_1(1 - L)]\}L \tag{9}$$

$$R^{e*} = [b_0 + a_0 b_1(1 - L) + b_2 L]/[1 - a_1 b_1(1 - L)]. \tag{10}$$

From equation (9), it is easy to establish that in order to ensure that the incidence of tree planting will be the same on inherited land, which is equal to T^* when $L = 0$, and on private land, which is equal to T^* when $L = 1$, the following equality must hold:

$$a_0 + a_1(b_0 + b_1) = (a_0 + a_1 b_0)/(1 - a_1 b_1). \tag{11}$$

From equation (10), it is straightforward to establish that equation (11) holds only when the expected equilibrium land rights on inherited land after tree planting are equalized with the maximum rights, that is, $b_0 + b_2$. This is not unreasonable if tree planting confers strong private rights.

One may argue that tree planting is a function of not only the land rights but also other exogenous variables (X), such as the market price of tree crops. Then, equation (5) may be rewritten as

$$T = a_0 + a_1 R^e + a_2 X, \tag{12}$$

where a_2 is a parameter. In this case it can be shown from equations (12) and (8) that the reduced-form tree-planting function has different intercepts and slope coefficients of X for different land tenure institutions if the equilibrium expected land rights on inherited land fall short of the maximum. However, if tree planting is sufficiently profitable, so that the equilibrium land rights on inherited land reach the maximum, tree planting is independent from the manner of land acquisition and affected uniquely by X. This can be easily ascertained from equation (12) by assuming that R^e is always equal to $b_0 + b_2$ under any land tenure institution. To the extent that tree crop production is more profitable than shifting cultivation of food crops, it may not be unreasonable to assume that tree planting is sufficiently profitable.

In other words, tree planting is independent of the manner of land acquisition if tree planting creates the maximum land rights permitted in an area. If this null hypothesis is correct, we expect that the land tenure dummy is insignificant in the tree-planting function. It is easy to prove that the same conclusion holds even when there are more than two land tenure types if tree planting creates the maximum rights.

If land rights are sufficiently strengthened after tree planting, subsequent management of tree crop fields will be no different among parcels with different land tenure institutions. Otherwise, the management intensity will be positively correlated with the strength of land rights. We test these conflicting hypotheses by comparing net revenue and labor use per hectare among different land tenure institutions in Chapters 3 to 6.

As Boserup (1965) emphasizes, fallow land is not unused; it is used for restoring soil fertility. Thus, fallowing can be considered as a kind of investment. Then our arguments developed in this section can be applied for the choice of fallow. Unlike the case of tree planting, however, fallowing does not require labor input or management effort; hence, it can easily be confused with underutilized or abandoned land, which tends to weaken land rights if it has any effect. Thus, we hypothesize that stronger initial land rights lead to larger proportions of fallow land in the shifting-cultivation area.

Analysis of Common Property Resource Management

One of the major challenges of this study is to develop a quantitative methodology to assess the efficiency of management of common property resources. In this subsection, we develop an analytical framework to apply to the behaviors of users of common property resources.

The theoretical approach we propose is to compare the allocation of labor in extraction activities from common property under different management rules. If access to common property is unrestricted for community members, a farmer will allocate his or her labor between resource extraction (or forest clearance) and other activities until the private marginal product of labor (MPL_c) is equal to the wage rate (W), that is, point E in Figure 1.4. This point, however, is not the optimum from the viewpoint of the community, because each farmer's extraction activity reduces the resources available for other community members. This open-access case corresponds to the case of *The Tragedy of the Commons* envisaged by Hardin (1968).

The social optimum is attained when $f_1 = w$ holds (see point E' in Figure 1.4). Thus, the privately optimum labor input is greater than the socially optimum level. If the number of users is sufficiently large, the private marginal product approaches the social average product (Dasgupta and Heal 1979:55–73).

FIGURE 1.4 Allocation of labor input for extraction activity from the commons

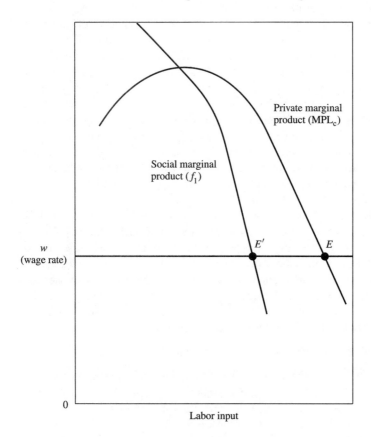

The social optimum can be attained only if everybody agrees to behave cooperatively. In order to ensure such behavior, noncooperative behavior must be detectable and punished with sufficient penalty so as to deter such behavior. This optimum corresponds to the social optimum if the resources were fully privatized under the condition of zero transaction costs (de Meza and Gould 1992). Whether private property can be protected without unduly high transaction costs will depend, among other things, on the nature of common property resources. If they are common-pool resources, as defined by Ostrom (1990), the private-property regime may not work because of the difficulty of excluding nonowners from exploiting resources. The ability to protect private property may depend on the size of holding because even minor products are easily protected on a small piece of land adjacent to a home.

Theoretically it has been demonstrated that in order to ensure cooperative behavior among members of a group, sufficiently effective and credible retaliation strategies must exist that punish those who violate collective agreements and reward those who honor them (for example, Seabright 1993). There are several preconditions for such mechanisms to work in a rural community. First, there should be an expectation of repeated agreements, because one-period agreements offer limited opportunity to punish or reward. Second, the future benefits and costs must be important for each individual. Third, the behavior of individual members must be observable with some positive probability by at least some other members of the group. Fourth, there must be a social mechanism to disseminate relevant information on the behavior of individual members to the group. Fifth, defection (cooperation) should result in the loss (buildup) of a member's reputation, leading to the termination (renewal) of his or her participation in the communal activity, which is potentially beneficial to each member if everyone observes the agreement. If these conditions are met, the maximization calculus of individual members points toward cooperation under the assurance that others will also cooperate (Runge 1981, 1984, 1986).

From an empirical point of view, the size and homogeneity of group, the degree of trust, the importance of reputation in the community, social stability, and users' time horizons are considered to be the more important factors affecting the effectiveness or the cost of collective action (Ostrom 1990; Meinzen-Dick, Rasmussen, and Jackson 1996). It is hypothesized that coordination failure can occur owing to unequal distribution of the benefits and costs of collective action and to the lack of assurance of receiving the benefits. To explore these issues further, detailed analysis of the rules and functions of collective action, which mediate between individual and collective interests, is required (Runge 1986; Wade 1987; Curtis 1991; Bromley 1992; Ostrom 1994).

In our observation there are two types of management rules to reduce overexploitation of forest resources: one is to restrict labor allocation to the forest by restricting the "open" days, and the other is to regulate the manner of resource extraction by restricting the use of tools and extraction of live trees and branches. In our statistical analysis in Chapter 8, we estimate the labor allocation function in which labor time for resource extraction is regressed on rules of restricting labor allocation and other variables expected to affect the enforcement cost of such rules, such as the size and heterogeneity of user group. Using the predicted value of labor allocation, we also estimate the firewood collection function, in order to assess the effectiveness of the regulation of resource extractions.

Land Tenure Institution and Equity

What would be the effects of the evolution of property rights institutions on equity? Specifically, would individualization of land rights create a larger disparity of access to land among community members? What will happen to women's rights and welfare when property rights are individualized? Will the establishment of common property with clear rules of resource extraction promote, maintain, or deteriorate equity? These are the major analytical issues about equity that this study attempts to address.

It can be assumed that asset distribution is fairly equitable under communal tenure when land is abundant and investment in both physical and human capital is minimal. In fact, the per capita distribution of land among households under the communal ownership system is generally equal, because this system is designed to achieve and preserve equitable distribution of land and income among community members, thereby ensuring communal solidarity and food security. As land becomes scarce and valuable, however, the distribution of land may become more skewed. We postulate that whether the individualization of land rights creates significant inequity through accumulation of land by a small number of people depends on the existence of scale economies or on whether the optimum scale of farm operation increases after new farming systems are adopted. If significant scale economies do not exist, incentives for selected individuals to accumulate large areas of land will be weak. On the contrary, if large-scale economies exist, land may be accumulated by a few; hence, large income disparities may emerge with changes in farming systems associated with the individualization of land rights. We empirically examine this point by estimating profit functions in which farm size is an explanatory variable.

Another important factor affecting equity is the factor-use bias of new farming systems. Since nearly all rural households have access to labor, changes in the production function in a labor using direction, as described in Figure 1.2, will promote equity. Thus, the extent to which changes in property rights institutions and farming systems increase labor demand is an important issue for social equity. In order to assess such effect, we estimate the labor use function in which property rights institutions are included as explanatory variables.

In our observation, huge inequities have been created by land policies of both colonial and postcolonial governments, which granted leasehold and freehold titles to large landholders. Since land and tenancy transactions between peasants and large landholders are often restricted, a dual agrarian structure is created in which land is scarce in the peasant sector and abundant in the largeholder sector. This is observed in Uganda and Malawi. One of the justifications for the creation of large-scale farming units is the existence of scale economies. However, if significant scale economies do not exist and large farms use land and other natural resources extensively, as in the case of unit isoquant $I_0 I_0$ in Figure 1.2, the operation of large farms will be detrimental not only to the efficiency of farming but also for equity.

Even if technical scale economies do not exist, wealthy people may further accumulate wealth with the individualization of land rights, because only the rich may be able to afford to invest in land and trees. Preferential access to cheap formal credit by rich farmers with titled land will reinforce this tendency (Feder et al. 1988). To the extent that the rich acquire more secure land rights than the poor, the rich may also have stronger incentives to invest for long-term benefits. A counterargument is that since the principal input required for investment in land and trees is labor, poor households endowed with cheap labor may have an advantage over the rich.[9] Thus, who among differential income classes is most likely to invest in land and trees remains an empirical question. We explore this issue by including the farm size as one of the explanatory variables in the tree-planting function.

When land is abundant, migrants can "purchase" uncultivated village land by making small gifts to the community chief as a token of appreciation. Since migrants are generally poor, their acquisition of land becomes more difficult once land becomes scarce and more valuable. Indeed, in many cases migrants acquire cultivation rights by renting in land in areas where land rights are individualized. In areas where land rights are less individualized, so that individual rights to rent out are not established, migrants may not be able to find opportunities to rent in land. One question that arises is to what extent the individualization of land rights promotes tenancy contracts. Another question is the extent to which tenancy contracts contribute to the reallocation of land from land-rich and labor-poor households to land-poor and labor-rich households, given the inherent imperfection of agricultural labor markets due to asymmetric information (Hayami and Otsuka 1993). Tenancy markets, if they work efficiently, will be conducive to both efficiency and equity, as tenancy transactions tend to equate operational land-labor ratios across farms. We test the efficiency of land tenancy markets, as well as other factor markets, by assessing the effects of factor endowment on the labor inputs and profits of farm operation per unit of land.

Individualization of land rights may change the relative strength of land rights between husbands and wives. For example, in certain areas of Ghana where women traditionally were not allowed to own land, they began to acquire land ownership rights when they helped their husbands plant and manage cocoa trees (see Chapter 3). It may well be that when demand for women's labor in planting trees increases, greater land rights are given to them to enhance their work incentives. In other areas where women are denied rights to own trees, men's land rights appear to increase when they plant trees. These intrahousehold issues associated with the evolution of property rights are issues that have not yet been rigorously explored.

Who gains most from common property resources is a critical question in assessing the equity implications of the establishment of common property with clear rules of resource extraction. Do the rich and the powerful control the use of common property resources to their advantage at the expense of the poor? Or do the poor extract greater amounts of resources from the commons by allocating

---

9. Although the rich may be able to hire laborers for investment activities, the enforcement of labor contracts may be costly.

30   *Keijiro Otsuka and Frank Place*

more labor to such activities? Does the social norm or a sense of social justice in the community play any role in allocating rights of access to common property to the poor? These issues are addressed by assessing the impact of farm size and caste status on the allocation of labor to the extraction of resources from community forests in the case study of the hill region of Nepal (Chapter 8).

References

Alchian, A. A., and Harold Demsetz. 1973. The property right paradigm. *Journal of Economic History* 16 (1): 16–27.

Anderson, Terry L., and Peter J. Hill. 1990. The race for property rights. *Journal of Law and Economics* 33 (2): 177–197.

Angelsen, A. 1999. Agricultural expansion and deforestation: Modelling the impact of population, market forces, and property rights. *Journal of Development Economics* 58 (1): 185–218.

Atwood, David A. 1990. Land registration in Africa: The impact on agricultural production. *World Development* 18 (5): 659–671.

Ault, D. E., and G. L. Rutman. 1979. The development of individual rights to property in tribal Africa. *Journal of Law and Economics* 22 (2): 163–182.

Azhar, R. A. 1993. Commons, regulation, and rent-seeking behavior. *Economic Development and Cultural Change* 42 (1): 115–129.

Baland, Jean-Marie, and Jean-Philippe Platteau. 1996. *Halting degradation of natural resources: Is there a role for rural communities?* Oxford: Clarendon Press.

Barbier, Edward B., and Joanne C. Burgess. 1997. The economics of tropical forest land use options. *Land Economics* 73 (May): 174–195.

Bardhan, Pranab. 1993a. Analytics of the institutions of informal cooperation in rural development. *World Development* 24 (4): 633–639.

———. 1993b. Symposium on management of local commons. *Journal of Economic Perspectives* 7 (4): 87–92.

Besley, Timothy. 1995. Property rights and investment incentives. *Journal of Political Economy* 103 (5): 913–937.

Boserup, Ester. 1965. *Conditions of agricultural change.* Chicago: Aldine.

Bromley, Daniel W., ed. 1992. *Making the commons work: Theory, practice, and policy.* San Francisco: International Center for Self-Governance.

Bruce, J. W., and S. E. Migot-Adholla, eds. 1994. *Searching for land tenure security in Africa.* Dubuque, Iowa: Kendall/Hunt.

Cleaver, K., and G. A. Schreiber. 1994. *Reversing the spiral: The population, agriculture, and environment nexus in sub-Saharan Africa.* Directions in Development Series. Washington, D.C.: World Bank.

Curtis, Donald. 1991. *Beyond government: Organizations for communal benefit.* London: Macmillan.

Dasgupta, Partha S., and G. M. Heal. 1979. *Economic theory and exhaustible resources.* Cambridge: Cambridge University Press.

Deacon, R. T. 1994. Deforestation and the rule of law in a cross-section of countries. *Land Economics* 70 (4): 414–430.

de Meza, David, and J. R. Gould. 1992. The social efficiency of private decisions to enforce property rights. *Journal of Political Economy* 100 (June): 561–580.

Demsetz, Harold. 1967. Toward a theory of property rights. *American Economic Review* 57 (2): 347–359.

Ehui, Simeon K., Thomas W. Hertel, and Paul V. Preckel. 1990. Forest resource depletion, soil dynamics, and agricultural productivity in the tropics. *Journal of Environmental Economics and Management* 18 (March): 136–154.

Feder, Gershon, and David Feeny. 1993. The theory of land tenure and property rights. In *The economics of rural organization: Theory, practice, and policy,* ed. Karla Hoff, Avishay Braverman, and J. E. Stiglitz. Oxford: Oxford University Press.

Feder, Gershon, and Raymond Noronha. 1987. Land rights systems and agricultural development in Sub-Saharan Africa. *World Bank Research Observer* 2 (2): 143–169.

Feder, Gershon, Tongroj Onchan, Yongyuth Chalamwong, and Chira Hongladarom. 1988. *Land policies and farm productivity in Thailand.* Baltimore: Johns Hopkins University Press.

Fortmann, Louise, and John Bruce. 1988. *Whose trees?: Proprietary dimensions of forestry.* Boulder, Colo.: Westview Press.

Gardner, Roy, Elinor Ostrom, and James Walker. 1990. The nature of common-pool resource problems. *Rationality and Society* 2 (July): 335–358.

Grafton, R. Q. 2000. Governance of the commons. *Land Economics* 76 (4): 504–517.

Hardin, Garret. 1968. The tragedy of the commons. *Science* 162 (3859): 1243–1248.

Hayami, Yujiro. 1997. *Development economics: From the poverty to the wealth of nations.* Oxford: Oxford University Press.

Hayami, Yujiro, and Keijiro Otsuka. 1993. *The economics of contract choice: An agrarian perspective.* Oxford: Clarendon Press.

Hayami, Yujiro, and V. W. Ruttan. 1985. *Agricultural development: An international perspective.* Baltimore: Johns Hopkins University Press.

Jodha, N. S. 1986. Common property resources and rural poor in dry regions of India. *Economic and Political Weekly* 21 (27): 1169–1182.

Johnson, O. E. G. 1972. Economic analysis, the legal framework, and land tenure systems. *Journal of Law and Economics* 15 (1): 259–276.

Kaimowitz, David. 1995. *Livestock and deforestation in Central America in the 1980s and 1990s: A policy perspective.* EPTD Discussion Paper No. 9. Washington, D.C.: International Food Policy Research Institute.

Kaimowitz, David, and Arild Angelsen. 1998. *Economic models of tropical deforestation: A review.* Bogor, Indonesia: Center for International Forestry Research.

McIntire, John, Daniel Bourzat, and Prabhu Pingali. 1992. *Crop-livestock interaction in Sub-Saharan Africa.* Washington, D.C.: World Bank.

McKean, Margaret, and Elinor Ostrom. 1995. Common property regimes in the forest: Just a relic from the past? *Unasylva* 46 (180): 3–15.

Meinzen-Dick, Ruth, L. N. Rasmussen, and L. A. Jackson. 1996. Local organization for natural resource management: Lessons from theoretical and empirical literature. International Food Policy Research Institute. Mimeo.

Mendelsohn, Robert. 1994. Property rights and tropical deforestation. *Oxford Economic Papers* 46 (5): 750–756.

Nugent, Jeffrey B. 1993. Between state, markets, and households: A neoinstitutional analysis of local organizations and institutions. *World Development* 21 (4): 623–632.

Ostrom, Elinor. 1990. *Governing the commons: The evolution of institutions for collective action.* Cambridge: Cambridge University Press.

———. 1994. Constituting social capital and collective action. *Journal of Theoretical Politics* 6 (4): 533–568.

Peluso, Nancy. 1992. *Rich forests, poor people.* Berkeley: University of California Press.

Pingali, Prabhu, Y. Bigot, and Hans P. Binswanger. 1987. *Agricultural mechanization and the evolution of farming systems in sub-Saharan Africa.* Baltimore: Johns Hopkins University Press.

Pinstrup-Anderson, Per, and Rajul Pandya-Lorch. 1994. *Alleviating poverty, intensifying agriculture, and effectively managing natural resources.* Food, Agriculture, and the Environment Discussion Paper 1. Washington, D.C.: International Food Policy Research Institute.

Platteau, Jean-Philippe. 1996. The evolutionary theory of land rights as applied to Sub-Saharan Africa: A critical assessment. *Development and Change* 27 (1): 29–86.

Runge, C. Ford. 1981. Common property externalities: Isolation, assurance, and resource depletion in a traditional grazing context. *American Journal of Agricultural Economics* 63 (4): 595–606.

———. 1984. Strategic interdependence in models of property rights. *American Journal of Agricultural Economics* 66 (5): 807–813.

———. 1986. Common property and collective action in economic development. *World Development* 14 (5): 623–635.

Ruthenberg, Hans. 1980. *Farming systems of the tropics.* Oxford: Clarendon Press.

Seabright, Paul. 1993. Managing local commons: Theoretical issues in incentive design. *Journal of Economic Perspectives* 7 (4): 113–134.

Shepherd, Gill. 1991. The communal management of forests in the semi-arid and sub-humid regions of Africa: Past practice and prospects for the future. *Development Policy Review* 19 (1): 151–176.

Stoorvogel, J. J., E. M. Smaling, and B. H. Janssen. 1993. Calculating soil nutrient balances at different scales: I. Supra-national scale. *Fertilizer Research* 35: 227–235.

Wade, Robert. 1987. The management of common property resources: Collective action as an alternative to privatization or state regulation. *Cambridge Journal of Economics* 11 (2): 95–106.

———. 1988. *Village republics: Economic conditions for collective action in South India.* Cambridge: Cambridge University Press.

White, T. Anderson, and Runge, C. Ford. 1994. Common property and collective action: Lessons from cooperative watershed management in Haiti. *Economic Development and Cultural Change* 43 (1): 1–42.

Wilson, Paul N., and G. D. Thompson. 1993. Common property and uncertainty: Compensating coalitions by Mexico's pastoral Ejidatarios. *Economic Development and Cultural Change* 41 (2): 299–318.

World Bank. 1990. *World development report.* New York: Oxford University Press.
———. 1996. *African development indicators 1996.* Washington D.C.: World Bank.
———. 2000. *World development report.* New York: Oxford University Press.
World Resources Institute, United Nations Environmental Programme, United Nations
    Development Programme, and World Bank. 1998. *World resources 1998–99.* New
    York: Oxford University Press.

2 Quantitative Methodology

KEIJIRO OTSUKA AND FRANK PLACE

In our theoretical framework, land tenure institutions and collective action are chosen by communities for efficiency and equity purposes, and the choice is hypothesized to be determined by population pressure, commercialization of agriculture, policies, and natural and social environments (see Figure 2.1). Natural environments refer to the physical environments, such as topography, altitudes, and temperature, that influence the innate comparative advantage of an area for food production, agroforestry, woodland, and rangeland. Policy environments may encompass not only policies directly imposed on the community, such as land titling and ownership of land by the state, but also the quality and influence of government ministries and the judicial system. These in turn affect the choice of appropriate land tenure institutions. Social environments refer to social customs and social power structures, as well as social capital created through the long history of cooperation among community members (Putnam 1993). One of the critical variables is residential mobility, which influences the extent to which social capital can be sustained, as the theory of repeated games suggests (for example, Pearce 1992).

We assume that these five sets of forces affecting the choice of institutions and the effectiveness of collective action are essentially exogenous to the community (that is, not affected by the actions of the community). Of course, this assumption may not always be warranted. For example, the population growth of the community will be affected by the stock of uncultivated and accessible forestland within a community. Certain aspects of social environments, for instance, the extent of mutual trust in the community, may be more legitimately considered as endogenous, while other aspects, for instance, the tradition of matrilineal or patrilineal inheritance, can be assumed exogenous. Where an endogeneity problem occurs (that is, where one or more of the sets of forces are influenced by community actions), the analytical and empirical methods will need to be modified. We must also note that the exogenous forces may be interrelated; for example, government agricultural policies may affect the population growth rate and the extent of commercialization in agriculture in certain

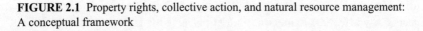

FIGURE 2.1 Property rights, collective action, and natural resource management: A conceptual framework

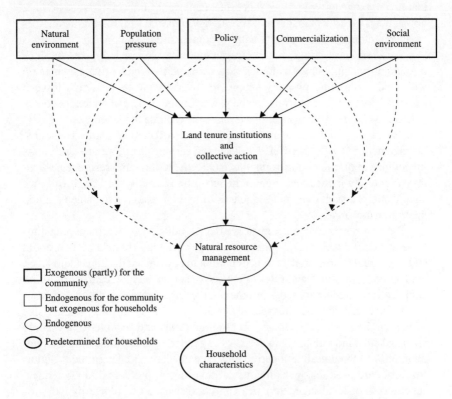

communities. We have to bear in mind these complexities in formulating statistical methodologies.

Some of the exogenous variables would affect natural resource management directly, as well as indirectly through their effects on the institutional choice. For example, growing population pressure may not only induce greater individualization of land rights but also promote directly the conversion of forests and rangeland to crop fields and the intensification of land use. There are, however, other sets of variables that may affect institutional choice but not natural resource management directly. Good examples are traditional inheritance rules; patrilineal systems under which use right of land is bequeathed to a farmer's sons can easily evolve into individual rights systems, whereas matrilineal systems in which members of a large extended family have partial rights to land tend to preserve extended family ownership systems. Although inheritance rules affect land tenure institutions, such rules per se would not affect natural resource management directly. Another example may be land titling; possession of land titles will strengthen individual land rights but not necessarily affect the manner of natural resource management directly. Information on exogenous variables that affect land rights and collective action but not natural resource management is critically important for distinguishing between direct and indirect effects within complex processes.

In some cases, land tenure institutions are imposed on communities through formal policy, for example, state ownership of land, private ownership with land titling, and publicly supported forest users' associations. In such cases, the focus of the analysis can be placed on the impact of the exogenously determined land tenure institutions on natural resource management.

However, land tenure institutions may be affected by natural resource management in the longer run. As discussed earlier, inappropriate land rights institutions may lead to unsustainable management of natural resources, which may eventually induce a change in the institution (see Figure 1.3). Ideally we should analyze such dynamic sequences of natural resource management and institutional change.

Natural resource management is affected not only by land tenure institutions, collective action, and some exogenous variables but also by household and individual characteristics. It is important to note that at the household level, land tenure institutions and rules of collective action may be regarded as either exogenous or predetermined, even though they are endogenous at the community level. Similarly, such household characteristics as family size and the size of the family's land endowment (in absolute terms and relative to household size) and such individual characteristics as gender, age, and educational attainment prior to the investment period may be considered predetermined. If plot-level data are used for the estimation of investment, profit, and labor demand functions, plot-level characteristics can be also used as predetermined variables. Furthermore, within a community, the five sets of exogenous factors specified in the upper portion of Figure 2.1 can be considered fixed and common for all households. These considerations imply that the critical variables in the analysis of natural resource management at the household level are land tenure and collective action and household and individual characteristics.

In order to analyze the efficiency of common property resource management, we need detailed household data on the allocation of labor time, grazing, and other resource extraction activities. Particularly in the case of woodland or forest resource management, the data requirements are demanding because many types of resources are extracted from the commons, for example, firewood, poles, timber, grasses, and leaf fodder. Such data collection would be impossible in a community survey. Thus, we propose to perform two sets of analyses based on two different types of surveys focusing on different aspects of the causal relationships illustrated in Figure 2.1. The first analysis may be termed an extensive study of communities located over wide areas endowed with different natural, social, market, and policy environments and different human and natural resources. The second analysis is an intensive study of households in selected communities, where different land tenure institutions and farming systems coexist.

Survey Methodology

Extensive Study

Our central hypothesis is that land tenure institutions will evolve in response to changing relative factor scarcities, which are affected by population pressure and commercialization of agriculture. We also postulate that the evolution of farming systems is affected by both natural and social environments. Needless to say, land tenure institutions are also directly affected by government land policies. Based on our theoretical framework, we propose to estimate the function explaining the incidence of land tenure (LT) institutions using the extensive community survey data:

$$LT = F \text{ (natural environment, population pressure, policy,}$$
$$\text{commercialization, social environment)}$$
$$= F(Z), \tag{1}$$

where Z stands for the five sets of variables that are considered to be mainly exogenous to the community. LT may be measured by the proportion of area under different land tenure institutions. Measurement issues are likely to arise in the specification of LT, because there are both written and unwritten rules on bundles of land rights available in rural communities. Explanatory variables to be used depend on the specific nature of the problem addressed. Population pressure may be endogenous, as might other social environment variables, and wherever possible instrumental variable estimation methods should be applied. Otherwise, it is preferable to use lagged variables, such as population density in the past. If land tenure institutions are solely policy-determined, this equation has no relevance.

An evolutionary model of land tenure institutions implies that the institutional choice is path-dependent, which suggests that LT in equation (1) is affected by changes in the stock of the natural resources in the past. It is therefore useful to specify an explanatory variable representing the condition of natural resource base in the past, if the data are available. The use of aerial photographs taken in the past is one way to obtain such data.

In order to examine changes in the stock of natural resources at the community level, we use changes in indicators, such as changes in the proportions of primary forest, woodlands, common property forest, and areas devoted to food, tree crops, and pastures in the community, as well as changes in vegetation or tree cover. These indicators of changes in natural resource stocks (ΔNR) can be regressed on LT and other relevant variables:

$$\Delta NR = NR_t - NR_0 = G \text{ (LT, } Z,' NR_0), \tag{2}$$

where NR_t and NR_0 pertain to the stock of natural resources at t-th and base periods, respectively, and Z' refers to a subset of exogenous varibles (Z) that direcly affect natural resource management.

A couple of remarks are in order about the estimation of equation (2). First, since the indicators are changes in stocks, they are affected by past as well as present values of the explanatory variables. It is desirable to analyze changes in the indicators of natural resource stocks, since it would purge out the influence of variables that equally affect the amount of the stock at two points in time. Use of aerial photographs and satellite images taken at different points of time is particularly useful for constructing appropriate dependent variables. Second, where the LT indicator is an endogenous variable, it is important to apply appropriate estimation methods. In the case studies of Malawi, Nepal, and Japan, the endogeneity is taken into account in the empirical specification of recursive equation systems. In the case of Uganda and Vietnam, the major land tenure institutions that are studied are legitimately considered exogenous. In the case of Ghana and Sumatra, community-level indicators of natural resource management are not available, and therefore we used recall data at the household level, using quick individual household surveys that complemented the extensive community survey. In these cases, we treated inherited and allocated family land tenure as either exogenous or predetermined for households and analyzed their effects on forest clearance and tree planting. Third, in estimating equation (2), the possibility of U-shaped changes in the stock of natural resources, envisaged in Figure 1.3, should be taken into account by including the state of natural resources in the base period.

Given the cross-sectional nature of the data set, it is difficult to analyze the historical paths of changes in land tenure institutions and natural resource management. In order to shed some light on this issue, we used the individual household survey data to trace out historical changes in the relative importance of various modes of land transfers, such as different types of inheritance (for example, from father or mother), inter vivos gifts, family allocation, forest clearance, private purchase, and land rental, for Ghana, Indonesia, and Malawi.

Intensive Study

Although the analysis of the extensive survey data is expected to provide an overview of the evolutionary process of land tenure institutions and their consequences, it does not provide us with a clear picture of how natural resources are managed by users. Furthermore, in analyzing extensive survey data we take the impact of household characteristics into account only by using "aggregate" socioeconomic variables for each community (for example, the proportion of minority ethnic groups with different inheritance rules). In order to examine how land tenure institutions and household characteristics affect natural resource management practices, we need to conduct detailed household surveys in selected communities where different land tenure institutions coexist.

As already argued, it may be reasonable to assume that land tenure institutions are exogenous or predetermined in the analysis of household data, so long as they are determined by the community or the large extended family. If, however, the strength of land rights can be changed by individual farmers, for instance, by investing in land using one's own resources and labor, they must be regarded as endogenous. In such cases, either a simultaneous equations system must be formulated,[1] or preexisting land tenure institutions or the modes of land acquisition, rather than ex post land rights, must be used as explanatory variables to ascertain causality.

Using household survey data, we would first like to assess the impact of land rights on investment in land and trees using plot-level data:

INVESTMENT = H (ML, characteristics of plots and household),   (3)

where ML stands for the modes of land acquisition, which are often used as land tenure variables in the intensive survey analysis. The modes of land acquisition are not subject to change or highly open to choice, unlike land rights, and, hence, they may be considered as predetermined. The effects of ML may be insignificant, if investment in trees sufficiently strengthens land rights, as was explained in Chapter 1. Wherever relevant, we acknowledge the possibility of simultaneous equation bias and take it into account in the interpretation of the estimation results. Note that Z variables do not appear in this equation, as they are fixed and common in a selected village.

Since land tenure institutions are often different on different plots of land, it is desirable to estimate equation (3) at the plot level. Characteristics of households should include variables related to both human and physical capital endowments. Particularly important will be variables representing wealth, such as the size of land ownership and cattle, and gender of plot managers if men and women own or operate different plots of land. We are particularly interested in whether the rich invest more resources per hectare and whether the strengthening of women's land rights promotes investment in land improvements.

In order to isolate the effect of the plot-level tenure variable, we apply the household-level fixed effects model as much as possible (this controls for the effect of unobservable household characteristics) when we estimate equation (3), as well as equation (4) specified below. Earlier application of the fixed effects model in similar context is found in Place and Hazell (1993). We also use alternative specifications to test the effect of key household-level variables that

---

1. If there are a large number of land tenure institutions prevailing within a village, which can be expressed only by the institutional dummies, it is not feasible to apply simultaneous equation methods.

are noted above. Furthermore, to control for correlations of error terms across plot-level observations, we also apply the random effects model where feasible.

Clearance of virgin forest is one form of investment for future benefits, and, accordingly, the dependent variable in equation (3) may be area acquired by clearing unclaimed forest. In this case, household data will be more appropriate for the analysis, simply because the decision to acquire new land is initiated and acted on by households. This creates the need to develop household-level tenure variables.

Second, we would like to assess the relative profitability of different farming systems, for example, shifting cultivation versus sedentary food crop production or tree crop production, which correspond to unit isoquants of $I_0 I_0$, $I_1 I_1$, and $I_2 I_2$ in Figure 1.2, respectively. For this purpose, we propose to estimate the profit function:

$$\text{PROFIT} = I \text{ (ML, characteristics of plots and household)}, \qquad (4)$$

where profit may be measured by the residual profit per hectare, which can be obtained by subtracting costs of nonland inputs (including the imputed value of labor) from the value of outputs. The profit thus computed is supposed to correspond to returns to land and management effort and efficiency. We do not use prices as explanatory variables, because they do not vary meaningfully within a community. If perennial crops are grown, the age of trees must be included as an explanatory factor, and the present value of profiles of investment costs and flows of expected profits must be assessed to compare their profitability with that of annual crops. The quality of land also needs to be controlled for, in order to distinguish the "pure" effect of land rights institutions on profit from possible indirect effects through relationships with land quality. The effect of ML may be insignificant, if long-term investment sufficiently strengthens land rights and if equation (4) is estimated after controlling for the effects of tree and other stock variables. Characteristics of plots should include variables representing the history of cropping patterns, which can be used to assess the sustainability of various farming systems.

Important variables to be included among household characteristics are farm size, the endowment of land relative to family labor, and gender of cultivator possessing use or ownership rights. Farm size is used to assess the significance of scale economies or diseconomies. The owned land-family labor ratio is used to examine the efficiency of factor markets, as factor endowments will not affect the efficiency of production if competitive factor markets operate so as to equalize land-labor ratios across different plots. Whether ownership by gender has any significant influence on the profitability of farming has important implications for the intrahousehold allocation of land rights.

The analysis of profitability is complementary to the analyses of the evolution of land tenure institutions and investment behavior. If we observe that land tenure institutions evolve toward individualized tenure and that such change promotes investment in land and trees, we ought to find a higher profitability for the new farming systems that required prior investment.

Similar to equation (4), we would like to estimate the impact of land tenure institutions on labor use per unit of land under different farming systems:

$$\text{LABOR/LAND} = J \text{ (ML, characteristics of plots and household).} \quad (5)$$

A critical question is the impact of new farming systems on the demand for labor, which may be differentiated by gender. The estimation of equation (5) examines the validity of the theory of induced institutional innovation, which asserts that increased population pressure on limited natural resources leads to the adoption of new institutions that save the use of natural resources (for instance, land) relative to labor.

Data Collection Methodology

The first task in the data collection phase was to identify major issues in the management of land and trees in a particular region through literature review, examination of secondary data, and informal exploratory surveys. We have found informal surveys to be particularly useful, because good prior studies on property rights and collective action are often unavailable. Even if available, the information is sometimes obsolete, as these institutions are dynamic and can be site-specific. Since we need to obtain a variety of information through questionnaire surveys, the pretesting of survey questionnaires was essential.

In the extensive study, we applied either random sampling of communities located over wide areas or stratified random sampling with stratification based on demographic factors and access to markets. A community may be defined as a single village or as large as a group of three to five villages, particularly when aerial photographs were used to assess the management of land and trees. However, when studying common property forests, which are often used by more than a single community, the forest itself is a more relevant study unit. Sixty to 100 communities or forests were chosen in each country or each major region within a country depending on the complexity of the issues to be studied.

Various data sources and data collection methods were used in the extensive study, which included (1) secondary data on demographic variables, climatic variables, and farming practices; (2) official data on land titles; (3) data on spatial variability of the physical environment, land use, vegetative cover, and other indicators of natural resource management, obtained from the analysis of aerial photographs and satellite images; (4) direct measurement of indicators of natural resource management, such as density of young seedlings and mature trees, their diameters at breast height, and the composition of valuable species of plants; (5) community survey data obtained from group interviews of key informants on socioeconomic variables, such as land rights, rules of resource use, access to markets, agricultural practices, and the development of

TABLE 2.1 Overview of sample size

Country	Extensive Study		Intensive Study	
	Number of Communities	Number of Households	Number of Communities	Number of Households
Ghana	60	420	10	200
Sumatra				
(Indonesia)	60	300	4[a]	200[a]
Malawi	57	570	8	141
Uganda	64		6	98
Vietnam	56		4	200
Nepal—hill	100[b]	500	6	120
Nepal—inner Tarai	102[b]			
Japan	61[b]		8[b]	61[c]

[a]Including case study of rubber agroforestry, which is not reported in this book.
[b]The number of sample forests.
[c]The number of sample plots in selected forests.

credit, labor, and land markets; and (6) brief household survey data on the history of use of natural resources (farmland, forests, and woodlands) and modes of farmland acquisition. We applied these data collection methods in the particular research sites where they were appropriate. For example, supplementary brief household surveys were conducted in Ghana, Sumatra, and Malawi, where village-level data on land use, land area, or inheritance practice were either unavailable or unreliable. Sample sizes are shown in Table 2.1.

Particular attention was paid to the bundle of land rights and indicators of natural resource management and collective action. For classification of land use, as well as estimation of areas under different land tenure institutions in a community, the technique of resource mapping based on interviews with villagers and aerial photographs was found to be very useful.

Selection of appropriate communities for the intensive household survey was based on the results of the extensive survey. We chose communities with contrasting characteristics in terms of prevailing land tenure institutions, farming systems, and degradation or protection of natural resources. Four to 10 villages were chosen for the household survey (Table 2.1). Sample sizes depended not only on the complexity of issues but also on the accuracy and coverage of data necessary for our statistical analyses. Since we are interested in the estimation of tree planting, profit, labor use, and production functions of resource extraction activities, we tried to obtain accurate labor and wage data.

In the intensive survey, both qualitative and quantitative information on the practices of natural resource management has been sought. We also attempted to obtain data on family composition, inventory of assets, histories of acquisition of assets and land use, current production, and nonlabor input use, in addition to property rights.

Overview of Case Studies

Countries Selected

We have chosen northern Vietnam, western Sumatra, hill and inner Tarai regions of Nepal, western Ghana, central Uganda, and Malawi, as well as central Japan, as study sites with a view to drawing comparative perspectives between Asia and Africa. Malawi, Ghana, and Sumatra have been chosen to analyze the evolution of communal land tenure institutions in diverse natural, social, and policy environments, whereas Uganda and Vietnam have been chosen to identify the effects of communal, state, and private ownership on natural resource management. Nepal and Japan have been selected to address the issue of common property resource management.

Table 2.2 provides some general economic, demographic, and forest resource indicators at the national level for each country. First of all, it is obvious that Japan is the most wealthy, distinct from the remaining countries because of its very high income, low dependence on agriculture, high rate of urbanization, high population density, low growth rate of population, and stable forest cover. It is clearly at a different stage of development than the other countries, and the welfare of its citizens is less dependent on the natural resource base. Yet we found it illuminating to compare the experience of evolutionary changes in community forest management toward the individualized system in postwar Japan with community forest management in contemporary Nepal. The remaining discussion in this subsection focuses on the six developing countries.

Four countries stand out as among the poorest countries in the world, with 1995 GNP per capita figures of $240 or less: Vietnam, Nepal, Uganda, and Malawi. For these countries, poverty alleviation through economic growth is the paramount policy objective. In these same countries, the vast majority of the population resides in rural areas (more than 80 percent), and the agricultural sector is an important contributor to the GDP. This means that strategies for short-term growth and poverty alleviation are likely to be aimed at agriculture and the rural sector. Thus, there are likely to be many conflicts, in the short run, between meeting these objectives and at the same time improving the long-term management of natural resources. However, increasing the efficiency of natural resource management in poor rural areas creates opportunities to achieve poverty reduction and the improvement of the natural resource base. Although the average household income is considered to be noticeably higher in Ghana and particularly in Indonesia, the populations in our sites in western Ghana and Sumatra are also very poor because of the maldistribution of income across regions.

TABLE 2.2 General characteristics of study countries

Country	GNP per Capita (US$ in 1995)	Agriculture as Percentage of GDP, 1995	Population Density, 1993	Annual Population Growth Rate, 1980–93	Percentage of Population in Rural Areas, 1993	Annual Rate of Forest Area Change, 1980–95
Ghana	390	46	69	3.3	65	−1.2
Sumatra (Indonesia)	980	17	98	1.7	67	−0.8
Malawi	170	42	89	4.2	87	−1.2
Uganda	240	50	77	2.4	88	−0.9
Vietnam	240	28	215	2.2	80	−1.0
Nepal	200	42	148	2.6	87	−0.9
Japan	39,640	2	329	0.5	23	0.0

SOURCES: World Resources Institute et al. (1996, 1998).

High levels of population growth among the poorer countries and in Ghana hamper efforts to increase per capita income growth. Malawi had an extremely high population growth rate of 4.2 percent, and since most of the absolute increase occurred in rural areas, the demand for land resources increased significantly. We expect that a significant amount of land had been converted into agriculture in Malawi and Ghana, with pressures almost as high as in Nepal, Uganda, and Vietnam. It is likely that population growth alone is behind much of the deforestation reported in Table 2.2, where the annual rate of deforestation varied between 0.8 and 1.2 percent among the developing countries between 1980 and 1995. Although Indonesia does not suffer from similarly high population growth, it nonetheless is characterized by a high proportion of population in rural areas, coupled with traditional shifting cultivation widely practiced in the outer islands. Thus, population growth would contribute to deforestation rates there as well. Although population densities differ across countries, within each there are large pockets of heavily populated areas, for example, areas with population densities exceeding 200 persons per square kilometer. In such areas, a large share of land had been previously converted to agriculture, and key natural resource management issues pertain to those related to agricultural resources, including agroforestry.

Characterization of Study Sites

There are similarities and dissimilarities among our seven study sites (see Table 2.3). Both the Ghana and Sumatra sites are characterized by the communal ownership systems. Moreover, both sites have a comparative advantage in agroforestry over pure food production under shifting cultivation, owing to hilly or mountainous topography on which annual crops cannot be grown sustainably without large investment. In western Sumatra, large areas of primary forests still exist in the national park, even though some portions have been converted to irrigated paddy fields, crop fields under slash-and-burn farming systems, and fields of commercial trees such as rubber, coffee, and cinnamon. In western Ghana, primary forests have largely disappeared and been replaced either by crop fields under shifting cultivation or by cocoa fields.

Although Malawi is also characterized by communal ownership, mixed food crop and tree systems are less profitable as compared with food cropping systems than in Ghana or Sumatra, as many areas are characterized by flat topography. There are also communally owned forests on hilly portions of Malawi, but they are largely open access except for small and infrequent Village Forest Areas strictly protected by cooperation between village organizations and the Forestry Department. Most community woodlands have been converted to crop fields in this country (with the exception of the sparsely populated north). The Uganda sites contain communal, private, and state-owned areas. Coffee is grown in hilly and humid areas nearer to Lake Victoria, and charcoal is a major product of woodlands in the rest of the areas, which are generally

TABLE 2.3 Characterization of study sites

Country	Land Tenure	Major Products of Agroforest/Forest	Topography
Ghana	Communal	Cocoa	Hilly
Sumatra (Indonesia)	Communal	Rubber, cinnamon, and coffee	Hilly/ mountainous
Malawi	Communal/ common property	None/minor forest products	Flat/hilly
Uganda	Communal/private/ state	Coffee/charcoal	Hilly/flat
Vietnam	State/private	Timber and fruit	Mountainous
Nepal—hill	Common property	Firewood, fodder, grass, and leaf litter	Mountainous
Nepal—inner Tarai	Common property (collective and centralized management)	Timber	Hilly
Postwar Japan	Common property (collective and individual management)	Timber	Mountainous

flat and dry. As in Malawi, woodlands have been degraded and converted to crop fields in most areas.

In northern Vietnam, natural forests in mountainous areas had been seriously denuded as a result of the expansion of food cultivation area until the end of the 1980s, when Vietnam launched major economic reform programs, including privatization of land tenure. The village area typically consists of flat lowland, mostly occupied by paddy land, and forestland on mountainous areas. Although the whole area is state-owned, use rights over forestland for 50-year periods have been distributed to individual farmers in selected areas in recent years. This policy has stimulated regeneration of forests by protection and planting of timber, fruit, and other perennial trees through the decisions of farmers. Firewood and other minor forest products are amply available from remaining forests and wooded areas in the Vietnam sites.

In contrast, those minor forest products are extremely scarce in the hill region of Nepal, where community forests are seriously degraded. In this particular environment, as in mountainous areas in prewar Japan (McKean 1992), common property systems with strict management rules of extraction regarding these minor products have emerged in selected locations. In the inner Tarai region of Nepal, which is flatter and has better access to markets, timber is a major forest product. In Japanese timber forests during the postwar period, both collective and individualized management systems coexist, even though forest-land is commonly owned by the community.

Land Use Systems and Land Tenure Institutions

Our basic hypothesis is that land tenure institutions change over time to achieve socially more efficient resource allocation. If so, the choice of land tenure institutions ought to be governed by land use systems, as the desirable land tenure insitutions are different for different land use systems. This seems to be the case in practice, as is demonstrated in Table 2.4. In customary land areas where agro-forestry has a comparative advantage, individualization of land tenure institutions has been taking place. This is consistent with our hypothesis that land tenure institutions change to stimulate investment in trees. On the other hand, in customary land areas where continuous food cultivation has a comparative advantage, land tenure institutions are individualized in some places (e.g., flat areas of Uganda) but not so in other places (e.g., Malawi and paddy fields in Sumatra). One interpretation is that similar to the case of investment in tree planting, efforts to invest in land improvement conferred strong land rights where such investment was profitable. Individualized land rights are also established in paddy fields in Vietnam, as the government has approved individual use rights.

Although it may not be costless to protect tree and food crops, it is much more costly to protect minor forest products, such as firewood, feed grasses, and

TABLE 2.4 Comparison of land use systems and land tenure institutions across study sites

Land Use Systems	Characteristics of Land Tenure Institutions	Study Sites
Agroforestry	Individualization	Ghana, Sumatra, hilly areas of Uganda
Crop fields for continuous cultivation	Individualized/collective	Flat areas of Uganda, Malawi, Sumatra/Vietnam
Nontimber forests	Unregulated common property	Malawi
	Emergence of regulated common property	Hill regions of Nepal
Timber forests/ plantations	Privatized or centralized management of common property	Inner Tarai region of Nepal, Japan
Timber forests/ fruit orchards/tea	Individualized	Vietnam

fodder. This is because these products tend to be grown in areas away from residential areas and can be harvested almost continuously through the year and detection of loss can be difficult. Moreover, unlike tree and food crop production that requires work effort, no such effort is required for management of nontimber forests. Thus, what is at stake is protection but not work effort and incentives in production activities. Our hypothesis is that common property regimes could be more efficient than private and other ownership systems when resources extracted from common property are minor forest products. In fact, nontimber forests are "managed" under common property regimes in Malawi and the hill region of Nepal. Such a relationship is illustrated in Table 2.5. In a comparison of the two countries, road systems are relatively well developed in Malawi, and thus access to markets is relatively favorable. Therefore, farmers can purchase chemical fertilizer and firewood at the markets. In contrast, the hill villages in Nepal are highly isolated, and farmers cannot survive without a local supply of firewood, leaf fodder, and feed grasses. This may be the major reason why the use of nontimber forest resources is largely unregulated in Malawi, whereas it is regulated strictly in an increasing number of hill forests in Nepal.

The protection of timber is less costly than that of minor forest products, as timber is bulky and difficult to haul without being detected by other members of the community. In addition, timber production requires management of trees through such silvicultural activities as weeding, pruning, and thinning. Thus, strong work incentives provided by private and other ownership systems are indispensable for proper management of timber trees. We therefore argue that the management of timber forests is more efficient under private land tenure than under common property systems. If the protection of timber is costly, for example, because of a threat of grazing, a combination of common property and private property systems, in which protection is carried out communally and management is carried out individually or by central management committee, may be optimum. Consequently, timber forests are often managed by privatized and cen-

TABLE 2.5 Hypothesized relationships among cost of protection, management intensity, and efficient land use and land tenure systems

Cost of Protection	Management Intensity	
	Low	High
Low	Crop fields for shifting cultivation	Agroforestry, crop fields for continuous cultivation, timber forests/ private ownership
High	Nontimber forests/ common property	Timber forests/centralized community management

tralized management systems in Japan and Nepal. In Vietnam, farmers chose to manage sloped land parcels for timber and other tree crop production individually, rather than collectively, following the allocation of individual use rights. As illustrated in Table 2.5, this is likely because, like agroforestry and continuous food cultivation, timber and tree crop production in Vietnam is management-intensive, which requires relatively low cost of protection of tree resources.

We expect that the more detailed comparative analyses of land tenure institutions and the characteristics of dominant natural resources in the chapters that follow will shed new light on the conditions under which different land tenure institutions and farming systems emerge and function efficiently.

Focus and Organization of the Book

This book consists of five parts. Following this introduction in Part I, Part II addresses the issues of evolution of customary land tenure institutions and its consequences on the management efficiency of forest, agroforest, and cropland and the equity implications between the rich and poor and between men and women, based on case studies in Ghana, Sumatra, and Malawi. We test the hypothesis that communal ownership systems generally evolve toward individual systems with increased population pressure and other changes by estimating functions explaining the incidence of various land tenure institutions using extensive survey data. Then we test whether tree planting and preservation of tree resources were facilitated by the shift to individualized ownership of land using the same data set. Our general contention is that the efficiency of tree resource management improves with strengthened individualized land rights. To corroborate this point, we estimate tree-planting, profit, and labor use functions using household data.

Part III is concerned with the impacts of different land tenure institutions on resource management based on the comparison of communal, state, and private land ownership in Uganda and state land ownership and the more individualized ownership system recently introduced in Vietnam. In these countries, major land tenure institutions that stipulate the land rights of the state, landowners, and occupants of customary land have been determined by authorities above the community level. Our studies focus on the consequences of land policies on the management of forest resources, tree planting, the efficiency of farming, and the intensity of labor use.

Part IV is devoted to the exploration of the conditions under which the common property regime is a viable and efficient institutional arrangement based on the case studies of hill and inner Tarai forests in Nepal and forests in central Japan. How efficiently common property forest is managed is explored in Nepal by using data of forest conditions generated by aerial photos and data of households' resource extraction patterns from the commons and in Japan by using parcel-level data.

The impact of women's land and tree rights on farmland and tree resource management is a final area of emphasis in this study. It is well known that traditional systems of land and tree tenure are particularly discriminatory against women. In many parts of Africa, women are traditionally not allowed to plant trees, because tree planting would be viewed as usurping the rights or decision-making power of males. With respect to farmland, the lack of or weak tenure rights for women are likely to reduce their incentives to invest in agroforestry or other land improvements bringing future benefits. In the case of woodlands or forests on which women depend to provide fuel, water, fodder, and medicines to their family, they may have clear incentives to organize collective action so as to ensure sustainable management of those renewable resources. In areas where land rights are privatized, women's access to land, trees, and other forest resources is likely to change. We propose to identify how far women's rights to land and trees are suppressed compared with men and to assess the consequences of such restricted rights on the efficiency and welfare outcome of forest and farm resource management. The gender analysis is carried out particularly in the context of western Ghana and western Sumatra, where land tenure institutions have been transformed from communal to individualized ownership.

The summary of research findings and policy implications is discussed in Part V. In particular, we advocate the establishment of profitable agroforestry and the promotion of incentive-compatible forestry projects as ways to reduce poverty and restore tree-based environments in areas where they have a comparative advantage by enhancing the efficiency of resource allocation.

References

McKean, Margaret A. 1992. Management of traditional common lands (*Iriaichi*) in Japan. In *Making the commons work: Theory, practice, and policy,* ed. D. W. Bromley. San Francisco: ICS Press.

Pearce, David G. 1992. Repeated games: Cooperation and rationality. In *Advances in economic theory: Sixth World Congress,* ed. Jean-Jacques Laffont. Cambridge: Cambridge University Press.

Place, Frank, and Peter Hazell. 1993. Productivity effects of indigenous land tenure in Sub-Saharan Africa. *American Journal of Agricultural Economics* 75 (1): 10–19.

Place, Frank, Michael Roth, and Peter Hazell. 1993. Land tenure security and agricultural performance in Africa: Overview of research methodology. In *Searching for land tenure security in Africa,* ed. J. W. Bruce and S. E. Migot-Adholla. Dubuque, Iowa: Kendall/Hunt.

Putnam, Robert D. 1993. The prosperous community: Social capital and public life. *American Prospect* 13 (1): 35–42.

World Resources Institute, United Nations Environment Programme, United Nations Development Programme, and World Bank. 1996. *World resources 1996–97.* New York: Oxford University Press.

———. 1998. *World resources 1998–99.* New York: Oxford University Press.

PART II

Evolution of Customary Land Tenure

3 Agroforestry Management in Ghana

AGNES QUISUMBING, J. B. AIDOO,
ELLEN PAYONGAYONG, AND KEIJIRO OTSUKA

Ghana is a predominantly agricultural country, and 95 percent of its total area of 239,000 square kilometers is potentially suitable for agriculture. In the 1990s, the agricultural sector accounted for about 44 percent of the GDP and employed about 59 percent of the labor force (World Bank 1998). In the 1970s, the latest date for which statistics are available, its contribution to foreign exchange earnings was 62 percent, and it produced 60 percent of industrial raw materials (Land Use Planning Committee of Ghana 1979). Its importance for national development therefore cannot be disputed.

If agriculture is the engine of growth of the Ghanaian economy, the cocoa sector is its hub. Growth trends in the country's economy have been critically influenced by the performance of the cocoa sector.[1] Over the past two decades, however, both cocoa production and cocoa prices on the world market have been declining. The country's output dropped from 401,000 metric tons in 1975 to 159,000 metric tons in 1983 and, after rebounding slightly, has stagnated at around 280,000 metric tons for the past 10 years. Nonetheless, the importance of cocoa still remains high for the economy; cocoa contributes 24 percent of foreign exchange earnings (Institute of Statistical, Social, and Economic Research 1995), whereas 18 percent of the total population of the country is in the cocoa sector (Ghana Statistical Service 1995). For most households in southwestern Ghana, it is the main, if not the only, source of livelihood. The population of cocoa farmers is likely to increase as cocoa frontier areas continue to attract migrants. Furthermore, the government has adopted a price incentive policy that increased the proportion of domestic to world cocoa prices from 6 percent in 1983 to 50 percent in the mid-1990s.

We are grateful for constructive comments on the earlier draft by George Benneh.

1. For example, when cocoa production fell by 9.6 percent from 1993 to 1994, the agricultural growth rate dropped from 2.5 percent to 1.0 percent, and the growth rate of the entire economy declined from 5.0 percent to 3.8 percent (Institute of Statistical, Social, and Economic Research 1995).

The indigenous method of cocoa production has remained essentially unchanged. Although new hybrid varieties are being introduced, cultivation is still based on extensive use of land with no application of chemical fertilizer and minimal use of pesticides. Since the soil of the natural forest is inherently fertile, farmers have a strong desire to clear forests for cultivation. In fact, because virgin forests have been cleared to produce cocoa and food crops under shifting cultivation for the past hundred years, it is estimated that Ghana's rainforest area has declined from 8.2 million hectares to 2.1 million hectares (Ortsin 1998). Out of 2.1 million hectares, 1.7 million hectares are reserve forest areas. It will not be long before the remaining forests outside the reserves disappear altogether. Given the high population growth rate and declining trend of cocoa production, the improvement of land use practices to sustain the cocoa industry is becoming an increasingly important issue.

Population pressure on limited land resources has resulted in shorter fallow periods under shifting cultivation, which has reduced soil fertility and, hence, sustainability of shifting cultivation. In the case of cocoa production, cocoa and food crops are intercropped for the first few years, and after cocoa trees mature, only cocoa is cultivated on the land. Consequently, the expansion of cocoa area entails a reduction of food cultivation area. Whether the expansion of cocoa area at the expense of area devoted to food crops is desirable for farmers remains to be verified. Moreover, the role of customary land tenure in the allocation of limited land resources for food cultivation, fallow, and cocoa production is not well understood.

All land used for cocoa cultivation in Ghana is under customary land ownership, in which land use rights have traditionally been granted to the extended family, even though the ultimate ownership rights were vested in the village chief (Asenso-Okyere, Atsu, and Obeng 1993). Tenure arrangements, however, have been evolving toward individualized ownership over time. When population was small and virgin forests were abundant, migrants were allowed to clear forests for cultivation, and this process resulted in the rapid reduction of forest areas, as vividly described by Hill (1963). With the disappearance of virgin forests, migrants lost such opportunities and instead sought tenancy and caretaker (or labor) arrangements (Benneh 1989). Meanwhile, land tenure arrangements for the indigenous population have also undergone substantial changes from ownership by the extended family under the uterine matrilineal inheritance system to more individualized ownership systems. This chapter attempts to explore the causes of evolutionary changes in customary land tenure institutions and their consequences on the efficiency of land use for food production, fallow, and cocoa production.

The organization of this chapter is as follows. An overview of the customary land tenure institutions in western Ghana is presented in the next section. We then discuss the sampling strategies used in the extensive and intensive studies along with a description of the study sites. In the section on the extensive survey study, we present major hypotheses followed by the estimation of functions explaining the choice of land tenure institutions and the mode of land acquisition. The section on the intensive study consists of subsections on major hypotheses and the estimation of a cocoa-tree-planting function, a fallow choice function, and net revenue and labor allocation functions for cocoa cultivation and food crop cultivation. Finally, the overall policy implications from both studies are discussed in the last section.

Customary Tenure Systems in Western Ghana

Uncultivated forestland is owned by the community or village, and the village chief serves as the custodian of forest area. In reality, village forest is open access for the community members, as was the case also for migrants when forestland was abundant (Berry 1963; Hill 1963; Robertson 1982). Thus, the clearance of forest is easily approved by the chief, so long as forestland is available. Forest clearance requires a large effort, and those who clear forests are rewarded by relatively strong individual rights to land. Such individually rewarded land rights are further strengthened if land converters make long-term or permanent improvements in the land, such as tree planting. Land rights, however, tend to become weaker if land is put into fallow over extended periods. The majority of people in western Ghana belong to the Akan ethnic group, which practices uterine matrilineal inheritance, whereas a number of inhabitants in migrant villages belong to non-Akan ethnic groups, which are generally subject to the patrilineal inheritance system. The mode of land transfer has been evolving over time. When virgin forests were abundant, forests were appropriated primarily by young males before marriage mainly for production of food crops. Traditionally, in the Akan matrilineal system, this type of land was either bequeathed to nephews or allocated to other male members of the extended family, in accordance with the decision of the family head. Wives and children were left with no rights to a man's property if he died intestate (Brydon 1987). Uncultivated fallow land was often allocated temporarily to members of the extended family, who possessed small landholdings. More recently, the appropriated village land is increasingly being transferred directly to one's wife and children, and even the family land is often transferred to them with the consent of the family members, particularly after the land was planted either wholly or partially with cocoa trees. Such inter vivos transfers are termed "gifts" in our study areas, and individual rights on such land are firmly established.[2] It is believed that gifts are used to circumvent existing matrilineal rules so that children may become heirs to

---

2. Such inter vivos gifts are formalized by the recipient's presenting ritual drinks to family elders and other witnesses in the *aseda* (thanksgiving) ceremony. The drink is the physical expression of appreciation for the gift and is crucial so that the transfer of land rights by gift will not be contested in the future. When a husband gives land to his wife and children, it is their responsibility to provide the drinks, although a husband may secretly do so if the recipients cannot afford it.

their parents' land (Migot-Adholla et al. 1993). Land rights have also been more clearly individualized among migrants, who either have nuclear families or practice patrilineal inheritance in which a relatively small number of sons within a single family are qualified to inherit their father's land. In contrast, a large number of heirs, including brothers and nephews of the deceased, are qualified for inheritance under uterine matrilineal systems.

Individualization or privatization of land rights amounts to the demise of traditional matrilineal inheritance, that is, the allocation of cultivated land among male members within the husband's extended families. Instead, land will be transferred to the most preferred persons at will by the landowner. Individualization, along with greater scarcity of land, will also promote the development of land rental and sale markets. The degree to which such market transfers of land contribute to production efficiency is another important empirical question.

The process of individualization of land tenure institutions may have been strengthened by the passing of the Intestate Succession Law (ISL, PNDCL 111) in 1985, which provides for the following division of the farm: three-sixteenths to the surviving spouse, nine-sixteenths to the surviving children, one-eighth to the surviving parent, and one-eighth in accordance with customary inheritance law (Awusabo-Asare 1990). Thus, the law allows children and wives to gain access to land that they were previously denied under traditional law.[3]

Study Sites

We conducted an extensive survey of 60 villages in the most active cocoa-growing regions in Ghana: the Western Region, the Brong-Ahafo Region, and the Ashanti Region in 1996/97 (Figure 3.1). In the Western Region, two areas were surveyed covering two districts each, the Wassa area and the Sefwi area. Sefwi and Wassa have different migration and settlement histories and are administratively and linguistically distinct, although the languages are related. Cocoa cultivation has historically spread from the Eastern Region toward the Ashanti and Brong-Ahafo Regions in the 1940s and 1950s and farther toward the frontier area of the Western Region during the 1950s and 1960s (Berry 1963; Hill 1963). The diffusion of cocoa to Wassa and Sefwi continued in the 1970s and 1980s. We randomly selected 15 villages each in the Brong-Ahafo and Ashanti Regions and 15 each in Wassa and Sefwi, of which 9 are predetermined to be indigenous villages and 6 are migrant villages. A group interview with village leaders and other members was conducted to obtain information about land rights under different land tenure institutions, among other

---

3. Interestingly enough, the common interpretation of the ISL is one-third each among spouse, children, and maternal family. This is remarkably similar to the *abusa* share tenancy arrangement, which is discussed subsequently.

things.[4] Population census data collected in 1984 were also obtained for 58 villages.[5] Data on village land area, total as well as cultivated and uncultivated areas, however, are not available. In order to construct indicators of population pressure at the village level, we conducted a survey of seven randomly selected households in each village.[6] We also obtained information about the mode of land acquisition and cocoa planting and yields from these sample households. Unless otherwise indicated, the extensive survey data used in this chapter come from the survey of seven households in each of the 60 villages.

For the intensive survey, we conducted a survey of households in 1996/97, which were surveyed by the World Bank in 1987/88 in 10 selected villages in the Wassa area of western Ghana (Migot-Adholla et al. 1993). With the exception of reserve areas, virgin forests have already disappeared in our study sites. Our study sites are mostly hilly, and the deterioration of forest environments has resulted in soil erosion and other negative environmental externalities. Cocoa fields are usually covered by tall shade trees, as cocoa trees are grown better in shade. The establishment of cocoa agroforestry in sloping land would reduce soil erosion and contribute to the partial restoration of tree biomass and biodiversity (Gockowski, Nkamleu, and Wendt 2001). Valuable timber trees, however, are not grown as shade trees, because farmers are not allowed to own such trees.

We originally intended to create a panel data set by revisiting those households surveyed in the earlier World Bank study. However, land tenure status in the previous survey was not clearly defined, and parcels owned by women in male-headed households were not included.[7] Furthermore, because of the

---

4. Since people seldom consider the land rights under different land tenure institutions explicitly and systematically, it took considerable time to arrive at consensus on each question. This experience led us to believe that it is not feasible to obtain accurate information on land rights from interviews with individual households.

5. As the migrant population increased, migrants, who tend to live in the periphery of indigenous villages, eventually formed new villages. Two of our migrant villages had not yet been established by 1984. Although we attempted to compute the population growth rate at the village level from 1970 to 1984, it was not possible to do so, because of the establishment of new villages and associated changes in village areas.

6. We had previously conducted a survey of 15 households in each village. Because of the extreme complexity of land tenure institutions, the use of local and varying measurement units for land areas, and inexperience of enumerators, this data set suffered from inaccuracy manifested in unbelievably large numbers and the lack of information about land parcels owned by female household members. Therefore, we subsequently conducted another survey of seven households in each village and paid more careful attention to consistency and plausibility of replies by our respondents and to ownership of land by women. We found that, as of 1997, women own about 10 percent of land in indigenous villages and 8 percent in migrant villages.

7. The only parcels managed by women in the World Bank study were in female-headed households. Also problematic are the lack of distinction between patrilineal and matrilineal inheritance rules and between female household heads and female plot managers in male-headed households and the lack of information on the intensity of tree planting. Neither was the productivity of cocoa and food crop cultivation considered separately.

FIGURE 3.1 Location of study sites in Ghana

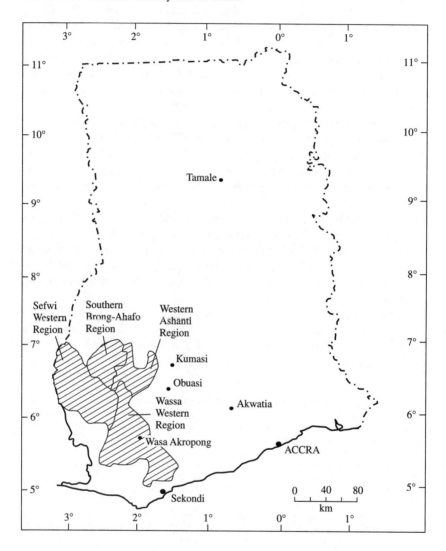

changing distribution of area across land tenure types, the World Bank samples no longer correspond to the actual distribution of land by tenure status in 1996. We also found the sample size of 150 randomly selected households in the earlier survey too small for our purpose, considering the complexity of the prevailing land tenure institutions. Thus, after conducting a census survey of 1,878 households in the 10 survey villages, we chose 281 households based on stratified random sampling of pure owners, pure tenants, pure caretakers (who manage mature cocoa fields, usually for absentee owners), owners-cum-tenants, owners-cum-caretakers, and tenant caretaker households.[8] Sample sizes were allocated to the 10 villages in proportion to village population, and to the extent possible, the earlier sample households that agreed to be reinterviewed were included.

For each sample household, we collected information on land tenure status and land use of all parcels, which are defined as contiguous areas of land acquired at the same time through a single mode of acquisition. We also collected land use histories for all these parcels, including previous land use and dates when land was converted to different uses. From all the fields currently held by the household, we then randomly sampled mature and young cocoa fields and food-producing fields managed separately by men and women and by tenants, owners, and caretakers if different field managers coexisted in the same household.[9]

Extensive Study

Land Use and Land Rights

Annual crop fields and fallow areas under shifting cultivation, including secondary forests, exist along with cocoa fields in our study sites (Benneh 1987, 1989). Table 3.1 summarizes the land use patterns, average farm size, and person-land ratio in indigenous and migrant villages. Indigenous villages tend to have larger farm sizes, a lower person-land ratio, and a large area devoted to bush-fallow land. Cocoa area per farm, however, is slightly lower in indigenous villages than in migrant villages. Indigenes are the original owners of land from whom migrants acquire land and are thus more likely to have larger landholdings.[10] Migrants are also more likely to have acquired land through rental agreements that require cocoa planting.

Table 3.2 shows the distribution of currently adopted inheritance rules by Akans and non-Akans in indigenous and migrant villages.[11] Among the tradi-

---

8. A total of 281 households were interviewed, but 23 were dropped for various reasons (including noncompletion of questionnaires for all three rounds). This brings the total to 258 households. The household tenure status can only be created for 257 households, since the tenure variable for some fields is missing in one household. Our subsequent discussion refers to the 257 remaining households.

9. A field is defined as a portion of a parcel characterized by the same cropping pattern.

10. An alternative hypothesis is that migrants are individuals who self-select into growing cocoa. This explanation, however, is unlikely to be important, given massive immigration not of isolated individuals but of whole extended families or clans into our study regions from outside. In fact, massive migration from the eastern to the western frontier regions has been a major process in the development of the cocoa industry in Ghana (Hill 1963).

11. We used data obtained from 408 households rather than the full sample of 420, because of missing and inconsistent data from 12 households.

TABLE 3.1 Land use patterns, farm size, and person-land ratio in 1997 in selected villages in western Ghana

	Sample Size	Bush-Fallow–cum–Forest Area per Farm	Cocoa Area per Farm	Total Farm Size[a]	Person-Land Ratio
	(number of villages)	(hectares)	(hectares)	(hectares)[a]	(persons/hectare)
Indigenous villages	36	5.50	4.99	11.98	1.16
		(44.30)	(48.90)	(100.00)	
Migrant villages	24	3.21	5.41	9.53	1.31
		(37.10)	(59.10)	(100.00)	

SOURCE: Extensive survey.

NOTE: Numbers in parentheses pertain to the average percentages of cocoa and bush-fallow–cum–forestland to total farm area.

[a]Total includes small areas used for other purposes.

TABLE 3.2 Distribution of currently adopted inheritance rules by ethnic group and type of village

	Number of Sample Households	Matrilineal	Intestate Succession Law[a]	Patrilineal
		(percentage)		
Akan people:				
Indigenous villages	235	45.1	40.4	14.5
Migrant villages	120	41.7	40.8	17.5
Non-Akan people:				
Indigenous villages	11	0.0	18.2	81.8
Migrant villages	42	7.1	11.9	80.9

SOURCE: Extensive survey.

[a]Common interpretation of the Intestate Succession Law is one-third equal sharing among spouse, children, and maternal family.

tionally matrilineal Akans, the percentage of households reporting that they follow the ISL is quite high (about 40 percent), and some households even report the practice of patrilineal descent. In contrast, among non-Akans, the predominant pattern of inheritance is patrilineal (80 percent), and only 12 to 18 percent of households follow the ISL. It appears that the ISL has little effect on patrilineal inheritance practice, in which land tenure systems are inherently more individualized.

Table 3.3 presents the distribution of land by mode of acquisition in migrant and indigenous villages. Inherited land accounts for a smaller share of land than land received as gift, particularly in indigenous villages. Transfer of land to sons as gift has been practiced historically (Hill 1963), but the incidence of gifts to wives seems to have increased in recent periods.[12] The larger share of gift land would reflect a shift to individualized property rights, reducing the matriclan's control over land. In indigenous villages, the share of temporarily allocated family land is also larger than inherited land, suggesting that the importance of allocated family land also increased at the expense of inherited land.

As may be expected, appropriated village forestland with permission from the village chief accounts for a larger share in indigenous villages than in migrant villages, even though indigenes migrating to nearby migrant villages ap-

---

12. We examine historical changes in importance of gifts and other modes of land transfer using intensive household survey data later in this chapter. See Quisumbing et al. (2001) for a related analysis of the impact of the individualization on land rights of men and women in western Ghana.

TABLE 3.3 Distribution of area under different land tenure regimes in western Ghana

	Indigenous Villages	Migrant Villages
	(percentage)	
Allocated family land	22.4	8.5
Inherited family land	13.2	17.9
Appropriated village forestland	18.1	9.7
Purchased village forestland	0.4	12.4
Received as gift	33.0	25.8
Privately purchased	3.8	5.2
Acquired through renting	1.0	3.3
Currently renting	6.6	15.5
Others	1.5	1.7

SOURCE: Extensive survey.

propriated land from the chiefs of their original villages. More often, migrants acquired village forestland by purchase through presenting tributes, the most important of which was schnapps, to the chiefs of indigenous villages. Hill (1963) observed that the chiefs were glad to seize the opportunity of selling land outright to enterprising migrants. As uncultivated forestland has disappeared, renting land under share tenancy arrangements, called *abusa* (one-third of land ownership for the tenant) and *abunu* (50:50), has become the primary means for migrants to acquire access to land (Robertson 1982; Boadu 1992). In these tenancy contracts, tenants are requested to plant cocoa trees usually on bushland and manage cocoa trees until the whole field is planted to cocoa, at which time land ownership, rather than output, is usually divided between tenant and landowner (Asenso-Okyere, Atsu, and Obeng 1993).[13] The fact that renting is widely practiced with ultimate division of land ownership between the contracting parties suggests that land ownership rights have been strongly individualized so as to allow for the alienation of land that was formerly to be transferred to other family members. This inference is reinforced by the nonnegligible incidence of private land purchase, which has traditionally been prohibited.[14]

---

13. The major harvesting season of cocoa extends from October to January. We suspect that the major reason for dividing land rather than sharing output lies in the difficulty for the owner to check cocoa output accurately. If output cannot be measured accurately, the tenant may be able to cheat the owner. See Otsuka, Chuma, and Hayami (1992) and Hayami and Otsuka (1993) for surveys of share tenancy literature.

14. Since we did not anticipate the prevalence of private land purchase, we failed to ask about land rights on privately purchased land in our formal group interviews. However, informal interviews suggest that strong rights, comparable to those of gifts, are conferred to individuals who purchase land using their own funds. If purchase is financed by a group of extended family members, however, individual land rights are rather weak.

In order to measure the strength of the individualization of land rights under different land tenure institutions, we asked through group interviews whether the following six rights exist: (1) to plant and replant trees, (2) to rent out land, (3) to pawn, (4) to bequeath, (5) to give, and (6) to sell. The numbers in Table 3.4 show the average number of cases in which farmers have rights without approval from family members or the village chief. The weakest land rights are observed in temporarily allocated family land, in which even tree planting is not allowed. Thus, if land tenure security at the time of tree planting determines investment incentives, we expect to observe that cocoa trees are seldom planted in allocated family land. Land rights are also weak in inherited land among matrilineal Akan households, which is in contrast to the case of patrilineal households bestowed with fairly strong rights on inherited land. It seems that land rights are more easily individualized in patrilineal society, as the interests in the same piece of land are shared primarily by a small circle of individuals, consisting of a father and his sons.

Strong land rights are also observed in formerly village forestland, whether appropriated by indigenes or purchased by migrants. The rights are somewhat stronger in migrant villages presumably because migrants are less subject to the tradition of the family ownership of land. Strong land rights accrue on cleared forestland, because efforts to clear forest are rewarded by strong individual land rights. The strongest land rights are observed in tree-planted land received as gift by the current landholder. Gifts are usually made by a father to his children and sometimes to his wife, after seeking consensus from

TABLE 3.4 Index of land rights under different land tenure regimes in western Ghana

	Indigenous Village	Migrant Village
Temporarily allocated family land		
Food cropland from father	0.1	0.1
Food cropland from family	0.5	0.3
Inherited family land		
Akan (matrilineal)	1.1	1.0
Non-Akan (patrilineal)	n.a.	3.3
Village forestland		
Appropriated by indigenes	3.0	3.4
Purchased by migrants	3.0	3.9
Tree-planted land transferred as gift		
From father	4.9	5.3

SOURCE: Based on group interviews in extensive survey.

NOTE: The following six rights are considered: (1) plant or replant trees; (2) rent out land; (3) pawn; (4) bequeath; (5) give; and (6) sell. The numbers in this table show the average number of cases in which farmers have rights without approval from family members or village chief. "n.a." refers to "not applicable."

members of the extended family. The strong rights are conferred to reward the effort exerted to plant and grow trees. This observation indicates that incentives to plant trees on allocated family land and inherited land may be strong if individual land rights are strengthened by planting trees, as was demonstrated in Chapter 1. It is a mistake to assume that incentives to invest in land governed by customary land tenure rules are universally very weak.

Determinants of Land Tenure at the Village Level

It was postulated in Chapter 1 that population pressure on land induces changes in customary land tenure institutions from family ownership (for example, acquired through allocation and inheritance) to individualized ownership (for example, through gift). We hypothesize in the context of Ghana that the advent and widespread adoption of gifts serve the role of providing incentives to invest in trees. As is emphatically argued by Platteau (1996), however, this autonomous process of evolution of land rights institutions will not lead to the establishment of complete private ownership system with land titling, which completely internalizes externalities associated with incomplete or insecure land ownership.

Note that in order to transfer land through gift, the agreement of the lineage head (*abusuapanin*) and other members of the extended family or lineage (*abusua*) must be obtained. Thus, the incidence of gifts is determined not only by the characteristics of the household that received land but also by those of the extended family. It is therefore appropriate for our hypothesis testing to use village-level data on population pressure and the incidence of gifts and other land tenure systems. Thus, we constructed estimates of the proportions of land under (1) family ownership (that is, allocated and inherited land) and individualized ownership acquired by (2) gift, (3) forest clearance, and (4) private purchase and renting, using data from the survey of seven households per village. We then estimated the following reduced-form functions explaining the incidence of the various land tenure institutions using a common set of explanatory variables:

$$S_i = a_{0i} + a_{1i} \text{ (population pressure indicators)}$$
$$+ a_{2i} \text{ (proportion of migrant population)}$$
$$+ a_{3i} \text{ (a vector of other village characteristics)}$$
$$+ a_{4i} \text{ (regional and area dummies)} + e_i, \tag{1}$$

where S_i stands for the proportion of i-th type of land ($i = 1, \ldots, 4$), a_{ji} are parameters, e_i is the error term, and all explanatory variables are village-specific except for regional dummies.[15] Population pressure is measured by the person-

---

15. Since the sum of S_i is unity, it is redundant to estimate the four share functions except to show the significance of coefficients directly.

TABLE 3.5 Means of other explanatory variables for village-level regression analysis on land tenure choice

	Indigenous Village	Migrant Village
Distance to nearest market town (km)[a]	13.9	18.6
Proportion of nonfarm households in 1984 (percentage)[b]	8.2	4.2
School attendance ratio in 1984 (percentage)[b]	26.0	21.0
Proportion of migrant population in 1995[a]	31.5	87.2

SOURCES: Extensive survey; 1984 Population Census.

[a]Based on group interviews.

[b]Based on population census.

land ratio as a proxy for population density. We hypothesize that the person-land ratio has a positive effect on the incidence of individualized forms of land tenure.

Village characteristics include distance to the nearest market town, the proportion of nonfarm households, school attendance ratios, and the proportion of migrants in the population (Table 3.5). School attendance ratio is used to capture the average quality of human capital and thus the quality of labor in the community. It is clear that migrant villages are located in more remote areas with less access to nonfarm jobs. There was, however, not much difference in primary school attendance ratios in 1984 between indigenous and migrant villages.

Since some categories were nonexistent in some villages, the proportion in various land tenure categories would be bounded upward by 100 and downward by 0. We thus applied the two-limit tobit estimation method, and the results are exhibited in Table 3.6. We also included the percentage of female-headed households and the percentage of Akan households in each village among the regressors, but none of these variables was significant, and regressions with these variables are not reported. It is possible that there is not much variation in these variables across villages; gender differences in household structure and inheritance practices are more likely to affect household-level outcomes. Moreover, village-level variables created from only seven household observations per village may not capture intravillage variation adequately.[16]

The coefficient of the person-land ratio is positive and highly significant in the gift equation, which supports our hypothesis that population pressure induced institutional innovation toward individualized land tenure. One may argue that person-land ratio is endogenous and thus that the estimated coefficient is biased. It is, however, unreasonable to assume that the prevalence of gift leads

---

16. We did not include the indigenous village dummy because it is highly correlated with the proportion of migrants in the population ($r = -.70$).

TABLE 3.6 Determinants of proportions of areas under different land tenure institutions at the village level: Tobit regression

	Family Land[a]	Gift	Village Forestland	Market Acquisition Land[b]
Intercept	0.476**	0.197*	0.041	0.044
	(3.86)	(1.99)	(0.32)	(0.51)
Person-land ratio	−0.070	0.183*	−0.009	−0.073
	(−0.71)	(2.33)	(−0.09)	(−1.05)
Proportion of migrant population	−0.001**	0.0003	−0.0003	0.001**
	(−2.47)	(0.62)	(−0.43)	(2.66)
Distance to town	−0.003*	−0.002	0.006**	−0.0001
	(−1.70)	(−1.40)	(2.99)	(−0.06)
Proportion of nonfarm households	−0.002	0.002**	0.0002	−0.001
	(−1.46)	(2.42)	(0.20)	(−0.94)
School attendance ratio in 1984	0.348	−0.313	0.243	0.222
	(1.46)	(−1.64)	(0.97)	(1.33)
Wassa dummy	−0.065	−0.038	0.090	0.002
	(−1.14)	(−0.84)	(1.57)	(0.06)
Sefwi dummy	−0.096	0.03	0.084	−0.011
	(−1.55)	(0.61)	(1.34)	(−0.25)
Brong-Ahafo dummy	−0.147**	0.017	0.018	0.101**
	(−2.62)	(0.38)	(0.32)	(2.57)
Log likelihood	32.06	44.95	26.64	43.02
Chi-square	20.05	16.31	17.75	29.21
p-value	0.01	0.04	0.02	0.0003
Number of observations	58	58	58	58

NOTE: Two-limit tobit estimates; ancillary parameter σ not reported. *t*-statistics in parentheses. One-tailed tests.

[a]The sum of inherited and allocated family land areas.

[b]The sum of areas purchased, rented, and acquired through past renting.

*.05 level

**.01 level

to an increased person-land ratio, as gifts are not available to migrants. In any case, the person-land ratio is closely correlated with the incidence of gift. As expected, the proportion of migrant population is negatively associated with the share of family land. Because migrants have less access to village forestland, they acquired cultivation rights mainly by renting in land or sometimes purchasing land from indigenes, as is indicated by positive coefficient of the proportion of migrant population in the market acquisition land equation. Strictly speaking, migration is endogenous, and migrants are likely to seek villages that are known to sell land. The negative effect of the migrant population on access to village forestland indicates that the opportunity for migrants to acquire village forestland has been largely exhausted.

Other variables are insignificant except in two cases. First, distance to town has a positive effect on the proportion of forestland, which indicates that remaining forests are largely concentrated in areas quite remote from roads and urban centers. Second, the Brong-Ahafo dummy also has a negative effect on the proportion of forestland and a positive effect on acquired nonforest land, suggesting that land tenure institutions have evolved toward market-based transactions in this region. This is not surprising because Brong-Ahafo was one of the earlier destinations of the westward geographical movement of cocoa area from the Eastern Region (Hill 1963).

Recall that the person-land ratio and shares of land areas under different land tenure institutions were estimated from data obtained from interviews of seven households in each village. In all likelihood, owing to the small number of observations per village, they are subject to measurement errors. Nonetheless, it is remarkable to find a significant relationship between population pressure and the emergence and widespread adoption of gifts in customary land areas.

Determinants of Land Acquisition at the Household Level

The village-level regressions are useful to identify factors affecting the choice of land tenure institutions, but we cannot assess how households choose among different land tenure institutions and how these choices are interrelated. Thus, we use household-level data to analyze the behavior of households regarding the acquisition of land. Although it is reasonable to assume that the acquisition or clearance of forestland, rental and purchase of land, and the development of agroforests reflect choices made by an individual household, the acquisition of land through inheritance and family allocations is determined primarily by the extended family.

Table 3.7 shows the average year of land acquisition by land tenure, together with proportion of cocoa area and cocoa yield, which are examined in the next section.[17] Several important observations can be made. First, village forestland was acquired in the earliest years. This is partly because village forestland was acquired primarily by young unmarried males and partly because forestland had been exhausted mostly in the 1970s. Clearing forestland to establish one's own farm was a rite of passage for young Ghanaian males. Among our respondents, the average age at marriage was 25 years, and they

---

17. We analyzed the determinants of cocoa tree planting and yield at the parcel level using the extensive survey data (see Quisumbing et al. 2001). We do not report the results here, because the results using the intensive household data are similar and more reliable.

TABLE 3.7 Proportion of area planted to cocoa trees before acquisition and in 1997, average year of land acquisition, and cocoa yield in 1997 by land tenure type in western Ghana

| | Average Year of Land Acquisition | Proportion of Cocoa Area | | Yield[a] |
		Before Acquisition	1997	
		(percentage)		(kilograms/ hectare)
Acquired village forestland				
Indigenous villages	1975	0.0	62.2	172.7
Migrant villages	1968	0.0	68.8	258.6
Inherited land				
Indigenous villages	1980	28.0	35.9	184.8
Migrant villages	1979	40.2	53.3	316.1
Allocated family land				
Indigenous villages	1983	16.7	38.8	139.4
Migrant villages	1990	24.2	46.4	150.9
Land received as gifts				
Indigenous villages	1982	20.5	50.8	167.2
Migrant villages	1983	25.2	64.4	176.6
Acquired land though renting				
Indigenous villages	1987	19.1	60.8	203.2
Migrant villages	1975	29.2	70.0	316.4
Rented land				
Indigenous villages	1990	2.6	46.9	142.1
Migrant villages	1989	2.2	55.4	111.0
Purchased land from nonfamily				
Indigenous villages	1984	3.6	48.9	170.7
Migrant villages	1983	3.8	62.4	202.6

SOURCE: Extensive survey.

[a]Production per farmland planted to cocoa.

would have cleared forestland roughly 19 years ago, in 1976. The last time forestland was acquired from the chief or through purchase of village land was in 1989. Second, the transfer of family land through inheritance, allocation, and gift would have occurred for the average household in the early 1980s. Third, except for the case of land acquisition through land rental in migrant villages where migrants acquired cultivation rights in earlier years, the acquisition of land through renting and private purchase generally occurred in later years.[18]

---

18. Renting land is a traditional practice for migrant households. Many early migrants who could not afford to purchase land engaged in share tenancy contracts; the recent increase of renting among indigene farmers may indicate the exhaustion of other traditional modes of acquiring land.

The above observations indicate that a man follows a sequential decision-making process with respect to land acquisition over his life cycle: if forestland is available, he acquires it through clearance when he is young, acquires family land through inheritance, allocation, and gift when he gets married, and later acquires additional land through renting and private purchase. There is a possibility that the acquisition of forestland by clearing depends on how much land is anticipated to be allocated or inherited in future. This is, however, unlikely to be important, because how much family land is transferred to a particular individual is the decision of the extended family, which often consists of more than 40–50 members. Although forestland is largely open access, forest clearance requires a great deal of hard work. Moreover, forests in accessible areas have increasingly disappeared over time. It is therefore reasonable to specify a recursive system of equations in which, first, the acquisition of forestland is determined by exogenous forces; second, the acquisition of family land is explained by the amount of forestland acquired as well as the exogenous forces; and finally, the acquisition of land through market transactions is accounted for by the entire set of predetermined land areas under different land tenure institutions and other exogenous factors. That is:

$$\text{Forestland} = b_0 + b_1 \text{ (vector of exogenous variables)} + e_1 \qquad (2)$$

$$\text{Family land or inheritance} = c_0 + c_1 \text{ (vector of exogenous variables)} \\ + \gamma \text{ (forestland)} + e_2 \qquad (3)$$

$$\text{Purchased or rented land} = d_0 + d_1 \text{ (vector of exogenous variables)} \\ + \delta_1 \text{(forestland)} + \delta_2 \text{(family land)} + e_3, \qquad (4)$$

where b_i, c_i, and d_i are parameters and e_i is an error term.

The exogenous variables in our estimation include the age of the household head, the year of marriage (a proxy for the start of own farming), years of schooling, a dummy for patrilineal household, a dummy for being a migrant to the village, distance to town, and regional dummies. We test two specifications: in the first, we use current holdings of forest- and family land as regressors in the subsequent equations; in the second, we use forest- and family land acquired prior to the first date of acquisition of family land and acquired nonforest land, respectively. The second definition imposes a more rigorous definition of predetermined forest and family landholdings.

We hypothesize that the egalitarian motive of customary land tenure institutions leads to a reduction in the amount of family land transferred to a household if the latter has already acquired village forestland. The transfer of family land will be also smaller in the case of patrilineal households as land tenure institutions are more clearly individualized. We also hypothesize that if land acquired through forest clearance and transfer of family land is insufficient, additional land will be acquired through renting and purchase. In other words, increased scarcity of land induces the development of land rental and sale markets.

Since certain types of land are not observed in a number of sample households, and because unobservable village characteristics may affect land acquisition decisions, we applied Honore's (1992) tobit estimation method with village fixed effects.[19] The results are shown in Table 3.8. The first column shows the determinants of forest area acquisition by households. The age of the household head has a positive and highly significant effect, which indicates that cultivable primary forests have largely disappeared in recent years as a result of the clearance of primary forests on a first-come basis. The dummy for being a migrant to the village has a positive effect on acquired forestland. This may reflect migrant households' strong desire to acquire land for cultivation, given the availability of forestland in the village.[20] The dummy for a patrilineal household has a negative effect on forest acquisition. Patrilineal households, which usually consist of long-distance non-Akan migrants, have no rights to clear forests, unlike short-distance Akan migrants.

The next two columns display the estimation results for the acquisition of family land including gifts. We initially hypothesized that the prior acquisition of forestland would have a negative coefficient, in line with the view that communal land tenure institutions are designed to achieve equitable distribution of land. In the first specification, in which current forestland was used as an explanatory variable, however, this coefficient is not significantly different from zero. In the second specification, using the strict definition of predetermined forestland led to nonconvergence of the estimates, and this variable was dropped from the regression for family land. In both specifications, patrilineal households and those who have migrated to their current villages of residence also have smaller areas of family land because they do not inherit family land in the area of relocation. The coefficient of years of schooling is positive, which may be taken to imply that the amounts of schooling and landholdings of the extended family are positively correlated.

According to the last two columns, forestland has a negative and significant coefficient, while the coefficients of family land are negative but only one of them is weakly significant (10 percent). This indicates that households seek additional land through renting and purchase when the traditional meth-

---

19. This estimator is preferred because it is both consistent and asymptotically normal under suitable regularity conditions and assumes neither a particular parametric form nor homoskedasticity.

20. This result may appear inconsistent with the negative effect of the proportion of migrant population on the share of acquired forestland reported in Table 3.6. Note, however, that a dummy for patrilineal household is included in Table 3.8 but not in Table 3.6. The results from Table 3.6 suggest that the positive effect on forest clearance of being born in nearby indigene villages is outweighed by the negative effect of patrilineal long-distance migrant households.

ods of land transfer are insufficient. In short, land scarcity stimulates land market transactions. The negative coefficients of acquired forestland and family land also imply that land market transactions transfer land from land-rich to land-poor households. There is also indication that better-educated household heads are able to acquire land through renting or purchase, probably because these require previous savings, managerial ability, and access to information. Better-educated individuals may also be engaged in nonfarm activities that provide easier access to cash for purchasing land.

Summary and Conclusions for Extensive Study

Under increasing population pressure, shifting cultivation becomes unsustainable because gradual decreases in the fallow period reduce soil fertility. Under such conditions, more labor-intensive and land-saving farming systems must be established. Doing so requires investment in land, but incentives to invest may be weak or close to nonexistent under traditional communal land tenure institutions, which are characterized by family or clan ownership of land with weak individual land rights. We found, however, that customary land tenure institutions have evolved toward individualized systems. We also obtained evidence that households with little land through inheritance or forest clearance are more likely to acquire land through markets. This evolution has been facilitated by the stipulation of the customary land tenure institutions that confers strong individual land rights to those who exert efforts to clear forest and to invest in land improvement, including tree planting. So long as population continues to grow, the profitability of long-term investment for intensified land use will further increase, which will either sustain or accelerate the evolution of customary land tenure institutions.

The observations that tree planting confers the right to pass land as a gift and that land received as a gift has strong rights imply that it is not necessarily land tenure security but, more important in our observation, expected *changes* in land tenure security that affect incentives to invest in tree planting and management. This is one of the major issues we address using the intensive household survey data in the next section.

Intensive Study

Major Hypotheses for Intensive Study

We postulate that evolutionary changes in customary land tenure institutions have taken place to achieve greater efficiency in the use and allocation of land for food crop production and cocoa agroforestry. Shifting cultivation implies that land will be periodically put to fallow in order to restore soil fertility. However, because of tenure insecurity under traditional land tenure institutions,

TABLE 3.8 Determinants of land acquisition at the household level: Tobit regression with village fixed effects

	Forestland	All Family Land	All Family Land[a]	Acquired Nonforest Land	Acquired Nonforest Land
Forestland (current)		-0.08 (-0.39)		-0.35* (-1.79)	
Forestland (predetermined)[b]			—[c]		-0.28* (-1.75)
Family land (current)				-0.67* (-1.93)	
Family land (predetermined)[b]					-1.02 (-1.52)
Age of household head	9.19** (2.38)	0.38 (1.12)	0.17* (1.69)	0.37 (1.44)	0.04 (0.43)
Year of first marriage of household head	0.56 (0.21)	-0.24 (-0.63)	0.12 (0.88)	-0.04 (-0.17)	-0.25* (-1.98)

	(1)	(2)	(3)	(4)	(5)
Dummy for household head born outside village	49.85*	−26.12	−5.38**	9.34*	7.07
	(2.13)	(−1.59)	(−3.29)	(2.12)	(0.84)
Years of schooling of head	−6.16	2.10**	0.46**	0.56*	0.44**
	(−1.62)	(3.07)	(3.27)	(1.91)	(2.63)
Dummy for patrilineal household	−90.54*	−10.21*	−4.68**	3.63	1.98
	(−2.16)	(−1.75)	(−2.90)	(1.14)	(0.22)
Chi-square	18.1	31.1	277.2	32.5	230.4
p-value	0.2	0.0	0.0	0.0	0.0
Number of observations	386	386	386	386	386

NOTE: Least absolute deviations estimator. t-statistics in parentheses. One-tailed tests.

[a] Family land includes allocation, inheritance, and gifts.

[b] Predetermined landholdings consist of land acquired prior to the first date of acquisition of land in the dependent variable category.

[c] Not included because of nonconvergence.

* .05 level

** .01 level

there is no strong guarantee that the cultivator can keep fallow land for his or her own use in the future. The most feasible strategy to guarantee use rights is to use the land continuously. Thus, we hypothesize that tenure insecurity induces the shortening of the fallow period, which is suboptimal from the cultivator's viewpoint.

In contrast, if trees are planted, individual tenure security is enhanced, and rights to give land to desired heirs are strengthened. It is therefore reasonable to hypothesize that incentives to plant cocoa trees are affected not only by tenure security but also by its expected changes after tree planting. If tree planting enhances tenure security, incentives to carry out subsequent management of trees through such activities as weeding and pruning may be high. In particular, weeding when trees are young has pervasive long-term impact on the growth and future productivity of cocoa trees. Thus, once trees are planted, management efficiency may not be so different among parcels under different land tenure regimes. In short, we expect that incentives to keep land fallow, plant trees, and manage them could be different even for parcels with the same tenure status (for example, inherited land), depending on the initial level of land tenure security and its expected changes due to tree planting. Using household-level data, we test these hypotheses by estimating tree-planting, fallow choice, and net revenue functions.

Land Tenure and Land Use

Table 3.9 shows the distributions of all fields and selected fields by land use type. Cocoa trees begin to produce output starting from the fourth to fifth year. We classify cocoa fields into mature cocoa fields from which cocoa can be harvested and young cocoa fields intercropped with food crops. Although the number of mature cocoa fields is smaller than the number of young cocoa fields, mature cocoa fields are much larger. This is because cocoa trees are planted gradually from one portion of the parcel to the next, with new fields being merged with other tree-planted fields. Although the majority of cocoa fields are cocoa monocrop fields, there are cocoa fields intercropped with other perennials. Fallow land occupies a large area, whereas land devoted entirely to food crops is less common. This is because food crops and cocoa are traditionally grown in an intercropped farming system: food crops are planted while the cocoa trees are still young, and once the cocoa trees are too tall to provide adequate sunlight for food crops, food is no longer grown as an intercrop. Growing food and cocoa intercrops also takes advantage of weeding labor, since the ground around young cocoa trees has to be kept free from weeds. Since cultivators often do not know the length of the fallow period on all their parcels, our data on the duration of the fallow period for all selected fields are incomplete. However, available information indicates that the fallow period commonly ranges from 5 to 10 years.

We oversampled food crop fields for the collection of detailed production data. Usually various food crops are grown together in an intermingled manner

TABLE 3.9 Distribution and size of operational landholdings for all sample and selected sample fields, by land use type

	All Fields		Selected Fields		
	Number	Size	Number	Size	Number of households
		(hectares)		(hectares)	
Mature cocoa	504	1.85	276	2.02	213
Young cocoa	701	0.60	218	0.67	187
Food only	197	0.52	112	0.53	106
Fallow only	548	2.37	0	n.a.	n.a.
Food and fallow	12	0.54	6	0.43	6
Others[a]	39	1.65	0	n.a.	n.a.
Total	2,001	1.42	612	1.25	249

SOURCE: Intensive survey.

NOTE: All sample fields refer to all fields of sample households, whereas selected sample fields refer to those fields selected for the detailed input and output survey. A field is defined as a portion of a parcel characterized by the same cropping pattern. "n.a." refers to "not available."

[a]Fields entirely planted to kola or palm oil trees.

in the same field, and we identified 12 crop types, including maize, plantain, cassava, and yams. We collected one-year production data, but a few crops, such as plantain, need more than a year to bear fruit and are continuously cultivated for two to three years in our survey area. Thus, when we estimate the net revenue function of food crops, in order to control for the effects of crop mix, we used estimates of the proportions of various crops as explanatory variables, assuming that various crops grown together in multiple-crop fields account for equal proportions of land area. As may be expected, there are only a small number of mixed fallow-crop fields.

Table 3.10 describes the distribution of land use according to prevailing land tenure categories. Among our sample villages, seven are indigenous villages inhabited primarily by Akan people subject to matrilineal inheritance, and three are migrant villages inhabited mostly by migrants generally following patrilineal inheritance. Our sample consists of 85 percent matrilineal, 9.4 percent patrilineal, and 5.6 percent mixed households. According to Table 3.10, temporarily allocated family land is more important than inherited land. Renting has become a common way for migrants to obtain access to cultivable land. Tenants are contracted to plant and establish cocoa trees. Migrants, as well as young Akan men, also work as caretakers in mature cocoa fields, for which they commonly receive one-third of harvested crop output. A non-negligible number of fields are borrowed from nonrelatives.

As in the extensive survey villages, the weakest land rights are observed in temporarily allocated family land, in which even tree planting is not allowed

TABLE 3.10 Distribution of all sampled fields under different land tenure regimes, by land use type

	Mature Cocoa	Young Cocoa	Food Only	Fallow Only	Food/ Fallow	Others	Total
			(number of fields)				
Allocated family land	42	62	42	83	3	6	238
Inherited family land	29	27	5	432	2	3	109
Appropriated village land	52	74	18	64	0	8	216
Purchased village land	26	19	7	24	0	2	78
Received as a gift	188	293	72	202	5	16	776
Privately purchased	12	25	5	19	0	0	61
Acquired through renting	16	8	0	7	0	0	31
Currently renting	78	185	23	88	0	3	377
Caretaking	61	5	8	10	1	1	86
Borrowing from nonrelatives	n.a.	3	17	8	1	n.a.	29
Total	504	701	197	548	12	39	2,001

SOURCE: Intensive survey.

NOTE: "n.a." refers to "not available."

(see Table 3.4). Land rights are also weak in inherited land among matrilineal Akan households. Yet about one-half of allocated and inherited fields are planted to cocoa according to Table 3.11. Although we did not formally collect data on land rights on borrowed land, our field interviews indicate that borrowed land has even weaker rights than allocated and inherited land. The proportion of fields planted to cocoa trees is relatively high in fields received as gifts (Table 3.11). This observation indicates that incentives to plant trees on allocated family land and inherited land may be strong if individual land rights are strengthened to permit transfer of family land as a gift by planting trees.

Actually, transfer of land to a man's wife and children as an inter vivos gift is not a new phenomenon. According to Figure 3.2, which shows changing relative importance of different modes of land transfer over time based on recall data of our respondents, gift transfers were already practiced in the 1960s. It is also important to point out that there was no noticeable increase in the incidence of gift after the enactment of the ISL in 1985, which strongly indicates that internal forces, rather than the law, led to the increasing incidence of gift as a mode of land transfer.

Determinants of Cocoa Tree Planting

Table 3.11 shows the proportion of cocoa fields in the total land area of a parcel in 1997, compared with land use patterns before acquisition. Cocoa trees

TABLE 3.11 Distribution of land use before acquisition and in 1997, by land tenure type

	Before Acquisition[a]			1997	
	Forest	Cocoa[b]	Others[c]	Cocoa[a,b]	Fallow in Shifting Cultivation Area[d]
	(percentage)				
Allocated family land	10.8	3.2	86.1	44.8	65.6
Inherited land	11.4	25.2	63.3	52.8	87.2
Appropriated village land	92.8	0.9	6.3	60.6	78.0
Purchased village land	87.2	1.9	10.9	59.2	77.4
Land received as a gift	17.9	5.6	76.5	63.3	73.1
Privately purchased	14.5	9.1	76.4	60.7	79.2
Acquired through renting	42.3	15.4	42.3	77.4	100.0
Currently renting	19.0	6.3	74.7	70.3	79.3
Caretaking	0.0	90.7	9.3	77.6	55.2
Borrowing from nonrelatives	0.0	0.0	100.0	10.3	30.8

SOURCE: Intensive survey.

[a]Percentage refers to proportion in total land area.

[b]Including both mature and young cocoa fields.

[c]Including food production and fallow fields.

[d]Percentage refers to proportion of fields.

have been planted in 44.8 percent of allocated parcels and 52.8 percent of inherited parcels, which suggests that the level of tenure security alone does not determine the incidence of tree planting. The proportion of cocoa fields in 1997, however, is somewhat higher in parcels with stronger land rights, such as appropriated and purchased village land. The proportions are also high in the case of renting and caretaking, because tenants are assigned to plant trees and workers are employed to take care of mature trees. In land received as a gift, the proportion of area under cocoa prior to acquisition was very small. Most of the parcels without trees that were later transferred as gifts had been inherited or allocated family land used for shifting cultivation and were given after tree planting by the father of the recipient, especially in Akan households (45 percent). This confirms that gifts are being used as a way to transfer land to designated heirs rather than to let it revert to the matriclan after death.

The maintained hypothesis of this analysis is that cocoa tree planting is sufficiently more profitable than shifting cultivation, which seems reasonable in view of the continued expansion of cocoa area. We also provide supporting evidence later in this chapter. We assume that land tenure institutions may differ within each household, depending on the gender of the parcel owner, the mode of land acquisition, and consequently the tenure status of field managers.

FIGURE 3.2 Proportion of land acquisition by type and year in Ghana, five-year moving averages

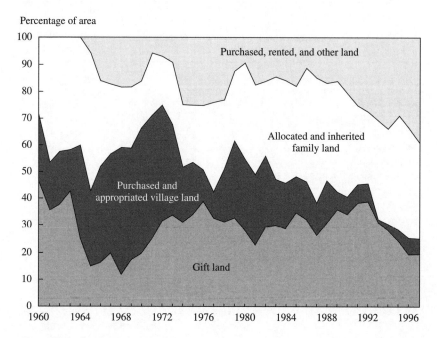

SOURCE: Extensive survey.

In order to control for possible correlation between land tenure variables and unobservable household characteristics, we estimated a tobit with household fixed effects for the proportion of area planted to cocoa.[21]

In explaining the proportion of area planted to cocoa, we included 10 land tenure dummies represented by the mode of land acquisition (allocated family land [both patrilineal and matrilineal], patrilineal inheritance or gift, gift in matrilineal households, appropriation of village land, purchase of village land, private purchase, current renting, acquisition through renting in the past, caretaking, and borrowing), with matrilineal inheritance as the base of comparison.[22] We assume that the mode of land acquisition can be considered as predetermined with respect to the tree-planting decision. We also included cur-

---

21. Since the proportion of area planted to mature cocoa is censored upward at 100 percent and downward at 0, we applied a two-limit tobit procedure with household dummy variables.

22. Because of the small number of observations in the patrilineal categories, allocated family land in patrilineal villages was aggregated with allocated family land in matrilineal villages; patrilineal gifts and inheritance, having the same degree of strength of land rights in the Wassa Region, were aggregated into a single category.

rent parcel characteristics, such as the distance from house to parcel, parcel size, years since acquisition, and its squared term. In the cocoa-planting function, years since acquisition and its square capture effects related to the timing of investment. We also control for characteristics of the parcel at the time of acquisition, including dummies for previous land use (forest or cocoa) and the real farm-gate cocoa price. It is expected that since virgin forest is more fertile than previously cultivated fallow land, parcels that were previously covered by forest may induce tree planting.[23] We included cocoa prices at the time of acquisition to control for the possibility that the surge in cocoa prices in the 1980s stimulated a conversion of land to cocoa. Finally, we included the educational attainment of the parcel manager and a dummy variable for the gender of the parcel owner.

The estimation results are shown in the first column of Table 3.12. Parcel size has a negative and significant effect on the proportion planted to cocoa, implying that an inverse correlation exists between parcel size and tree planting. This indicates that the transactions undertaken through the land rental market, not to mention the land sales market, are imperfect, because some portions of the parcel could have been rented for tree planting if the land rental market worked effectively (Hayami and Otsuka 1993).

Although one may expect that more secure land rights have a positive and significant effect on tree planting, the results are not consistent with such expectations. Trees are more likely to be planted by the previous landholder in land bequeathed as gift as compared with land inherited and allocated. This would be largely explained by the fact that tree planting is a prerequisite for transferring land as a gift. The coefficient on privately purchased land is positive but insignificant, and that on patrilineal gift and inheritance is negative and insignificant. This is surprising, since these categories have the strongest individualized rights. Thus, although tenure security may have a positive effect on tree planting, as argued by Besley (1995), its effect is not dominant. We also find positive and significant effects of land under caretaking, rental, and land acquired through renting, since cocoa planting or harvesting is the major task under these contractual arrangements. The dummy for a female parcel owner has a positive but insignificant effect on the proportion of area planted to cocoa, suggesting that there is no significant difference between male and female parcel owners with respect to tree planting.[24]

---

23. López (1997) found that biomass had a positive effect in his estimation of production functions using regional data from western Ghana. He attributes this effect to the positive production externality arising from the effect of biomass on protection from soil erosion and flooding, but we consider it more plausible to interpret that the biomass is positively correlated with soil fertility.

24. It is also possible that, if women receive land only after it has been planted to cocoa, subsequent observations will not reveal any difference between male and female parcel owners in the probability of planting cocoa.

TABLE 3.12 Determinants of current land use at the parcel level: Tobit and logit regressions with household fixed effects

	Proportion of Parcel Planted to Cocoa	Probability Shifting Cultivation Area Is Fallow
	Tobit with Household Dummies	Fixed-Effects Logit[a]
Current parcel characteristics		
Distance to parcel	0.04	0.78**
	(1.94)	(2.71)
Parcel size (ha)	−0.01**	2.35**
	(−2.35)	(6.53)
Years since acquisition	0.12*	0.05
	(2.09)	(0.74)
Years since acquisition squared	−0.00	−0.00
	(−1.50)	(−0.09)
Woman-owned parcel	0.17	1.93
	(1.66)	(1.78)
Schooling of parcel owner	0.01	0.34
	(0.59)	(1.32)
Characteristics of parcel at acquisition		
Dummy for forest	0.01	—
	(0.13)	
Dummy for cocoa	0.23**	—
	(2.54)	
Real cocoa farmgate price	−0.00	—
	(−0.23)	
Land tenure dummies		
Allocated land	−0.22	−2.38*
	(−1.56)	(−2.16)
Land received as gift	0.34**	−1.50
	(2.80)	(−1.59)
Patrilineal gift or inheritance	−0.23	0.32
	(−1.13)	(0.28)
Appropriated village land	0.26	0.41
	(1.54)	(0.32)
Purchased village land	0.30	1.71
	(1.47)	(0.79)
Privately purchased	0.14	1.38
	(0.72)	(0.90)
Rented	0.43**	0.18
	(3.23)	(0.19)
Ownership through renting	0.71**	—
	(3.53)	

(continued)

TABLE 3.12 *Continued*

	Proportion of Parcel Planted to Cocoa	Probability Shifting Cultivation Area Is Fallow
	Tobit with Household Dummies	Fixed-Effects Logit[a]
Caretaker	1.08**	−0.15
	(6.58)	(−0.12)
Borrowed from nonrelatives	−0.71**	−4.43**
	(−3.29)	(−2.70)
Constant	0.07	—
	(0.19)	
Log likelihood	−438.91	−110.29
Chi-square	503.98	168.35
p-value	0.00	0.00
Number of observations	688	483

NOTE: Two-limit tobit estimates; ancillary parameter and household dummies not reported. *t*-statistics in parentheses. Because of the small number of observations in the patrilineal categories, allocated family land in patrilineal villages was aggregated with allocated family land; patrilineal gifts and inheritance, having the same degree of strength of land rights, were aggregated into a single category.

[a]Estimated using field-level data for all fields, for households with more than one field devoted to shifting cultivation.

*.05 level

**.01 level

Determinants of Fallow Choice

We now examine the choice to keep a field fallow in land solely devoted to shifting cultivation, that is, land either devoted to food crops or left fallow, using data from all fields enumerated by respondents.[25] Close to three-quarters of all field area under shifting cultivation is left fallow (Table 3.11). A smaller proportion of fields is left fallow on land borrowed from nonrelatives (30.8 percent) and allocated family land (65.6 percent). Since it is difficult to measure the proportion of fallow area accurately, and given that almost three-quarters of all field area under shifting cultivation is fallowed, we estimated a conditional (fixed effects) logit model, in which the dependent variable is the probability that a parcel under shifting cultivation will be totally devoted to

---

25. We use information on all fields, not just the sample fields, in this regression. Although we could have estimated this equation using parcel-level data, fields are a finer level of disaggregation. The number of observations is larger using data for all fields, but we do not have information on previous uses of the field, since this was collected only for the sample fields. Regressions that included information on previous land use, for those fields for which information was available, showed that these variables were insignificant.

fallow. We use the same regressors as in the cocoa-planting regression, with the exception of the dummies for previous land use, cocoa price, and the dummy for ownership through renting. Since land acquired through renting would already have been planted to cocoa trees, sample fields in this analysis do not include this tenure type. Results are shown in the second column of Table 3.12. The most significant factors affecting the decision to leave land fallow are the distance to the field, the size of the field, and the dummies for allocated and borrowed land. Thus, larger and more distant fields are more likely to remain fallow. Consistent with our hypothesis that land with insecure tenure is less likely to remain fallow, the dummies for allocated and borrowed land have negative and significant coefficients, and they are significantly different from those of individualized tenure variables. That is, individuals holding allocated family land have a stronger incentive to continue cultivating it, rather than face the risk of losing use rights to another member of the extended family. This conclusion will be strengthened if fathers tend to choose less productive land for family allocation. In this case, from an agronomic perspective allocated land would have to be more often left fallow. Likewise, individuals who borrow land from nonrelatives have very little reason to keep it fallow, since borrowing is undertaken to obtain land on which to raise subsistence crops.

However, we do not have clear evidence that stronger land tenure security results in less frequent fallow periods. One of the reasons may be the strong security of use rights on inherited land compared with other land tenure categories. Moreover, we were not able to control for the effect of soil fertility, which would be critically determined by the fallow periods before the current cultivation.

Determinants of Net Revenue of Mature Cocoa

Data on gross revenue, paid-out costs, and the net revenue or cash income per hectare of mature cocoa fields, together with data on labor hours and the relative contribution of women and children within the household, are shown in Table 3.13. Since dried cocoa is sold only to the village office of the state cocoa marketing board, the revenue data are expected to be highly accurate. We made three visits to the respondents in a year to obtain accurate labor data. Paid-out cost accounts for roughly 15 percent of gross revenue, consisting mainly of payments to hired labor. Chemical fertilizers were not applied, and only a small number of farmers use pesticides, albeit in small amounts. Net revenue, defined as total revenue less paid-out costs, represents the return to land and family labor. There is no strong association between average age of trees and revenue, even though there appears to be some declining trend.

For mature cocoa, the major task is harvesting, which may start as early as October and is completed in March. Cocoa farming is highly labor-intensive; if a person works for seven hours per day, the average labor input amounts to

TABLE 3.13 Gross revenue, paid-out cost, net revenue, and labor inputs of mature cocoa production at the field level, by average age of cocoa trees

Average Age of Cocoa Trees	Number of Observations	Gross Revenue	Paid-out Cost[a]	Net Revenue	Total Labor Hours per Hectare	Percentage Women and Children
4	15	402	62	325	460	27
5	21	636	56	564	669	34
6	19	534	59	452	695	36
7	14	515	36	464	314	32
8	19	658	49	584	602	35
9	18	488	43	423	627	30
10	9	674	37	614	468	33
11	12	531	69	447	571	34
12	12	674	126	531	451	32
13	10	341	43	286	458	34
14	6	497	26	451	398	23
15	7	338	47	273	503	34
16	7	564	60	486	582	35
17	6	319	39	267	446	43
18	7	412	51	344	362	29
19	5	408	88	306	432	25
20–24	23	343	58	273	378	27
25–29	13	396	37	350	328	22
30 and over	18	381	54	319	467	33

SOURCE: Intensive survey.
[a]1,000 cedis per hectare.

70 days per hectare. As with revenue, there is no strong trend in labor requirements associated with aging of trees. Family labor of women and children, particularly the wife, accounts for about one-third of labor total inputs. The labor
market for harvesting is relatively active, and hired labor contributes to roughly
40 percent of total labor inputs.[26]

In order to identify the effects of land tenure institutions on the intensity
of cocoa farming, we estimated net revenue and labor use functions per hectare
using village-level and household-level fixed and random effects models. We
present only the results for the random effects model with plot-level heterogeneity in Table 3.14.[27]

In addition to the land tenure dummies, characteristics of the parcel at acquisition, and current parcel characteristics found in the tree-planting and fallow
choice regressions, we also include the age of trees and the number of kola trees,
oil palm, and other trees on the parcel. It is possible that the presence of other
trees may affect labor use as well as net revenue from cocoa if competition exists among different tree species because of overcrowding. It is remarkable to find
from Table 3.14 that no land tenure variables are significant in the net revenue
functions.[28] These results support the hypothesis that management intensity of
cocoa fields tends to be equalized owing to the establishment of secure land tenure
after tree planting, regardless of the mode of land acquisition. The insignificant
effect of renting is also interesting, as it suggests that share tenancy arrangements
are fairly efficient not only in Asia but also in some parts of Africa (see Hayami
and Otsuka 1993 for the case of Asia). While field size has a negative effect on
net revenue, the coefficient is insignificant. Although it may appear that women
enjoy lower net revenues from cocoa, these effects are not significant.

The estimation results of the labor use function provide added support for
our hypothesis; again, no land tenure variables are significant. Field size has a
negative and significant coefficient, which suggests that because of the imperfection in factor markets (for example, labor markets), large fields are less intensively cultivated. The presence of other trees on the parcel also increases labor input per hectare, and new cocoa varieties, particularly *Amazonia,* appear

---

26. Wages, however, are substantially different among the 10 villages, even for the same
tasks, which indicates segregation of local labor markets due to labor market imperfections or high
transaction costs. These 10 villages are located fairly far apart, and it would take several hours by
motor vehicle to go from one remote village to another remote village in a different direction. Because of the noncomparability of wages, we did not impute the cost of family labor using prevailing wages to estimate profits.

27. We also estimated the functions with village-level fixed and random effects, but none of
the household-level characteristics (the numbers of male and female adult workers) was significant.
Although sample sizes are smaller for the household random effects results, this is the preferred
specification, since within-household estimators control for household-level heterogeneity. Hausman tests do not indicate that fixed effects are significant, and Breusch-Pagan Lagrange-Multiplier
tests show that parcel-level heterogeneity is important.

28. This finding is robust to the choice of estimation method, whether fixed or random effects.

TABLE 3.14 Determinants of net revenue from mature cocoa production and total labor use at the field level: Random effects

	Net Revenue	Labor Use per Hectare
Current field characteristics		
Distance to field	−30.26	−23.91
	(−0.93)	(−0.86)
Field size (ha)	−11.21	−56.42*
	(−0.38)	(−2.32)
Years since acquisition	20.17	24.29
	(0.98)	(1.40)
Years since acquisition squared	−0.44	−0.33
	(−1.01)	(−0.88)
Woman-owned field	−90.31	162.88**
	(−1.34)	(2.89)
Schooling of field owner	−0.19	−4.49
	(−0.02)	(−0.49)
Number of kola trees per hectare	5.96	0.92
	(0.89)	(0.17)
Number of oil palm trees per hectare	2.99	−4.40
	(0.18)	(−0.32)
Number of other trees per hectare	9.95	43.04**
	(0.80)	(4.01)
Characteristics of parcel at acquisition		
Dummy for forest	−103.74	−79.45
	(−0.68)	(−0.62)
Dummy for cocoa	325.98	−96.87
	(1.55)	(−0.54)
Tree characteristics		
Amazonia dummy	62.91	−388.29*
	(0.29)	(−2.15)
Hybrid dummy	−50.68	−389.84
	(−0.21)	(−1.95)
Average age of trees	−7.87	−0.39
	(−0.39)	(−0.02)
Age of trees squared	−0.01	−0.10
	(−0.03)	(−0.29)
Land tenure dummies		
Allocated and matrilineal	112.06	−277.17
	(0.32)	(−0.94)
Land received as gift	128.70	−182.35
	(0.40)	(−0.67)
Patrilineal gift	319.23	468.45
	(0.70)	(1.22)
Appropriated village land	367.29	−96.31
	(0.94)	(−0.29)

(continued)

TABLE 3.14 *Continued*

	Net Revenue	Labor Use per Hectare
Purchased village land	30.52	−226.82
	(0.07)	(−0.63)
Privately purchased	—	—
Rented	104.45	−56.80
	(0.32)	(−0.21)
Ownership through renting	73.97	−241.71
	(0.19)	(−0.72)
Caretaker	−67.45	57.14
	(−0.19)	(0.19)
Constant	245.37	829.92**
	(0.64)	(2.59)
Breusch-Pagan Lagrangian Multiplier Test (*p*-value)	5.06 (0.02)	3.87 (0.05)
Hausman Specification Test (*p*-value)	14.67 (0.91)	18.55 (0.73)
Number of observations	105	105

NOTE: Z-statistics within parentheses. Dummies for allocated patrilineal land, borrowing, and inherited patrilineal land were dropped because of collinearity with the fixed effects.

*.05 level

**.01 level

to use less labor. It is also noteworthy that labor use is significantly higher on woman-owned fields.

Determinants of Net Revenue of Food Crops

We perform a similar analysis for food crop production on young cocoa and pure crop fields. Since there seem to be few, if any, investment opportunities in food crop fields, there is no theoretical reason to assume that land tenure security affects the intensity of cultivation. According to Table 3.15, gross revenue and net revenue from pure food crop fields are much higher than those from mixed crop fields, except in the first two years of cocoa cultivation. The relatively high revenue from young cocoa fields clearly explains the advantage of cocoa and food intercropping. Paid-out costs and labor hours, however, are much higher in the initial year of cocoa cultivation, owing to the high labor requirement of establishing cocoa fields. Although total labor input and net revenue per hectare are higher in pure food cultivation than cocoa cultivation, the intensity of cultivation is much higher in cocoa cultivation. Typically food crops are produced in two consecutive seasons under shifting cultivation, and land is left fallow for nearly eight years on average. Therefore, roughly speaking, in shifting cultivation, the average net revenue per year is 90 cedis, and the average labor input is 220 hours, both of which are far smaller than the annual

TABLE 3.15 Gross revenue, paid-out cost, net revenue, and labor inputs of food crop production of young cocoa and pure food crop fields

Type of Crop and Years of Cultivation	Number of Observations	Gross Revenue[a]	Paid-out Cost[a]	Net Revenue	Total Labor Hours per Hectare	Percentage Women and Children	Average Fallow Period
Young cocoa[b]							
Less than 1 year	52	253	79	171	1,401	41	15.60 (5)
1st year	40	489	32	452	894	51	9.96 (72)
2d year	49	443	36	397	616	35	11.91 (54)
3d year	28	271	66	189	687	32	7.87 (24)
4th year	14	207	46	142	274	15	7.86 (7)
Pure food crops	98	494	38	456	1,106	48	7.73 (56)

SOURCE: Intensive survey.

NOTE: All figures, except those for the average fallow period, are derived from the selected sample fields (total 612 fields). The figures for average fallow period prior to the current cultivation are derived from the entire sample fields (total 2,001 fields). Information on the average fallow period, however, is available for only a limited number of fields, which is indicated within parentheses in the last column of the table.

[a] 1,000 cedis per hectare.

[b] "Young cocoa" refers to those cocoa fields intercropped with food crops.

revenue and labor hours in cocoa cultivation. Thus, the switch from shifting cultivation to cocoa cultivation is consistent with the evolutionary view of farming systems postulated by Boserup (1965) and the view of induced innovation formulated by Hayami and Ruttan (1985).

In order to identify the effects of land tenure institutions on net revenue and total labor use in young cocoa and pure food crop fields, we estimated net revenue and labor use functions per hectare using village-level and household-level fixed and random effects models. Again, since random effects are the preferred specification, we present only the random effects results in Table 3.16.[29] Since cocoa is intercropped with a variety of food crops in different combinations, we included the proportion of area planted to each of the food crops present in the field (for example, the proportion devoted to cocoyam in 1997) as well as their interactions with a dummy variable indicating that young cocoa is grown in the field. We also included dummy variables for the age of the cocoa trees, with trees less than a year old as the reference category. Since 34 percent of the sampled food crop fields have a female cultivator other than the male or female manager, we include a dummy variable for the presence of another female cultivator or field manager. This person is typically the wife of the male field manager, or a co-wife in the case of a female manager. All other regressors are identical to those in Table 3.14.

The results, presented in Table 3.16, are very similar to those for mature cocoa fields. Neither net revenue per hectare nor labor use is significantly different in fields under different land tenure regimes. The difficulty of identifying crop mix may be partly responsible for the failure to obtain significant effects of land tenure systems. Yet tree age dummies significantly affect labor use, as would be expected. Relative to trees less than a year old (the excluded category), labor use per hectare in succeeding years is significantly less. Consistent with the earlier finding that land under allocated family tenure is less likely to be left fallow, the coefficients of the family allocation dummies are negative in the net revenue function, even though they are not significant. Given that a major proportion of labor input is provided by women and children, it is not surprising that gift transactions have evolved to increase their incentive to provide labor in establishing cocoa. Note that there are no significant differences in either net revenue per hectare or labor use per hectare depending on whether or not a field is managed by a woman. Thus, the transfer of land to women through gifts has improved gender equity without sacrificing production efficiency. Last, even if the presence of another female cultivator increases labor input, the effect on net revenue is insignificant.

---

29. Similar to our regressions for mature cocoa, although we estimated the functions with village-level fixed and random effects, none of the household-level characteristics were significant. Moreover, Hausman tests do not indicate that fixed effects are significant, and Breusch-Pagan Lagrange-Multiplier tests show that parcel-level heterogeneity is important.

TABLE 3.16 Determinants of net revenue and total labor use of food production of young cocoa and pure food crop fields: Random effects

	Net Revenue	Labor Use per Hectare
Current field characteristics		
One-year-old cocoa dummy	137.16	−333.36
	(0.92)	(−1.45)
Two-year-old cocoa dummy	40.37	−865.12**
	(0.22)	(−3.03)
Three-year-old cocoa dummy	30.42	−296.57
	(0.14)	(−0.87)
Four-year-old cocoa dummy	−388.63	−1,243.33**
	(−1.58)	(−3.37)
Distance to field	−12.06	−79.53
	(−0.31)	(−1.12)
Field size (ha)	136.73	−1,309.15
	(0.31)	(−1.84)
Years since acquisition	−16.24	−5.37
	(−1.53)	(−0.29)
Years since acquisition squared	0.21	0.12
	(1.02)	(0.35)
Woman-owned field	73.88	−37.42
	(1.11)	(−0.32)
Schooling of field owner	−5.73	−9.15
	(−0.55)	(−0.44)
Presence of other female cultivator	62.07	344.14
	(0.57)	(1.70)
Number of kola trees per hectare	−5.90	9.76
	(−1.62)	(1.53)
Number of oil palm trees per hectare	−1.54	−4.35
	(−0.69)	(−1.29)
Number of other trees per hectare	−13.24	7.86
	(−1.68)	(0.64)
Characteristics of parcel at acquisition		
Dummy for forest	−100.35	−259.08
	(−0.58)	(−0.82)
Dummy for cocoa	−83.75	33.46
	(−0.39)	(0.09)
Land tenure dummies		
Allocated and patrilineal	−871.69	−349.12
	(−1.41)	(−0.35)
Inherited and patrilineal	−444.22	−918.66
	(−0.79)	(−1.01)
Allocated and matrilineal	−224.99	−268.74
	(−0.68)	(−0.50)

(continued)

TABLE 3.16 *Continued*

	Net Revenue	Labor Use per Hectare
Land received as gift	−80.57	−50.31
	(−0.25)	(−0.10)
Patrilineal gift	2.22	−174.40
	(0.01)	(−0.28)
Appropriated village land	13.89	−187.35
	(0.04)	(−0.28)
Purchased village land	521.82	−252.12
	(1.30)	(−0.36)
Privately purchased	−408.32	−634.57
	(−1.09)	(−1.05)
Rented	−165.79	−174.86
	(−0.50)	(−0.33)
Ownership through renting	—	—
Caretaker	—	—
Borrowed from nonrelatives	−232.53	322.56
	(−0.47)	(0.42)
Constant	728.01*	1,947.47**
	(2.03)	(3.29)
Breusch-Pagan Lagrangian Multiplier		
Test (*p*-value)	230.00 (0.13)	8.70 (0.00)
Hausman Specification Test (*p*-value)	20.18 (1.00)	19.29 (1.00)
Number of observations	151	151

NOTE: Z-statistics in parentheses. Aside from variables shown in this table and village/household dummies, we used 11 variables representing proportion of different food crops and their interaction terms with young cocoa.

*.05 level

**.01 level

Land Tenure and Land Distribution

The evolution of customary land tenure institutions toward individualized ownership may lead to an inequitable distribution of landholdings. In order to quantify the relative contribution of land under different tenure categories to the overall inequality of land distribution, we apply a decomposition analysis of the Gini measure of landholding inequality as developed by Fei, Ranis, and Kuo (1978) and Pyatt, Chen, and Fei (1980) for household data.

The Gini decomposition formula is given by $G(Y) = s_i PG(Y_i)$, where $G(Y)$ equals the Gini ratio of total operational landholdings, Y_i pertains to landholdings of the i-th tenure type, s_i equals average share of i-th type of land, and $PG(Y_i)$ equals the pseudo-Gini of landholding inequality. If $PG(Y_i)$ is greater (smaller)

TABLE 3.17 Overall Gini ratio of operational landholdings and contribution by land component

	Land Share	Pseudo-Gini Ratio
Allocated family land	0.11	0.25
Inherited family land	0.04	0.82
Appropriated village forestland	0.12	0.66
Purchased village forestland	0.04	0.75
Received as gift	0.37	0.35
Privately purchased	0.02	0.59
Acquired through renting	0.02	0.35
Currently renting	0.19	0.15
Borrowing from nonrelatives	0.08	−0.08
Overall	1.00	0.34

SOURCE: Intensive survey.

than $G(Y)$, distribution of i-th type of landholding is less (more) equitable than the average, thereby contributing to the expansion (contraction) of inequality in the overall landholding distribution (see Appendix in this chapter for further details). Results of computations using household data on operational landholdings from the 10 intensive survey villages are shown in Table 3.17.

The overall Gini ratio is 0.34, which is relatively small by international standards, indicating the relatively egalitarian distribution of operational holdings. Compared with the overall Gini ratio, the pseudo-Gini coefficient is particularly small for allocated family land, which strongly suggests that egalitarian motives prevail in the decision to allocate family land. In contrast, inheritance is inequality-increasing, whereas gifts have a neutral effect on land distribution. Note that the prevalence of family land allocation and gifts has increased while that of inheritance decreased. Therefore, in all likelihood, these changes in customary land tenure institutions from inheritance to family allocation and gifts have improved the equality of land distribution.

Appropriation and purchase of village forestland were possible only for elder indigenes and early migrants, contributing to inequality of land distribution. Not surprisingly, private land purchase also contributes to landholding inequality. It is more remarkable to find that the pseudo-Gini ratio of current renting, which accounts for 19 percent of operational land area, is small. Also noteworthy is the negative ratio of borrowing from nonrelatives. It is clear that renting significantly contributes to the equalization of operational holdings by reallocating land from land-rich to land-poor households.

To conclude, there is no indication that the evolution of customary land tenure institutions results in a highly skewed distribution of operational landholdings.

Summary for Intensive Study

The results of the intensive survey study provided evidence consistent with the extensive survey study. Based on the analysis of the extensive survey, we proposed that tree planting is affected not only by the strength of current land rights but also by expected changes in land tenure security due to tree planting. We argued, therefore, that whether the incidence of tree planting is lower under less secure, family tenure institutions is an empirical question. We also predicted that in the shifting-cultivation area the proportion of fallow land is higher for parcels with more secure land tenure. Last, we postulate as a null hypothesis that management intensity is not significantly different between family land and other types of land.

Our findings show that although there is a tendency for more secure land rights to have a positive effect on tree planting, such effect is generally insignificant. We conclude that although tenure security would have a positive effect on tree planting, as argued by Besley (1995), its effect is not of overwhelming importance. In other words, the traditional land tenure institutions are generally not inefficient with respect to the decision to plant trees. However, we have obtained evidence that land is less often left fallow in parcels allocated temporarily by family, which indicates the inefficiency of land use in shifting-cultivation area under this type of the customary land tenure systems.

Last, we find that net revenue and labor use in both mature cocoa fields and young cocoa and food crop fields are not significantly affected by land tenure institutions.

These results do not refute the hypothesis that management intensity of cocoa fields tends to be equalized, owing to the establishment of secure land tenure after tree planting, regardless of the mode of land acquisition. This suggests that, given the almost complete individualization of land rights under some land tenure categories, traditional land tenure institutions in customary areas of western Ghana have been sufficiently individualized to achieve farm management efficiency comparable to private ownership.

Policy Implications

As in other places in Africa, virgin forests have already been cleared by poor farmers in western Ghana. This has occurred because of the absence of a mechanism that controls forest clearance under customary land law coupled with continued and rapid population growth due primarily to the influx of migrants. The major question is how to restore the tree resource base for environmental benefit while simultaneously improving the welfare of poor farmers. In this study, by examining the determinants of cocoa tree planting and the relative profitability of cocoa production compared with shifting cultivation of food crops, we explored whether it is feasible to meet the two goals of environmental and welfare improvement through the development of cocoa agroforestry.

In cocoa-growing areas of Ghana we observed that customary land tenure institutions have evolved toward individualized ownership systems, which provide appropriate incentives to plant cocoa trees and manage cocoa agroforestry. It is likely that such evolutionary changes have taken place to stimulate the establishment of cocoa agroforestry, which is found to be more profitable than shifting cultivation. Thus, the development of cocoa agroforestry will contribute positively to the improvement of farmers' incomes by enhancing the intensity and the efficiency of land use.

The efficiency might be particularly high if valuable timber trees are grown as shade trees, which are required for proper growth of cocoa trees. Wild shoots of valuable timber trees, if grown on cocoa fields, however, are immediately cut by farmers, because they are not allowed to own such trees, and mature trees are felled by logging companies without making due compensation for damaged cocoa fields. The current policy, which prohibits the ownership of valuable timber trees, needs to be replaced by a new policy that respects the rights to private ownership of any trees grown on private land.

The development of cocoa agroforestry not only enhances the intensity and efficiency of land use from the private point of view but also improves social efficiency as trees grown on sloped fields reduce soil erosion and increase tree biomass. Considering environmental benefits and private benefits that accrue to poor cocoa farmers, public efforts should be directed toward the development and the promotion of profitable agroforestry systems through research, extension, and improvement of marketing systems. To our knowledge, however, no serious attention has been paid to the importance of developing profitable agroforestry systems for the benefits of both efficiency and equity.

Appendix: Gini Decomposition Formula

In order to examine whether the individualization of customary land tenure institutions and the activation of land market transactions have resulted in inequitable distribution of landholdings, we apply a decomposition analysis of the Gini measure of inequality as developed by Fei, Ranis, and Kuo (1978) and Pyatt, Chen, and Fei (1980) for the operational landholdings of households. This decomposition formula is designed to assess the inequality of distribution of particular types of land relative to the distribution of overall landholding. Note, however, that the computed percentage contribution of overall inequality by land components under the Gini decomposition rule may be substantially different from the decomposition of an alternative measure of inequality (Shorrocks 1983). We have chosen the Gini decomposition formula because of the popular use of Gini ratios in the economic analysis.

The Gini decomposition formula is as follows:

$$G(Y) = \Sigma \, s_i \, R(Y, \, Y_i) \, G(Y_i)$$
$$= \Sigma \, s_i \, \mathrm{PG}(Y_i), \qquad\qquad\qquad (5)$$

where $G(Y)$ equals Gini ratio of total operational landholding; Y_i equals landholding of i-th tenure type; s_i equals share of i-th type of land; $R(Y, \, Y_i)$ equals the rank correlation ratio; $G(Y_i)$ equals Gini ratio of i-th land; and $\mathrm{PG}(Y_i)$ equals the pseudo-Gini ratio of landholding inequality. The rank correlation ratio is defined as

$$R(Y, \, Y_i) = \mathrm{Cov} \, \{Y_i, \, r(Y)\} \, / \, \mathrm{Cov} \, \{Y_i, \, r(Y_i)\}, \qquad\qquad (6)$$

where $r(Y)$ and $r(Y_i)$ denote ranking of households in terms of Y and Y_i, respectively. It is clear that R is unity if $r(Y) = r(Y_i)$. Otherwise, R is shown to be less than unity. In general, the larger the correlation between Y and Y_i, the larger is R.

In the computation of $G(Y)$, households are ranked in accordance with Y, but in the case of $G(Y_i)$ they are ranked in accordance with Y_i. In order to adjust this difference, the rank correlation appears in the formula. In fact, $R(Y, \, Y_i) \, G(Y_i)$ is equal to the pseudo-Gini ratio, $\mathrm{PG}(Y_i)$, which is obtained if we use ranking of households in accordance with total landholding Y in the computation of component Gini ratio for Y_i.

If $\mathrm{PG}(Y_i)$ is greater than $G(Y)$, the distribution of i-th type of landholding is less equal than other types of land. Thus, we make a comparison between $\mathrm{PG}(Y_i)$ and $G(Y)$, to assess whether i-th type of landholding is inequity-increasing or inequity-decreasing. The importance of $\mathrm{PG}(Y_i)$ in overall inequality is weighted by its share in the overall landholdings.

References

Alchian, A. A., and Harold Demsetz. 1973. The property rights paradigm. *Journal of Economic History* 16:16–27.

Asenso-Okyere, W. K., S. Y. Atsu, and I. S. Obeng. 1993. Communal property resources in Ghana: Policies and prospects. Discussion Paper No. 27. Institute of Statistical, Social, and Economic Research, University of Ghana, Legon.

Ault, David E., and Gilbert L. Rutman. 1979. The development of individual rights to property in tribal Africa. *Journal of Law and Economics* 22:163–182.

Awusabo-Asare, Kofi. 1990. Matriliny and the new intestate succession law of Ghana. *Canadian Journal of African Studies* 24:1–16.

Barrows, Richard, and Michael Roth. 1990. Land tenure and investment in African agriculture: Theory and evidence. *Journal of Modern African Studies* 28:265–297.

Bassett, Thomas J. 1993. Introduction: The land question and agricultural transformation in Sub-Saharan Africa. In *Land in African agrarian systems,* ed. T. J. Bassett and D. E. Crummey. Madison: University of Wisconsin Press.

Benneh, George. 1987. Land tenure and agroforestry land use systems in Ghana. In

Land, trees, and tenure, ed. J. B. Raintree. Nairobi: International Centre for Research in Agroforestry, and Madison: Land Tenure Center.

————. 1989. The dynamics of customary land tenure and agrarian systems in Ghana. In *The dynamics of land tenure and agrarian systems in Africa,* World Conference on Agrarian Reform and Rural Development. Rome: Food and Agriculture Organization.

Berry, Sara. 1963. *No condition is perfect: The social dynamics of agrarian changes in Sub-Saharan Africa.* Madison: University of Wisconsin Press.

Besley, Timothy. 1995. Property rights and investment incentives. *Journal of Political Economy* 103:913–937.

Boadu, Fred. 1992. The efficiency of share contracts in Ghana's cocoa industry. *Journal of Development Studies* 29:108–120.

Boserup, Ester. 1965. *The conditions of agricultural growth: The economics of agrarian change under population pressure.* London: George Allen and Unwin.

Bruce, John W., and Shem E. Migot-Adholla. 1993. *Searching for land tenure security in Africa.* Dubuque, Iowa: Kendall/Hunt.

Brydon, Lynne. 1987. Women in the family: Cultural change in Avatime, Ghana, 1900–80. *Development and Change* 18:251–269.

Demsetz, Harold. 1967. Toward a theory of property rights. *American Economic Review* 57:347–359.

Feder, Gershon, and David Feeny. 1993. The theory of land tenure and property rights. In *The economics of rural organization: Theory, practice, and policy,* ed. K. Hoff, A. Braverman, and J. E. Stiglitz. Oxford: Oxford University Press.

Feder, Gershon, and Raymond Noronha. 1987. Land rights systems and agricultural development in Sub-Saharan Africa. *World Bank Research Observer* 2:143–169.

Fei, J. C. H., Gustav Ranis, and S. W. Y. Kuo. 1978. Growth and family distribution of income by factor component. *Quarterly Journal of Economics* 92:17–53.

Ghana Statistical Service. 1995. *Ghana living standard survey.* Accra, Ghana: Ghana Statistical Service.

Gockowski, James, Blaise Nkamleu, and John Wendt. 2001. Implications of resource use intensification for the environment and sustainable technology systems in the central African rainforest. In *Tradeoffs or synergies: Agricultural intensification, economic development, and the environment,* ed. D. R. Lee and C. Barrett. Wallingford, U.K.: CAB International.

Hayami, Yujiro. 1997. *Development economics: From the poverty to the wealth of nations.* Oxford: Oxford University Press.

Hayami, Yujiro, and Keijiro Otsuka. 1993. *The economics of contract choice: An agrarian perspective.* Oxford: Clarendon Press.

Hayami, Yujiro, and Vernon W. Ruttan. 1985. *Agricultural development: An international perspective.* Baltimore: Johns Hopkins University Press.

Hill, Polly. 1963. *The migrant cocoa-farmers of southern Ghana: A study in rural capitalism.* Cambridge: Cambridge University Press.

Honoré, Bo. 1992. Trimmed LAD and least squares estimation of truncated and censored regression models with fixed effects. *Econometrica* 60:533–565.

Institute of Statistical, Social, and Economic Research. 1995. *The state of Ghanaian economy.* Legon, Ghana: University of Ghana.

Johnson, O. E. G. 1972. Economic analysis, the legal framework, and land tenure systems. *Journal of Law and Economics* 15:259–276.

Land Use Planning Committee of Ghana. 1979. *The national land use report.* Accra, Ghana: Land Use Planning Committee of Ghana.

Lopez, Ramon. 1997. Environmental externalities in traditional agriculture and the impact of trade liberalization: The case of Ghana. *Journal of Development Economics* 53:17–39.

Migot-Adholla, Shem E., George Benneh, Frank Place, and Steven Atsu. 1993. Land, security of tenure, and productivity in Ghana. In *Searching for land tenure security in Africa,* ed. John W. Bruce and Shem E. Migot-Adholla. Dubuque, Iowa: Kendall/Hunt.

Ortsin, G. 1998. Natural resource utilization and community participation. Paper presented at the National Workshop on Land Use Planning for Sustainable Land Management, Accra, Ghana.

Otsuka, Keijiro, Hiroyuki Chuma, and Yujiro Hayami. 1992. Land and labor contracts in agrarian economies: Theories and facts. *Journal of Economic Literature* 30:1965–2018.

Place, Frank, and Peter Hazell. 1993. Productivity effects of indigenous land tenure in Sub-Saharan Africa. *American Journal of Agricultural Economics* 75:10–19.

Platteau, Jean-Philippe. 1996. The evolutionary theory of land rights as applied to Sub-Saharan Africa: A critical assessment. *Development and Change* 27:29–86.

Pyatt, G., C. Chen, and J. C. H. Fei. 1980. The distribution of income by factor components. *Quarterly Journal of Economics* 95:451–473.

Quisumbing, A. R., E. Payongayong, J. B. Aidoo, and K. Otsuka. 2001. Women's land rights in the transition to individualized ownership: Implications for tree resource management in western Ghana. *Economic Development and Cultural Change,* forthcoming.

Robertson, A. F. 1982. *Abusa:* The structural history of an economic contract. *Journal of Development Studies* 18:447–478.

Shepherd, Gill. 1991. The communal management of forests in the semi-arid and sub-humid regions of Africa. *Development Policy Review* 19:151–176.

Shorrocks, A. F. 1983. The impact of income components on the distribution of family income. *Quarterly Journal of Economics* 98:310–326.

World Bank. 1998. *The World Development Indicators 1998 CD-ROM.* WinSTARS Version 4.01. Washington, D.C.: World Bank.

4 Agroforestry Management in Sumatra

S. SUYANTO, THOMAS P. TOMICH,
AND KEIJIRO OTSUKA

Indonesia is endowed with rich tropical rainforests in its outer islands, including Sumatra, Kalimatan, and Irian Jaya. These are primary forests covering more than 100 million hectares of the nation and representing 10 percent of the world's remaining tropical forest (World Bank 1998). Rapid deforestation, however, has been taking place in this country, which has been the second most conspicuous in the world in terms of lost forest area. FAO (1990) estimates that forest cover of the country had declined from 74 percent to 56 percent during the past 30–40 years. The World Bank (1990) reports that the estimated deforestation rate was 1 million hectares per year in 1990, which is 67 percent higher than in 1981.

Population pressure is considered to be the most important factor underlying the rapid deforestation in Indonesia. Using provincial data, Fraser (1998) finds a strong inverse correlation between population density and forest cover. The population of Indonesia increased dramatically from 77 million in 1950 to almost 195 million in 1995. The majority of the population still relies on agriculture as a source of employment and income. In 1990, 57 percent of the labor force was engaged in agriculture, which contributed to 16.5 percent of the GDP.

Forest conversion for farming purposes by traditional shifting cultivators and spontaneous migrants is an immediate cause of deforestation (Dick 1991). In addition, the establishment of large private estates for the production of timber and commercial tree crops, government-sponsored resettlement schemes (called transmigration), and forest fires have also significantly contributed to deforestation in Indonesia.

The rate of reduction in forest area in Sumatra is the highest in the nation (Dick 1991). The forest cover in Sumatra decreased from 72 percent in 1950 to 48 percent in 1985, whereas it declined from 88 percent to 72 percent for the same period in Kalimatan (Fraser 1998). As a result of rapid population growth, population density increased from 17 people per square kilometer in 1930 to 85

We are grateful for constructive comments on the earlier draft by Robert Deacon, Yujiro Hayami, and Iwan Azis. This chapter draws partly on Otsuka et al. (2001) and Suyanto and Otsuka (2001).

people per square kilometer in 1995 in Sumatra. How to preserve forest conditions while providing sufficient job opportunities for the growing population is a major development issue in Sumatra.

The major farming system in Sumatra has changed from shifting-cultivation systems to more intensive, tree-based farming systems. The traditional shifting cultivation with a long fallow period has become unsustainable, as the land frontier has gradually closed. In fact, as population pressure increases and land becomes scarce, the fallow periods tend to become too short for sustainable food crop production. Agroforestry systems, which produce such commercial trees as rubber (*Hevea braziliensis*), cinnamon (*Cinnamomum burmannii*), and coffee (*Coffea canephora*), have become common in the study areas where shifting cultivation used to be practiced on sloped areas (de Foresta and Michon 1990). If successful, the development of agroforestry will contribute to the enhancement of incomes in rural population and the prevention of soil erosion and other negative consequences of deforestation.

Establishment of agroforestry requires significant investment in the form of work effort in land preparation, tree planting, weeding, and pruning, for which property right institutions need to provide appropriate incentives. As elsewhere, customary land tenure institutions in Sumatra seem to evolve toward individualization with greater tenure security, which would have a positive influence on the development of agroforestry and the intensity of land use.

Yet little is known about the evolution of customary land tenure institutions and their consequences on land use and agroforestry management in Sumatra, not to mention appropriate polices the government should adopt to support efficient and equitable evolution of the customary land tenure institutions. The purposes of this study are to identify the causes of the land tenure evolution and to assess its consequences on the efficiency of land and tree resource management.

Organization of this chapter is as follows. Following the introductory section, we present characteristics of land tenure institutions with a special focus on changes from joint family ownership of land to individual ownership that is accompanied by changes from matrilineal to egalitarian or even to patrilineal inheritance systems. After identifying major empirical issues and specifying the testable hypotheses, we carry out econometric analyses to test those hypotheses, separately for extensive and intensive survey studies. We also attempt to analyze the effects of newly emerging land rental and land market transactions on the equity of operational landholdings. The final section discusses policy implications of the findings.

Customary Tenure Systems in Sumatra Sites

In the extensive survey conducted in 1995, we selected 60 villages randomly with probability proportional to village population from four districts in Suma-

FIGURE 4.1 Location of study sites in Sumatra

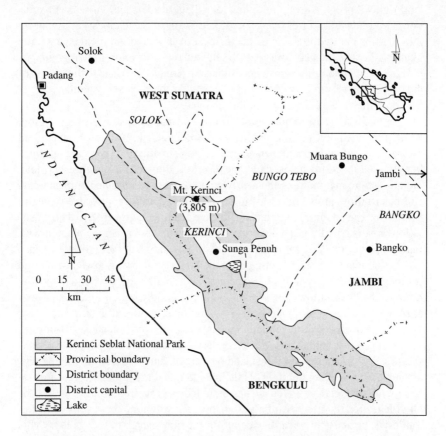

tra: Solok in West Sumatra Province, Kerinci, Bungo Tebo, and Bangko in Jambi Province along the buffer zone of the Kerinci Seblat National Park (see Figure 4.1). Solok, which we call the high region in this study, is located at the highest elevation, more than 1,000 meters above sea level. The major tree crop is coffee, though the area planted to cinnamon has been increasing. Kerinci is called the middle region, where cinnamon is a major tree crop. Bungo Tebo and Bangko are adjacent districts located in a low-lying area, where rubber is the major tree crop. Since our sites in these two districts are similar in terms of ethnic composition, climate, and topography, we lump them together and call this the low region.[1]

---

1. For more information on the dominant farming systems in Sumatra, see Angelson (1994, 1995) for shifting cultivation, Aumeeruddy (1994) on cinnamon, and Barlow and Muharminto (1982), Barlow and Jayasuriya (1984), Gouyon, de Foresta, and Levang (1993), and Penot (1997) on rubber.

We collected information about the prevailing land tenure institutions and land rights through a group interview of village leaders and farmers. In addition, we conducted a brief interview of five farmers in each location to inquire into the manner and the date of acquisition of land and the incidence of tree planting. For the intensive survey, we selected two cinnamon-growing villages in Kerinci and two rubber-growing villages in Bungo Tebo. Since the results of the two intensive survey studies (cinnamon and rubber) are very similar, we report only the case of cinnamon in this chapter.[2]

Traditionally, the major ethnic groups—Minangkabau in the high region, Kerinci in the middle region, and Melayu Jambi in the low region—have relied on wet rice cultivation, and, hence, areas along streams and rivers are predominantly used for paddy fields. Paddy fields are surrounded by agroforestry plots, including both mature trees and newly planted trees intercropped with annuals, and bush-fallow plots under shifting cultivation. Natural forests are typically located in the mountainous terrain farther from village centers. The bush-fallow area originally was converted from primary forests and is planted with food crops periodically for a few seasons followed by another fallow period.

As shown in Table 4.1, villages in the high region are endowed with large paddy areas, whereas paddy fields account for a small portion of land in the low region. The bush-fallow area is smallest in the middle region in terms of both absolute area and relative proportion in the total exploited area. In contrast, large tracts of bush-fallow remain in the low region. Unfortunately, official statistics do not distinguish between secondary forest, which is a part of the bush-fallow system, and primary forest, and farmers' estimates of primary forest area are subject to substantial errors. Thus, we estimated the primary forest area by subtracting the total exploited area estimated by a group of farmers from the total village area reported by official statistics. According to the results shown in Table 4.1, primary forests still account for the lion's share of village land. This may be explained partly by the fact that a relatively well-protected national park accounts for about 58 percent of the area in the high region and 74 percent in the middle region, according to farmers' estimates, and partly by steep slopes of mountainous areas unsuitable for cultivation. Although we cannot provide concrete evidence, we have an impression that our estimation procedure resulted in overestimation of primary forest areas.

While all primary forestland in Indonesia is officially owned by the state, native people in our sites believe that forestland belongs to their community and is controlled by village chief, with the possible exception of forests in Kerinci Seblat National Park, which was established in 1985. Farmers, however, continue to encroach on the park, and boundary disputes have often occurred between local farmers and park officials. Usually farmers obtain permission to clear forestland from the village chief before carrying out clearance. Once the forestland is cleared, strong land rights are granted to farmers.

---

2. See Suyanto, Tomich, and Otsuka (2001b) for the case study of rubber.

TABLE 4.1 Land use patterns and population size in selected villages in Sumatra

| | Sample Size | Exploited Area in 1995[a] | | | Total Village Area[b] | Primary Forest Area[c] (ha) | Population in 1993[b] | Population Density in 1993[d] |
		Paddy Fields	Agroforestry Plots	Bush-Fallow				
		(hectares)						(persons/ square kilometer)
High region	24	259 (31)	377 (45)	204 (24)	5,143	4,303	1,764	34
Middle region	19	151 (19)	526 (66)	125 (16)	3,173	2,371	1,340	42
Low region	17	102 (9)	594 (55)	385 (36)	6,735	5,654	772	11

SOURCE: Extensive survey.

[a]Numbers in parentheses are proportions in exploited area in percentage terms.

[b]Based on Agricultural Census (Bureau of Statistics).

[c]Estimated by subtracting total exploited area from total village area.

[d]Population divided by village area.

Population density is highest in the middle region and lowest in the low region. None of the selected villages is newly settled, and more than 90 percent of them were established before the Dutch period ended in 1942. Low population density in the low region may be explained partly by the paucity of paddy fields in this area, whereas the rich endowment of flat fertile area suitable for rice cultivation and the high profitability of cinnamon would explain the highest population density in the middle region.

The three major ethnic groups all follow matrilineal inheritance and matrilocal residence systems, even though the inheritance system has undergone substantial transformation over time (Kahn 1980; Errington 1984). Traditionally lineage land, particularly that for paddy fields, has been owned collectively by a group of kin members, and this group usually consisted of a grandmother, her husband, children, and grandchildren. Land is bequeathed to sisters, nieces, and daughters of a woman who passed away, in accordance with the decision of a lineage head. The head is selected from among uncles, that is, a male member of the second generation, who exercises strong authority regarding land inheritance. The basic principle of land allocation is to maintain equity among lineage members.

According to our interviews with farmers, it is primarily husbands who make farm management decisions under this version of the matrilineal system, even though they have no customary land rights. Traditionally no single member of a lineage had complete ownership rights, and land transactions were strictly prohibited. Although formal approval by a lineage or community head is required for clearing community-owned forests, such approval is easily granted. Women are the custodians of lineage and family land and are expected to oppose the transfer of land to nonfamily members. Nowadays lineage land occupies only small areas in our sample villages.

Land under joint family ownership, which is inherited and owned jointly by daughters, is much more common than lineage ownership. The major difference from lineage tenure is that land is owned by a smaller number of family members. A system of rotating land use among sisters' families is often practiced for the cultivation of wet rice fields to prevent excessive fragmentation. All types of decisions regarding land use, inheritance, renting, and mortgaging are made jointly by sisters and their husbands without the intervention of other lineage members.

Joint family land tenure has developed along two paths. In the first form, lineage members agree to divide lineage land into joint family land, usually at the time of inheritance. In the second, daughters jointly inherit private land, which was acquired either by opening forestland or by purchasing already exploited bush-fallow land. Although the sale of lineage and family land traditionally has been prohibited, such land actually can be sold with the consent of the family members. In fact, the sale of land ownership rights is the most common method of land transfer among village population in recent years in our intensive study sites, as is shown later in this chapter. This would reflect the increasing scarcity of cultivable forestland. Such transactions are witnessed by village leaders and family members of both sellers and buyers to ensure proper protection of the transacted property. In this way, private-property rights on land have been firmly established.

Single family ownership is also emerging. Like joint family ownership, daughters inherit land under single family ownership, but ownership rights are more individualized. Another form of the single family ownership system has appeared in which sons are permitted to inherit some land, even though daughters inherit shares greater than or at least equal to those of sons. In some areas, the patrilineal system, in which only sons individually inherit the land, has also emerged. As in the case of Ghana, tree planting is usually a prerequisite for transforming jointly owned family land to a single family land at the time of inheritance. Compensation payments from those who have acquired single family land after tree planting to those who used to have joint ownership rights are sometimes made. Single family ownership could also have evolved from inheritance of private lands.

In these ways, the traditional matrilineal inheritance system in Sumatra has eroded considerably and given way to more individualized systems.

Major Issue and Hypotheses

If tree planting rights do not exist, incentives to tree planting are suppressed. Similarly, if rights to rent out, bequeath to desired heirs, and sell do not exist, expected returns to investment for those who plant and grow trees will be reduced (Besley 1995). As population pressure increases, the comparative advantage of agroforestry over shifting cultivation tends to increase, because net revenue from shifting cultivation decreases owing to declining fallow period and its negative impact on soil fertility.[3] The critical question is whether more secure land tenure institutions are induced to develop in order to capture larger benefits from investment in tree planting. It must be also pointed out that there may be security rewards from efforts to invest in land improvement in general, rather than investment in tree planting alone. Based on the theoretical framework developed in Chapter 1, we postulate the following hypotheses:

Hypothesis 1: More secure individualized land tenure institutions will develop in response to increasing scarcity of land relative to labor in order to reap benefits from investing in the establishment of agroforestry. In other words, this hypothesis suggests that increasing scarcity of land induces the development of an institutional rule stipulating that tree planting increases land rights.

---

3. Our study of rubber-growing villages (Suyanto, Tomich, and Otsuka 2001b) finds that shifting cultivation of upland rice is no longer profitable.

The individualization of land tenure institutions, however, is less likely to occur if profitable investment opportunities are limited. This is the case for paddy fields, in which only minor investments in the maintenance of traditional and simple gravity irrigation systems are required. In our empirical study, we compare the difference in land tenure institutions among paddy fields, bush-fallow areas, and tree crop fields, using extensive survey data obtained from the group interviews.

We are interested in exploring the causes of deforestation and the determinants of the development of agroforests. For this analysis, we use household data on the manner of land acquisition collected from five households in each of 60 randomly selected communities. Since inheritance is determined by the parent generation, it is assumed that inherited land area is given for (that is, not a choice of) individual households.

Hypothesis 2: Population pressure, manifested in both reduction of inherited land area per household and an increase in households size, increases the land area acquired by the clearance of forest.

In our observation, primary forest areas are largely open access, at least for community members, even though the village chief is supposed to be a custodian of communally held primary forest areas. As a result, forests have been cleared on a first-come basis, which has led to the rapid exhaustion of forest-land and its conversion to cropland including agroforest areas in many locations.[4] Since we expect that forests were more abundant in earlier years, older household heads are more likely to have had better access to forestland in their youth, and, hence, their acquired forest areas would be larger.

Hypothesis 3: Age of household head positively affects the amount of land acquired through forest clearance.

It is considered that the development of profitable agroforesty systems will help prevent deforestation (Tomich and van Noordwijk 1996). An implicit assumption of this argument is that the development of agroforest increases the demand for labor, which otherwise might have been allocated to the clearance of forest. In addition, the increased wealth due to the development of agroforest may reduce the supply of labor for such hard work as clearance of forests. Angelsen (1995, 1999) does not concur, arguing that the pace of deforestation would depend on the profitability of land use, so that the opportunity to grow profitable perennial crops will accelerate the speed of deforestation. In our view, the arguments of Angelson are valid if labor markets are well developed. Therefore, even where labor demand for agroforestry management increases, if labor markets are developed and agroforestry is profitable, labor can be hired to clear the forest. Thus, whether the development of agroforest deters or promotes deforestation is an empirical question (Kaimowitz and Angelsen 1998).

---

4. See the model of Anderson and Hill (1990), which describes how rapidly unused open-access land will be exploited when the property rights are conferred to those who have opened the land.

We examine this issue by assessing the effect of inherited agroforestry land on the area of cleared forestland.

Tree planting has played a catalytic role in the establishment of individual rights, because, as in the case of Ghana, tree planting confers stronger individual rights (see regression models specified in Chapter 1). Therefore, incentives to plant trees and carry out subsequent management activities are embedded in customary land tenure rules. As a null hypothesis, we would like to postulate the following:

Hypothesis 4: Given the expected increase in tenure security after tree planting, tree planting and the management efficiency of agroforestry are independent from initial tenure security levels under different land tenure institutions.

We test this hypothesis by estimating tree-planting function using extensive survey data and profit function using intensive household survey data. We also estimate the internal rate of return to investment in tree planting under different land tenure institutions based on the results of the estimated profit function.

Reflecting the establishment of clear private land rights, tenancy contracts are widely observed. If factor markets, including land rental and labor markets, are perfect, household endowments of land and labor should not affect factor proportions across farms, since households will rent land or hire labor so as to equalize them. As a result, we expect that production cost, revenue, and profit per unit of area are independent from household factor endowments.

Hypothesis 5: Household factor endowments do not affect production efficiency because of resource reallocation effects of efficient factor markets.

We expect that factor markets are induced to work more efficiently when land becomes scarce and, hence, valuable, because the economic cost of inefficient resource allocation becomes higher.

It is widely believed that the individualization of land rights results in inequitable distribution of land. Considering that customary land tenure institutions are designed to achieve equitable distribution of land among community members, the conventional view has some force. Yet the degree to which the individualization of land rights leads to inequitable distribution of land is not known. As in the study of Ghana in Chapter 3, we examine this issue by performing the analysis of decomposition of Gini ratios by land tenure category.

Extensive Study

Property Rights and Land Use

Through group interviews, we obtained estimates of the proportions of land under different land tenure institutions by type of land use. Since measurement of areas under different land tenure at the village level has never been done, such data are necessarily crude and subject to errors. Thus, we combine similar land tenure categories, such as single family ownership by daughters and by daughters and sons in order to reduce measurement errors associated with the finer classification of land tenure categories. Nonetheless, as is demonstrated in Table 4.2, some clear tendencies can be observed. First, lineage land is observed mostly in bush-fallow areas and in limited areas of paddy land. Second, joint ownership is dominant for paddy fields in the middle and low regions but accounts for only 3.1 to 19.4 percent of bush-fallow and smaller portions of tree crop plots in all regions. Third, single family ownership is more important than joint ownership except for paddy fields. Fourth, private ownership tends to be predominant in tree crop plots and accounts for a sizable portion of bush-fallow.

The fact that area under joint family and lineage ownership is generally small in all the regions indicates erosion of the traditional matrilineal inheritance system. A major exception is bush-fallow area, in which lineage land remains observed in relatively large areas. In our Sumatra sites, private ownership rights acquired by clearing forest are strong while the acquired land is cultivated, but they become weaker once it is left fallow and subject to traditional inheritance rules unless trees are planted.[5] This explains why joint family ownership is more prevalent for bush-fallow than for tree fields.

In order to assess the strength of property rights under different land tenure institutions, we asked a group of farmers in each village whether the cultivating household possesses rights to rent out under share tenancy, rent out under fixed-rent leasehold tenancy, pawn, and sell with and without approval of family or lineage leaders, or both, for the various tenure categories. Theoretically, the right to rent out under share tenancy is the weakest right followed closely by the right to rent out under leasehold tenancy,[6] whereas the strongest right rests in the right to sell without approval. Pawning is problem-ridden, because if a pawner cannot repay the loan, the land may eventually be confiscated by a pawnee. Except for the case of lineage-owned paddy fields, in which there is no individual right to sell at all, farmers' answers were either "yes without approval" or "yes with approval," for all categories. Therefore, we characterized the strength of individual land rights in terms of the number of rights without requiring approval (see Table 4.3).[7] Since there is no difference in land rights

---

5. The role of trees in establishing land claims was noted by one of the earliest Europeans to publish on Sumatra. Marsden (1811:69), drawing on his experience living in Sumatra in the late sixteenth century, long before rubber and coffee were introduced, wrote that "property in land depends on occupancy, unless where fruit-bearing trees have been planted." For a more recent analysis, see Angelson (1995).

6. This could be because there is stronger incentive to mine the soil under leasehold tenancy than share tenancy, because the whole marginal product accrues to leasehold tenants, unlike share tenants, who receive only a portion of incremental output. See Otsuka, Chuma, and Hayami (1992) for a survey of the literature on the land tenancy contracts in agrarian economies.

7. Besley (1995) constructs a similar variable and treats it as a continuous variable for the regression analyses. This procedure is problematic: unless the differences in land rights between all contiguous land tenure categories are equal, the land right index should be treated as an ordinal rather than a cardinal variable.

TABLE 4.2 Distribution of area under different land tenure institutions by land use type

	Lineage Ownership	Joint Family Ownership	Single Family Ownership	Private Ownership I (Purchase)	Private Ownership II (Clearance)
			(percentage)		
Paddy field					
High region	2.2	9.0	75.7	7.9	4.1
Middle region	10.4	63.9	6.3	5.5	7.8
Low region	0.0	64.6	29.2	6.1	0.1
Tree plots					
High region	3.1	5.2	41.8	10.4	37.1
Middle region	4.7	1.5	61.7	13.5	18.5
Low region	0.0	3.0	45.6	12.4	38.7
Bush-fallow area					
High region	15.5	8.5	36.3	5.2	32.6
Middle region	10.3	19.4	43.1	14.3	12.5
Low region	22.5	3.1	41.7	5.7	27.0

SOURCE: Extensive survey.

NOTE: Numbers in some rows do not add up to 100 percent because of the small area of land under state ownership.

TABLE 4.3 Index of land property rights under different land tenure institutions

	Lineage Land	Joint Family Ownership	Single Family Ownership I (Daughters)	Single Family Ownership II (Daughters and Sons)	Private Ownership (Purchased and Cleared)
Paddy field					
High region	0.5	0.8	1.6	3.2	3.6
Middle region	0.8	2.2	2.0	2.8	3.9
Low region	n.a.	2.7	2.0	n.a.	3.8
Upland field[a]					
High region	0.0	(0.6)	1.6	2.0	3.1
	(0.6)	(0.6)	(1.9)	(2.0)	(2.0)
Middle region	0.8	0.9	1.9	2.9	3.8
	(0.5)	(0.8)	(2.0)	(2.0)	(2.0)
Low region	0.0	1.0	1.0	2.8	3.8
	(0.5)	(0.5)	(1.7)	(1.7)	(2.0)

SOURCE: Extensive survey.

NOTE: Four rights are considered: rights to rent out under share tenancy, rent out under leasehold tenancy, pawn, and sell. Numbers refer to the average number of rights without obtaining approval of the family or lineage members, or both (maximum = 4.0). For upland fields, rights to plant and replant are also considered, and the average number of rights are shown in parentheses (maximum = 2.0). "n.a." refers to "not applicable."

[a]Upland field refers to both agroforestry plots and bush-fallow.

between bush-fallow and agroforestry plots for the same tenure category, these two types of land are combined under the category of upland fields. Needless to say, less individualized tenure categories are found more widely in bush-fallow plots.

Individual land rights under lineage ownership are very weak, possessing at best the right to rent out under share tenancy. It is interesting to observe that individual land rights for paddy fields under joint family ownership in the middle and low regions are comparatively high, even greater than the land rights under single family ownership by daughters in these two regions. It appears that individual land rights under joint family ownership have been strengthened by the deliberate agreement of the extended family members.

Except for this somewhat anomalous phenomenon, land rights are stronger under single family ownership than joint family ownership, and within single family ownership, the rights are stronger in the case of ownership by both daughters and sons. But even under single family ownership by daughters and sons, there is no right to sell without the approval of family members. The right to sell without approval is granted only to land acquired by clearing forests or by purchasing land. There is practically no difference in land rights between cleared and purchased land at the time of acquisition. Particularly in the middle and low regions, land rights in privately acquired land are close to complete ownership. Even in the high region, where individuals' rights over cleared and purchased land are weaker, it does not seem too difficult to obtain approval from one's family members in order to sell land. The major difference between private ownership in Sumatra and the Western world is the lack of official registration, so that land cannot be used as collateral for loans from banks. It is important to note that land rights acquired by clearing forests tend to decline over time if the land is planted to food crops and fallowed. How fast this decline occurs, however, is difficult to quantify.

Table 4.3 also compares tree rights on upland field under different land tenure institutions (see numbers in parentheses). Two rights are considered: rights to plant and replant trees. As in the case of land rights, we characterized the strength of individual tree rights in terms of the number of rights without requiring approval. It is clear that tree rights are markedly weaker under the collective ownership (lineage and joint family ownership) than under the individualized ownership (single family ownership and private ownership), which confers almost perfect tree-planting and -replanting rights. In the case of collective ownership, members of the group usually oppose tree planting because those who plant trees tend to demand strong individual ownership or long-term use rights on land.

The data in Tables 4.2 and 4.3 seem consistent with hypothesis 1, that land tenure institutions evolve toward individualized tenure in order to enhance incentives to invest in commercial trees in the face of increasing population pressure on land. On the other hand, investment in traditional irrigation works for paddy production requires a minimum of effort to maintain and repair these simple, small-scale facilities. Thus, less individualized land tenure for paddy fields is not as much of a problem from the standpoint of required investment incentives. If population pressure is the driving force toward individualization of land tenure institutions, we would expect to observe a predominance of more individualized tenure on tree crop plots in areas where population density and population growth rates are high.

Determinants of Land Tenure Choice

In order to identify the determinants of the choice of land tenure institutions, we estimated functions explaining the proportion of land under lineage, joint and single family ownership, and the two types of private ownership (that is, for purchased and cleared land) separately for paddy fields and tree crop plots. More specifically, we estimated the following functions while using a common set of explanatory variables:

$Y_{ij} = Y_{ij}$ (population density, population growth rate, proportion of paddy area, proportion of ethnic minorities, traveling time to subdistrict town, walking time to forest, regional dummies),

where Y_{ij} shows the proportion of i-th type of land ownership ($i = 1, 2, 3, 4$) on j-th type of land ($j = 1, 2$), and explanatory variables are all village-specific except regional dummies represented by middle and low region dummies. By definition, in principle, $\Sigma_i Y_{ij} = 100$ percent.[8] This equation corresponds to equation (1) in Chapter 2.

Means of explanatory variables by region are exhibited in Table 4.4. Population density in 1983, the earliest census year for which consistent village population statistics are available, was highest in the middle region and lowest in the low region. Annual average population growth rate for 1983–93, however, was low in the middle region, indicating the high population pressure on limited land resources in this region. Annual population growth rates were around 1 percent. Out-migration seems to have taken place, partly because of limited availability of unexploited land suitable for cultivation and partly because of ample job opportunities provided by commendable growth of nonfarm sectors until the recent Asian economic crisis arose. Percentage of paddy area is included to capture the special importance of paddy fields for supplying food. The percentage is computed from data in Table 4.1. In this measure, the high region is located in the most favorable area, with paddy fields covering 5.7 percent of the village land. The percentage of outsiders was highest in the middle region, most of whom were migrants from Java and settled in this region before the 1980s. The Javanese are not matrilineal, and their inflow might have

---

8. The sum, however, does not add up to 100 percent in some cases because of the small area of land under state ownership.

TABLE 4.4 Means of explanatory variables for village-level regression analysis on land tenure choice

	Population Density in 1983	Annual Average Population Growth Rate, 1983–93	Percentgae of Paddy Field	Percentage of Outsiders	Traveling Time to Subdistrict Capital	Walking Time to Forest
	(person/square kilometer)	(percentage)			(minutes)	(minutes)
High region	37.9	1.1	5.7	1.6	35.3	50.6
Middle region	53.1	1.0	3.7	4.6	20.4	194.8
Low region	11.5	1.0	1.2	1.4	29.7	171.6

SOURCE: Extensive survey and 1983 population census.

affected the traditional land ownership systems in these matrilineal societies. Travel time to the subdistrict capital by motorcycle was included to take into account the impact of access to local markets, whereas walking time to the nearest forest was included to capture the effects of proximity of residential areas to remaining forests. Partly as a result of its well-maintained infrastructure, travel time to the subdistrict capital was shortest in the middle region. Because little forestland is left near villages, walking time to the nearest forest was as long as approximately three hours in both the middle and low regions. Thus, farmers often build cottages and stay there overnight when they work in newly cleared fields. In the high region, walking time is shorter, but villages are often surrounded by the national park, which has been strictly protected in recent years. These observations suggest that the availability of forestland suitable for cultivation has been declining.

We estimated 13 regression functions; the estimation results are shown in Table 4.5, excluding the case of lineage ownership of paddy field and tree plots, which occupied small areas. Since Y_{ij} are truncated below zero, we applied the tobit estimation method.[9]

The validity of hypothesis 1, that population pressure promotes the individualization of land tenure, can be tested by examining whether higher population density and greater population growth rates are associated with greater incidence of private ownership and smaller incidence of family ownership. In order to reduce simultaneous equation bias possibly arising from the endogeneity of the population variables, we used population census figures from the past.[10] Consistent with our hypothesis, population density has a negative and significant effect on the incidence of joint family ownership and positive and significant effects on the incidence of single family ownership and private ownership through purchase in the case of paddy field. Since all forest areas suitable for conversion to paddy cultivation have been exhausted, individualization took the form of replacing collective ownership by single family ownership and inducing market transactions in land. Note that the middle and low region dummies have positive effects on the proportion of joint family ownership and negative effects on the proportion of single family ownership in the paddy field equations. These results are consistent with the observation from Table 4.3 that land rights for joint family tenure in the middle and low regions were similar to or even stronger than land rights of single family ownership. According to the estimation results of the determinants of land tenure in agroforestry plots, higher population density seems to have promoted private ownership by stimulating the clearance of forests at

---

9. Since tree crop plots under single family ownership existed in all sites, tobit and ordinary least squares (OLS) regressions are identical in this case. According to the OLS estimation, R^2 is 0.39.

10. Note that the results of our statistical test must be qualified to the extent that population variables are endogenous.

TABLE 4.5 Determinants of proportion of area under different land tenure institutions by land use type at the village level: Tobit regressions

	Paddy Fields				Agroforestry Plots			
	Joint Family	Single Family	Purchased	Cleared	Joint Family	Single Family	Purchased	Cleared
Intercept	21.29	75.29	3.54	5.73	−0.74	56.58	7.44	27.74
	(2.66)	(8.46)	(1.31)	(0.38)	(−0.06)	(7.09)	(1.46)	(3.41)
Population Density	−0.20*	0.21*	0.11**	0.13	0.22	−0.47**	0.07	0.27*
	(−1.67)	(1.91)	(2.75)	(0.42)	(1.00)	(−3.13)	(0.07)	(1.80)
Population Growth	0.39	−3.16	−0.32	4.07	−3.74	−4.88**	−2.45	6.36**
	(0.19)	(−1.34)	(−0.41)	(1.13)	(−1.06)	(−2.23)	(−1.74)	(2.83)
Percentage of paddy area	0.28	−0.27	0.00	−7.73**	−1.45	2.11**	−0.85	−1.35*
	(0.47)	(−0.31)	(0.00)	(−2.29)	(−1.11)	(2.48)	(−1.52)	(−2.01)
Percentage of outsiders	−7.04**	−0.16	0.04	3.45**	0.47	−0.49	0.26	0.23
	(−4.22)	(−0.21)	(0.17)	(3.03)	(0.90)	(−1.32)	(1.08)	(0.56)
Travel time to town	−0.10	−0.07	0.02	−0.24	−0.14	−0.05	0.15**	−0.02
	(−0.91)	(−0.58)	(0.50)	(−1.41)	(−0.78)	(−0.56)	(2.50)	(−0.02)
Travel time to forest	0.11	0.37	−0.29	−1.10	−0.14	−0.47	1.15*	−1.73
	(0.17)	(0.37)	(−0.91)	(−0.35)	(−0.08)	(−0.53)	(2.09)	(−1.12)
Middle region	75.09**	−87.38**	−4.20	−7.76	−30.44	29.90**	−0.77	−25.99**
	(8.79)	(−8.65)	(−1.43)	(−0.55)	(−1.89)	(3.61)	(−0.15)	(−3.03)
Low region	51.28**	−45.34**	0.85	−35.40	−18.31*	0.47	−2.03	8.19
	(6.39)	(−5.02)	(0.29)	(−1.85)	(−1.31)	(0.06)	(−0.39)	(0.96)
Log likelihood	−221.57	−204.45	−171.51	−67.40	−80.53	−257.83	207.60	−232.10
Sample size	55	55	55	55	58	58	58	58

NOTE: Numbers in parentheses are *t*-statistics.

* .05 level

** .01 level

the expense of single family ownership. The effect of population density on joint family ownership, however, is insignificant presumably because of the small area remaining under this ownership (see Table 4.2). Like population density, higher population growth resulted in lower incidence of single family ownership and higher incidence of private ownership through clearance of forests.

It is interesting to observe that percentage of paddy area tends to have negative effects on the clearance of forest, which is different from the effect of population variables. This is expected, because the larger endowment of paddy fields, which produce more grain per unit of area than upland fields, lessens the population pressure on land. Percentage of outsiders is associated negatively with the incidence of joint family ownership of paddy fields, suggesting that the inflow of outsiders helped undermine the traditional family ownership system of the matrilineal society. There is a possibility of reverse causation that outsiders migrated to villages where land tenure institutions are highly individualized so that they could rent in land. However, outsiders seem to have acquired paddy land in the distant past by clearing the remaining forest areas suitable for paddy cultivation, which is reflected in its positive coefficient in the cleared area regression for paddy fields.

By and large, both travel time to the subdistrict town and walking time to forests have no significant effects on the distribution of land ownership, with the exception of the positive effects of both variables on the incidence of purchased agroforestry plots. The former result indicates that the more remote locations are the only places where people are willing to sell land at a reasonable price. The latter result, which points to the high incidence of purchase of the existing agroforestry plots in areas where there is little forest near the village, is tenable.

To sum up, statistical evidence indicates that population pressure induces the individualization of land ownership, even though we cannot rule out the possibility of simultaneous equation bias. A major question is the relative speed by which primary forest and bush-fallow areas have been converted to commercial tree plots planted to rubber, cinnamon, and coffee under different land tenure institutions. If the major source of tree plots is primary forest, agroforestry development comes at the expense of the natural environment. On the other hand, if tree plots were primarily converted from bush-fallow, this development brings environmental benefits. These are the issues to which we now turn.

Determinants of Deforestation and Land Purchase

In order to obtain more accurate information on the distribution of upland under different land tenure institutions, let us examine the data from a brief individual household survey. Our total sample size consists of 300 households—5 households each in 60 villages. Since we hope to be able to assess the behavior of households regarding deforestation, we focus on 273 households that actually owned upland fields including land acquired through forest clearance. Similarly, we pay particular attention to the 231 households that have ever acquired bush-fallow and forestland for the analysis of the development of agro-forestry. The difference, which is 42 households, acquired upland planted to trees from the beginning. In this survey, we failed to obtain reliable data on joint family land areas, as individual respondents could not correctly estimate the areas of land owned by the extended family, particularly when it is "unused" or under fallow. So we focus on inheritance by single family under the matrilineal, newly emerging egalitarian and patrilineal inheritance systems and cleared and privately purchased land.

Table 4.6 demonstrates the manner of acquisition of upland fields. First, we found that the proportion of inherited land is well below 50 percent, suggesting that the importance of inheritance has declined over time. This seems to be a consequence of increasing population pressure on land inherited from the earlier generation. It appears that the proportion of purchased land has increased, even though land transaction has traditionally been prohibited. The proportion of inherited land is highest in the high region, partly because the settlement of villages in this region is earlier.

We also found that the average upland area per household in the low region is higher than in the high and middle regions. This indicates less population pressure on land in the low region compared with the other two regions. It must be also pointed out that the land acquired by forest clearance is quite high in the low region, because of greater availability of forests in this region.[11] Usually, newly cleared forestlands are located in distant areas, whereas purchased lands are commonly located in areas not far from residential areas.

It would be reasonable to assume that acquisition of land through forest clearance and acquisition through purchase are the choices made by an individual household, while the acquisition of inherited land is determined by the parental generation. In the low region, land was first acquired by inheritance, followed by forest clearance and purchase (Table 4.6). In the high and middle regions, although forest was acquired in the earliest years, there is not much difference from the dates of purchase and inheritance. Even though forestlands tend to be acquired earlier, it seems reasonable to assume that young farmers are able to predict relatively accurately how much land they will acquire through inheritance in the near future. This is because in the case of single family ownership qualified heirs can be clearly defined, so that inheritance decisions by parents are public knowledge for their heirs. Although heirs do not know when parents will die, they can temporarily use parents' land until inheritance. If they perceive that land to be received as inheritance will not be sufficient, they will acquire more land by clearing forest or purchasing. Therefore, it is reasonable to assume that the amount of inherited land areas, either actual or expected, influences individual decisions to acquire land. We also

---

11. The data exhibited in Table 4.6 are largely consistent with the data shown in Table 4.1. We further examine land tenure distribution in the intensive survey sites later in the chapter.

TABLE 4.6 Average upland area per household and average year of land acquisition by manner of land acquisition and site

Land Acquisition	High Region (hectares)	(percentage)	(acquisition)	Middle Region (hectares)	(percentage)	(acquisition)	Low Region (hectares)	(percentage)	(acquisition)
Inherited by									
Daughters	0.48	42	1984	0.13	10	1981	0.81	20	1982
Daughters and sons	0.00	3	1982	0.18	14	1982	0.00	0	—
Sons	0.03	0	—	0.07	5	1981	0.41	10	1981
Forest clearance	0.49	42	1981	0.40	31	1980	1.84	42	1988
Purchase	0.15	13	1982	0.51	39	1982	1.06	26	1988
Total	1.17	100	—	1.29	100	—	4.12	100	—

SOURCE: Brief individual household survey in extensive survey villages.

NOTE: Households that have never inherited land have been excluded.

assume that the reduction in inherited land area per household reflects the severity of population pressure, as the population growth must have exceeded the pace of forest clearance over the past few decades. We hypothesize that as the size of inherited land decreases, farmers attempt to clear more forest, even though newly cleared areas may be small, or purchase more land.

In order to identify the determinants of the choice of upland acquisition, we estimated functions explaining the areas of land acquired by forest clearance and purchase. The explanatory variables in our regressions include the area of inherited land, interaction of inherited land with two inheritance system dummies with the base for comparison being inheritance by daughters, the percentage of trees planted at the time of acquisition of inherited land, age of household head, schooling of head, owned paddy area, and the number of male and female workers between 16 and 60 years of age. Although one may think that owned paddy area is endogenous, actually it is largely inherited (see Table 4.2). We believe that it is legitimate to assume that the inherited land areas are determined by parents and, hence, exogenous for current generations.

The average paddy area was larger in the low region (0.8 hectare) and the high region (0.6 hectare) than in the middle region (0.3 hectare), reflecting the comparatively abundant endowment of paddy land relative to population outside the middle region. There were no appreciable differences in the proportion of trees planted in inherited land among the three regions, which is about 40 percent of the area. There were also no noticeable regional differences in the age and schooling of household head and the number of male and female workers per household. Since there are different inheritance systems, we used interaction terms of inherited land area with two inheritance system dummies in our specification of the regression function.

Because of the nonexistence of certain types of land acquisition in a number of sample households, and because unobservable characteristics of villages may affect land acquisition decisions, we applied the tobit estimation method with village fixed effects. The estimation results are shown in Table 4.7.

The first column shows the determinants of acquired forest areas through forest clearance or deforestation. As we expected, inherited land has a negative and significant effect on deforestation. This is consistent with hypothesis 2, that increasing population pressure on limited land is a major cause for deforestation. Although the tobit beta coefficient is −0.97, the marginal effect of a 1 percent increase in inherited land on forestland is −0.37,[12] which indicates that decreases in inherited land are not well compensated for by increases in forestland. Interaction terms of inherited land with two inheritance dummies, however, were not significant, suggesting that there is no substantive difference in the decision to clear forest among matrilineal, bilateral, and patrilineal inheri-

---

12. We calculated the marginal effect following the formula proposed by McDonald and Moffitt (1980).

TABLE 4.7 Determinants of land acquisition at the household level: Tobit regression with village fixed effects

	Forest Clearance	Purchase
Intercept	−2.88	−3.88
	(−1.40)	(−1.49)
Inherited upland	−0.99**	−0.26
	(−2.75)	(−0.65)
Interaction of inherited upland and dummy	−0.07	1.52
for bilateral inheritance	(−0.07)	(1.36)
Interaction of inherited upland and dummy	0.69	−0.16
for patrilineal inheritance	(1.25)	(−0.16)
Percentage of area planted to trees in	−0.01	−0.02*
inherited upland	(−1.43)	(−2.00)
Age of head	0.05**	0.02
	(2.50)	(0.67)
Schooling of head	0.09	0.16*
	(1.13)	(1.78)
Owned paddy area	0.93*	1.19*
	(2.11)	(2.02)
Number of male workers	0.60*	0.42
	(1.71)	(0.98)
Number of female workers	0.25	0.10
	(−0.74)	(0.26)
Log likelihood	−306.32	−254.13

NOTE: Numbers in parentheses are t-statistics.

*.05 level

**.01 level

tance systems. From this result we may be able to conclude that the traditional matrilineal inheritance system under single family ownership provides incentives to invest in forest clearance as strong as the more recent bilateral and patrilineal inheritance systems.

Owned paddy area has a positive and significant effect on deforestation, which suggests that wealthier farmers tend to clear more forestland by employing hired laborers. This interpretation is reinforced by the fact that the purpose of forest clearance is to establish agroforest, which also requires labor and capital. The finding that paddy land ownership has a positive effect on forest clearance may seem contradictory to our earlier finding that the proportion of paddy land tends to have negative effects on the proportion of cleared forestland. It must be noted, however, that we applied the village-level fixed effects model in Table 4.7, so that the effects of the availability of paddy and forestland in the village are controlled for. The earlier analysis, in contrast, did not control for such village-specific effects. Thus, it is likely that in villages endowed with relatively large paddy areas the demand for new forestland is smaller, but among farmers it is the rich who can afford to invest in clearance of forests.

The percentage of area planted to trees has a negative effect but is not significant. Therefore, the hypothesis that the development of profitable agroforestry deters deforestation is not supported by our data. The net effect will depend on the labor-using effect of agroforestry and development of labor market, as we discussed earlier.[13] The age of the household head has a positive and significant effect on deforestation. This result is consistent with hypothesis 3, that the older the household head, the greater would have been access to forestland in one's youth. Hence, acquired forestland area would be larger. We also found a significant influence of the increasing number of male workers on deforestation. Since clearance of forest requires hard work by male workers, this result is not surprising.

The second column shows the estimation results of the determinants of purchased land. Owned paddy area has a highly positive effect on the purchase of land, which indicates that wealthier farmers tend to purchase larger areas of upland. We also found that schooling of the household head has a positive and significant effect, suggesting that more educated farmers tend to buy more land. Unexpectedly, inherited land has an insignificant effect on purchased land. Interaction terms of inherited land with the two inheritance dummies are also insignificant. The percentage of area planted to trees has a negative and significant effect. It may well be that the larger demand for labor in agroforestry deterred purchase of additional land.

Determinants of Development of Agroforestry

Under customary law, relatively strong individual rights are granted to those who plant trees not only in Sub-Saharan Africa (for example, Shepherd 1991, chap. 3) but also in Sumatra. Under such an institutional rule, an individual community member who has acquired land through inheritance as well as through other means may have strong incentives to plant trees in order to obtain secure individual land rights. Table 4.8 shows the average acquired forest and bush areas by household and the incidence of tree planting (development of agroforest) by manner of acquisition and region. The percentages of bush-fallow and forest area converted to agroforests are high in all regions. Furthermore, the incidence of tree planting tends to be higher in cleared forest and inherited land than in purchased land, with the exception of the high region. The purchase in the high region, however, was unimportant. These observations indicate that incentives to invest in tree planting are not simply determined by the

---

13. According to Suyanto, Tomich, and Otsuka (2001b), rubber agroforestry requires substantially more labor than upland rice cultivation under shifting cultivation, which is a major alternative farming system in the low region.

TABLE 4.8 Average areas of acquired forest- and bushland per household and the incidence of tree planting by manner of acquisition and site

Land Acquisition	Acquired Bush and Forest Area	Area Planted to Trees
	(hectares)	(percentage)
High region		
Matrilineal inheritance	0.33	69
Egalitarian inheritance	0.00	n.a.
Patrilineal inheritance	0.00	n.a.
Forest clearance	0.62	79
Purchase	0.08	95
Tenancy	0.03	78
Total/average	1.06	77
Middle region		
Matrilineal inheritance	0.13	95
Egalitarian inheritance	0.12	90
Patrilineal inheritance	0.04	77
Forest clearance	0.48	94
Purchase	0.42	71
Tenancy	0.16	77
Total/average	1.33	84
Low region		
Matrilineal inheritance	0.55	74
Egalitarian inheritance	0.00	n.a.
Patrilineal inheritance	0.12	45
Forest clearance	1.93	71
Purchase	0.35	29
Tenancy	0.01	100
Total/average	2.96	66

SOURCE: Brief individual household survey in extensive survey villages.

NOTE: Tree-planted areas at the time of land acquisition have been excluded. "n.a." refers to "not applicable."

strength of land rights or the level of land tenure security but also by the expected changes in land rights after tree planting.

In order to identify the determinants of the development of agroforests, we estimated a tree-planting function in which area planted to trees is a dependent variable. The explanatory variables included the area of inherited land, interaction terms of inherited land with two inheritance dummies, purchased land, age of household head, owned paddy area, the number of male and female workers 16 to 60 years of age, and outsider dummy. The estimated function corresponds to equation (3) specified in Chapter 2.

Since some households have not planted trees, and because unobservable characteristics of villages may affect the tree-planting decisions, we applied the tobit estimation method with village fixed effects model while using household data. The estimation results, including the estimated marginal effects, are shown in Table 4.9. We found that the estimated marginal effects are almost similar to the estimated tobit beta coefficient, which reflects the high incidence of tree planting.

Both forestland and inherited land have positive and highly significant effects on tree planting. Purchased land also has a positive but weaker effect, judging from its significantly smaller coefficient than the coefficients of forest- and inherited land. Thus, the incentive to plant trees in purchased land is lower,

TABLE 4.9 Determinants of area planted to commercial trees: Tobit regression with village fixed effects

	Beta coefficients	Marginal effect
Intercept	−0.54	
	(−1.38)	
Forestland area	0.77**	0.73**
	(25.67)	
Inherited land area	0.69**	0.65**
	(8.63)	
Interaction of inherited land area	−0.17	−0.16
and dummy for bilateral inheritance	(−0.74)	
Interaction of inherited land area	0.19	0.18
and dummy for patrilineal inheritance	(0.76)	
Purchased land area	0.38**	0.36**
	(5.43)	
Age of head	0.01	0.01
	(1.00)	
Schooling of head	0.03*	0.03*
	(1.67)	
Owned paddy area	0.19*	0.18*
	(1.73)	
Number of male workers	0.16*	0.15*
	(1.99)	
Number of female workers	−0.14*	−0.13*
	(−2.01)	
Outsider dummy	0.12	0.11
	(0.29)	
Log likelihood	−223.97	

NOTE: Numbers in parentheses are *t*-statistics.

*.05 level

**.01 level

even though the strength of purchased land rights is much higher. Because of the secure land right, farmers probably do not have to rush in planting trees. In contrast, if land use is limited to food crops grown under shifting cultivation, individual rights acquired through forest clearance tend to diminish over time. When land is under fallow, other members of the community can claim the right to use this "unused" land (Marry and Michon 1987). Relatively strong individual ownership rights, however, are granted if trees are planted. Under such institutional rules, an individual community member who has cleared forestland would have strong incentives to plant trees in order to establish secure land rights. Similar to this case, if individual household members have not planted trees on bush-fallow land received by inheritance, there is a possibility for other members of the extended family to claim the "unused" land.

The interaction terms of inheritance dummies (egalitarian inheritance by daughters and sons and patrilineal inheritance by sons only) do not have significant coefficients. It appears that the incentives to invest in tree planting are more likely and more strongly affected by expected changes in land rights after tree planting than the level of land rights before tree planting. These findings are consistent with hypothesis 4. Similar phenomena are reported by a case study of cocoa planting in western Ghana (Chapter 3). Our result, however, is quite different from the findings of Besley (1995), who uses the data set from western Ghana to show statistically that stronger land rights lead to a higher incidence of tree planting. We would argue that Besley's methodology of simply counting the number of rights (for example, rights to rent out and sell) to measure the tenure security without considering the relative importance of each right leads to biased estimation.[14] The number of male workers has a positive and significant effect on tree-planted areas, whereas the number of female workers has a negative and significant effect. These results are plausible, since the establishment of agroforest requires primarily male labor (Barlow and Muharminto 1982). Finally, we found that more educated farmers tend to establish agroforest more actively.

Summary for Extensive Study

According to the results of the extensive study, population pressure is positively associated with individualization of land tenure institutions in indigenous societies. The conclusion that population pressure is a causal factor, however, will have to be qualified, to the extent that the population variables are not truly exogenous. The extent of individualization, however, was different for different types of land. Ownership of paddy land is least individualized, which is consistent with the small investment requirement for paddy field. Thus, joint family ownership still prevails in many areas. The ownership of bush-fallow land

---

14. Moreover, tree planting is expressed by binary variable in Besley's study, which is inadequate where tree-planting areas and densities are significantly different.

is more individualized than paddy fields but less so than agroforestry plots. In fact, joint family–cum–lineage ownership accounts for about one-fourth of bush-fallow but for much less than 10 percent of agroforests. These observations are consistent with our contention that, as in Ghana (Chapter 3), both clearing forests and planting trees enhance individual ownership rights under these indigenous land tenure institutions. These institutional rules seem to reflect the general principle that labor effort for long-term investments is rewarded by stronger individual land rights.

We also obtained evidence that reduction in inherited area results in deforestation in Sumatra and that wealthier farmers clear forests and develop agroforestry more actively. It is found that the development of agroforestry did not exert a strong influence on the pace of deforestation. Therefore, we question the validity of the argument that the development of agroforestry deters deforestation significantly. If it is desirable to preserve primary forest from the social or global viewpoint, measures other than the promotion of profitable agroforestry need to be implemented.

The statistical analysis indicates that the proportion of area planted to trees is higher in formerly forest- and inherited land than in purchased land and that the difference in the strength of land rights between matrilineal and egalitarian inheritance does not have any effect on the pace of tree planting. These results support our hypothesis that the incentive to invest in tree planting is affected not only by strength of individual land rights but also by expected changes in land rights after tree planting. In other words, customary land tenure institutions have built-in incentive mechanisms that ensure active tree planting. In all likelihood, therefore, farmers in customary land areas invest in tree planting if agroforestry is profitable. The establishment of profitable agroforest, in turn, will contribute to the improvement of the well-being of farmers residing in mountainous areas and to the improvement of natural environment, to the extent that it replaces bush-fallow area.

It is observed that inequality between rich and poor farmers may increase in the process of deforestation and the development of agroforestry, as wealthy farmers clear forests and develop agroforests more actively than poor farmers. How to achieve equitable development of agroforestry without sacrificing its profitability is a major challenge we now face.

Intensive Study

Property Rights and Land Use

In order to explore to what degree individualized land rights stimulate the efficient management of agroforests, we conducted an intensive household survey in two typical cinnamon-growing villages in Kerinci District in Jambi Province (see Figure 4.1). Almost all inhabitants belong to the Kerinci ethnic group, which traditionally has practiced matrilineal descent. We conducted a random sample survey of 50 households in each of the two contiguous villages, which have similar topographical, ecological, and socioeconomic environments. Three rounds of the household survey were conducted in August/September 1996, February/March 1997, and August 1997.

As shown in Table 4.10, we found a total of 695 fields cultivated by our sample households under joint family ownership, other ownership systems, and tenancy and borrowing arrangements. Out of 695, 239 were lowland paddy fields. Note that a rotation system of cultivation is common under the joint family ownership system, in which only qualified households cultivate the land in a particular year. Therefore, we found 99 paddy fields cultivated by members of joint families other than selected sample households during the 1996/97 wet season and focused on the 140 paddy fields actually cultivated by our sample households in this study. Among these, 82 percent were irrigated by traditional simple gravity systems using streams flowing from nearby mountains, while the rest were rainfed. The average size of paddy field was less than half a hectare, and a typical household owned two to three paddy plots, including jointly owned plots.

Upland fields were divided into 155 young cinnamon fields with trees 1 to 3 years of age, 264 productive cinnamon fields with trees age 4 to 13, and 37 bush-fallow fields. A considerable number of cinnamon fields were intercropped with coffee, even though cinnamon trees predominated. To simplify

TABLE 4.10 Distribution and average size of owned/cultivated and sample plots by land use

	Owned/ Cultivated Plots[a]		Sample Plots		
	Number	Average Size	Number	Average Size	Number of households
		(hectares)		(hectares)	
Total	695	0.96	378	0.75	100
Lowland rice fields	239	0.48	140	0.47	88
Young cinnamon fields[b]	155	1.20	63[c]	0.70	46
Productive cinnamon fields[d]	264	1.18	175[c]	0.99	79
Bush-fallow	37	1.60	0	—	33

SOURCE: Intensive survey.

[a]Owned under joint family ownership, owner-cultivated under other ownership systems, and cultivated under tenancy and borrowing arrangements.

[b]Young cinnamon fields refer to those with trees aged one to three years.

[c]Excluding those cinnamon fields intercropped with coffee.

[d]Productive cinnamon fields refer to those with trees aged four years and above.

the analysis of profitability, we chose 63 young and 175 productive fields entirely planted to cinnamon for the detailed survey of production, input use, and cost.[15]

Most of Indonesia's cinnamon is produced in the Kerinci Valley, where our study sites are located.[16] There, the main cinnamon harvest (when trees are felled) occurs after 8 to 10 years of growth. Coppices regrow after harvesting, and this process can be repeated three times in most cases. Because of the declining rate of regrowth, trees are usually replanted after the fourth harvest. Minor output is "produced" when certain branches are pruned beginning with four years after planting or regrowth. Among the young cinnamon fields in our sample, 16 percent were converted from bush-fallow land after clearance, 22 percent were established after clearing old cinnamon fields and replanting, and 62 percent were derived from regrowth after the main harvest. Young fields were intercropped with annual crops, mostly with chili; in our sample, 62 percent were intercropped in the first year, 21 percent in the second year, and 5 percent in the third year. Intercropping intensity declines primarily because of the increasing competition for sunlight with growing trees.

Bush-fallow fields, which accounted for a small proportion of area, were generally located in areas far from village centers and were formerly planted to food crops. Only one-third of our sample households owned such land, which reflects the near exhaustion of easily accessible cultivable land in the Kerinci Valley. At present, some of them are secondary forests.[17] Farmers sell standing cinnamon trees to local traders, who offer prices to farmers based on their own assessment of the value of cinnamon in the field. Taking advantage of this practice, we employed traders in our survey and requested them to assess the value of standing cinnamon trees in all productive sample fields. We define the sum of the estimated value of trees and actual sale value of minor output as "potential value of output" and the potential value of output minus total nonland cost as "potential profit." We used both of these variables in our statistical analysis. In our survey we also measured the elevation and slope of plots to obtain information on land quality. Land quality may be affected not only by its physical characteristics but also by soil fertility, which is considered to be critically affected by the previous land cover (that is, forest, cinnamon field, or bush fallow). Thus, we also investigated the previous land cover of our sample plots.

---

15. Insofar as coffee is a minor crop, the choice between cinnamon alone and cinnamon intercropped with coffee seems to be of secondary importance.

16. Indonesian cinnamon (*Cinnamomum burmanii*)—also called "cassiavera"—accounts for roughly two-thirds of the world supply of this species, which is ground from the bark. It is a different species than that in South Asia (*Cinnamomum verum*). The bark of the South Asian species can be removed without cutting down the living trees. In the main harvest of Indonesian cinnamon, however, trees are felled before the bark is removed.

17. The choice between growing cinnamon trees and maintaining bush-fallow fields is not explicitly analyzed in this study because of the minor importance of the latter.

It is expected that soil fertility is higher on land that has just been cleared from natural forests.

The prevailing land tenure institutions differ somewhat between lowland paddy fields and upland cinnamon fields. Table 4.11 shows the land tenure distribution of all sample plots by land use type. There were a variety of land tenure institutions in lowland paddy fields, ranging from joint family ownership to private tenure and to share and fixed-rent tenancy. It is remarkable that the traditional matrilineal inheritance system (joint family tenure with inheritance by daughters) has almost completely given way to inheritance by daughters and sons alike, in both joint family and single family ownership systems. Because of the predominance of this egalitarian inheritance system, we use the combined subcategories in joint family and single family ownership systems in our statistical analysis. In the case of joint family ownership, a household that has the right to cultivate in a particular year also has rights to rent out under both share and fixed-rent tenancy and to pawn without permission of other members of the "joint family." Land rights are much weaker in the case of borrowing from relatives, a system with no formally required payments in which the cultivator basically has only usufruct rights. In the case of all other tenure institutions, including single family ownership, respondents indicated that the cultivator possesses perfect rights including the right to sell without anybody's permission, even though land cannot be used as collateral for credit from formal financial institutions. The common arrangement under share tenancy was 2/3:1/3 output sharing for tenant and landowner without cost sharing. Such an output sharing arrangement is sometimes observed elsewhere in Asia (Hayami and Otsuka 1993).

TABLE 4.11 Land tenure distribution of sample plots by land use type

Land Tenure Categories	Lowland Rice	Young Cinnamon	Productive Cinnamon
		(percentage)	
Joint family	24	0	0
Daughters	3	0	0
Daughters and sons	21	0	0
Single family	28	37	43
Daughters	2	3	3
Daughters and sons	22	27	38
Sons	4	6	1
Borrowing	8	18	14
Private—purchase	10	18	24
Private—forest clearance	1	14	9
Share tenancy	19	14	10
Fixed-rent tenancy	11	0	0

SOURCE: Intensive survey.

The land tenure institutions of cinnamon fields were much more individual-ized. First of all, there was no joint family ownership in this type of land. As in the case of paddy fields, the rights to rent out under leasehold and share contract, pawn, and sell without permission of any family and lineage members existed not only under private ownership but also under single family ownership. Renting under share tenancy contracts has also been observed, in which revenue from cin-namon was shared equally between landowner and tenant if planting or replant-ing was carried out by the tenant, and shared at 2/3:1/3 between them if trees were established prior to the tenancy. For annual crops intercropped with cinnamon seedlings, harvests were shared equally if current inputs were provided by the landowner, or wholly given to the tenant if the tenant provided inputs. Share ten-ants and borrowers have cultivated the currently occupied land for 4.0 and 5.6 years, respectively, on average. The distribution of land tenure institutions was essentially no different between young and productive cinnamon fields.

Based on recall data, Figure 4.2 traces out changes in the manner of ac-quisition of upland fields in terms of ratios of areas.[18] It is clear that as the im-portance of forest as a source of acquired land declined, the relative importance of single family ownership increased in the 1970s. As forestland became scarcer in the 1980s and 1990s, purchase of land became the predominant mode of land acquisition. It must be noted that the purchase of land became dominant because the right to sell land was bestowed under single family ownership. Fig-ure 4.2 also suggests that the process of the evolution of land tenure institution has been relatively continuous and smooth.

Table 4.12 shows land use by land tenure before the current cohort of cin-namon trees were established. The data show that 13 percent of both young and productive cinnamon fields under single family ownership previously were bush-fallow, and 87 percent were cinnamon fields. In the latter case, either cinnamon was replanted or coppiced after the previous cinnamon harvest. Significant num-bers of cinnamon fields have been purchased, and many others are operated un-der borrowing arrangements and share tenancy contracts, indicating that land market institutions are functioning. In the case of privately owned plots acquired by clearing natural forest, 44 to 47 percent had been used as cinnamon fields be-tween the periods after forest clearance and before the establishment of current trees, 20 to 33 percent previously were bush-fallow land, and fewer than one-third of the plots were converted directly from primary forest.

Revenue, Cost, and Profit

In order to analyze how the prevailing land tenure institutions affect the profitability of cinnamon and paddy production, we estimated the residual

---

18. It must be pointed out that since data are based on recall of current population, in all like-lihood, the trend shown in Figure 4.2 understates the importance of the more traditional manners of land acquisition, such as inheritance under joint family ownership, in earlier years.

FIGURE 4.2 Proportion of land acquisition by land tenure in Kerinci

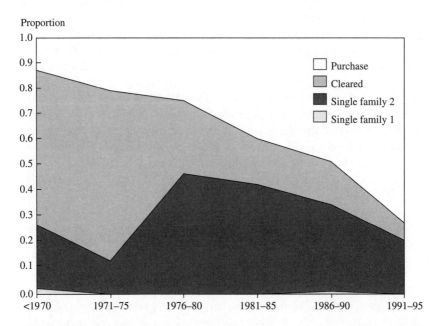

NOTE: "Single family 1" refers to ownership through inheritance by a daughter. "Single family 2" refers to ownership by daughter and son separately.

profit, defined as gross revenue minus both actual and imputed costs of hired and family labor, and current and capital inputs. The residual profit thus defined is intended to measure the contribution of land, management inputs, and the intensity of family labor effort, which cannot be directly measured. Since tenure security determines incentives to manage fields for future benefits, it is reasonable to assume that after controlling for land quality, the differences in the residual profit can be attributed to the differences in tenure security. We therefore regressed the estimated residual profit on the land tenure variables and variables representing land quality, among other things.

Labor, particularly family labor, is the major cost item in the production of paddy and cinnamon. In order to estimate the total cost of production, we imputed the cost of family labor by activity and gender by using the relevant prevailing wage rates of hired laborers. Wages of both male and female workers in the same activity under the same contractual arrangement (that is, daily wage or piece rate contract) were quite uniform across our sample observations, suggesting that a standard wage existed in each activity in our sites. We also found that both daily wages and piece rate contracts coexisted in many activities in

TABLE 4.12 Previous land use of current cinnamon fields by land tenure type

	Young Cinnamon			Productive Cinnamon		
	Bush-Fallow	Cinnamon	Forest	Bush-Fallow	Cinnamon	Forest
	(percentage)					
Single family	13	87	0	13	87	0
Borrowing	9	91	0	33	67	0
Private—purchase	0	100	0	21	79	0
Private—clearance	33	44	22	20	47	33
Share tenancy	11	89	0	22	78	0

SOURCE: Intensive survey.

both paddy and cinnamon production and that daily wages were substantially lower than daily earnings under piece rate contracts.[19]

Wage income per day used for the imputation of family labor costs ranged from 4,500 to 6,500 rupiah ($1.88 to 2.71) for men and from 3,400 to 3,900 rupiah ($1.42 to 1.63) for women.[20] Since family laborers are expected to work more intensively than daily wage workers, we used daily earnings under piece rate contracts for the imputation whenever such contracts prevailed.[21]

Although unreported in tabular form, several important observations can be made on labor use per hectare of paddy production by activity and land tenure institution. First, labor use per hectare, both total and by activity, was quite similar across different tenure systems, which suggests that tenure effects on labor allocation were relatively small. Second, the average rice yields were also similar and clustered around 2.1 tons per hectare. Third, labor use was very high in absolute terms, amounting to slightly more than 200 days per hectare, even though the traditional, six-month varieties were grown. In fact, it is generally greater than that observed in well-irrigated paddy fields growing modern, high-yielding rice varieties in other parts of Asia, which are considered highly labor intensive (David and Otsuka 1994). The high labor intensity suggests that paddy area was scarce relative to labor in our sites. Fourth, the proportion of female labor was about one-half, implying that both men and women worked more or less equally in paddy fields. There was, however, specialization of work

19. Such uniform differences between daily wages and daily earnings under piece rate contracts are widely observed in rice-growing areas of Asia, which may be attributed to incentive-enhancing and self-selection effects of the latter contract (David and Otsuka 1994).

20. The prevailing exchange rate of approximately US$1.00: 2,400 rupiah in 1996/97 was applied for the conversion from Indonesian rupiah to U.S. dollars.

21. Since no woman was engaged in cinnamon harvesting as a hired laborer, we used the average female wage for other activities (land preparation, planting of annual crops and seedlings of cinnamon, crop care, and harvesting of annual crops) for the imputation of women's family labor cost in cinnamon harvesting.

TABLE 4.13 Labor use in cinnamon fields by age of trees and laborers' gender

Age of Trees	Number of Sample Plots	Men	Women	Total
(years)			(person-days/hectare)	
1	21	57.3	51.9	109.2
		(85)	(78)	(82)
3	21	20.6	25.4	46.0
		(67)	(58)	(62)
5	29	15.1	5.5	20.7
		(58)	(85)	(65)
7	30	17.6	17.4	35.0
		(27)	(9)	(18)

SOURCE: Intensive survey.

NOTE: Numbers in parentheses are proportions of family labor. For simplicity, only labor data for tree of selected ages are shown.

by gender; women worked primarily in weeding and harvesting, whereas men were engaged mostly in land preparation. The proportion of hired labor seasonally migrating from neighboring areas was approximately two-thirds, primarily because the selected villages are endowed with much more fertile paddy fields than neighboring areas. The large reliance on hired labor also indicates that the labor market is well developed in this area.

Table 4.13 shows labor use per hectare in cinnamon fields by laborers' gender and age of trees. It is clear that in cinnamon fields, too, men and women worked more or less equally. Labor use per hectare is particularly high in the first year owing to heavy labor requirements for land preparation and planting of both cinnamon and annual crops. From the second year, labor requirements tend to decline as the proportion of fields planted to food crops and weeding requirements declined. Family labor is used mostly in the first three years, whereas hired labor is heavily employed for such simple tasks such as weeding in later stages of tree growth.

Using average wages to impute family labor costs, we examined estimates of revenue, total cost, and the residual profit of rice production by land tenure institution, including the costs of current inputs (such as seeds and chemical fertilizer) and capital services (water buffaloes for land preparation, trucks for hauling, and mechanical threshing). The costs of current inputs and capital accounted for only a small portion of total cost,[22] whereas labor accounted for about 50 percent. This is not surprising given the labor-intensive paddy cultivation system employed in the study area. It is observed that not only gross rev-

---

22. We also imputed the cost of family-owned buffalo and threshing machines, even though they were relatively minor cost items.

enue but also the cost of each item and the residual profit were quite similar among different land tenure institutions. Borrowed land, which exhibits lower values of revenue, total cost, and profit, is an exception to this pattern. These observations suggest that, despite differences among the prevailing tenure institutions, these institutional differences do not have a significant influence on the efficiency of paddy production. This may be explained partly by the fact that although the lack of tenure security may affect long-term investment incentives, rice is an annual crop, and the simple gravity irrigation system requires little investment to establish or maintain. It may also be the case that practices that would degrade land, which in principle would arise under the rotation system of jointly owned plots, were effectively prevented by mutual enforcement mechanisms operating in the joint ownership arrangements within extended families.

The potential value of production, labor costs, current input costs (mostly chemical fertilizer for annual crops), and the potential profit of cinnamon fields are shown by age of trees in Table 4.14. For young cinnamon plots, data are shown by plantation or regrowth. Plantation after clearance of different types of fields (old cinnamon field, bush-fallow field, or forest) was combined because of the limited number of observations and the similarity of costs of clearance

TABLE 4.14 Potential value, production costs, and potential profit of upland cultivation by age of cinnamon trees

Age	Potential Value[a] (1)	Labor Cost[b] (2)	Cost of Current Inputs (3)	Total Cost (2) + (3)	Potential Profit (1) − (2) − (3)
(years)			(1,000 rupiah)		
1 (Plantation)	457	649	126	775	−318
1 (Regrowth)	553	328	66	394	158
2 (Plantation)	214	134	2	135	79
2 (Regrowth)	154	282	11	293	−140
3 (Plantation)	38	256	8	264	−226
3 (Regrowth)	82	198	9	206	−124
4	1,071	209	2	211	860
6	2,441	119	2	121	2,319
8	4,096	98	0	98	3,995
10	6,408	64	19	83	6,325
12	9,271	83	0	83	9,189

SOURCE: Intensive survey.

[a]Actual revenue from food production for age 1 to 3 years and the value of cinnamon trees estimated by traders for age 4 years and above. Only data for trees of selected ages are shown.

[b]Imputed cost of family labor by the prevailing wages plus cost of hired labor.

among the three cases. The total cost was substantially higher and the value of production lower in planted fields than in coppiced fields in the first year primarily because of the cost of clearing fields before planting. In the second year, however, the total cost became higher and revenue smaller in coppiced fields because of the larger labor requirements for weeding due to the omission of slash-and-burn operation. The difference in production cost, as well as the residual profit, became smaller by the third year. For the productive fields with trees aged four years and above, differences between planting and coppicing were negligible. The potential value of production and potential profit increase monotonically with the age of trees. Note that production and cost data in the very old fields must be interpreted with caution; since cinnamon trees are generally felled between 8 and 10 years of age, data for older trees probably are subject to selection bias.

Econometric Analysis

In this section, we estimate the revenue or potential value, total cost, and actual or potential residual profit functions separately for paddy, young cinnamon, and productive cinnamon fields by the ordinary least squares regression method. The specification of estimated functions is based on the basic methodology developed in Chapter 2 (see equation [4]). Dependent variables are expressed as values per hectare. Since the residual profits are negative in some cases, we used a linear specification. In this specification, the estimation of one of the three functions is redundant except for the direct demonstration of the significance of the estimated coefficients. We assume that land tenure institutions, represented by modes of acquisition, are predetermined for each household. In order to take into account the effect of household specific factors, we applied the random effects model for the estimation pertaining to the productive cinnamon.[23] We have 140 parcels for this analysis, after excluding parcels of those households cultivating only one parcel.

Means of explanatory variables, other than land tenure variables, are shown by type of field in Table 4.15. The majority of sample fields were acquired more than 10 years ago. Both young and productive cinnamon fields were located far from residential areas. Household characteristics represented by paddy and cinnamon area owned, endowment of male and female family workers, and age and schooling of the male household head were not substantially different across different types of fields.

---

23. We did not apply the household-level fixed or random effects model to the statistical analysis of young cinnamon fields because only a small number of households cultivated two or more parcels. We show only the results of random effects estimation for the productive cinnamon because the Hausman test shows that household-level unobservables are not significant, indicating that random effects is the preferred specification. The Breusch-Pagan test also indicates the importance of random effects.

TABLE 4.15 Means of explanatory variables for plot-level analysis on lowland rice and upland crop production by type of field

	Paddy Land	Young Cinnamon	Productive Cinnamon
Year of land acquisition	1983	1986	1983
Walking time (minutes)	24.3	76.6	86.3
Altitude (m)	n.a.	1,058	1,082
Slope (degree)	n.a.	10.16	11.66
Owned paddy area (ha)[a]	1.05	0.95	1.21
Owned cinnamon area (ha)	4.01	4.68	6.00
Number of male workers[b]	1.16	1.14	1.11
Number of female workers[b]	1.27	1.24	1.26
Age of head	43.3	40.3	42.9
Schooling of head (years)	8.0	7.1	8.1

SOURCE: Intensive survey.

NOTE: "n.a." refers to "not analyzed."

[a]Including areas under joint family ownership.

[b]Number of male or female family members between 16 and 60 years of age.

Estimation results of gross value of output, total cost, and the residual profit functions for paddy production are shown in Table 4.16, in which joint family ownership is used as the base for comparison of land tenure effects. The fits of the regressions are poor, as reflected in low values of R^2. None of the coefficients of the three land tenure dummies is significant in any of the three functions, which supports our hypothesis that the prevailing land tenure institutions do not affect farm management efficiency. These results are consistent with earlier findings by Place and Hazell (1993) that land tenure institutions do not affect crop yields in customary land areas of selected Sub-Saharan countries.

The two tenancy variables are not significant either, which is consistent with the general finding that land tenancy contracts do not distort work incentives in Asia (Hayami and Otsuka 1993). Moreover, there also is no strong evidence that resource endowments of households significantly affect profitability of paddy production, even though owned paddy areas and the number of male family workers affect gross revenue and total costs. The overall findings are consistent with hypothesis 5, that factor markets, including land rental and hired labor markets, function well so as to equalize factor ratios among different fields.

Table 4.17 presents the estimation results for young cinnamon fields. Since production differed with the age of trees and previous land cover (Table 4.14), we used two dummies for tree age and three interaction terms between tree age and regrowth dummies. As might be expected, the dummy variables have

TABLE 4.16 Determinants of gross value of output, total cost, and residual profit of rice production

	Gross Value of Output	Total Cost	Residual Profit
Intercept	2001.0	1589.7	411.3
	(5.42)	(5.69)	(1.71)
Rainfed dummy	−8.77	−40.6	31.8
	(−0.05)	(−0.31)	(0.28)
Walking time	−1.02	0.12	−1.15
	(−0.34)	(0.05)	(−0.59)
Age of head	0.70	−5.30	6.00
	(0.11)	(−1.14)	(1.50)
Schooling of head	−3.31	6.43	−9.74
	(−0.19)	(0.48)	(−0.85)
Owned paddy area	−178.2*	−201.6**	23.4
	(−2.45)	(−3.67)	(0.49)
Owned cinnamon area	28.2	16.0	12.2
	(1.45)	(1.08)	(0.96)
Number of male workers	152.6*	113.2*	39.4
	(1.75)	(1.72)	(0.69)
Number of female workers	41.1	−26.1	67.2
	(0.41)	(−0.34)	(1.02)
Single family	7.88	−15.0	7.13
	(−0.43)	(−0.11)	(0.06)
Private	225.5	303.2	−77.7
	(0.82)	(1.45)	(−0.43)
Borrowing	−389.0	−133.9	−255.1
	(−1.46)	(−0.66)	(−1.47)
Share tenancy	−260.5	−215.6	−44.9
	(−1.29)	(−1.41)	(−0.34)
Fixed-rent tenancy	−32.5	−85.7	53.2
	(−0.14)	(−0.50)	(0.36)
R-squared	0.109	0.164	0.121

NOTE: Dependent variables are expressed as values per hectare. Numbers in parentheses are t-statistics.
*.05 level
**.01 level

significant coefficients in several cases. As a result, R^2 statistics generally are high. Yet neither land and labor endowment variables nor the share tenancy dummy is significant, rendering added support to the hypothesis that factor markets work well. Furthermore, none of the land tenure variables except borrowing is significant, which supports the hypothesis that the customary land tenure institutions provide sufficient tenure security comparable to private ownership.

TABLE 4.17 Determinants of gross value of output, total cost, and residual profit for young cinnamon fields

	Gross Value of Output	Total Cost	Residual Profit
Intercept	731.88	1484.98	−727.37
	(1.16)	(2.26)	(−1.10)
Second-year dummy (2D)	−308.49*	−415.52*	24.09
	(−1.83)	(−2.37)	(0.14)
Third-year dummy (3D)	−563.86**	−461.58**	−113.53
	(−3.45)	(−2.71)	(−0.66)
Regrowth dummy × 1D[a]	118.66	−308.47*	385.01**
	(0.85)	(−2.11)	(2.61)
Regrowth dummy × 2D[a]	−86.91	−64.93	34.45
	(−0.50)	(−0.36)	(0.19)
Regrowth dummy × 3D[a]	118.95	−128.27	227.52
	(0.72)	(−0.74)	(1.30)
Walking time	−0.90	−0.95	0.23
	(−1.13)	(−1.14)	(0.27)
Slope	4.05	−1.64	5.71
	(0.68)	(−0.26)	(0.91)
Altitude	−0.047	−0.51	0.46
	(−0.09)	(−0.93)	(0.84)
Age of head	2.77	−3.33	5.63
	(0.63)	(−0.72)	(1.21)
Schooling of head	−6.98	−17.95	10.45
	(−0.58)	(−1.44)	(0.83)
Owned paddy area	−43.14	−58.28	9.18
	(−0.85)	(−1.10)	(0.17)
Owned cinnamon area	−15.35	5.37	−18.88
	(−1.12)	(0.38)	(−1.31)
Number of male workers	−38.66	−5.43	−40.90
	(−0.65)	(−0.09)	(−0.65)
Number of female workers	59.10	151.44*	−78.85
	(0.83)	(2.04)	(−1.05)
Private—purchase	−159.83	−100.507	−62.93
	(−1.43)	(−0.86)	(−0.54)
Private—clearance	−219.06	−23.12	−152.82
	(−1.40)	(−0.14)	(−0.93)
Share tenancy	−87.28	−57.02	−40.23
	(−0.64)	(−0.40)	(−0.28)
Borrowing	−337.32**	−36.52	−299.33*
	(−2.91)	(−0.30)	(−2.46)
R-squared	0.536	0.411	0.416

NOTE: Dependent variables are expressed as values per hectare. Numbers in parentheses are t-statistics.

[a]Interaction term between dummy for regrowth of trees and dummy for first year (1D), second year (2D), or third year (3D) of cultivation.

*.05 level

**.01 level

Regarding borrowed land, which does not conform to the general pattern, it may well be that land that is lent is of inferior quality. This is consistent with the observation that revenue from borrowed land was significantly lower even though production costs are comparable to costs under single family ownership.

Finally, Table 4.18 presents results for productive cinnamon fields using the random household effects model.[24] In this model, we used nine tree age dummies and four variables related to land quality, namely, slope, altitude, and two dummy variables representing the previous land cover. Partly reflecting the fact that the age of trees is largely uniform in the same field unless the field is very old, most coefficients of tree age dummies are not only positive, as may be expected, but also highly significant. Altitude has negative and significant effects on the potential value and profit, which is consistent with the common perception of farmers in this area that trees grow less well and water content of bark tends to be higher at higher altitudes within the Kerinci Valley. The area of land cleared from forest has a weakly significant positive effect on the potential value.

It is remarkable to find that neither the factor endowment variables nor private land tenure, share tenancy, and borrowing dummies have significant effects on potential value, total cost, and potential profit. The former result indicates that factor markets work well in customary land areas of Sumatra. The latter result strongly supports our hypothesis formulated in Chapter 2 that customary land tenure institutions have been sufficiently individualized to ensure tenure security.

Estimation of Internal Rates of Return

In order to assess the profitability of investments in cinnamon trees, we computed the internal rate of return by land tenure type under the assumption of an eight-year interval between major cinnamon harvests based on the estimated profit functions shown in Tables 4.17 and 4.18. In computing net profits, we assume that bush-fallow land is cleared in the first growth cycle and that cinnamon trees are regrown three times thereafter, which was reported to be the common practice by farmers.[25] We used the average values of variables pertaining to plot and household characteristics and their estimated coefficients, and the coefficients of tree ages and land tenure dummies. Results for profit function estimates for young cinnamon trees were used to derive cash flows for the first three years. The cost function estimates for productive trees were used for cash flows from fourth to seventh years. Finally, the profit function result for pro-

---

24. Considering the possibility of selection bias arising from the fact that some cinnamon trees were harvested after the eighth year, we reestimated all three functions by excluding those fields whose trees were nine years of age and older. Both the magnitude and significance of the remaining variables, however, remain largely unchanged.

25. The estimated internal rates of return were almost unchanged when we assume that trees were harvested every 10 years.

TABLE 4.18 Determinants of potential value, total cost, and potential profit functions for productive cinnamon fields: Household random effects

	Potential Value	Total Cost	Potential Profit
Intercept	4880.0	273.1	4597.5
	(2.73)	(2.34)	(2.58)
Age 5 dummy	417.9	−45.1	458.4
	(0.65)	(−1.07)	(0.71)
Age 6 dummy	1684.0**	−17.3	1712.7**
	(2.64)	(−0.42)	(2.68)
Age 7 dummy	2708.9**	−60.9	2774.3**
	(4.56)	(−1.57)	(4.66)
Age 8 dummy	2920.5**	−34.3	2975.5**
	(4.45)	(−0.80)	(4.53)
Age 9 dummy	4786.9**	19.5	4776.2**
	(4.68)	(0.29)	(4.65)
Age 10 dummy	5702.3**	−81.7	5789.7**
	(8.37)	(−1.84)	(8.49)
Age 11 dummy	6603.3**	−135.1*	6743.5**
	(6.33)	(−1.99)	(6.46)
Age 12 dummy	8308.0**	−119.7*	8436.8**
	(8.91)	(−1.97)	(9.04)
Age 13 dummy	10905.7**	−131.1	11055.7**
	(7.21)	(−1.32)	(7.30)
Slope	−3.4	0.57	−4.2
	(−0.21)	(0.57)	(−0.26)
Altitude	−3.7*	−0.1	−3.6*
	(−2.34)	(−1.00)	(−2.25)
Dummy for forest before	2136.6*	128.0	2029.5
	(1.71)	(1.57)	(1.62)
Dummy for bush-fallow before	−15.0	−4.6	−1.7
	(−0.03)	(−0.16)	(−0.00)
Walking time	0.5	−0.12	0.63
	(0.02)	(−0.71)	(0.24)
Private—purchase	−433.7	25.1	−461.8
	(−0.91)	(0.80)	(−0.97)
Private—clearance	−261.5	−44.3	−202.0
	(−0.31)	(−0.81)	(−0.24)
Share tenancy	925.6	−23.6	970.8
	(1.49)	(−0.58)	(1.57)
Borrowing	1016.9	−9.0	1020.9
	(1.82)	(−0.25)	(1.84)
R-squared	0.650	0.082	0.650

NOTE: Dependent variables are expressed as values per hectare. Numbers in parentheses are *t*-statistics.

*.05 level

**.01 level

ductive cinnamon was the basis for the estimate of profit from the main harvest in the eighth year.

The estimates of internal rates of return are 42 percent for single family ownership, 29 percent for private ownership through purchase, and 31 percent for private ownership through clearance of forest. Note that these estimates are not significantly different, as none of the land tenure dummies was significant in the regression analyses of profits and cost on both young and productive cinnamon fields. The estimated returns are quite high, which indicates that cinnamon is quite profitable.[26] The high profitability of cinnamon production is consistent not only with the expansion of cinnamon areas in Kerinci but also with the transformation of the customary land tenure system toward individualization, which is conducive to investment in trees. Very similar results were obtained from the companion case study of rubber agroforestry in Sumatra (Suyanto, Tomich, and Otsuka 2001).

These high rates of return on investment may be explained in part by the lack of access to credit because of the credit market imperfection, which in turn may be explained partly by the absence of collateral value of land due to the lack of land titles, as argued by Feder et al. (1988). In any event, since these high rates of return are found under private ownership as well as traditional tenure systems, they cannot be attributed to any deficiency of customary land tenure institutions.

Land Tenure and Land Distribution

The evolution of customary land tenure institutions toward individualized ownership may lead to inequitable distribution of landholding. In order to quantify the relative importance of the various land components under different land tenure institutions in accounting for the overall inequality of land distribution, we apply a decomposition analysis of the Gini measure of landholding inequality as developed by Fei, Ranis, and Kuo (1978) and Pyatt, Chen, and Fei (1980) for household data.

The Gini decomposition formula is given by $G(Y) = \Sigma s_i \, PG(Y_i)$, where $G(Y)$ equals the Gini ratio of total operational landholdings, Y_i equals landholding of i-th tenure type, s_i equals average share of i-th type of land, and $PG(Y_i)$ equals the pseudo-Gini of landholding inequality. If $PG(Y_i)$ is greater (smaller) than $G(Y)$, distribution of i-th type of landholding is less (more) equitable than the average, thereby contributing to the expansion (contraction) of inequality in the overall landholding distribution (see Appendix of Chapter 3 for further details). Computation results are shown in Table 4.19.

---

26. It is estimated that during the period from 1981 to 1996 the real domestic price of cinnamon increased by 7 percent per year. If farmers expect an increasing trend in the cinnamon price, the estimated internal rates of return may still underestimate farmers' expected returns.

TABLE 4.19 Overall Gini ratio of operational landholding and contribution by land component

	Land Share	Pseudo-Gini Ratio
Single family—matrilineal	0.02	−0.362
Single family—egalitarian and patrilineal	0.33	0.373
Private—forest clearance	0.22	0.565
Private purchase	0.23	0.472
Renting	0.21	0.171
Overall	1.00	0.382

SOURCE: Intensive survey.

The negative pseudo-Gini coefficient of landholding under the matrilineal-type single family ownership implies that the distribution of this type of land is negatively correlated with the distribution of other types of land. Since the income share of this type of land is negligibly small, its impact on the overall Gini coefficient is small. As might be expected, the pseudo-Gini ratio of single family land acquired by egalitarian and patrilineal land inheritance is smaller than the overall Gini ratio, implying that this type of land is relatively equally distributed. The pseudo-Gini of the acquired forestland is a major component of landholding that contributed to the inequitable distribution of land. As we have seen from Table 4.7, households endowed with larger paddy fields and large number of male family workers acquired more forestland, which seems to have resulted in the inequitable distribution of landholding. Privately purchased land is another inequality-increasing component of land distribution. Yet it is remarkable to find that the pseudo-Gini ratio of land renting is exceedingly small, which implies that land rental transactions contributed to the reduction of inequality. As a result, the overall Gini ratio is not widely different from the Gini ratio of single family ownership with egalitarian inheritance.

Thus, contrary to popular belief, there is no strong evidence that the evolution of customary land tenure institutions toward individualized ownership significantly widened the inequality of operational landholding.

Summary for Intensive Study

The intensive household study provided added support for our hypothesis that traditional land tenure institutions in customary land areas have evolved over time toward more individualized ownership. Otherwise, it would be difficult to interpret the absence of the significant effects of the modes of land acquisition on the efficiency of production. Farm management efficiency under single family ownership is comparable to that under private ownership in both lowland paddy and upland cinnamon production. The efficient management of cinnamon fields under single family ownership is particularly noteworthy, as this suggests that sufficiently strong incentives to invest in management of agroforestry exist under this newly emerging ownership system. Furthermore, the estimated internal rates of return to investment in cinnamon trees support the hypothesis that investment in cinnamon trees has high payoffs. This explains why uncultivated bush-fallow land has largely disappeared and has been replaced by more intensive use of land through tree planting in our study sites. It is highly likely that the conversion of bush-fallow land to cinnamon fields was facilitated by the individualization of customary land tenure systems.

We also have obtained evidence that land rental and labor markets allocate resources efficiently among households endowed with different proportions of land and labor. Tenure security established under the prevailing land tenure institutions is likely to have contributed to the formation of effectively functioning land markets because security of ownership is a prerequisite for efficient land market transactions. Furthermore, renting is found to contribute to the equitable distribution of operational landholdings.

In sum, the evolution of customary tenure institutions and factor markets seems effective in achieving an efficient allocation of resources and investments in agroforestry in an equitable manner.

Policy Implications

At present, property rights in land are well recognized and respected among community members, so that there does not seem to be much room for improving investment incentives by strengthening individual rights within indigenous communities. However, we do not mean to suggest that a land-titling program is unnecessary to enhance management efficiency further in the long run. Because of the lack of official titles, land cannot be used as collateral for credit from formal financial institutions. But, as others have recognized for the case of Sub-Saharan Africa (Feder and Noronha 1987; Migot-Adholla et al. 1991), there also are important questions about the administrative feasibility and cost-effectiveness of formal land titling. The cost will be particularly high or even prohibitive if land is owned jointly and land title is to be given only to a single person or household. An important observation is that such cost may not be excessively high for upland fields in Sumatra owing to clear individualization of land rights. The expansion of formal credit institutions into these relatively remote areas and the establishment of official land title will become increasingly important as further intensification of the land use is required. Unusually high internal rates of return to investment in cinnamon agroforestry may attest to the significant imperfection of credit markets in our sites.

The finding that equally efficient incentives exist for investment in and management of agroforestry among different land tenure institutions has important implications for both equity and efficiency from the social point of view.

First of all, we have to recognize that rural people in hilly and mountainous areas, such as our study sites, are generally very poor and that in such areas agroforestry has a comparative advantage over food production. In order to reduce the incidence of poverty, it is recommended that profitable agroforestry systems should be established, given that the efficient land tenure institutions are in place. Investments in research of new technologies and their extension, investment in social infrastructures, and improvement of marketing systems are examples of measures to enhance the profitability of agroforestry. Due consideration, however, must be paid to the fact that relatively wealthier farmers tend to develop agroforestry more actively.

The development of agroforestry on sloped fields will contribute to the reduction in soil erosion, siltation, flooding, and other negative externalities and the improvement in tree biomass. Such contribution justifies the support for the development of agroforestry from the social point of view.

However, it is unrealistic to expect local communities to supply sufficient substitutes for natural forests' many ecological and environmental services, including abatement of negative environmental externalities of land use change (for example, smoke that impedes aviation and harms public health) and global public goods (for example, carbon sequestration and biodiversity conservation). The analysis in this chapter shows, however, that natural forests are largely open access under the communal land tenure institutions, and, hence, they have been exploited by the desire of local farmers to acquire cultivation fields. No effective mechanism exists to compensate these farmers directly for production and investment opportunities forgone in favor of natural forest conservation. The search for workable, incentive-compatible institutional mechanisms that can clarify, monitor, enforce, and compensate for a more socially optimal mix of agricultural production and environmental services deserves high priority. Our hope is that insights from this research on the dynamics of indigenous land tenure institutions can contribute to constructive approaches to address these complex natural resource policy issues.

References

Anderson, T. L., and P. J. Hill. 1990. The race for property rights. *Journal of Law and Economics* 33:16–27.

Angelsen, Arild. 1994. From rice to rubber: The economics of shifting cultivation and deforestation in Kec. Seberida, Sumatra. Paper presented at the International Symposium on Management of Rainforests in Asia, March 23–26, Jevnaker, Norway.

———. 1995. Shifting cultivation and deforestation: A study from Indonesia. *World Development* 23:1713–1729.

———. 1999. Agricultural expansion and deforestation: Modeling the impact of population, market forces, and property rights. *Journal of Development Economics* 58 (1): 185–218.

Aumeeruddy, Yildiz. 1994. Local representation and management of agroforest on the periphery of Kerinci Seblat National Park, Sumatra: Indonesia, people and plants. Working Paper No. 3. Paris, Division of Ecological Sciences, UNESCO.

Barlow, Colin, and S. K. Jayasuriya. 1984. Problems of investment for technological advance: The case of Indonesian rubber smallholders. *Journal of Agricultural Economics* 35:85–95.

Barlow, Colin, and Muharminto. 1982. The rubber smallholder economy. *Bulletin of Indonesian Economic Studies* 18:86–119.

Besley, Timothy. 1995. Property rights and investment incentive. *Journal of Political Economy* 103:913–937.

Boserup, Ester. 1965. *The conditions of agricultural growth: The economics of agrarian change under population pressure.* London: George Allen and Unwin.

David, Cristina C., and Keijiro Otsuka, eds. 1994 *Modern rice technology and income distribution in Asia.* Boulder, Colo.: Lynne Rienner.

de Foresta, H., and G. Michon. 1991. Indonesia agroforest system and approach. In *Harmony with nature,* ed. Y. S. Kheong and Lee Su Win. Proceedings of the International Conference on Conservation of Tropical Biodiversity. Kuala Lumpur: Malayan Nature Society.

Dick, J. 1991. Forest land use, forest use zonation, and deforestation in Indonesia: A summary and interpretation of existing information. Background paper to UNCED for the State Ministry for Population and Environment (KLH) and the Environmental Impact Management Agency (BAPEDAL).

Errington, Frederick K. 1984. *Manner and meaning in West Sumatra: The social context of consciousness.* New Haven: Yale University Press.

Feder, Gershon, and R. Noronha. 1987. Land rights systems and agricultural development in sub-Saharan Africa. *World Bank Research Observer* 2 (2): 311–320.

Feder, Gershon, Tongroj Onchan, Yongyuth Chalamwong, and Chira Hongladarom. 1988. *Land policies and farm productivity in Thailand.* Baltimore: Johns Hopkins University Press.

Fei, J. C. H., Gustav Ranis, and S. W. Y. Kuo. 1978. Growth and family distribution of income by factor component. *Quarterly Journal of Economics* 92 (1):17–53.

Food and Agriculture Organization of the United Nations (FAO). 1990. *Situation and outlook of forestry sector in Indonesia.* Vol. 1, *Issues, findings and opportunities.* Jakarta: Ministry of Forestry, Government of Indonesia, and FAO.

Fraser, A. I. 1998. Social, economic, and political aspects of forest clearance and land-use planning in Indonesia. In *Human activities and the tropical rainforest,* ed. B.K. Malonoey. The Netherlands: Kluwer Academic Publisher.

Gouyon, Anne, Hubber de Foresta, and Patrice Levang. 1993. Does jungle rubber deserve its name? An analysis of rubber agroforestry systems in Southeast Sumatra. *Agroforestry System* 22:181–206.

Hayami, Yujiro. 1997. *Development economics: From the poverty to the wealth of nations.* Oxford: Oxford University Press.

Hayami, Yujiro, and Keijiro Otsuka. 1993. *The economics of contract choice: An agrarian perspective.* Oxford: Clarendon Press.

Hayami, Yujiro, and Vernon W. Ruttan. 1985. *Agricultural development: An international perspective.* Baltimore: Johns Hopkins University Press.

Johnson, O. E. G. 1972. Economic analysis, the legal framework, and land tenure systems. *Journal of Law and Economics* 15 (1): 259–276.

Kahn, Joel S. 1980. *Minangkabau social formation: Indonesia peasants and the world economy.* Cambridge: Cambridge University Press.

Kaimowitz, David, and Arild Angelsen. 1998. *Economic model of tropical deforestation: A review.* Bogor, Indonesia: Center for International Forestry Research.

Marry, Fabienne, and Genevieve Michon. 1987. When agroforest drives back natural forest: A socio-economic analysis of a rice-agroforest system in Sumatra. *Agroforestry System* 5:27–55.

Marsden, William. 1811. *The history of Sumatra.* Reprint of 3d ed. Singapore: Oxford University Press.

McDonald, J. F., and R. A. Moffit. 1980. The use of tobit analysis. *Review of Economics and Statistics* 62:318–321.

Migot-Adholla, Shem, Peter Hazell, Benoit Blarel, and Frank Place. 1991. Indigenous land rights systems in sub-Saharan Africa: A constraint on productivity? *World Bank Economic Review* 5 (1): 155–175.

Otsuka, Keijiro, Hiroyuki Chuma, and Yujiro Hayami. 1992. Land and labor contracts in agrarian economies: Theory and fact. *Journal of Economic Literature* 30:1965–2018.

Otsuka, Keijiro, S. Suyanto, Tetsushi Sonobe, and Thomas P. Tomich. 2001. Evolution of customary land tenure and development of Agroforestry: Evidence from Sumatra. *Agricultural Economics* 25 (1): 85–101.

Penot, Eric. 1997. From shifting agriculture to sustainable rubber complex agroforestry systems (Jungle Rubber) in Indonesia: A history of innovations, production, and adoption process. Paper presented at the ICRAF/CORNELL University Workshop on Indigenous Strategy for Intensification of Shifting Cultivation in Southeast Asia in Bogor, June.

Place, Frank, and Peter Hazell. 1993. Productivity effects of indigenous land tenure in sub-Saharan Africa. *American Journal of Agricultural Economics* 75:10–19.

Pyatt, G., C. Chen, and J. C. H. Fei. 1980. The distribution of income by factor components. *Quarterly Journal of Economics* 95 (3): 451–473.

Shepherd, Gill. 1991. The communal management of forest in the semi-arid and sub-humid regions of Africa. *Development Policy Review* 1:151–176.

Suyanto, S., and Keijiro Otsuka. 2001. From deforestation to development of agroforestry in customary land tenure areas of Sumatra. *Asian Economic Journal* 15 (1).

Suyanto, S., Thomas P. Tomich, and Keijiro Otsuka. 2001. Land tenure and farm management efficiency: The case of smallholder rubber production in customary land areas of Sumatra. *Agroforestry Systems,* forthcoming.

Tomich, T. P., and M. van Noordwijk. 1996. What drives deforestation in Sumatra? In *Montane mainland Southeast Asia in transition,* ed. Benyaven Rerkasem. Chiang Mai, Thailand: Chiang Mai University.

World Bank. 1990. *World development report.* New York: Oxford University Press.

———. 1998. *The world development indicators 1998 CD-ROM.* WinSTARS Version 4.01. Washington, D.C.

5 Tree and Cropland Management in Malawi

FRANK PLACE, REDGE MASUPAYI,
AND KEIJIRO OTSUKA

Malawi is one of the poorest countries in the world, with 63 percent of the population estimated to live in poverty (World Bank 1996). It is also heavily reliant on its agricultural sector, not only for employment, as is common with most other countries in Sub-Saharan Africa, but also for income generation. In 1993, agriculture accounted for 39 percent of GDP and 94 percent of export earnings (World Bank 1996). Obviously, any program designed to confront the immediate poverty problem must address agricultural productivity. As Malawi's history indicates, this is no easy feat in a country that is landlocked and has but a single rainy season.

Malawi in fact did invest heavily in an agriculturally led growth strategy between the 1960s and 1990s. This was aimed primarily at increasing production through the large estate sector, and the government facilitated this by expropriating land from traditional chiefs and leasing it to large estate holders at low fees (Pryor 1990). It also restricted smallholders from effectively producing and marketing certain commercial crops, which had the effect of creating a pool of cheap labor for the estates. Although this strategy did generate significant export revenues, mostly from tobacco production, it did not make a significant dent in alleviating rural poverty. One of the reasons is that the government was a monopoly purchaser of maize in the country and producer prices were set very low, acting as a tax on smallholder maize producers (Sahn and Arulpragasam 1991a).

The effect of this producer tax on output was partially offset by significant state expenditures in subsidized credit and inputs for smallholder maize production. The focus on maize helped to solidify the dominance of maize in smallholder production systems, where it occupied more than 80 percent of cultivated land in the early 1990s. Smale (1995) reports that just before the complete removal of input subsidies and movement toward liberalization of maize output markets, a Green Revolution had occurred in Malawi, with the area under hybrid maize rising from 7 percent to 24 percent between 1988 and 1992. Al-

We are particularly grateful for valuable comments on an earlier version by Peter Dewees and Davies Ng'ong'ola. This chapter draws on Place and Otsuka (2001a, 2001b).

though this is encouraging, the increase in household income resulting from a switch to improved maize varieties is low because the value of maize per unit area is low relative to other cash crops such as tobacco (Zeller, Diagne, and Kisyombe 1997). Fortunately, the government then removed production controls (through marketing quotas) on burley tobacco for the smallholder sector. On the whole, farmers in the relevant agroecological zones have responded enthusiastically by incorporating burley tobacco into their farming systems.[1]

The pace of rural population growth and demand for agricultural land, urban demand for fuelwood, and the recent expansion of the smallholder tobacco program have heightened the concern of policymakers over the state of the natural resource base and its ability to sustain rural agricultural growth. They have taken note that in Malawi, as elsewhere in Sub-Saharan Africa, there has been a significant change in its landscape cover. Although reliable figures are hard to come by, the Forestry Department estimates the annual deforestation rate to be 1.3 percent per year in the 1980s (World Resources Institute 1994). This has raised concern about the future supply of fuelwood and other tree products and environmental services (French 1986; Hyde and Seve 1993; Dewees 1995). Much of the deforestation is believed to be linked to conversion of communally owned *miombo* woodlands into agricultural land. This includes expansion onto steep slopes and other fragile lands in many cases. Bojo (1994) presents data suggesting that the consequent effects on soil erosion create serious costs to the Malawian economy.

Malawi policymakers, having few resources at their disposal, must make critical choices concerning the type of land use patterns that will prevail in the future. There will likely be trade-offs between growth and sustainability, and regardless of the choices made, patterns of investment will need to intensify. Unfortunately, there is little understanding of the dynamic process leading up to the current land utilization pattern or to related effects on productivity and the stock of natural resources. This study will provide new evidence as to how communities and households have managed their land and tree resources and what factors seemed to be most important in their decisions. This information is valuable to policymakers who continue to struggle with the twin objectives of alleviating poverty in the short run and preserving the natural resource base in the long run so that future generations may have access to high-quality income-generating assets.

In this study we are concerned primarily with the influence of land tenure on land use, tree resource management, agricultural investment, and agricultural productivity in Malawi. Our study focuses on the customary sector, which occupies about 70 percent of land area in Malawi (Sahn and Arulpragasam 1991b). In this sector, cultivators are small peasants (with the exception of fron-

---

1. After the time of this research, prospects for tobacco growers worldwide seem to have worsened owing to accelerated changes in public opinion in the north.

tier areas in the north-central region), and many of them suffer from severe poverty. Although previous research has explicitly questioned the appropriateness of certain customary tenure systems in providing incentives for woodland management and agricultural investment (Mkandwire 1983–84, 1992; Dickerman and Bloch 1991; Coote, Luhanga, and Lowore 1993a, 1993b; Nankumba 1994; Lowore et al. 1995), there have been surprisingly few quantitative tests of these hypotheses. Following an overview of the customary tenure system in Malawi, these hypotheses are more clearly developed in the separate studies of tree management and agricultural efficiency.

The organization of this chapter is as follows. An overview of the customary land tenure systems in Malawi is presented in the next section. We then discuss the sampling strategies used in the extensive and intensive studies along with a description of the study sites. The discussion of the extensive "community" study is subdivided into sections on hypotheses, development of econometric models, description of key variables, a discussion of results, and a conclusion. The section following this repeats this format, but for the intensive "household" study. Finally, the overall policy implications drawn from both studies are found in the last section.

Customary Tenure Systems in Malawi

There is no single customary tenure system in Malawi, and many of the differences derive from the practices of individual ethnic groups. However, a few characteristics of the tenure systems appear to hold across most of Malawi. First, all customary land falls under the paramount administration of a traditional authority (or chief), and these boundaries are well established and documented. The vertical structure of traditional administration is fairly consistent, with village headmen acting as custodians of land within a clearly defined village area. Where land is plentiful, they remain with some allocative authority, but their powers are now largely confined to dispute settlement. Village headmen allocate land to individuals as well as to heads of families. The heads of families, once they receive allocated land, have direct management control of lands and are the first to be sought by family members in search of land. Virtually all customary land is transferred through allocation by a traditional leader or, more commonly today, through inheritance. Land is normally shared among all legitimate heirs. The individual right of land sale is not known throughout the rural customary sector of Malawi (except in the case in which the land had been converted to a formal leasehold with the state).

The communal tenure system can be first distinguished between cultivated and noncultivated land. Cultivated land, as described above, is mainly under the control of families, and therefore village headmen and chiefs do not have much authority over the land. This is not to say that land rights are individualized. The family head and other members may exert considerable influence over the transfer of land rights. Noncultivated land, mainly in the form of open woodland, is normally under the custodianship of a clan, a village headman, or perhaps a higher traditional authority (for example, a leader among a group of headmen). The woodlands can be considered as common property, as they are owned by the community and used jointly by community members for collection of firewood, other natural resources, and grazing. These lands, however, appear to be virtual open-access resources for community members, with only a few operational rules on user group membership or use rates (see Coote, Luhanga, and Lowore 1993a, 1993b; Lowore et al. 1995). Thus, conversion of woodlands into farmland has proceeded without serious impediment in most areas of Malawi, even in the case of migrants. One notable exception is the Village Forest Area (VFA) system initiated in the 1920s, rekindled recently by the Forestry Department, in which communities demarcate woodland areas to be placed under special management rules (which appear to emphasize conservation over sustainable use).

Within cultivated land, as noted above, the dominant mechanism for land transfer is through inheritance. In this context, customary tenure systems can be distinguished according to descent practices, namely, matrilineal or patrilineal, and relatedly to residency practices, namely, patrilocal or matrilocal. The system as practiced by the Ngoni or Tumbuka is both patrilineal and patrilocal. Land is passed from father to son(s), and the sons continue to reside in the father's village, normally bringing in a wife from another village. The Chewa, the most populous group in Malawi, had traditionally practiced a matrilineal-cum-matrilocal system (Hirschmann and Vaughan 1983, 1984). Typically, a daughter would receive land from her parents (or other relatives, such as her uncle) upon marriage to a man from outside her village.[2] The husband was said to be initially under *chikamwini,* or a probationary period, during which he had to prove his worthiness to the wife's parents. This system is akin to matrilineal systems observed in some parts of Asia, such as Sumatra (Chapter 4). In matrilineal systems in which the couple moves to or otherwise resides in the husband's village, the husband traditionally acquired land from a village headman or family leader in his village.

The matrilineal-cum-matrilocal system, because of relatively weak land rights for husbands, is expected to provide the least incentives for long-term resource management, both of woodlands and of agricultural land. The first incentive problem is when the husband is residing in the wife's village only on a temporary basis. During this phase, the husband has very weak tenure security over this land.[3] Apart from the probationary period under the matrilocal sys-

---

2. The practice of transmitting land from uncles to nieces and nephews, though documented in the literature, appears to have declined considerably according to our informal interviews.

3. Such a view led to the resolution by the ruling party in 1969 to discourage the practice of *chikamwini* in favor of residence in the husband's village (Nankumba 1994).

tem, a major incentive problem under the matrilocal/matrilineal system arises upon divorce or death of a wife. In such cases, the male is expected to leave his wife's village (Nankumba 1994), which reduces his incentives to undertake long-term investment. Furthermore, he may have restricted land rights under the matrilineal system, because the land rights are also possessed by the wife's family. Although incentives for wives may be equally weak under the patrilocal/ patrilineal system, the incentive problem is likely to be less pronounced because the husband is considered the head of household under both systems (Mkandawire 1983–84).

As land became scarce, different scenarios or modifications of the traditional matrilocal/matrilineal practice emerged, suggesting the existence of demand for its change. First, males unable to find land in their wife's village were now obtaining land from their Chewa parents. Second, some males were shortening or completely circumventing the probationary *chikamwini* period by offering other gifts to the wife's parents. The right of males to relocate their family in their own village became formalized in the institution of *chitengwa* (Nankumba 1994). Males were often actively seeking to gain control over land from outside their wives' villages. In a study in Lilongwe Agricultural Development Division (ADD), Nankumba (1994) found that more than 80 percent of the sampled Chewa households had some access to land in more than one village.

Study Sites

The data for the extensive study come from 57 enumeration areas throughout Malawi, which is the smallest unit for which boundaries are documented and can thus be transferred onto maps with relative ease.[4] Enumeration areas are designed to have roughly the same population and thus are different in size depending on the density of population. Our sample had a range of size from 180 to 5,580 hectares; the mean was 1,271 hectares (or about 4 by 3 kilometers). Excluded from the sample were enumeration areas in the extreme north and south (Karonga and Shire Valley) and those corresponding to towns and gazetted state land (see Figure 5.1). The remaining enumeration areas were selected by a stratified random process in which 15 each from the northern, north-central, south-central, and southern regions of Malawi were selected. This stratification was made to ensure a variation in population density and tenure type, both of which are known to vary from north to south in Malawi.

For the intensive study, we attempted to control for differences among ethnic groups and the broad ecological and economic conditions associated with geographical location, while at the same time allowing for variation in tenure arrangements. This could be accomplished only by finding an appropriate site

---

4. Aerial photographs for 60 sites were analyzed for land use and tree cover change, but 3 were not visited for field surveys because of logistical difficulties.

FIGURE 5.1 Location of study sites in Malawi

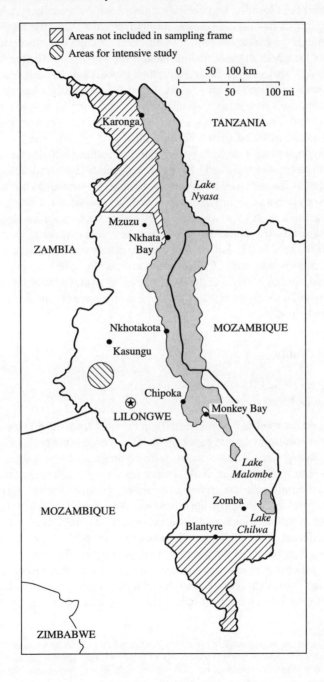

that was fairly small in total size. The north-central region of Malawi offered the possibility of locating households within a confined area that received their land through several different means: through the wife's family in her home village, through the husband's family in his home village, and others, including cases in which both the wife and husband were new to the village. We chose Kasungu ADD to examine the intensification process and tree management under different woodland scarcity levels. Local forestry officers helped to identify possible sites within high woodland cover, medium woodland cover, and low woodland cover areas. We selected one cluster of villages from each of the three areas and included eight villages in all.

The process of selecting households was rather complex because we wished to ensure the inclusion of households operating under different tenure arrangements. Because of the complexity of the tenure arrangements, it was too costly to develop a sampling frame that would capture all the tenure subtleties. Instead, a quick census was used to stratify and select households according to broad tenure characteristics, that is, whether they were matrilocal, patrilocal, or other. Of the total of 138 households, approximately one-third were randomly selected from within each of these tenure groups. Once the surveys were administered, further analysis of the data enabled us to classify households more clearly, based not only on residency status but on source of land acquired, as is described below.[5]

Extensive Study

Defining the Property Rights and Natural Resource Variables and Hypotheses

Building on the models developed in Chapter 1 and from the previous discussion of the customary tenure sector of Malawi, we view the probability of the husband losing rights to land in the wife's village as the primary source of tenure insecurity (p in the model). Greater insecurity is anticipated within the matrilineal-cum-matrilocal tenure arrangement compared with others, especially the patrilineal-cum-patrilocal system. We found this insecurity arising under the matrilineal-cum-matrilocal system to be perceived consistently across different sites. Therefore the proportion of plots acquired under the matrilineal-cum-matrilocal system is used as a proxy for tenure insecurity. These matrilineal-cum-matrilocal systems are reported to be undergoing change, and our first investigation concerns an understanding of the factors leading to the transformation to more patrilineal or mixed systems. Our hypothesis is that

---

5. One of the inadequacies of the census was the reliance on birthplace to stratify households. This led to misclassification of some "migrant" households into the other group when in fact they may have migrated as children and received land from parents through matrilineal or patrilineal means.

there will be more erosion of the matrilineal/matrilocal system with increased population pressure and influence of markets and the urban sector.

The second set of questions is focused on the anticipated effect of the different customary tenure systems on selected natural resource management variables. In applying the theoretical framework developed in Chapter 1 to the case of Malawi, it is important to mention that, unlike other study sites, tree planting cannot improve the husband's security of tenure in his wife's village. This is because, regardless of the husband's actions, he has no rights to land in the wife's village and must leave upon death or divorce. Theoretically, there is more scope for tree planting to improve the husband's individual security in the patrilineal system. But in our patrilineal study sites, population densities are relatively low, and most sons are able to obtain adequate holdings through inheritance, thus reducing competition from within the extended family. Therefore, long-term investment on agricultural land will depend critically on the initial level of tenure security alone in both matrilineal and patrilineal societies.

This implies that we would hypothesize to observe less tree planting and greater reduction in tree cover within the matrilineal-cum-matrilocal system as compared with other systems.[6] Likewise, incentives to manage woodlands in a sustainable manner are low for males in this system, and we hypothesize that tree cover will have declined fastest under the matrilineal-cum-matrilocal system. In our study, we did not observe the presence of long-term investments that enhanced the profitability of maize, the most common crop. In the absence of such investments, we hypothesize that tenure security is not related to the change in crop yield. Last, we wish to test for the effect of tenure security on the pace of land conversion into agriculture. The discussion of equation (4) in Chapter 1 indicates that the link is ambiguous. Basically, the greater the net present value of profits from agriculture compared with woodlands, the more the effect of tenure security increases in magnitude. In the case of Malawi, it is likely that conversion of land will lead to higher *short-term profits* because the land would be fertile initially. Thus, tenure security increases incentives to invest in land conversion, as in the two-period model of Besley (1995). However, in the absence of promising long-term investments, *longer-term growth of profits* may be lower in agriculture. As is implied by the infinite horizon model of Mendelsohn (1994), tenure security promotes the choice of sustainable use of land. Hence, our model cannot predict unambiguously the direction of the effect of different customary tenure systems on the rate of conversion.

Econometric Modeling

At the community level, the proportion of land acquired through the matrilineal-cum-matrilocal system, population growth, tree cover change, land use change,

---

6. As shown below, however, the variation in tree cover on agricultural land is too small to permit econometric testing of this hypothesis.

and yield change may be considered as endogenous. We do not report our regressions on population growth because these are used mainly to derive predicted values to be used as regressors in the other models. We applied two separate models, one to explain current tenure patterns and the other to explain changes in natural resource management variables. With respect to the tenure regression, we applied a two-stage least squares method approach with population growth as an endogenous independent variable. We found that by interacting tenure with the location dummy variables, we are better able to distinguish tenure and location-specific factors. Because of this complexity, we could not treat the tenure variable as endogenous for methodological reasons.

The proportion of land received through the matrilineal-cum-matrilocal system is denoted by M. This is most strongly linked to ethnic group because traditionally ethnicity was a near perfect predictor of inheritance rules. Over time, the influence of ethnicity has eased owing to land pressure brought about by population density and growth as well as to interactions with the formal sector through markets and urban pull. In-migration is yet another mechanism through which local institutions are subjected to new influences and modifications. Last, the more recent the turnover of land to new occupants, the greater the opportunity for tenure systems to change. Thus, we postulate the following regression equation to explain the current proportion of plots acquired through the matrilineal-cum-matrilocal system:

$$M = f(\text{ETH}, N_0/X, G_N, D, X_{A0}/X, \text{YR}), \qquad (1)$$

where ETH denotes ethnic group; N_0/X is population density in the initial period, and G_N stands for the population growth rate; D is distance to urban centers; X_{A0}/X is the share of agricultural land in the initial period; and YR is the average date of plot acquisition.

According to equation (4) in Chapter 1, the degree to which land is converted to agriculture depends on the relative profits of agriculture versus woodlands. However, we do not possess direct measures of growth of profits for agriculture and woodland, so in actual estimation we use proxies that are expected to affect those key variables. First, we assume that the profitability of farming per unit of land in the base period is positively and closely correlated with yield of maize, which was estimated to occupy more than 72 percent of smallholder cultivated area (in pure stands and mixes) in Malawi in 1980 (Malawi Government 1984).[7] Second, we assume that the net benefit from woodland in the base period can be captured by the woodland tree cover density at the time. Third, we assume that growth in agricultural profit and growth in woodland profit are

---

7. Prices of maize and other crops were virtually uniform throughout Malawi because of a monopoly parastatal operating until recently. We do not have data on 1971 prices, but the coefficient of variation on 1995–96 maize prices at the sites was a paltry .08.

proportional to the rates of change in yield and tree cover, respectively. We note that population pressure on land may affect the growth rates of profit by changing the scarcity of foods and woodland products.

Assuming that each household maximizes the net benefit of investment and that all households in the community have common expectations about the growth rates of profit, the aggregate area converted from woodland to agricultural land at the community level is the sum of the converted areas by households. Thus, we postulate that the land conversion at the community level is affected by the following set of explanatory variables:

$$\Delta X/X = F(Y_0, D, X_{A0}/X, T_{N0}, N_0/X, G_T, M, G_Y, G_N), \qquad (2)$$

where the dependent variable (ΔX, which is the amount of land converted to agriculture) is normalized by total area of community (X) to adjust for differences in the total size of communities; Y_0 and T_{N0} denote yield and woodland tree cover in the initial period, respectively; and G_Y and G_T represent their expected growth rates. While Y_0, T_0, N_0/X, D, X_{A0}/X, and M are either predetermined or exogenous, G_N, G_Y, and G_T may be considered as endogenous variables. Since the rate of land conversion is assumed to be determined in the base period with the expectations of future growth rates of some key variables, the initial conditions play prominent roles. Factor and output prices do not appear in equation (1) because the price levels are assumed to be different cross-sectionally primarily because of different transaction costs, which are captured by the distance variable.

If the Boserupian hypothesis of intensification of the farming system takes place in response to population pressure (Boserup 1965), or if the Hayami-Ruttan thesis of induced technological innovation takes place in response to changing factor scarcities (Hayami and Ruttan 1985), G_Y will depend on population density and on access to output and input markets. There are indications that adoption of high-yielding maize technologies had occurred in some areas (Smale 1995), and we may expect that the Green Revolution was particularly successful in land scarce areas close to urban markets. Land tenure may matter in the growth rate of maize yield, to the extent that yield-enhancing investment plays a significant role. Changes in yields in the long run may also be affected by changes in land use and woodland tree cover. Thus, we assume the following functional relationship in the determination of yield growth:

$$G_Y = G_Y(Y_0, T_{A0}, M, N_0/X, D, X_{A0}/X, E, \Delta X/X, G_T, G_N), \qquad (3)$$

where T_{A0} is tree cover on agricultural land in the initial period and E is a vector of exogenous environmental factors, such as rainfall, which would affect yield growth.

Woodland management may depend on the homogeneity of community members, since this affects the cost of organizing community actions and enforcing agreements (Clarke, Cavendish, and Coote 1996; Matose and Wily

1996), and on the prevailing land tenure, as this affects the extent of myopic be-havior. Aside from the cost of mobilizing collective action, the rate of resource extraction will depend on the demand for woodland resources, which is affected by population density and access to markets, and the supply, which is governed by the initial endowment of woodland and the regeneration capacity of wood-land. It is also important to note that the Malawi government has attempted to promote tree cover by designating VFAs and by implementing tree-planting projects. Finally, pressure on woodland tree cover depends on profits from agri-culture that are affected by land use change and the growth of yield. These con-siderations lead to the formulation of the following functional relationship:

$$G_T = G_T(Y_0, T_{N0}, M, N_0/X, D, X_{A0}/X, H, A, GP, \Delta X/X, G_Y, G_N), \qquad (4)$$

where H represents the degree of homogeneity of community members, which may be measured by the proportion of the major ethnic group and the propor-tion of cattle-owning households using woodland for grazing; A represents an ability for woodland regeneration, measured by the prevalence of tree species with good coppicing ability; and GP corresponds to government policies, such as area under managed VFAs and implementation of tree-planting projects. In the estimation, we use changes in proportion of land under tree canopy cover for G_T.

Description of Natural Resource Management Indicators

For each enumeration area, aerial photographs were obtained for 1971–73 and 1995. The 1970s aerial photos are from a countrywide coverage. Both sets are at a scale of 1:25,000, which greatly facilitated the land use and tree cover in-terpretation and comparison. The minimum mapping unit (that is, area that can be effectively differentiated and given a unique land use or tree cover data point) is about 1 hectare.

Interpreters differentiated broad land use into agriculture, wetland, grass-land, forests, plantations, woodlands, woody regrowth (that is, bushland), rocky areas, marshes, built-up areas, and surface water. Within agriculture, there were several subcategories, including upland rainfed, irrigated, and wetland cultiva-tion. Within upland agriculture (which constitutes 99 percent of all sampled agricultural land), further differentiation was made according to tree cover with separate classes identified for under 2 percent cover, 2–5 percent cover, 5–10 percent cover, 10–20 percent cover, and 20–40 percent cover. Forests were dif-ferentiated in terms of normally stocked (averaging 80–100 percent) and de-pleted forest (averaging 50–60 percent). Woodlands and bushland (regrowth) were each differentiated into four tree cover classes: 2–20 percent, 20–40 per-cent, 40–60 percent, and 60–80 percent cover. Other land use categories were largely devoid of trees by definition.[8]

---

8. If there was significant tree cover, then the area would have been reclassified (for exam-ple, from grassland to woodland).

TABLE 5.1 Land use and land use change across study sites, 1972 and 1995

Land Use Category	Average Share across Sites in 1972	Average Share across Sites in 1995	Share Change Interval[a]	Most Positive Absolute Change in Share	Most Negative Absolute Change in Share
Agriculture	.515	.677	−.02 to .41	.73	−.32
Woodland and bushland	.330	.185	−.38 to .00	.10	−.66
Forest and plantations	.013	.002	.00 to .00	.07	−.63
Other	.142	.136	−.12 to .08	.35	−.18

SOURCE: Extensive survey.

[a]The interval that includes 80 percent of sites.

Table 5.1 displays some statistics on broad land use categories in the 1970s and in the 1990s using simple averages across the 57 enumeration areas.[9] Agriculture had the largest share of the enumerated land area in both years, averaging .515 in 1972 and .677 in 1995.[10] Roughly 20 percent of enumeration areas had an agricultural land share of more than .80 in 1972, but as many as 48.0 percent achieved the same proportion by 1995. Despite this, a few enumeration areas from the north of Malawi maintained relatively little agricultural activity during the period, and 10 of the 57 enumeration areas did not show any increase in aggregate agricultural land area over the study period. The change in share of agricultural land per enumeration area ranged from −.32 to +.73 across the study sites.

Most of the increase in land under agriculture was accommodated by a reduction in woodland and bushland. This broad category of land use had a mean share land area of .33 in 1972, which dwindled to .19 in 1995. About one-fourth of all enumeration areas had less than a .10 share of woodland in 1972, but the percentage of enumeration areas in the same category jumped to 60.0 percent by 1995. Nonetheless, about one-fifth of all enumeration areas retained a woodland area constituting at least a .40 share of land area in 1995 (mainly areas in the north). There were very few natural forests or plantations in the study sites. The number of enumeration areas with at least 1.0 percent forest cover was only five in both 1972 and 1995, and the share of land in this category remained

9. It is worthy to note that the 1995 land use estimates from our enumeration areas correlate very closely with those from a larger study designed to be representative of Malawi (Green and Mkandawire 1997).

10. Note that agriculture is a small proportion of land in the larger enumeration areas (in northern Malawi). Thus, the weighted share of land in agriculture is much lower, .50 in 1995, for example.

TABLE 5.2 Tree cover pattern across study sites, 1972 and 1995

Broad Land Use Category	Average Tree Cover across Sites in 1972	Average Tree Cover across Sites in 1995	Cover Change Interval[a]	Most Positive Absolute Change in Cover	Most Negative Absolute Change in Cover
Agriculture	.023	.020	−.02 to .01	.05	−.07
Nonagriculture	.243	.167	−.18 to .03	.14	−.61
Average	.173	.101	−.20 to .00	.06	−.57

SOURCE: Extensive survey.

[a]The interval that includes 80 percent of sites.

negligible over the entire period. The "other" category remained more or less constant at 13.6–14.2 percent. Most of this area is composed of village settlement areas, while in some, the low-lying grasslands (or *dambos*) are significant.

Table 5.2 displays some summary statistics pertaining to tree canopy cover across the enumeration areas. In 1972, the average canopy cover was estimated to be 17.3 percent of total land area, but the median was much lower, at 9.0 percent. More than half of the enumeration areas had a tree cover of under 10.0 percent, and four enumeration areas were virtually devoid of tree cover (under 1.0 percent cover). At the other extreme, about one-fourth of enumeration areas had a canopy cover of more than 30.0 percent; the highest recorded was 61.0 percent. By 1995, tree cover had fallen to an estimated cover of 10.1 percent (the median being only 3.3 percent). Some 14 enumeration areas had tree canopy covers of 1.0 percent or less. A nearly equal number (12), however, remained with relatively high tree canopy cover of more than 20.0 percent.

There are significant differences in tree cover according to whether the primary land use is agriculture or not. Table 5.2 shows that tree canopy cover in agricultural land is very low in the sites, estimated to be only around 2 percent in both years. This level of cover has remained constant across most enumeration areas as noted by the fact that the change in absolute tree cover was between −.02 and +.01 for 80 percent of the sites. Tree cover in nonagricultural areas is much higher but has shown a more marked decline. From a level of about 24.3 percent in 1972, tree cover in nonagricultural areas dropped to 16.7 percent, on average, across the study sites by 1995.[11] Some 44 sites experienced a decrease in nonagricultural land tree cover, while 9 showed an increase. Our

---

11. Again, note that because the northern enumeration areas are larger and have a greater tree density, the weighted average tree cover for Malawi would be much higher than indicated by our simple averages across sites.

TABLE 5.3 Important explanatory variables for extensive study sites

Variable	Northern Region	North-Central Region	Southern Region	Average
1971 population density (per km^2)	25.4	48.7	93.8	65.2
Annual population growth, 1971–95	3.91	5.24	3.44	4.10
Percentage of plots through matrilocal system	13.4	33.5	68.9	46.0
Distance to tarmac (km)	33.8	13.9	28.1	24.8
Distance between closest tarmac road and a major city (km)	76.8	115.2	89.7	95.1
1971 maize yield (kg/ha)	2,278	5,192	2,726	3,410
Average percentage change in maize yield, 1971–95	−44.4	−65.5	−51.5	−54.5
Average date of plot acquisition	1984	1984	1981	1982
Percentage of households with cattle in 1971	11.3	13.2	9.9	11.3
Percentage of households using fertilizer in 1971	30.0	35.5	24.9	29.3
Average distance to plots (km)	1.3	1.1	1.1	1.1
Average annual rainfall (mm)	1,004	867	907	915

data do not seem to support the contention of Hyde and Seve (1993: 286) that "the level of deforestation still exceeds the level of reforestation, but the rate of reforestation is rapid."

Data on average yields of important crops in 1971 and 1996 were collected through group interviews. Maize is the most important crop grown by smallholders in Malawi, and we received data on maize yields for 52 of 57 sites.[12] Reported yields for 1996 are considered to be fairly accurate, but those for some 25 years back are less so, as this stretches recall capabilities of respondents. Nonetheless, we feel that the relative changes in yields across sites are not systematically biased in any significant way and therefore provide at the minimum a useful ordinal ranking (see Table 5.3). The mean maize yield in 1996 was 1.1 tons per hectare, and only seven sites reported means of above 2 tons per hectare (this is a typical yield for unfertilized maize in a normal rainfall year). All but

---

12. Maize yield estimates were not obtained for five enumeration areas. For these, averages calculated from nearby enumeration areas were used.

three enumeration areas saw maize yields decline over the study period. In many cases the declines were substantial, and the mean decline in yield was 54.5 percent. The agricultural development strategy based on large-scale estate agriculture appears to have neglected significantly the development of small-holder agriculture (Kydd and Christiansen 1982; Kydd 1989; Dickerman and Bloch 1991; Sahn and Arulpragasam 1991a, 1991b).

Data for the explanatory variables in our model come mainly from group and household surveys conducted in each of the enumeration areas. Our field surveys consisted of interviews with a group of well-informed elders and local leaders at each site combined with surveys of 10 randomly selected households in each site. Secondary data sources were used for information on population, climate, and soils.

Table 5.3 displays information on many of the factors hypothesized to lead to changes in the management of natural resources. They are presented as averages by three zones. The north includes the 12 sites from Mzuzu ADD. This zone is distinguished by its relatively low population density and predominance of patrilineal ethnic groups, as can be seen from the low percentage of plots acquired under the matrilocal system. The north-central region includes sites in Kasungu and Salima ADDs and are grouped together because these two areas have witnessed the greatest expansion of the estate sector and associated population increase through migration (Christiansen 1984). The south is generally more heavily populated by matrilineal groups.

Table 5.3 confirms that our regional groupings are quite important. Population density in 1971 ranges from 25.4 per square kilometer in the north to 93.8 in the south. Growth of population is found to be significantly higher in the frontier zone, where estates had been formed and many families resettled. The higher growth rates of population are also reflected in the average date of acquisition of land plots, which is about three years earlier in the more populated southern region.[13]

The prevalence of matrilocal inheritance systems is strongest in the matrilineal south, weakest in the patrilineal north, and moderate in the transitional north-central zone. Overall, about half of all plots were acquired through the wife's family. Figure 5.2 shows that the percentage of plots acquired through village headmen has declined over time, as more land has come under direct control of households. There has been a steady, though not large, increase in the importance of the husband's family in providing land to new couples. While the importance of the wife's family increased during the 1970s and 1980s (as land held by village headmen disappeared), it experienced a slight decline in the 1990s. In our sample, 22.8 percent of sites reported that the Tumbuka or Ngoni, patrilineal groups, were the most prevalent groups. The Chewa, a matrilineal

---

13. Population growth and density were based on 1977 and 1991 figures, the two most appropriate census years. The values were used to extrapolate forward or backward to 1971 and 1995.

FIGURE 5.2 Proportion of land acquisition by source in central and southern Malawi

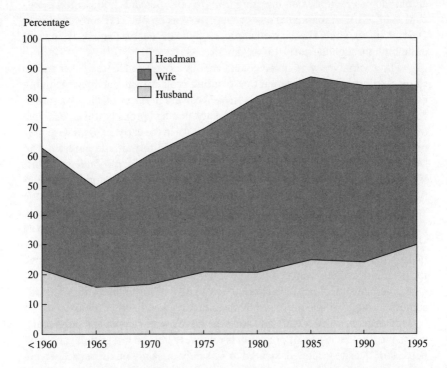

group, was clearly the most commonly found group; it was the most prevalent in 47.4 percent of enumeration areas. The remaining 29.8 percent of sites reported other traditionally matrilineal groups as the most common.

Two location factors were measured to approximate access to markets and off-farm employment opportunities: distance to a tarmac road and distance from the tarmac road to a major city (Mzuzu, Lilongwe, or Blantyre). There was significant variation in the responses for both. The mean distance to tarmac was 24.8 kilometers; this was notably higher (33.8) in the north and less in the north-central region (13.9). The latter is explained by the fact that a major tarmac route forms a loop through the north-central region. Mean distance between the closest tarmac road and a major city was much longer, 95.1 kilometers, and was similarly high in all regions.

Cattle holding is not as common in Malawi as it is in some other countries, as shown by the relatively low percentage of households with cattle in 1971 (11.3 percent). Few cows are milked, and cattle raising is a means of saving in Malawi (Blanc et al. 1996). The percentage has more or less stayed the same over time, and herd sizes are not large, either. Goats are more prevalent, with about one-third of households reporting to have at least one goat in 1996. The proportion of households using chemical fertilizer in the early 1970s was fairly similar across regions, ranging from 24.9 to 35.5 percent. Following liberalization of fertilizer marketing and pricing, this has dropped off considerably in 1995–96 in our study sites, but other reports indicate that fertilizer use remained quite high through the early 1990s (Smale 1995).

Three variables were obtained that are directly related to tree cover and its change. Information on external tree-planting projects was obtained including the approximate number of trees planted. The average across all sites was about 630 trees, but the average across the 13 sites that had projects was 2,762. Just over one-third of sites reported to have had VFAs in the early 1970s. These may not have actually corresponded to the VFAs as laid forth in the Forest Act in Malawi, but they nonetheless represent areas identified by respondents as different from ordinary *miombo* woodlands and managed, at least during some period, by the community. For those sites with such areas, about 40 percent of the area on average was under such schemes. The final variable was the coppicing ability (or ability to regrow after cutting) of trees, which is defined as the percentage of all trees on the landscape in 1971 having a high coppicing ability (calculated by weighting and scaling up from individual species). The average for the entire sample was 25.4 percent, though 20 parishes registered a 0.

Average annual rainfall across all sites was 915 millimeters. Rainfall was somewhat higher in the north (1,004 millimeters) than in other regions (867 to 907 millimeters). Soil texture and soil type were obtained only at a large scale; consequently the degree of precision is relatively low. In our sample, about 63 percent of the sites were considered to be sandy or sandy mixtures, 43 percent were clays or clay mixtures (there are some sandy-clays reported), and 47 percent were identified as having a fine texture as opposed to coarse. Data on slopes are not available. In order to isolate the effects of tenure and other explanatory variables from their clear relationship to regional effects, we include regional dummy variables in the regressions.

Econometric Analysis

ESTIMATION METHOD.   The first equation is the explanation of the proportion of plots acquired through the matrilineal-cum-matrilocal inheritance system. The results reported are from a two-stage least squares (2SLS) regression in which population growth is the dependent variable in the first stage. The model expressed in equations (2) through (4) contains three endogenous variables: land use change, woodland tree density change, and yield change. Land use change is reflected by the absolute change in the share of agricultural land in total enumeration area land. As indicated above, this change is nearly equal to the change (in the opposite direction) of woodland and bushland, so that the inclusion of one land use change in the model is sufficient. Theoretically, tree density change on agricultural land and nonagricultural land ought to be considered in the model. However, in practice, our data indicate very little change in tree cover density on agricultural land; in both the early 1970s and mid-1990s, a very low tree density is found. Because of the limited number of sample observations and the difficulties in identifying each of the equations, it was decided to exclude tree cover on agricultural land from the formal analysis. A third natural resource management variable is the change in yield. Since maize is the most commonly grown crop in Malawi, the change in yield of maize is used as the measure of yield change.

Although there may well be unidirectional or lagged relationships, or both, among the variables, we cannot a priori rule out a simultaneous equations structure. Consequently, both (2SLS) and three-stage least squares (3SLS) estimation procedures were used. Because the results were almost identical, only the two-stage least squares results, corrected for heteroskedasticity, are reported. In a three-equation model, especially one in which endogenous variables are clearly linked, satisfying the rank condition for identification can be difficult. Nonetheless, we feel that our choice of "identifying variables" is sound: ethnic group for population growth; altitude for land use change; coppicing ability of trees, presence of external tree-planting and management projects for tree cover change; and initial period use of fertilizer and average distance to plots for yield change.

It will be noted in Table 5.3 that many of the explanatory variables are linked to region. Since we are primarily interested in the role of tenure and because the degree of matrilocal/matrilineal tenure arrangements differs across region, we interact this continuous variable with regional dummies in the regression.

RESULTS.   Table 5.4 shows the results from the 2SLS regression explaining the proportion of plots acquired through the matrilineal-cum-matrilocal inheritance system. Several variables were found to be significant, and the *R*-squared value is quite high at .52. A lower proportion, or greater tenure security (for male heads of households), is related to the Chewa ethnic group (matrilineal) and traditional patrilineal groups as compared with non-Chewa matrilineal groups. Contrary to our expectations, after controlling for ethnic group, population density was positively correlated to greater tenure insecurity. This implies that more transformations toward the patrilocal/patrilineal system are occurring in the less densely populated frontier areas in the north-central region, which happen to be dominated by the Chewa. Predicted population growth was, however, not related to tenure security. Displaying a weaker link to the transformation of tenure systems were the distance variables. As hypothesized, the farther from a major city, the greater the proportion of plots acquired under the traditional matrilineal system. However, at the same time, results show that proximity to roads works in the opposite way. It is difficult to explain the opposing results from the distance variables.

Turning to the natural resource management regressions, the results from a 2SLS model are presented in Table 5.5. The *R*-squared measures in most of

TABLE 5.4 Determinants of proportion of plots acquired through matrilineal/matrilocal system: 2SLS regressions

Variable	Coefficient Estimate	t-Value
Constant	−12.409	−1.14
Chewa ethnic group	−.3067**	−4.12
Patrilineal ethnic groups	−.2699**	−2.65
Percentage of population in main ethnic group	.0014	0.63
Population density in 1970	.0193**	3.88
Square of population density in 1970	−.0001**	−3.28
Log of distance to paved road	−.0502	−1.76
Log of distance to major city	.0581	1.67
Share of agricultural land in 1970	.0641	0.31
Average date of acquisition of plots	.0061	1.12
Population growth[a]	.0220	0.88
R-squared value	.52	

[a]Fitted values from first-stage instrumental variable regression used.
**.01 level

the equations were very encouraging, ranging from .29 to .74. We review these results in separate subsections.

Change in Nonagricultural Land Tree Density: The change in woodland tree density is found to be related to tenure, but not in the consistent manner hypothesized earlier. In the northern region, more matrilineal-cum-matrilocal systems led to faster decline in tree cover. Although this was the expected result, similar relationships did not occur in the remaining two regions. This may reflect the tenure security effect as postulated or could also measure the effect associated with the influx of migrant groups into a relatively wooded area (that is, the matrilineal groups moving into the patrilineal north). These types of households may well have different long-term strategies than indigenes and make the creation and enforcement of conservation rules more difficult.

We found that tree cover change was higher (mainly smaller decreases) where VFAs occupied a larger share of the area. This was the expected result, as VFAs were identified by respondents as specially managed areas, implemented with the assistance of the Forest Department. The change in tree density was strongly and negatively related to the initial period tree density level, suggesting that change is more rapid the lower the scarcity value of the resource. Tree cover loss was found to be more severe in areas farther from major cities. This is contrary to expectations but may simply mean that woodlands nearer to cities were cleared prior to 1970 (this would be expected under virtual open-access conditions). Tree cover loss was also greater where yield change was higher (that is, less negative). This is not self-evident, but it may

TABLE 5.5 Determinants of tree cover change, yield change, and land use change: 2SLS regressions

Variable	Tree Cover Change	Yield Change	Change in Share of Agricultural Land
Constant	.486	2.860**	−1.168**
	(1.63)	(2.92)	(−2.00)
North-central zone	−.453**	.276	−.115
	(−3.03)	(1.08)	(−0.46)
Southern zone	−.580**	−.399	−.489
	(−2.94)	(−0.49)	(−1.62)
Percentage of population of main ethnic group	.0005		
	(0.97)		
1970 population density	.001	−.009	.016**
	(0.31)	(−0.69)	(2.11)
1970 population density squared	−.00001	.00005	−.00008*
	(−0.34)	(0.67)	(−1.77)
Log of distance to tarmac	−.0008	.022	−.026
	(−0.06)	(0.64)	(−0.92)
Log of distance from tarmac to major city	−.041**	−.173**	.008
	(−2.00)	(−2.73)	(0.24)
1970 log of yield		−.300**	.115
		(−4.07)	(1.60)
1970 share of land in agriculture	−.124	−.040	−.504
	(−0.89)	(−0.10)	(−1.54)
1970 woodland tree cover	−.800**		
	(−4.31)		
1970 census area tree cover			−.209
			(−0.32)
Proportion of trees that coppice well	.047		
	(1.21)		
1970 percentage of Village Forest Area to total area	.002**		
	(2.33)		
Log of trees planted by external projects	.003		
	(0.48)		
1970 percentage of households with cattle	.001	.002	.003
	(1.19)	(0.69)	(1.45)
1970 percentage of households using fertilizer		−.00071	
		(−0.54)	
Average annual rainfall		−.0002	
		(−1.24)	
Mean altitude			.0001
			(1.00)

(continued)

TABLE 5.5 *Continued*

Variable	Tree Cover Change	Yield Change	Change in Share of Agricultural Land
Average distance to plots		−.007	
		(−0.11)	
Whether sandy soils prevail		−.143*	
		(−1.85)	
1970 agricultural land tree cover		2.704	
		(0.63)	
Percentage of plots acquired by	−.913**	−.486	−.865
women in northern zone	(−2.05)	(−0.40)	(−0.91)
Percentage of plots acquired by	.054	−.395	−.506
women in north-central zone	(0.30)	(−0.65)	(−1.34)
Percentage of plots acquired by	.209	.754	.226
women in southern zone	(1.04)	(0.91)	(0.83)
Population growth[a]	.012	.035	.056
	(0.44)	(0.59)	(1.27)
Change in woodland tree cover[a]		.420	−.788*
		(0.88)	(−1.71)
Change in yield[a]	−.133**		.092
	(−2.26)		(0.64)
Change in share of agricultural land[a]	−.155	−.027	
	(−1.21)	(−0.06)	
R-squared	.74	.42	.29

NOTE: Figures in parentheses are *t*-values.

[a]Fitted values from first-stage instrumental variable regression used.

*.05 level

**.01 level

be that yield losses are not as great in areas where tobacco is more prevalent (from the impacts of greater income generation or fertilizer use), in which case we would expect greater removal of trees for tobacco drying. Finally, tree cover change is related to region. There has been greater tree density loss in the north-central region, characterized by estate development and high wood demands for tobacco drying and curing, and in the southern region, where demand for wood for fuel and shelter by a sweltering population is acute.

Change in Crop Yields: The strongest relationship appears to be the initial period yield, which shows a negative relationship. This may simply reflect the fact that respondents were much more aware of current day yields (which were relatively similar across enumeration areas) than they were of past yields (which varied much more). Yield decline was steeper the farther away from a major city. The latter result may capture the higher ratio of input costs to output prices leading to lower use of inorganic nutrient inputs in areas far away from major cities, especially in recent years where liberalization has led to significant reductions in fertilizer use. The rate of yield decline was less in areas of better soils (that is, where sandy soils were not prevalent), which is the expected result.

Change in Share of Agricultural Land: Population density has the expected positive effect on the rate of conversion of woodlands to agricultural land. The negative sign on the squared term indicates that this positive effect declines with population density and is maximized at a population density of 114 per square kilometer (exceeded by 19 percent of sites). Population growth was, however, not significantly related to conversion. Land use change was not related to the tenure variables, which may highlight the general characterization of woodland management as being open-access for community members.

Only one other variable was significant in the regression. Greater conversion to agriculture is associated with faster loss of nonagricultural tree cover. This would be anticipated if the resulting loss in tree cover lowered profits of woodlands relative to profits from conversion to agriculture. Surprisingly, land use change was not significantly related to initial share of agricultural land, though its coefficient estimate is rather high. This may be due to confounding effects between the initial share and population growth.

Summary and Conclusions for Extensive Study

First of all, it should be made clear that it is difficult to generalize our findings for all of Malawi, because of the considerable variation from north to south. In our discussions that follow, we have in mind the situation facing the central and southern regions, which are home to the majority of the population and which are facing more critical natural resource management choices. The north, with its relatively low population density, cannot be lumped in with the others in the following discussion, although it may face similar issues in the near future.

We found several trends in natural resource management that portend hard times ahead for rural households in Malawi. First, we found that in nearly all sites, yields of maize, the staple food crop, were perceived by respondents to have declined over the past 25 years. Second, although families and communities have hitherto been able to compensate for this by expanding agricultural areas, new uncultivated areas are becoming scant. In nine enumeration areas land once under woodlands has completely disappeared, and in most others the area under woodlands has decreased markedly. This supports the hypothesis that woodland has been excessively converted to farmland. Third, the conversion of land has had a dramatic and negative impact on aggregate tree density, since tree cover is many times greater on nonagricultural land than on agricultural land (16.7 compared with 2.0 percent in 1995). At the same time, we found little evidence of significant tree planting, though in some of the sites, tree density on agricultural land inched upward. Fifth, exacerbating the effect of land conversion on tree cover is the decrease in tree density on remaining woodlands (by about 33 percent).

In sum, the increasing scarcity of woodlands and their products has not yet manifested itself in sufficiently attractive incentives for their sustainable management. Given the high degree of poverty among rural households and the poor remuneration from maize production, it is unlikely that high profits from agricultural production have driven the conversion process. Instead, one must look at weaknesses in the management of woodlands themselves as contributing toward the seemingly low valuation attributed to their preservation and management.

It is difficult to assess the degree to which this apparent natural resource degradation is undesirable. However, considering the lack of woodland resource management and slight acceleration of degradation in areas where mixed tenure systems are operating, the pace of natural resource degradation almost certainly exceeds the socially optimal level. The rather likely possibility that resources have been degraded beyond the optimal rate implores us to ponder, in the policy implications section at the end of this chapter, how these trends can be reversed.

Intensive Study

Major Hypotheses for Intensive Study

Given the rise in importance of the hybrid maize/fertilizer package among smallholders (Smale 1995), it may not appear that tenure played a significant role in the choice of new technology. This is to be expected if investments and payoffs are of relatively short duration, and such findings have been observed elsewhere in Africa for crop production systems (Place and Hazell 1993). It is important to recognize that tenure security is expected to have an impact on longer-term investments as it affects the expected future benefits. Important examples are semifixed investments in trees and terracing. Adoption of tobacco growing might also require longer-term investment, partly because farmers normally have to join tobacco clubs for input and output market access, which requires investments in developing personal relationships and in a deposit to be used as security for loans. Since tobacco is entirely new to many farmers,[14] payoffs to tobacco growing are likely to follow a learning curve, a part of which involves learning appropriate rotational practices within their farms. Farmers who are unsure of their long-term residence in the village or security on the land may be less willing to adopt this crop.

---

14. An exception would be farmers who worked on tobacco estates.

As noted earlier, many farmers in our sample have opted to obtain leases on their parcels, thereby effecting a tenure conversion to the estate sector. Leases were obligatory for those wishing to grow tobacco before the 1990s. This is no longer the case, but some farmers find leases to be beneficial by providing some security for input credit and perhaps also to individualize the land rights (often in the name of the male head). Other than the time involved in obtaining the lease and the small annual fee required, a farmer must also obtain the approval of his or her village headman. The latter obligation has not proved to be difficult, at least in the case of Kasungu ADD. For the most part, the acquisition of leasehold will reflect determinants on the demand side, with the exception of rules governing minimum size of leasehold of 10 hectares.[15] Leasehold land, though there are conditions on its use and transfer, is similar to private land, and it is of great interest to analyze whether the farming performance under this institution outweighs that under the customary tenure institutions.

More formally, we intend to test the following hypotheses concerning the role of tenure security on agricultural investment and productivity:

Hypothesis 1: Greater tenure security, as measured by security of landholding for the male head of household, will lead to more rapid and expansive adoption of tobacco farming.

Hypothesis 2: Greater tenure security will lead to increased investment in land improvements.

Hypothesis 3: Greater tenure security will *not* lead to greater efficiency in crop production, except where long-term investments for enhancing productivity are available.

Unlike western Ghana and Sumatra, where the payoffs for investment in the establishment of agroforestry are high, lucrative investment opportunities are generally limited in Malawi. Moreover, investment in trees or other land improvements do not appear to be able to reduce the risks of losing rights to residence and land that males face in their wives' villages due to traditional rules regarding rights of husbands during probationary periods and following death of or divorce from their wives. Under such conditions, it is the level of tenure security rather than its expected change that affects investment decisions, as specified in hypotheses 1 and 2.

We may be tempted to hypothesize that because of the possibility of using land as collateral and the strong tenure security, the lease system leads to higher productivity and stronger incentives to invest than the customary land tenure institutions, as is forcefully shown by Feder et al. (1988) in Thailand. Considering, however, that tenure security is fairly well established under the

---

15. However, there are many leases held by farms smaller than 10 hectares in our sample. This means that the rule is not rigorously enforced, whether through accepting applications from smaller farms or through lack of size verification.

patrilineal system and that formal sector credit is not so important in Malawi, whether such a hypothesis holds is an empirical question.

Data Collection Methods

Much of the analysis in this chapter draws on data collected from a formal survey instrument. Each household was visited at least three times in order to reduce errors of reporting due to recall lapses. This was extremely important in that the survey sought to collect information on labor allocation and farm production. The information collected on labor captured, for one wet season month and one dry season month, the labor hours for all activities undertaken by the husband, the wife, the children, and others. For the largest maize and tobacco fields, information was collected on all labor time by task and type of laborer. Other inputs used on these fields, along with production figures, were also collected. A host of other variables were collected including basic farm and household characteristics, land acquisition, land rights, land use, and land improvements at the parcel level, as well as a detailed section on existing stocks of trees and planting behavior.

Household and Farm Characteristics

In order to understand the tenure security of households in Malawi with respect to their land, two variables are particularly important: the residency status of the household and the manner in which their land was acquired. For residency status, households could be residing in the husband's village, the wife's village, or a village where neither was born. Our sample is split equally among these three types (about 33.0 percent to each). For methods of land acquisition, we have information on both the type of transaction and the source of transaction (see Table 5.6). There was only one purchase of land reported among 187 land parcel acquisitions. The most common land acquisition modes were inheritance (36.9 percent), gift from relatives (32.1 percent), and allocation by village headmen (26.7 percent). These methods are common throughout Malawi, with the exception that in the southern regions, for some time little land has remained to be allocated by village headmen. Among these acquisitions was a range of sources. The most common source was the parents of the husband (35.3 percent), followed by the village headman (27.3 percent) and the wife's parents (15.0 percent). Other relatives accounted for a further 18.2 percent, while only a few transactions occurred among neighbors and friends (4.3 percent).

Based on resident status of the household and source of land acquisition, five distinct modes of land acquisition were created. Although these are defined at the parcel level, they also aggregate up to the household level as all but three households acquired all their land through the same method.

1. Matrilocal/matrilineal: Husband lives in wife's village, and the household acquired land from wife's relatives or the headman in her village.

2. Patrilocal/matrilineal: Wife lives in husband's village, and the household acquired land from wife's relatives.
3. Immigrants/village headman: Husband and wife live in new village and acquired land from village headman.
4. Matrilocal/patrilineal: Husband lives in wife's village, and the household acquired land from husband's relatives.
5. Patrilocal/patrilineal: Wife lives in husband's village, and the household acquired land from husband's relatives.

Table 5.6 shows that 37.4 percent of sampled parcels fall into the patrilocal/patrilineal category, which is expected to provide the strongest tenure security among the customary land tenure institutions. The matrilocal/patrilineal category (4) would seem to offer less, though relatively strong, security of tenure to males. Just over 17 percent of parcels are of this type. The patrilocal/matrilineal category (2) would seemingly offer less security because land passes through the wife. Some 15 percent of parcels have been identified as belonging to this group. The lowest security position for a male is the matrilocal/matrilineal category, in which he is a guest in his wife's village and farming on land acquired from her relatives (category 1). Nearly 20 percent of parcels fall

TABLE 5.6 Mode of acquisition of parcels and tenure security

Category	Percentage of Parcels (n = 187)
How parcel acquired	
Inherited	36.9
Purchased	0.5
Gift	32.1
Allocated	26.7
Rented/borrowed	3.7
From whom parcel acquired	
Wife's parents	15.0
Other relatives of wife	7.0
Husband's parents	35.3
Other relatives of husband	11.2
Village headman	27.3
Others	4.3
Tenure security groups	
Matrilocal/matrilineal	19.3
Patrilocal/matrilineal	15.0
Immigrant/village headmen	11.2
Matrilocal/patrilineal	17.1
Patrilocal/patrilineal	37.4

SOURCE: Intensive study.

TABLE 5.7 Descriptive statistics for regression analysis

	Matrilocal/ Matrilineal Households	Patrilocal/ Patrilineal Households	Full Sample
Number of households	28	53	138
Number of parcels	36	70	187
Female household head (percentage)	10.7	0.0	2.9
Age of household head (mean)	40.7	38.6	40.6
Years farming in village (mean)	8.8	12.2	11.5
Some off-farm income (percentage)	46.4	37.7	35.7
Farm size (mean, ha)	1.7	5.6	5.0
Adult equivalents (mean)	2.4	2.9	2.7
Has lease (percentage of parcels)	36.1	51.4	47.6
No right to give land away (percentage of parcels)	33.3	7.1	15.5
No right to select heir for land (percentage of parcels)	33.3	11.4	16.6
Distance to tarmac road (mean, km)	13.5	13.5	13.1
Distance to nearest market (mean, km)	8.6	6.3	7.1

SOURCE: Intensive survey.

into this category. A final category, immigrant/village headman, is difficult to rank in terms of tenure security, though its security is clearly less than that of patrilocal/patrilineal. This category contains the fewest number of parcels of any of the tenure security groups (11.2 percent).

Table 5.7 displays some of the general characteristics of sampled households in aggregate and for the hypothesized least and most secure categories. There are few reported female-headed households, and the majority are found among the matrilocal/matrilineal households. The mean age of the household head was 40.6 and was slightly higher among matrilocal/matrilineal households than for patrilocal/patrilineal households. But this is reversed for the number of years of farming in the village where the patrilocal/patrilineal households have tended to farm for longer. The finding of shorter periods of farming in wives' villages supports the observations by Mkandawire (1983–84) that males often seek to leave their wives' villages in favor of land in their own village when possible. About 36 percent of the households reported some off-farm employment mainly involving agricultural labor or trade. There is no significant difference in off-farm employment between matrilocal/matrilineal and patrilocal/ patrilineal households.

Average farm size is 5 hectares, at least twice as large as the farms farther south, where population pressure is acute. For this variable, there is quite a significant difference across mode of land acquisition. By far, the smallest farms are reported in the matrilocal/matrilineal group, where the average is only 1.7 hectares. Surprisingly, these farms are operated by approximately the same number of family workers as those in other modes of land acquisition. The relatively small farms in the matrilocal/ matrilineal system might reflect demands for land from a larger number of competing heirs than under the patrilineal system, which has a clearly defined set of heirs (that is, limited to sons). Just under half of the parcels sampled had been converted to leaseholds. In the sample, households with leases had farms averaging nearly 8 hectares in size, compared with about 2.5 hectares for those without leases. The matrilocal/matrilineal group was least likely to obtain a leasehold, this being most likely related to the rather small farm sizes and difficulty in establishing individual rights.

No household claims the right to sell land, but there are varying degrees in the ability to exercise other types of rights, for example, rights to give land and to choose an heir freely. Patrilocal/patrilineal households (Table 5.7) claim more individualized rights. While matrilocal/matrilineal households responded that they had no right to give their land away for one-third of their parcels, patrilocal/patrilineal households mentioned this in only 7.1 percent of cases. Households were located, on average, 13.1 kilometers from a tarmac road, and this was consistent across the modes of land acquisition. Major markets were located about half this distance, 7.1 kilometers on average, and the distance reported by matrilocal/matrilineal households was slightly above the average.

Agricultural Investment and Production Variables

The uptake and expansion of tobacco growing by smallholder farmers in Malawi represent the most important recent change in Malawian agriculture. We consider the growing of tobacco an investment by farmers for several reasons. First, for those unfamiliar with the crop, agronomic and economic success will follow a learning curve path whereby farmers require some time to optimize the production of tobacco within their farm fields. Second, there are institutional linkages to be developed for the procurement of inputs and for the marketing of outputs. Third, where tree resources are limited, there is the added investment in constructing drying sheds and in some cases planting trees for this purpose. Table 5.8 shows that the average farmer in the sample had been growing tobacco for 9.9 years and now devotes 29.5 percent of his or her farm area to tobacco production. Patrilocal/patrilineal households began growing tobacco much earlier and now cultivate it on a larger scale than do matrilocal/ matrilineal households.

In addition to the investment in tobacco, Malawian farmers practice several other types of investments to support the production of both maize and tobacco. Data were collected on the prevalence of different types of investments on 455 fields operated by sampled households. At this observational level, the frequency of almost all investments is low. Thus we present here the prevalence of investments at the household level. The incidence of investment displayed

TABLE 5.8 Descriptive statistics: Dependent variables for intensive survey study

	Matrilocal/ Matrilineal Households	Patrilocal/ Patrilineal Households	Full Sample
Years farming tobacco	5.1	13.0	9.9
Proportion of area under tobacco	25.4	33.1	29.5
Percentage of households planting trees	50.0	77.4	65.9
Percentage of households destumping	31.0	48.1	39.1
Percentage of households terracing or leveling	58.6	63.0	60.9
Percentage of households investing in water management	13.8	24.1	21.0

in Table 5.8 in terms of percentages of households undertaking various invest-ments shows considerable variation across the modes of land acquisition. Tree planting was practiced by nearly two-thirds of all sampled households. Most of the trees were planted for poles that are used in the tobacco-drying process, indicating that tree planting is affected by indirect market incentives noted also in Dewees (1995). The likelihood of planting was much greater among patrilocal/patrilineal households than for their matrilocal/matrilineal counter-parts. Leveling and terracing are also common improvements made (60.9 per-cent of households), followed by destumping (39.1 percent) and water man-agement such as drainage (21.0 percent). These types of investments follow the same pattern of increased likelihood in patrilocal/patrilineal households, with the widest difference in destumping.

Production input and output data were collected on the largest maize and tobacco fields for each household.[16] In total, there were 117 burley tobacco plots for which information was recorded, 68 hybrid maize fields, and 58 local maize fields. Profits were calculated as the value of output less purchased input costs, less hired labor, and less the imputed value of all adult labor (using mar-ket wages) from the household. Profit thus calculated is supposed to capture the returns to land, management input, and superior work effort. By crop, Table 5.9 clearly shows that tobacco is much more profitable than maize, with average profits nearly 10 times as high (see also Zeller, Diagne, and Kisyombe 1997). At the same time, to attain these high levels, tobacco requires more labor and purchased inputs. Access to these inputs as well as the need to rotate tobacco within the farm help to explain why only minor proportions of total farm area are taken up by tobacco. In our sample, hybrid maize was not attractive com-pared with local maize. Yields were not much higher, perhaps reflecting the

---

16. We chose the largest fields to minimize recall errors.

TABLE 5.9 Descriptive statistics: Crop production data for intensive survey study

Variable	Local Maize	Hybrid Maize	Burley Tobacco
Number of observations	58	68	117
Husband's hours per hectare	266.4	321.7	457.8
Wife's hours per hectare	271.6	350.8	473.3
Hired hours per hectare	74.4	51.3	79.5
Purchased inputs per hectare (Malawi kwacha)	304.7	570.8	1,531.6
Nitrogen applied per hectare (median kg)	3.3	6.5	40.9
Profits per hectare (Malawi kwacha)			
Full sample	795.3	620.7	6,241.7
Matrilocal/matrilineal	666.9	477.4	4,724.6
Patrilocal/patrilineal	859.7	410.1	6,722.1

very low use of fertilizer inputs (median of about 6 kilograms of nitrogen per hectare), and there were some additional costs for labor and seed. Table 5.9 also shows that average profits per hectare for tobacco were lower in matrilocal/matrilineal households (4,724.6 Malawi kwacha [MK], where $1 = 16 MK) than in patrilocal/patrilineal households (6,722.1) and again for local maize. However, neither difference was statistically significant at the 5 percent level.

Econometric Models

We use several independent regression models to test the hypotheses outlined earlier. Before testing them, we investigate the factors determining the acquisition of a leasehold in a parcel-level logit regression model. The actual and predicted leasehold values are then used later as explanatory variables in analyses of production efficiency. The relationship between the presence of a lease and investments is not analyzed because of lack of information on the timing of acquisition of a lease.

A second set of regressions addresses the adoption and spread of tobacco growing at the household level. Two dependent variables are examined, the years since the farmer began growing tobacco and the proportion of the farm area under tobacco (calculated as an average of the proportion of area under tobacco during the previous three seasons). For each, a zero indicates nonadoption, and as such tobit models are used.

A third set of regressions concerns the incidence of four different types of land improvements: tree planting, destumping, terracing/leveling, and water management (for example, drainage). Data on these variables are in binary form, and as such logit models are employed. For tree planting and destumping, the number of trees present at the time of land acquisition was used as an additional explanatory variable. We study the impact of tenure (through the mode of land acquisition) and other factors at the household level, as the proportion of fields improved (the unit at which land improvement data were collected) is too low for almost all types of investments.

A fourth set of regressions examines the impact of tenure security and other factors on profits per hectare for two crops, maize and burley tobacco.[17] We separate tobacco from maize because a priori it is hypothesized that tenure security might play a more significant role in tobacco production than in maize production, since the former requires additional investment.[18] These models are run at a plot level using ordinary least squares (OLS) and applying a linear specification, since the presence of negative profit values precluded a logarithmic transformation. Prices of inputs and outputs do not enter the profit function, as they were essentially constant across sampled households in the same locality.

The final set of regressions examines the intensity of labor and cash inputs for maize and tobacco. The issues addressed here include the question of whether land tenure institutions affect allocation of factor inputs and the extent to which factor markets function toward the equalization of the factor intensities across farms managed by households with different factor endowments. The inputs examined are the intensity of the husband's labor input (for cases in which a husband is present), the intensity of the wife's labor (for cases in which a wife is present), the intensity of hired labor, and the intensity of purchased inputs (seed, fertilizer). As in the case of profits, OLS regression models are used.

Tenure security is captured by the five modes of land acquisition identified earlier. The regression models include a set of four dummy variables with the matrilocal/matrilineal tenure category omitted as the base comparison case. Other variables used as explanatory variables include farm size, farming experience, access to markets measured by distance, family labor endowment/owned land radio, and village dummies.[19]

Econometric Results

THE ACQUISITION OF LEASEHOLD.   Table 5.10 presents the results of a logit model used to explain the acquisition of a leasehold at the parcel level. None of the mode of land acquisition variables is significant in comparison with the base case of matrilocal/matrilineal tenure, indicating that nontenure variables are more important. The number of years the household has been farming in the current village is the most highly correlated to the acquisition of a leasehold. This confirms the statements noted earlier that leaseholds used to be required for tobacco production and marketing. Two other variables, inherited

---

17. Data were collected separately for local and hybrid maize. However, we found that there was no significant difference between the two in terms of mean yields, so we pooled them together for this analysis, utilizing a crop variety dummy as an explanatory variable.

18. Pooling the crops in a model did not lead to any changes in significance among the independent variables.

19. Family labor endowment is calculated by summing up the family members each weighted by his or her adult equivalent factor, which is dependent on age.

TABLE 5.10 Determinants of the acquisition of lease: Logit regression

Variable	Estimate	t-Statistic
Constant	−2.241	−2.94
Patrilocal/matrilineal tenure	.666	1.09
Matrilocal/patrilineal tenure	−.862	−1.38
Patrilocal/patrilineal tenure	−.296	−0.57
Immigrant/village headman tenure	−.070	−0.11
Inherited land size	.060	1.65
Primary school education	.573	1.23
Postprimary education	.991*	1.95
Polygamous household	−.237	−0.48
Years farming in village	.047**	3.86
Village 1	1.641*	2.25
Village 2	−.253	−0.31
Village 3	.978	1.41
Village 4	.979	0.98
Village 5	.713	0.90
Village 6	.323	0.50
Village 7	1,166	1.54
Log likelihood		
Percentage of leased parcels correctly predicted	64.0	
Percentage of nonleased parcels correctly predicted	76.3	

*.05 level
**.01 level

land size and postprimary education, are positively related to the acquisition of a leasehold and are of the expected direction. These may be related to wealth levels and suggest that wealthier households self-select themselves into the pool of leaseholders. Last, the acquisition of a leasehold is generally unrelated to village location, with the exception of one case. This indicates that the absence of significant institutional incentives or disincentives (for example, prohibition by some village headmen) for leasehold acquisition.

ADOPTION OF TOBACCO.   Table 5.11 displays the results of regressions on two dependent variables, the years farming tobacco and the proportion of farm area under tobacco. Patrilocal/patrilineal households are found to have adopted tobacco much earlier and to have allocated a higher proportion of land area to tobacco compared with matrilocal/matrilineal households. Matrilocal/patrilineal households are likewise more likely to have adopted tobacco growing earlier on. These results confirm our hypothesis that owing to the investment and learning curve associated with tobacco growing, households that have

TABLE 5.11 Determinants of adoption of tobacco farming: Tobit regression

Variable	Years Farming Tobacco	Proportion of Area under Tobacco	Proportion of Area under Tobacco
Constant	−7.517	.229	.234
	(−2.09)	(3.34)	(3.38)
Patrilocal/matrilineal tenure	3.025	.072	.077
	(1.21)	(1.42)	(1.49)
Matrilocal/patrilineal tenure	5.530**	.020	.031
	(2.41)	(0.41)	(0.57)
Patrilocal/patrilineal tenure	8.967**	.078*	.099*
	(4.61)	(1.90)	(1.67)
Immigrant/village headman tenure	2.850	−.002	.011
	(1.00)	(−0.04)	(0.17)
Farm size	.160*	−.002	−.001
	(1.71)	(−0.91)	(−0.50)
Age of household head	.214**		
	(4.35)		
Years farming in village		−.0001	.0004
		(−0.06)	(0.23)
Labor/land ratio village		−.010	−.007
		(−0.84)	(−0.74)
Distance to paved road	.003	−.005	−.004
	(0.01)	(−0.98)	(0.96)
Village 1	2.732	.110	.113
	(0.89)	(1.79)	(1.83)
Village 2	−.507	.058	.058
	(−0.16)	(0.93)	(0.92)
Village 3	.729	.095	.094
	(0.25)	(1.61)	(1.60)
Village 4	5.659	.154	.165
	(1.35)	(1.81)	(1.88)
Village 5	2.258	.123	.125
	(0.52)	(1.42)	(1.44)
Village 6	2.330	.111	.088
	(0.54)	(1.25)	(1.27)
Village 7	8.720*	.183*	.204*
	(2.35)	(2.49)	(2.41)
Predicted years farming tobacco			−.003
			(−0.49)

NOTE: Figures in parentheses are *t*-values.

*.05 level

**.01 level

acquired land through patrilineal channels have greater incentive to adopt tobacco, ceteris paribus.

Other variables related to the speed of uptake are farm size and age of household head. Both of these signs are of the expected positive direction. Farmers who had grown tobacco for eight years or more had to have larger farms, because of the restrictions on tobacco growing set forth by the government. The positive result on age of household head simply reflects the fact that younger households could not have been growing tobacco for many years. Perhaps surprisingly, the proportion of area under tobacco is not related to farm size. This shows that tobacco growing is on the whole scale neutral.

INVESTMENT IN LAND IMPROVEMENTS. Table 5.12 shows the results of logit regression models for four types of investments made since land acquisition, tree planting, destumping investment, terracing and leveling investment, and water management investment. Among the mode of land acquisition variables, most of the signs are of the hypothesized direction, and a few statistically significant results are obtained. Patrilocal/patrilineal households are more likely than matrilocal/matrilineal households to have invested in tree planting and destumping since acquisition of their land. Matrilocal/patrilineal households are also more likely to have planted trees. These results are in line with hypothesis 2 and suggest that patrilineal households may undertake destumping and tree planting (mainly poles) as an overall strategy of increasing tobacco production. The other significant finding is that those households that were composed of immigrants and that received land from the village headman are more likely to have been destumped; this is not surprising because such land is more likely to have been uncultivated woodland.

It is also of interest to note that none of the land tenure variables is significant in the terracing, leveling, and water management investment regressions. Although we failed to obtain relevant information during the field survey, similar to the case of commercial tree planting in Ghana and Sumatra, investments in terracing, leveling, and water management may to some extent increase expected land rights, when they are originally weak. If such institutional rules exist, investment incentives can be equally strong under different land tenure institutions, as was discussed in Chapter 1. Whether this is indeed the case needs to be examined by careful follow-up studies.

Farm size is generally not important except with respect to water management, in which case the investment is more likely to be observed on larger farms. The number of years farming in the village is positively linked to tree planting, which is expected, but surprisingly not related to other types of land improvements. Also insignificant are variables reflecting relative factor endowment and market access. Overall, this may show that these investments are divisible and provide returns that are unaffected by the size of farm and household. The village dummies are most significant for the tree planting and destumping investments, which reflects the different tree cover conditions among villages.

TABLE 5.12 Determinants of land investments: Logit regressions

Variable	Tree Planting	Destumping	Terracing or Leveling	Water Management
Constant	−1.683	.349	.881	−2.249
	(−1.76)	(0.36)	(0.92)	(−1.93)
Patrilocal/matrilineal tenure	.920	−.019	.283	.575
	(1.25)	(−0.02)	(0.42)	(0.71)
Matrilocal/patrilineal tenure	1.463*	−.216	.471	−.839
	(1.95)	(−0.30)	(0.74)	(−0.97)
Patrilocal/patrilineal tenure	1.431*	1.249*	.328	−.021
	(2.30)	(2.15)	(0.64)	(−0.03)
Immigrant/village headman tenure	−.133	2.101**	.093	−2.047
	(−0.15)	(2.61)	(0.13)	(−1.55)
Farm size	.022	−.046	.037	.082*
	(0.54)	(−1.31)	(1.17)	(2.37)
Years farming in village	.070**	.017	−.005	.007
	(2.61)	(0.75)	(−0.24)	(0.28)
Labor/land ratio	.149	.071	.175	−.052
	(0.85)	(0.39)	(0.97)	(−0.23)
Distance to market	−.040	−.013	−.035	.042
	(−0.94)	(−0.30)	(−0.87)	(0.87)
Village 1	1.569	−2.551**	−1.483	−.441
	(1.69)	(−2.72)	(−1.68)	(−0.33)
Village 2	2.897*	−1.370	−.847	.373
	(2.26)	(−1.50)	(−0.92)	(0.32)
Village 3	.611	−2.229*	−.283	.632
	(0.77)	(−2.59)	(−0.33)	(0.63)
Village 4	1.118	.009	−.427	.036
	(0.93)	(0.01)	(−0.40)	(0.03)
Village 5	−.026	−2.279*	−1.143	.374
	(−0.03)	(−2.14)	(−1.15)	(0.31)
Village 6	.924	−1.462	−1.343	−.243
	(1.22)	(−1.86)	(−1.68)	(−0.24)
Village 7	.406	−2.290*	−.197	1.566
	(0.48)	(−2.46)	(−0.21)	(1.46)
Number of trees present at acquisition of farm	−.002	.002		
	(−0.62)	(0.48)		
Percentage of improved farms correctly predicted	90.1	54.7	79.8	20.7
Percentage of unimproved farms correctly predicted	44.7	79.8	33.3	99.1

NOTE: Figures in parentheses are *t*-values.

*.05 level

**.01 level

PROFITS AND INPUT USE.   Regression results on profits per hectare for tobacco and maize are shown in Table 5.13, where model 2 adds the actual presence of lease variable and model 3 adds the predicted presence of lease variable. The results show that mode of land acquisition does not have a significant impact on plot-level profitability conditional on crop type. This supports our hypothesis 3, that tenure security does not affect incentives for current production.[20] The presence of a lease does have a highly positive effect on tobacco profits, but this effect disappears when using the predicted lease variable.[21] This means that it is unlikely to be the presence of the lease per se but other variables related to the acquisition of the lease, such as farmer skill and wealth, that affected profits. This argues against the possibility that the establishment of private ownership promotes efficient farming. Farm size is also not significant, which suggests that scale economies over small and medium-sized farms (as studied in our analysis) do not exist in tobacco and maize farming. Very few variables are related to profits per hectare, suggesting that there are no glaring impediments for farmers to attain similar levels of efficiency. The lone exception to this is that farming experience is positively related to tobacco profits, indicating that there is a learning curve associated with tobacco growing arising from the heavy use of inputs (labor and fertilizer) and the importance of rotation. There is also weak evidence that household female labor endowment is negatively associated with maize profits. Because labor is costed in the profit function, this implies that households may be overapplying female labor on maize fields. There is no difference in profits between hybrid and local maize, confirming similar findings noted by Zeller et al. (1997).

Tables 5.14 and 5.15 show the factor intensity regressions for maize and tobacco, respectively. Only one specification is reported for each, corresponding to model 1 in Table 5.13. For maize, it is clear that the larger endowment of male and female family labor relative to land resulted in the higher application of family labor inputs without significantly reducing hired labor inputs. Although this seems to indicate the existence of labor market imperfection, the extent of imperfection may not be too large, judging from the insignificant effect of the labor/land ratios in the profit regression. It appears that only those households with a relatively higher ratio of labor to land undertake significant husbandry practices on maize (for example, additional weeding), which brought about merely marginal net benefits. A higher male labor/land endowment is associated with more intensive use of purchased inputs on tobacco fields, indicating some degree of complementarity between the two (for exam-

---

20. This result is compatible with findings from elsewhere in Africa (for example, Place and Hazell 1993).

21. Because the predicted lease variable is based on a logit model, we used the bootstrapping technique in the second stage. This procedure verified that the conclusions from Table 5.11 remain valid.

TABLE 5.13 Determinants of profits per hectare: OLS regression

	Tobacco			Maize		
Variable	Model T-1	Model T-2	Model T-3	Model M-1	Model M-2	Model M-3
Constant	3039.3	2110.9	3129.9	1528.4	1572.9	1519.8
	(0.96)	(0.67)	(0.98)	(2.15)	(2.19)	(2.14)
Patrilocal/matrilineal tenure	−238.0	−591.6	−515.3	−310.2	−294.3	−208.1
	(−0.10)	(−0.24)	(−0.20)	(−0.58)	(−0.55)	(−0.37)
Matrilocal/patrilineal tenure	470.0	871.9	710.1	−271.1	−299.6	−352.7
	(0.20)	(0.38)	(0.30)	(−0.55)	(−0.60)	(−0.69)
Patrilocal/patrilineal tenure	836.3	794.3	844.8	−228.1	−234.8	−225.8
	(0.41)	(0.40)	(0.42)	(−0.54)	(−0.56)	(−0.54)
Immigrant/village headman tenure	602.9	715.9	499.0	302.1	269.2	318.2
	(0.23)	(0.28)	(0.19)	(0.52)	(0.46)	(0.55)
Leasehold	...	2960.4*	...	...	−155.4	...
		(2.02)			(−0.46)	
Predicted leasehold	...	...	1216.2	...	...	−304.5
			(0.59)			(−0.67)
Farm size	−34.2	−81.6	−48.7	−9.0	−7.9	−7.3
	(−0.33)	(−0.78)	(−0.46)	(−0.44)	(−0.38)	(−0.35)
Male labor/land ratio	931.1	492.2	999.0	−24.9	−9.1	−51.6
	(0.74)	(0.39)	(0.78)	(−0.09)	(−0.03)	(−0.19)
Female labor/land ratio	−833.6	−176.5	−851.2	−534.6	−570.4	−510.7
	(−0.54)	(−0.11)	(−0.55)	(−1.58)	(−1.64)	(−1.50)
Years farming in village	162.6*	109.9	132.3	−4.7	−3.1	3.1
	(2.35)	(1.50)	(1.53)	(−0.30)	(−0.20)	(0.16)

Good soil fertility	1229.6	1394.1	1248.3	140.1	182.3	179.3
	(0.77)	(0.89)	(0.78)	(0.46)	(0.57)	(0.58)
Good soil texture	−1253.1	−1246.4	−1267.4	173.4	168.6	182.7
	(−0.95)	(−0.96)	(−0.96)	(0.57)	(0.55)	(0.59)
Distance to market	26.9	54.7	41.8	−35.6	−38.7	−39.5
	(0.19)	(0.39)	(0.29)	(−1.16)	(−1.22)	(−1.26)
Hybrid maize	⋯	⋯	⋯	−291.5	−287.1	−306.1
				(−0.98)	(−0.97)	(−1.03)
Village 1	−2032.9	−2838.3	−3030.4	878.4	948.1	1068.0
	(−0.69)	(−0.96)	(−0.89)	(1.33)	(1.40)	(1.49)
Village 2	591.3	369.1	668.9	−529.1	−525.2	−589.2
	(0.20)	(0.12)	(0.22)	(−0.74)	(−0.73)	(−0.81)
Village 3	−523.8	−795.8	−1022.7	170.4	205.1	280.4
	(−0.21)	(−0.32)	(−0.38)	(0.29)	(0.35)	(0.46)
Village 4	−2026.6	−2365.7	−2562.7	−123.0	−72.0	−11.5
	(−0.59)	(−0.70)	(−0.72)	(−0.16)	(−0.09)	(−0.02)
Village 5	1155.1	810.2	1097.3	397.2	451.6	395.9
	(0.36)	(0.26)	(0.34)	(0.53)	(0.60)	(0.53)
Village 6	1273.1	1397.8	1115.9	−364.8	−375.3	−364.0
	(0.51)	(0.57)	(0.45)	(−0.65)	(−0.67)	(−0.65)
Village 7	2986.4	2203.3	2552.6	−62.3	8.7	16.2
	(1.03)	(0.77)	(0.85)	(−0.09)	(0.01)	(0.02)
R-squared	.15	.18	.15	.14	.14	.14

NOTE: Figures in parentheses are *t*-values.

*.05 level

TABLE 5.14 Determinants of factor intensity on maize: OLS regression

Variable	Husband Labor/Hectare	Wife Labor/Hectare	Hired Labor/Hectare	Cash Inputs/Hectare
Constant	197.6	182.6	19.3	−114.1
	(1.29)	(1.08)	(0.21)	(−0.50)
Patrilocal/matrilineal tenure	30.4	134.7	−15.1	−6.4
	(0.26)	(1.06)	(−0.21)	(−0.04)
Matrilocal/patrilineal tenure	−18.1	−11.8	−3.7	16.3
	(−0.17)	(−0.10)	(−0.06)	(0.10)
Patrilocal/patrilineal tenure	−23.0	−40.0	33.6	72.7
	(−0.25)	(−0.40)	(0.61)	(0.54)
Immigrant/village headman tenure	−44.2	−48.9	51.7	−7.0
	(−0.35)	(−0.35)	(0.68)	(−0.04)
Farm size	0.6	−1.0	0.5	−1.1
	(0.13)	(−0.20)	(0.18)	(−0.17)
Male labor/land ratio	115.0*	106.2	6.5	140.1
	(1.97)	(1.65)	(0.18)	(1.62)
Female labor/land ratio	169.6*	152.0*	−23.9	−149.8
	(2.32)	(1.89)	(−0.54)	(−1.39)
Years farming in village	−2.0	0.8	−0.9	−2.8
	(−0.58)	(0.20)	(−0.44)	(−0.57)
Good soil fertility	−36.1	−43.8	1.4	629.6**
	(−0.55)	(−0.61)	(0.04)	(6.49)

Good soil texture	-50.4	-35.4	18.3	-0.1
	(-0.76)	(-0.49)	(0.45)	(-0.01)
Distance to market	8.2	7.9	1.5	0.4
	(1.24)	(1.07)	(0.36)	(0.04)
Hybrid maize	16.7	66.6	-14.1	174.3*
	(0.26)	(0.94)	(-0.36)	(1.84)
Village 1	-79.8	-121.4	-32.4	655.1
	(-0.56)	(-0.77)	(-0.37)	(3.11)
Village 2	-124.3	-139.0	-36.4	71.0
	(-0.80)	(-0.81)	(-0.38)	(0.31)
Village 3	-38.1	-76.1	4.0	161.2
	(-0.30)	(-0.55)	(0.05)	(0.87)
Village 4	-25.1	79.9	-39.4	-22.5
	(-0.15)	(0.44)	(-0.39)	(-0.09)
Village 5	-331.6*	-268.6	-9.0	193.8
	(-2.05)	(-1.51)	(-0.09)	(0.81)
Village 6	-48.2	-72.2	76.0	150.0
	(-0.40)	(-0.54)	(1.03)	(0.84)
Village 7	-90.6	-115.6	159.5	199.1
	(-0.63)	(-0.73)	(1.82)	(0.94)
R-squared	.31	.27	.12	.42

NOTE: Figures in parentheses are t-values.

*.05 level

**.01 level

TABLE 5.15 Determinants of factor intensity on tobacco: OLS regression

Variable	Husband Labor/Hectare	Wife Labor/Hectare	Hired Labor/Hectare	Cash Inputs/Hectare
Constant	582.5	573.4	46.8	818.0
	(2.83)	(2.77)	(0.32)	(1.06)
Patrilocal/matrilineal tenure	−76.8	−26.3	−86.6	353.9
	(−0.48)	(−0.16)	(−0.76)	(0.59)
Matrilocal/patrilineal tenure	−8.5	−42.5	−5.9	−15.9
	(−0.06)	(−0.28)	(−0.06)	(−0.03)
Patrilocal/patrilineal tenure	−125.4	−199.8	−62.0	−107.6
	(−0.96)	(−1.51)	(−0.66)	(−0.22)
Immigrant/village headman tenure	−242.2	−293.6*	−134.7	318.3
	(−1.41)	(−1.70)	(−1.10)	(0.55)
Farm size	−6.8	−8.7	2.0	8.8
	(−1.02)	(−1.28)	(0.42)	(0.35)
Male labor/land ratio	74.6	37.2	−23.1	717.8*
	(0.91)	(0.45)	(−0.39)	(2.32)
Female labor/land ratio	43.9	57.0	−34.6	−465.4
	(0.44)	(0.56)	(−0.48)	(−1.23)
Years farming in village	0.8	3.1	1.9	12.6
	(0.17)	(0.68)	(0.59)	(0.75)

Good soil fertility	43.5	101.6	9.6	731.4*
	(0.42)	(0.98)	(0.13)	(1.88)
Good soil texture	-14.9	-14.3	-24.7	5.7
	(-0.17)	(-0.17)	(-0.40)	(0.02)
Distance to market	-4.0	-2.5	5.3	-49.2
	(-0.43)	(-0.27)	(0.80)	(-1.41)
Village 1	-94.7	-65.5	52.0	-220.1
	(-0.49)	(-0.34)	(0.38)	(-0.30)
Village 2	-263.6	-264.5	-60.9	-822.6
	(-1.34)	(-1.34)	(-0.43)	(-1.11)
Village 3	-48.7	-68.4	72.4	31.1
	(-0.29)	(-0.41)	(0.61)	(0.05)
Village 4	-95.0	-2.7	-88.1	-170.4
	(-0.42)	(-0.01)	(-0.55)	(-0.20)
Village 5	-94.6	-90.9	-29.2	1337.9
	(-0.45)	(-0.43)	(-0.20)	(1.71)
Village 6	-60.7	-58.0	105.9	-115.0
	(-0.38)	(-0.36)	(0.92)	(-0.19)
Village 7	-98.7	-113.5	222.5	899.5
	(-0.53)	(-0.60)	(1.66)	(1.27)
R-squared	.14	.16	.12	.20

NOTE: Figures in parentheses are t-values.

*.05 level

ple, the extra labor required for harvesting and drying tobacco when yields are high). Purchased input use was higher for hybrid maize than for local maize (about $12 per hectare), but as indicated earlier, these added inputs did not generate sufficiently higher returns. We believe that this is primarily because fertilizer prices were too high relative to maize prices.

The single statistically significant result among the mode of land acquisition variables is that wives in immigrant households expended less labor per hectare on tobacco compared with those in matrilocal/matrilineal situations.[22] Although one may expect a high effort level from women residing in their own village, it is not clear why the difference is significant only in this pairwise comparison. Reviewing other results from the tobacco regressions, we find that the household endowment of labor relative to land is not related to family labor intensity in contrast to the case for maize. This indicates that tobacco receives a priority for labor allocation within households endowed with smaller labor/land ratio. Farm size was not significantly related to input use, suggesting once again scale neutrality of efficiency in both maize and tobacco production.

Summary and Conclusions for Intensive Study

The dynamism of the agricultural sector as catalyzed by the removal of the restriction against smallholder tobacco growing has provided a very relevant testing ground for the influence of tenure on farmer decisionmaking. Our site comprises nearly all the possible land transfer mechanisms witnessed in wider areas of Malawi. Our results, in principle, can be extended beyond the confines of our study zone.

In terms of impacts on investment, we found that after controlling for other factors, farmers operating land acquired through patrilocal/patrilineal means compared with those acquiring land through matrilocal/matrilineal means were (a) adopting tobacco farming more quickly, (b) cultivating tobacco on larger areas of their farms, (c) more likely to invest in destumping, and (d) more likely to invest in tree planting. The results for other types of investments gave similar signs, but with lower statistical significance. Together, these findings support the hypotheses raised in this chapter and by others that the incentives for investment provided by the matrilocal/matrilineal tenure arrangement are weaker (for males who are key decisionmakers) than those in patrilineal descent systems.

Despite differences in longer-term investments, we found no differences in efficiency of plot-level crop production across the different modes of land acquisition. This is not surprising given that the types of land improvements that were affected by these arrangements may not have directly affected crop productivity. Once adopted, both the maize and tobacco production systems appear

---

22. When the predicted lease variable is included, the only change among tenure security variables is that the wives are found to work less on tobacco in immigrant households as compared with matrilocal/matrilineal households.

to be driven by short-term inputs yielding short-term benefits, thus implying that tenure will not play a major role. However, since tobacco is far more profitable than maize and grown more widely under the patrilineal system, it is clear that the average profit per farming area should be greater under this system.

The higher profitability of tobacco production as compared with maize, the widespread adoption of tobacco farming by smallholders, and the lack of scale economies in its production imply that the state's abolition of restrictions on to-bacco production by smallholders was justified. Furthermore, the lack of impact of lease on the profitability of tobacco production suggests that neither the creation of large leaseholders nor land titling will contribute to the enhancement of farming efficiency, not to mention their adverse impacts on social equity.

Another important finding in this study is the lack of significant impact of hybrid maize on profitability, which is in sharp contrast with the expansion reported by Smale (1995) and the reported success of the maize Green Revolution in neighboring countries, such as Zimbabwe (Eicher 1995). The impediment to achieving high payoff from hybrid maize is likely to be the unfavorable relative price of maize to fertilizer, which has dropped since the early 1990s in Malawi and in some other countries following liberalization of exchange markets, such as Zambia (Rusike et al. 1997).

Policy Implications

It will be beneficial to review briefly the major findings from the empirical research in order to develop policy recommendations. At the community level, population density was found to have its anticipated positive effect on the conversion of land into agriculture. However, interestingly, neither population density nor growth necessarily led to decreased yields or tree cover, implying that it is the quest for farm land, rather than local demand for fuelwood and other products, that leads to loss of tree cover. The weakening of the population effect on tree cover and yields is encouraging and suggests that, to some extent, some induced responses are occurring within communities.

We found that no particular customary tenure system could be singled out as providing poor incentives for long-term management of land and tree resources. However, our study has found evidence to suggest that tenure factors play a role on the demand side of the equation. There has been widespread conversion of woodlands throughout our study sites, demonstrating the lack of common property management of these resources. We found that tree density in remaining woodlands is lower in some areas where there appear to be some changes to traditional tenure systems from migration. There are likely to be more of these types of areas as extreme population densities in some areas force people to migrate. Thus, there will be an increased need for local institutions to develop or strengthen to ensure that natural resources are managed for the social good.

Connectivity to markets could play a role in raising long-term benefits from resources and improving household incentives to manage them. We found that proximity to major urban areas was positively associated with yield change and at the same time did not lead to degradation of tree resources or woodlands over the study period. Such a finding is similar to that found for Uganda (Chapter 6), where market integration was linked to significant tree-planting activities by households. The fear that infrastructure development will have deleterious effects on the environment is not supported by our analysis at two points in time, though this requires continued monitoring. There is clearly a role for governments to play here, and increased market connection can be a strategy to reduce poverty while simultaneously promoting natural resource management.

Although tree planting on farms has shown little movement in the aggregate, there seems to be better scope for increasing tree density on farms than on woodlands, where areas and tree densities have displayed a rapid decline. Aside from improved incentives to plant and manage trees on individual farms, the simple fact that most of the landscape (the north excepted) is already under agriculture leads us to this conclusion. But growing trees on farms in Malawi does not seem to be straightforward as noted by Dewees (1995). Our study found no perceptible increase in tree cover on agricultural land over the study period. This gives cause for concern because with the widespread uptake of tobacco by smallholders, demand for poles has increased sharply and pressure on remaining woodlands intensified. Impediments in terms of the flows of information and tree germplasm must be addressed.

What are the possible implications for land tenure reform as it pertains to improved investment on agricultural land? From a policy point of view, direct interventions aimed at the traditional tenure systems themselves would be difficult and risky and likely not a direction worth pursuing. First, customary land tenure institutions are so complex, diverse, and elusive that an appropriate intervention scheme can hardly be designed. Second, tenure systems are evolving toward the patrilocal/patrilineal arrangement without direct government intervention. Based on efficiency objectives, this is an appropriate direction in which to move, especially because significant productivity increases are required to affect the already high poverty rates. Most likely this can be hastened through the promotion of profitable investment opportunities. The fact that the patrilocal/patrilineal system has fostered adoption of the more profitable tobacco-farming system suggests that further transformation of customary land tenure institutions toward the patrilineal direction will take place. Such a tendency is likely to be strengthened, as payoffs to tree planting and other long-term investments increase with increasing scarcity of trees, land, and other natural resources. It is therefore expected that external support for these investments will bring about not only direct private benefits but also indirect benefits of transforming customary tenure institutions, aside from the external benefits of improving the natural resource base in a resource poor economy.

References

Besley, T. 1995. Property rights and investment incentives. *Journal of Political Economy* 103:903–937.

Blanc, F., R. Mathewman, A. Soldan, T. Norman, D. Chilombo, and M. Edelsten. 1996. A survey of value and utilization of cattle among smallholders in Central Malawi. *Journal of Farming Systems Research-Extension* 6:67–80.

Bojo, J. 1994. The cost of land degradation from a national perspective: An assessment of African Evidence. Paper presented at the Eighth International Soil Conservation Conference, December 4–8, New Delhi, India.

Boserup, E. 1965. *The conditions of agricultural growth: The economics of agrarian change under population pressure.* London: George Allen and Unwin.

Christiansen, R. 1984. The pattern of internal migration in response to structural change in Malawi, 1966–77. *Development and Change* 15:125–151.

Clarke, J., W. Cavendish, and C. Coote. 1996. Rural households and miombo woodlands: Use, value, and management. In *The miombo in transition: Woodlands and welfare in Africa,* ed. B. Campbell. Bogor, Indonesia: Center for International Forestry Research.

Coote, H. C., J. M. Luhanga, and J. D. Lowore. 1993a. Community use and management of indigenous forests in Malawi: The case of chemba village forest area. FRIM Report No. 93006. Forestry Research Institute of Malawi, Zomba, Malawi.

———. 1993b. Community use and management of indigenous forests in Malawi: The case of three villages in the Blantyre City Fuelwood Project Area. FRIM Report No. 93007. Forestry Research Institute of Malawi, Zomba, Malawi.

Dewees, P. A. 1995. Trees on farms in Malawi: Private investment, public policy, and farmer choice. *World Development* 23:1085–1102.

Dickerman, C., and P. Bloch. 1991. Land tenure and agricultural productivity in Malawi. LTC Paper 143. Land Tenure Center, Madison, Wisconsin.

Eicher, C. 1995. Zimbabwe's maize-based green revolution: Preconditions for replication. *World Development* 23 (5): 805–818.

Feder, G., T. Onchan, Y. Chalamwong, and C. Hongladaron. 1988. *Land policies and farm productivity in Thailand.* Baltimore: Johns Hopkins University Press.

French, D. 1986. Confronting an unsolvable problem: Deforestation in Malawi. *World Development* 14:531–540.

Fujisaka, S., W. Bell, N. Thomas, L. Hurtado, and E. Crawford. 1996. Slash and burn agriculture, conversion to pasture, and deforestation in two Brazilian Amazon colonies. *Agricultural Ecosystems and Environment* 59:115–130.

Green, R., and V. Mkandawire. 1997. Land relations and management of trees in Malawi: Land use change determination. Research report prepared for the International Centre for Research in Agroforestry, Nairobi, Kenya.

Hayami, Y., and V. W. Ruttan. 1985. *Agricultural development: An international perspective.* Baltimore: Johns Hopkins University Press.

Hirschmann, D., and M. Vaughan. 1983. Food production and income generation in a matrilineal society: Rural women in Zomba, Malawi. *Journal of Southern African Studies* 10:86–99.

———. 1984. Women farmers of Malawi: Food production in Zomba district. Institute of International Studies, University of California, Berkeley.

Hyde, W. F., G. S. Amacher, and W. Magrath. 1996. Deforestation and forest land use: Theory, evidence, and policy implications. *World Bank Research Observer* 11:223–248.

Hyde, W. F., and J. E. Seve. 1993. The economic role of wood products in tropical deforestation: The severe example of Malawi. *Forest Ecology and Management* 57:283–300.

Kydd, J. 1989. Maize research in Malawi: Lessons from failure. *Journal of International Development* 1:112–144.

Kydd, J., and R. Christiansen. 1982. Structural changes in Malawi since independence: Consequences of a development strategy based on large-scale agriculture. *World Development* 10:355–375.

Lowore, J. D., H. C. Coote, P. G. Abott, G. B. Chapola, and L. N. Malembo. 1995. Community use and management of indigenous forests and forest products in Malawi: The case of four villages close to Chimaliro Forest Reserve. FRIM Report No. 93008. Forestry Research Institute of Malawi, Zomba, Malawi.

Malawi Government. 1984. National sample survey of agriculture 1980/81, volume II. National Statistical Office, Zomba, Malawi.

Matose, F., and L. Wily. 1996. Institutional arrangements governing the use and management of miombo woodlands. In *The miombo in transition: Woodlands and welfare in Africa,* ed. B. Campbell. Bogor, Indonesia: Center for International Forestry Research.

Mendelsohn, Robert. 1994. Property rights and tropical deforestation. *Oxford Economic Papers* 46 (5): 750–756.

Mkandawire, R. M. 1983–84. Customary land, the state, and agrarian change in Malawi: The case of the Chewa peasantry in the Lilongwe rural development project. *Journal of Contemporary African Studies* 3:109–128.

———. 1992. The land question and agrarian change in Malawi: The changing dual character of Malawi's agriculture. University of Malawi, Lilongwe. Mimeo.

Nankumba, J. S. 1994. The potential of agroforestry technology under customary land tenure in Malawi: A case study of Lilongwe district. Bunda College, University of Malawi and International Centre for Research in Agroforestry. Mimeo.

Place, F., and P. Hazell. 1993. Productivity effects of indigenous land tenure systems in Sub-Saharan Africa. *American Journal of Agricultural Economics* 75:10–19.

Place, F., and K. Otsuka. 2001a. Population, land tenure, and natural resource management: The case of customary land areas in Malawi. *Journal of Environmental Economics and Management* 41 (1): 13–32.

———. 2001b. Tenure, agricultural investment, and productivity in customary tenure sector of Malawi. *Economic Development and Cultural Change* 50 (1).

Pryor, F. 1990. *The political economy of poverty, equity, and growth: Malawi and Madagascar.* Oxford: Oxford University Press.

Rusike, J., T. Reardon, J. Howard, and V. Kelly. 1997. Developing cereal-based demand for fertiliser among smallholders in southern Africa: Lessons learned and implications for other African regions. Food Security II Policy Synthesis Number 30. Mimeo.

Sahn, D. E., and J. Arulpragasam. 1991a. Development through dualism? Land tenure, policy, and poverty in Malawi. Cornell Food and Nutrition Policy Working Paper No. 9. Cornell University, Ithaca, New York.

————. 1991b. The stagnation of smallholder agriculture in Malawi: A decade of structural adjustment. *Food Policy* 16 (3): 219–234.

Smale, M. 1995. Maize is life: Malawi's delayed green revolution. *World Development* 23 (5): 819–831.

World Bank. 1996. *African development indicators 1996.* Washington, D.C.: World Bank.

World Resources Institute. 1994. *World resources 1994–95.* Oxford: Oxford University Press.

Zeller, M., A. Diagne, and V. Kisyombe. 1997. Adoption of hybrid maize and tobacco in Malawi's smallholder farms: Effects on household food security. In *Food security and innovations: Successes and lessons learned,* ed. F. Heidues and A. Fadani. Frankfurt: Peter Lang Press.

PART III

Impacts of Land Tenure Policy

6 Customary and Private Land Management in Uganda

FRANK PLACE, JOE SSENTEZA,
AND KEIJIRO OTSUKA

Uganda's potential for agricultural production, because of its inherently good soils and dependable rainfall, has long been recognized. In the early 1960s the country produced enough food for its population and exported other agricultural commodities (World Bank 1993). But the promise of sustained agricultural and economic growth was left unfulfilled by a long period of political instability beginning in the late 1970s. Thus, in 1995, Uganda ranked 13th poorest among Sub-Saharan African countries, in terms of average per capita income (World Resources Institute et al. 1998). The overwhelming majority of its people, about 90 percent, continue to reside in rural areas, and it is estimated that about 50–55 percent of them are poor. Therefore, the bulk of the poor in Uganda are dependent to a large extent on crop land and other natural resources for their livelihoods. In a few areas, expansion of agricultural land remains an option, but in most cases, poverty alleviation will require intensification strategies.

Within agriculture, productivity of farmers appears to be much less than its potential. Although increasing in recent years, food production per capita in the mid-1990s was still below its level in the early 1970s. Yields of several crops on-station far surpass those on farmers' fields (MPED 1996). Among the reasons for this are constraints on information flow to farmers (for example, poor extension services), absence of rural credit, and thus little use of improved seed or fertilizer. In fact, Ugandan farmers rank at the very bottom in the world in terms of fertilizer use per hectare or per capita. Furthermore, even though investments in infrastructure have been made, the ratio of output to input prices at the farmgate are low in many areas of Uganda (MPED 1996). At the same time, some of the traditional crops grown, such as banana and cassava, have been attacked by pests and diseases. There is some room for optimism, however. Uptake of high-value crops such as vanilla and passionfruit has increased, and farmers have increased production of maize to capitalize on increased regional market opportunities.

We are particularly grateful for valuable comments on an earlier version by W. Kisamba-Mugerwa. This chapter draws partly on Place and Otsuka (2001).

The prolonged focus on extensive agricultural production systems affected other natural resources. It is estimated that tropical high forest area was 7,000 square kilometers in 1990, representing about 3 percent of land area (World Bank 1993), while Langdale-Brown (1960) had estimated dense forest area to be more than 11,000 square kilometers in 1958 and more than 25,000 square kilometers in the mid-1920s. More recently, the annual rate of deforestation (including all types of natural forests) had been estimated to be about 0.9 percent between 1980 and 1990 (World Bank 1994). Given that the area under closed forest remains small, concern about the sustainability of woody biomass naturally directs one to the more abundant agriculture land, woodland, bushland, and wetland areas found on the landscape. As is documented in most countries in Sub-Saharan Africa, the area under agriculture has expanded significantly at the expense of formerly wooded areas (Hosier 1989). The other major demand on woody vegetation has been for charcoal to satisfy urban commercial and household needs. It is expected that rural households will be called on to supply an increasing proportion of the demand for wood products in Uganda.

The Museveni government came into power in 1986 and shortly thereafter embarked on a comprehensive structural adjustment program. A key feature of this program was to liberalize foreign exchange markets in order to encourage exports and attract foreign investment. Coupled with this adjustment was a relatively sound monetary policy and large inflows of donor money, and consequently price levels and currency rates were relatively stable throughout the 1990s. A large amount of foreign aid has been used to rehabilitate the woeful communication, energy, water, and transportation infrastructure. Other money has been used to rejuvenate agricultural research and extension.

One of the features of the Museveni government has been to decentralize many of the functions and responsibilities of government to local levels. For instance, people elect their representatives down to municipalities and district levels, and these officials have hiring power over several key positions, including extension agents. A pilot project that allows for more local financial autonomy is being tested in several districts. This fundamental change might be expected to benefit agriculture and natural resource management, both of which would appear to be important issues among the rural voting population.

The primary objective of this chapter is to examine the effect of tenure systems on the management of land and tree resources in Uganda. For land management, we focus on community-level choices of land use and tree cover and on household-level choices of land use, investment (including tree planting), and productivity. In doing so, we also identify the effect of other factors, for example, population pressure, on these same land management variables. A secondary objective is more basically to provide estimates of land use and tree cover change in Uganda, since quantitative data in this area are virtually nonexistent.

This chapter is organized as follows. The next section discusses the major tenure systems in Uganda and those that are observed in the study sites. We then describe the sites for the extensive and intensive studies. Discussion of the extensive study is subdivided into sections on hypotheses and econometric modeling; definition and description of key variables; econometric analysis; and summary and conclusions. The section following this presents the intensive study in much the same manner. A discussion of policy implications emanating from both studies is the focus of the final section.

Tenure Systems in Uganda

Across our study sites in Uganda, several land tenure systems were prevalent before 1975, and despite the de jure nationalization of all land in that year, the same tenure systems are recognized both in the perceptions of the population and in formal land tenure reform debates. The most widespread of the tenure regimes is customary land tenure, which is virtually the only tenure system operating in our eastern and northern sites. Customary lands in our sites were traditionally governed by clans that allocated plots of land to members. In many of the sites by the early 1900s, households had settled on lands and acquired strong permanent rights to specific parcels (Bazaara 1992). In some areas, power shifted from clans to chiefs following colonial intervention, but in 1966 kingdoms were formally abolished by the Ugandan government, and this led to loss of control over land by traditional authorities in some cases. Some urban elites seized this opportunity to claim customary lands, particularly those close to urban areas, through the newly developed Land Commission. All customary systems follow patrilineal rules of descent, and in our study region inheritance is the most common method of land acquisition.

In the Buganda region of central Uganda, the major tenure system is the *mailo* tenure system. Vast tracts of land, measured in units of square miles, were given to notables and elites by the colonialists beginning in the early 1900s and were known as private *mailo* land. A large area of land (958 square miles) went to the chief of the Buganda, known as the *kabaka*. Owners, lacking labor to till such large land areas, had received fees and rents by settling tenants (*kibanja*) on their land. Subsequently, tenants acquired legal protection against eviction in the 1928 Busuulu and Envujjo law that required landlords to pay tenants full compensation for any investments made. Furthermore, tenants benefited from the abolishment of rents under the 1975 land reform. Although only *mailo* owners may acquire titles to the land, many tenants have very strong rights over land they occupy, including the right to bequeath. Today, some *mailo* owners occupy and farm their land; however, in many areas, occupation of land is overwhelmingly by *kibanja* tenants

Other nonallocated land in the Buganda region was initially classified as Crown Land and included land considered as "waste." During the reign of traditional rulers, this land was loosely administered by chiefs and was akin to customary land, though Muhereza (1992) describes the management of this land as resembling an open-access resource. Settlers on these lands in the Buganda region face a different type of tenure security risk than do settlers on customary land in other regions because the Buganda region surrounds the capital, Kampala. The insecurity arises from the allocation of leaseholds on public land to wealthy individuals and elites without regard to other occupants on the land. In some highly publicized cases, these new settlers have evicted families ("squatters" under the law) that had occupied the land for several generations. It is difficult to know how many evictions there have been, but the local populations are well aware of them. Because of the increased potential for conflict over rights to these lands, we distinguish them from the customary areas in the eastern and northern sites and refer to such land as "public" land. Although it is clear that land rights of occupants of public land are weak vis-à-vis land authorities, the extent to which individual rights are established and respected by occupants is less clear.

Within each of these tenure systems, a rightful landholder may apply for a formal lease from the state. In doing so, the tenure over that land is transformed into the legally recognized category of leasehold. In reality, few leaseholds are taken out by occupants of customary land, and leaseholds are more common among *mailo* owners and recent settlers on public lands.

In the 1990s, the Ugandan government put into place a decentralized administrative network of Resistance Councils. The chairmen of these councils were often former traditional leaders, and they are now key players in land affairs, such as settling many types of disputes. The formalization of tenure administration at the local level has not led to significant transformations of tenure systems, nor has it prevented changes originating from the central government, such as the awarding of titles to land already occupied by other households. After this study was completed, a new Land Act was submitted to parliament and later enacted. Although this did not affect our empirical analyses, we shall refer to this in the policy section.

A review of the literature on the effect of tenure on natural resource management and agricultural productivity found only a few relevant empirical studies. A study was conducted in *mailo* and non-*mailo* areas of Luwero and Masaka Districts in the mid- to late 1980s. Kisamba-Mugerwa (1989) found that within *mailo* land there was considerable uncertainty as to future land rights. They also found that on land occupied by tenants it was the owner who especially felt insecure about long-term land rights, because of possible government land tenure reform favoring tenants. In contrast, they found little insecurity of losing rights in nearby lands operated under indigenous systems. Despite the existence of a "private" *mailo* tenure system, land rights are not necessarily individualized. A study in Mpigi District by Aluma et al. (1995) found that individual rights of sale were claimed by only 55 percent of *mailo* households. Studies of the effect of differences in tenure systems and tenure security on agricultural investment and productivity are lacking (the study by

Kisamba-Mugerwa [1989] is an exception). Although *mailo* tenant farmers have a strong perception that timber trees cannot be planted because the landlord will claim ownership (Nielsen, Guinand, and Okorio 1995), Place (1995) found that some types of tree planting were more common on *mailo* tenant farms than on *mailo* owner farms.

Study Sites

Extensive Study

The data for this study come from 64 parishes in 10 districts of Uganda (Figure 6.1).[1] The 10 districts form a circle around Lake Kyoga in east-central Uganda. These sites were selected for several reasons: presence of differing population densities, different tenure regimes, relative homogeneity of topography and agrozone, and availability of remote sensing material at two points in time. It is also important to note that our sites are largely free from organized tree-planting interventions, so that changes in tree resources at the level of a parish have not been exogenously influenced by government, nongovernmental organizations, and the like.

The sampling procedure was stratified random. Five parishes were selected from each district with the exception of Luwero, Mukono, and Kiboga, for which a greater number were selected to ensure an adequate number of *mailo* and public tenure cases. The sampling frame excluded all parishes above the size of 150 square kilometers to ensure that parish-level field data were meaningful (which eliminated only 2.1 percent of parishes across the 10 districts). A further stratification rule based on availability of recent aerial photos was established, but a random sample provided for sufficient numbers of parishes covered by aerial photographs, and the rule was invoked in only two parishes in the district of Mukono.

Although there are more subtle variances, the sites fall broadly within two agroecological zones. A drier zone cuts across the northern sections of Kiboga, Luwero, Mukono, Kamuli, and Iganga Districts, all located south of Lake Kyoga. Drier zones are also found as one moves to the north of Apac and Lira Districts. In some of the drier areas, soils tend to have higher sand to clay composition. Conversely, despite the wide geographical area covered by the study, the degree of variation in topography is quite low, with flat and gentle sloping areas predominant.

Population densities range widely; the highest 1991 population density (the most recent census year) recorded is 629/square kilometer in Bumasobo Parish in Mbale District, and the lowest is 26/square kilometer in Mugongo

---

1. The 10 districts are Mukono, Kamuli, Iganga, Tororo, Mbale, Kumi, Lira, Apac, Kiboga, and Luwero.

FIGURE 6.1 Location of study sites in Uganda

Parish in northern Mukono District. The percentage of urban population in or adjacent to the parishes is low, and agriculture is the main activity in all parishes. Within agriculture, coffee, maize, and plantain dominate in the more favorable areas; cassava, beans, and millet become more important in the drier areas. The importance of livestock varies considerably, with higher densities per land area (but lower numbers per household) found in the heavily populated parishes.

Intensive Study

We selected a border area between Mukono District and neighboring Kamuli District as the intensive study site. *Mailo* and public land are found in Mukono District, while customary land is found in Kamuli District. This particular east-west band contains sites that are nearly the same in terms of agroecological potential, access to roads, and population density. The Nile River runs between the two districts, and a lack of bridges means that there is relatively little exchange between the two districts despite their close proximity. We selected two parishes with similar flat to mildly sloping topography and located in a relatively high bimodal rainfall band suitable for coffee and plantain production. It was felt that if tenure effects on farm land management were important, they would be most pronounced in areas with higher agroecological potential and population density. The sites are Nabalanga Parish in a *mailo*/public land area and Bupadengo Parish in a customary area. Average annual rainfall is between 1,225 and 1,275 millimeters in the sites. The 1991 population density was 169 in Nabalanga and 233 in Bupadengo. Bupadengo is positioned along a tarmac road, and Nabalanga is a 7-kilometer drive from a tarmac road. Nabalanga is closer to Kampala, at 50 kilometers, than Bupadengo, which is approximately 116 kilometers from the capital city. Cattle numbers are low in both areas.

The extensive study found that at the parish level broad land use had stabilized in Nabalanga, where the share of land under agriculture was .74 in 1960 and .72 in 1995. The bulk of the remaining area was wetland. In Bupadengo, the share of land under agriculture moved upward from .74 in 1960 to .80 in 1995. Tree cover estimates over the whole parish decreased in both parishes over the 1960–95 period. In Nabalanga, the proportion of land area under tree canopy cover declined from .30 to .24. In Bupadengo, the decrease was more pronounced, from .43 to .21. Within the agricultural land use category, tree cover also declined in each site (contrary to most of the other sites). In Nabalanga, the decrease was larger, from .32 to .18, while in Bupadengo, the decrease was from .30 to .22. Because there were no tree planting projects in either location, comparisons of tree management are not distorted by this external factor.

A random sampling procedure for selecting households was followed in the customary sites, where all households operate under a customary tenure system. The only stratification made was on village within a parish, and households were selected from three villages in each.[2] In the *mailo* areas, a list of households was drawn up for each village found along with their tenure status: *mailo* owner, *mailo* tenant, or public land occupant. A sample of households from each was randomly chosen.

In total, 47 and 50 households were interviewed in Nabalanga and Bupadengo, respectively. Only 15 households operated more than one parcel (that is, contiguous areas of land acquired at the same time and through a single mode of acquisition), and each was enumerated for size, acquisition method, and land rights. Parcels were divided into numerous fields devoted to crop enterprises. All fields were enumerated for tree planting. For crop production inputs and outputs, the main coffee field was enumerated along with a random selection of two to three other farm fields.

---

2. Each parish had between four and six villages.

Extensive Study

Defining Key Variables

The baseline land use and tree cover data were generated from aerial photographs at a 1:30,000 scale taken mainly between 1955 and 1960. The source for the recent information for 42 parishes was also aerial photography. Aerial photographs at a scale of 1:60,000 taken in 1995 were used for 38 parishes, and 1:25,000 photos taken in 1989 were used for 4 parishes. Satellite images from 1989 were used for the remaining 22 parishes, which were not included in any recent aerial photography. All remote sensing data were taken during the dry season, and thus there was no interference from clouds. The mainly flat terrain also made photo interpretation relatively trouble-free. Any ambiguities were rectified through groundtruthing by the field survey team.

Details of the photo interpretation methodology can be found in Breyer (1996), but generally two types of data were generated. The first was a mapping of land use classes in all 64 parishes, using a 0.1 hectare minimum size of mapping unit. The land use classification scheme adopted distinguished between agricultural land, forests, plantations, woodland, bushland, grassland, wetland, urban land, barren land, and water. Forested land could be disaggregated into naturally stocked (virtually 100 percent canopy cover) or depleted forest (mainly 90 percent cover with a minimum of 80 percent). For our land use analysis, we use the term *forest* to include both natural forests and plantations, the latter of which was virtually nonexistent. Woodlands were nonagricultural lands on which tree cover of between 2 and 80 percent was found. A similar definition was used for bushland with the main difference that bushland contained woody vegetation primarily below 4 meters in height. However, since average height is rather difficult to confirm in aerial photo interpretation, woodlands and bushlands were later aggregated together in our analyses. Grasslands were areas with less than 2 percent woody vegetation. Land with vegetation cover similar to woodland, bushland, or grassland but that was within a visible field pattern was classified as agricultural land.

In the 42 parishes where recent aerial photographs were used, the woodland, bushland, and wetland classifications were further distinguished by four categories of tree cover density ranging from very dense (60–80 percent cover) to open (2–20 percent cover). For agricultural land, a second method was used to generate tree cover estimates involving a grid sampling of areas and the calculation of average tree cover from a number of sample observations.

Hence, for all 64 parishes, the area and proportion of land under the different land uses were calculated at two points in time. For the 42 parishes with recent aerial photo coverage, average parish tree cover could be assessed by taking a weighted average of tree cover in nonagricultural land (using tree cover classes) and tree cover in agricultural land (grid sample estimates). In nonagricultural land, these two types of variables were also calculated for each tenure classification within a parish after overlaying tenure boundaries on the land use maps. Tree canopy in agricultural land is estimated at only a parish level. The agricultural land samples were too costly to digitize, and consequently it proved very difficult to match samples with tenure boundaries in parishes with multiple tenures.

For our tenure variables, the general boundaries of the *mailo* tenure system are well known. To obtain more precise locations, we engaged our group respondents in drawing the boundaries between tenure systems in their parish using aerial photographs as aids. This proved to be quite informative and often involved traveling through the parish to engage additional key informants in discussions. In the end, the boundaries were drawn on sheets overlaid onto aerial photographs and digitized into a geographic information system database, so that they could be interacted with measures of land use and tree cover.

We classified tenure systems into three categories. The first is customary land, which is nearly all the land outside the *mailo*-area parishes. A second is *mailo* land, which constituted a large part of land area in the districts of Mukono, Luwero, Jinja, and Kiboga. The non-*mailo* land area within these four districts was classified as public land, comprising land formerly akin to customary land but that has recently been targeted by settlements of elites.

Description of Data

LAND USE AND TREE COVER VARIABLES. Table 6.1 shows some aggregate descriptive indicators pertaining to the land use variables. The mean share of agricultural land per parish increased from .57 to .70 between 1960 and 1995. The lowest share of agriculture recorded was .05 in 1960, but this increased to .15 by 1995. This expansion came largely at the expense of woodland and bushland, whose average share per parish fell from .28 to .18. Despite the fact that the large majority of parishes saw their share of woodlands decrease, nearly all parishes have some woodland or bushland remaining. The share of forested land fell by 50 percent, from .04 to .02 of total land area. In some cases, this reflected a complete depletion of forests—of 20 parishes with some forestland in 1960, 10 became completely deforested by 1995. There is significant variation in the current degree of woody vegetation and its change over time across the parishes. Taking the area under forest and woodland together, the absolute change in share of total parish area varies from + .28 to −.51.

Table 6.2 displays average tree cover per parish by broad land use category and for whole parishes after taking a weighted average. The average tree canopy cover proportion per parish was estimated to be .31 both in 1960 and in 1995 for the 42 parishes where the variable could be calculated. Tree densities conditional on broad land use categories were also relatively constant for the aggregate sample. However, in about 42 percent of parishes, the absolute

TABLE 6.1 Land use pattern in selected communities, 1960 and 1995

Land Use	Average Parish Share in 1960	Average Parish Share in 1995	Share Change Interval[a]	Most Positive Absolute Change in Share	Most Negative Absolute Change in Share
Agriculture	.57	.70	−.09 to +.46	.75	−.27
Forest	.04	.02	−.08 to .00	.01	−.71
Wood-, bush-, and grassland	.28	.18	−.31 to +.07	.27	−.55
Wetland	.11	.10	−.05 to +.02	.11	−.19

SOURCE: Extensive survey.

NOTE: $N = 64$.

[a]The interval that includes 80 percent of parishes.

TABLE 6.2 Tree cover pattern covered by recent aerial photos, 1960 and 1995

Land Use	Average Parish Share in 1960	Average Parish Share in 1995	Share Change Interval[a]	Most Positive Absolute Change in Share	Most Negative Absolute Change in Share
Agriculture	.23	.28	-.14 to +.31	.41	-.35
Forest	.94	.94	-.02 to .00	.10	-.05
Wood-, bush-, and grassland	.44	.42	-.19 to +.12	.31	-.35
Wetland	.21	.19	-.14 to +.16	.27	-.40
Average	.31	.31	-.05 to +.02	.30	-.36

SOURCE: Extensive survey.

NOTE: $N = 42$.

[a]The interval that includes 80 percent of parishes.

change in average tree cover was greater than plus or minus .10, and the range was from +.30 to −.36. Last, it is noteworthy to highlight the result that tree cover in agricultural land increased from .23 to .28.

Two points of clarification are worth noting about the observed aggregate tree canopy stability. First, canopy may not be an accurate measure of biomass. Large trees that are cut (for example, for charcoal) often grow back in several shoots that may form a wide canopy without a large woody biomass. Second, there is often a change in the composition of species, as is the case when land is converted from woodlands (for example, indigenous species such as *Combretum* spp.) to agroforestry or agricultural land (for instance, coffee, shade trees, and exotic fruits). Nonetheless, we believe that tree cover changes broadly capture trends of changes in biomass density. Particularly noteworthy is increased tree cover in agricultural land, which seems to have compensated, at least partly, for loss of biomass from conversion of nonagricultural land.

DRIVING FACTORS.   The variables hypothesized to be the main factors behind land use and tree cover change came principally from a survey instrument administered in each of 64 parishes. The respondents consisted of local leaders, respected elders, and agricultural officers. One meeting was often enough to obtain the necessary data, but in some cases the team traveled around to different parts of the parish to verify responses. A few variables, including soil type, rainfall, and population, were found from secondary sources The survey elicited information about infrastructure and distance to markets, ethnic composition and extent of in-migration, cropping and livestock activities, tree species composition, major tree-planting projects, and a set of tenure variables including rights over land and trees across broad tenure categories. Many variables captured both current and initial conditions in 1960.

Table 6.3 displays a general description of some of the important non-tenure variables hypothesized to affect land use and tree cover. The average population density among the parishes was 79 per square kilometer in 1960 and the range was from 9 to 461 (MFEP 1992). Population growth was high in all our sample parishes, with the mean annual growth rate on the order of 4.5 percent per year. As a result, the average population density increased to 164 in 1991. One of the reasons for the large increase is that central Uganda has in recent years been the major destination of migrants from the west (higher population densities) and the north (poor and risky agricultural environments). The extent to which this can continue in the future is questionable given the wide expansion of agriculture and reduced farm sizes. In terms of market integration, the two most important variables collected were 1960 distance to a tarmac road and distance to the major commercial center, Kampala. Several parishes were located on tarmac roads, and the mean and maximum distance to a tarmac road was 25 and 102 kilometers, respectively. The nearest parish to Kampala was 29 kilometers away, the mean distance was 181 kilometers, and the farthest was 435 kilometers.

TABLE 6.3 Key driving factors affecting land use and tree cover

Variable	Mean	Minimum	Maximum
1960 population density per km^2	79	9	461
1960–95 annual population growth (percentage)	4.5	−1.3	10.1
1960 distance to Kampala (km)	181	29	435
1960 distance to tarmac road	25	0	102
Long-term annual rainfall (mm)	1,230	1,070	1,575
Long-term number of dry days/year	82	43	123
Sandy soils (1 if yes)	.44	0	1
Coffee is a major crop (1 if yes)	.47	0	1

SOURCE: Extensive survey.

NOTE: $N = 64$.

The topography of the study sites was mainly flat or mildly sloping with the exception of only a handful of parishes in Mbale and Kiboga Districts. Soils were of two types, reddish brown clay-loams (56.2 percent) and those that were more sandy and shallow (Ollier et al. 1969). To assess climate, secondary data on average annual rainfall and the number of "dry days" (the number of days per year that are evaluated to be strictly unsuitable for crop growth) were obtained (FAO 1984). The average number of dry days ranged from a low of 43 to a high of 123 days, and average annual rainfall varied from 1,070 to 1,575 millimeters across the parishes, with the mean 1,230 millimeters. As far as tree characteristics are concerned, it is perhaps not surprising that in areas occupied by humans for several centuries, almost all the common trees found in the landscape coppice well (that is, regrow after cutting) as noncoppicing species would fail to reproduce. In virtually all parishes, respondents reported that the density of high-valued timber trees had fallen, and the median number per square kilometer fell from 47 to 18. Coffee was a significant crop in 30 parishes, or slightly under 50 percent. Our survey found that formally organized tree-planting projects (of noncoffee trees) occurred in only 7 parishes.

As discussed earlier, there were three main types of tenure regimes whose boundaries remained fixed throughout the study period in the study areas. Customary land was found in 37, or 57.8 percent, of the parishes (see Table 6.4). In 30 parishes, customary land covered the entire parish area and occupied about 50 percent of all land in the study area. The median farm size reported in customary areas in 1995 was 2 hectares. Table 6.4 shows that the percentage of land under agriculture was highest in customary tenure systems in both 1960 and 1995. Although this is consistent with our hypothesis that incentives to expand agriculture area and ease of doing so are strong under customary tenure systems, it is also true that higher population densities are observed in customary areas. We try to disentangle these effects in our econometric analysis below.

TABLE 6.4 Area and land use by type of tenure

Tenure Type	Percentage of Parishes Present	Percentage of Total Land Area	Percentage of Land in Agriculture in 1960	Percentage of Land in Agriculture in 1995
Customary	57.8	50.2	64.5	81.3
Mailo/lease	45.3	39.4	36.6	53.8
Public	37.5	10.4	19.1	28.0

SOURCE: Extensive survey.

NOTE: $N = 64$.

The *mailo* land tenure system was found in 29, or 45.3 percent, of parishes and constituted 39.4 percent of all land area in the study. Leasehold tenure was found in a handful of sites but constituted a large enough area for mapping in only two parishes. Because the characteristics of leasehold tenure are quite similar to those of *mailo* tenure (for example, large landowners, the majority of whom hold titles to land, and often with land leased to tenants), it is grouped together with *mailo* land for data analysis. There was considerable variation in the estimated proportion of *mailo* land occupied by owners and tenants in 1960 (ranging from 5 to 90 percent), but by 1995 tenants were reported to occupy the majority of *mailo* land in most parishes. Average farm size in 1995 was 2 hectares for tenants and 6 hectares for owner-cultivators. The median number of *mailo* owners in a parish was 12. Within *mailo* land, we also obtained estimates of the percentage of owners who were absentee. In 34 percent of *mailo* areas, virtually all *mailo* owners were resident, while the remaining two-thirds had moderate to high levels of absentee ownership.

Public land was found in 24, or 37.5 percent, of parishes, occupying 10.4 percent of total land area. Some public land remains gazetted or otherwise non-settled, but other public lands are occupied by households, some in government rice schemes (small plots) and others in more traditional farm settings (farms of a few acres). More recent government leasing of large tracts of land to elites had not occurred with any significance in our study sites. Of the three predominant tenure systems in the study areas, public land has the lowest share of agricultural land, though the rate of change over the 1960–95 period was high.

A series of questions about land rights were asked for all observed tenure categories. In all tenure categories, individual rights to plant trees and to cut nontimber trees were ubiquitous. The only tree right to exhibit much variation concerned the right to cut timber trees (for example, *Chlorophora excelsa*), which reflected differences in awareness that some of these tree species are legally protected. As for land rights, in only a few cases was the unrestricted right of sale observed. In the case of customary tenure, the unrestricted right of sale was completely absent, and consultation with extended family members was required. Free grazing, hence less exclusive rights to land, was reported for 32 percent of customary areas, 66 percent of *mailo* areas, and 42 percent of public lands. The higher percentage within the *mailo* tenure category likely reflects the fact that large and often absentee owners are unable to enforce exclusion rights.

Econometric Analysis

ESTIMATION METHODS.   We estimate the following equation to assess the effect of tenure, population, and other factors on the conversion of land into agriculture:

$$\Delta A/\text{PA} = f\,(\text{TEN, DIST, } N_0/\text{PA}, \Delta N/N, A_0/\text{PA}, E), \tag{1}$$

where the dependent variable is the change in agricultural area (ΔA) normalized by total parish area (PA) to adjust for differences in the total size of parishes. This equation corresponds to equation (2) in Chapter 2. The variable TEN captures the proportions of customary and *mailo* land tenure areas contrasted to the proportion of public land, which is the base and omitted case. These are further interacted with measures of exclusivity of tenure and, in the case of *mailo* land, the degree of absenteeism among *mailo* owners. There are two distance variables to represent DIST, one to the nearest tarmac road and another one to Kampala. Population density in the initial period (N_0/PA) is entered along with population growth ($\Delta N/N$). A_0/PA represents the initial share of parish land area under agriculture. Finally, E captures variables such as soil type, annual average rainfall, and number of days unsuitable for cultivation.

Equation (1) can be estimated using the full sample of 64 parishes. We assume a linear specification except as noted for population density (N_0/PA), for which we add a square term in order to test for positive but decelerating impacts of population pressure on the expansion of agricultural land due to the limitation of cultivable area. We hypothesize that population growth and environmental factors conducive to agricultural production have positive effects on the expansion of agricultural land. If the effect of distance is dominated by differences in wage rates, then greater distance (lower wage) will be associated with greater conversion of land. However, if distance is capturing effects of prices of outputs, the effect is somewhat less determinant, depending on ease of marketability of major products. Analogous to equation (1), we specify the functions explaining changes in tree density on agricultural (Δd_A) and non-agricultural land (Δd_N) as:

$$\Delta d_A = \Delta d_A\,(\text{TEN, DIST, } N_0/\text{PA}, \Delta N/N, A_0/\text{PA}, d_{N0}, d_{A0}, E) \tag{2}$$

$$\Delta d_N = \Delta d_N\,(\text{TEN, DIST, } N_0/\text{PA}, \Delta N/N, A_0/\text{PA}, d_{N0}, d_{A0}, E) \tag{3}$$

where the tree densities in the initial period (d_{N0}, d_{A0}) are included to test the hypothesis that lower tree density on nonagricultural land, as well as on agricultural land, induces tree planting on agricultural land and more strict control of tree felling on nonagricultural land. It is also of interest to assess the impacts of population pressure on the tree densities on agricultural and nonagricultural land. In estimating equations (2) and (3), we used tree canopy cover as a proxy for tree density. Since data on tree cover are available only for 42 parishes where aerial photos are available, we used the subsample for the estimation. In the case of equation (3), tree cover data are available conditional on land tenure system within parishes. We therefore use 67 observations for the actual estimation and use dummy variables for customary and *mailo* tenure systems (rather than the percentages used for the parish-level regressions of equations [1] and [2]).

Migration is common within our study sites, particularly within broad ethnic group boundaries (for example, the Busoga), and, hence, population growth could be considered as endogenous. We therefore apply the two-stage least squares (2SLS) regression functions in addition to the ordinary least squares regression in the estimation of equations (1) to (3).

RESULTS.   The results from the regressions of change in share of agricultural land are given in Table 6.5. The models were based on observations from all 64 parishes, and the resulting adjusted R-squared values were very encouraging, in the range of .60.[3] Each of the models are 2SLS regressions with population growth treated as endogenous, and each differs in terms of the specification of the tenure variables, as explained later. The results in Table 6.5 indicate that the change in agricultural land share is affected by land tenure regime. Customary tenure is positively related (in comparison to public land) to agricultural land conversion, in all models. This could imply the existence of weak indigenous institutional management of lands in which land clearing is not regulated. It could, however, also indicate a purposeful strategy on the part of indigenous institutions to respond to demands for agricultural land by its ever increasing constituents. The finding that "exclusive customary tenure" led to faster agricultural expansion than "more open access customary tenure" suggests that management of agricultural land is more profitable under the former than the latter owing to the difference in tenure security or the degree of individualization of land rights. There is no significant difference in land use change between *mailo* and public tenure systems in any of the models. There was further no significant difference in the change in agricultural land share within *mailo* areas differing on the basis of exclusivity of land rights or residency of owners.

---

3. We ran models after annualizing land use and tree cover change to account for differences in beginning and ending dates for remote sensing interpretation. The statistical significance of the models and of individual variables was unchanged from those presented here. Other explanatory variables, such as livestock density and other environmental variables, were found to have little statistical significance in other regression specifications.

TABLE 6.5 Determinants of change in share of agricultural land: 2SLS regressions

Variable	2SLS Model 1	2SLS Model 2	2SLS Model 3
Constant	.012	.024	−.0007
	(0.71)	(0.15)	(−0.00)
Share of customary tenure	.181*		.179*
	(2.08)		(2.09)
Exclusive customary tenure[a]		.191*	
		(2.25)	
Open customary tenure[a]		.077	
		(0.80)	
Share of *mailo* tenure	.026		
	(0.28)		
Exclusive *mailo* tenure[a]		−.006	
		(−0.06)	
Open *mailo* tenure[a]		.027	
		(0.29)	
Resident *mailo* tenure[a]			.089
			(0.86)
Absentee *mailo* tenure[a]			−.002
			(−0.02)
1960 population density	.0020**	.0015*	.0019**
	(2.52)	(1.89)	(2.45)
1960 population density squared	−.000003*	−.000003	−.000003*
	(−1.96)	(−1.58)	(−1.80)
Predicted population growth	.033*	.032*	.0364*
	(2.00)	(1.98)	(2.22)
Number of dry days	.0008	.001	.0008
	(0.90)	(1.08)	(0.85)
Distance to Kampala	−.00002	.00005	.00002
	(−0.07)	(0.14)	(0.07)
Distance to tarmac road	.0022**	.0019*	.0022**
	(2.60)	(2.13)	(2.68)
1960 share of agriculture land	−.651**	−.611**	−.663**
	(−7.67)	(−7.06)	(−7.86)
Adjusted *R*-squared	.59	.61	.60

NOTE: $N = 64$. Figures in parentheses are *t*-values.

[a]Interaction terms: tenure category × exclusivity of land right; *mailo* tenure × residence status of *mailo* owners.

*.05 level.

**.01 level.

Population variables were extremely important in explaining land use change. Increased agricultural land share was linked to higher population growth and higher population density, the latter at a nonlinear decreasing rate. This is consistent with a well-noted observation made by others (for example, Boserup 1965) and can be attributed to both increased benefits from and lower costs of conversion. The effect of population density shows that at low levels the change in share of agricultural land is high as families clear large areas for their farms. As population increases, the land frontier diminishes, and eventually new families must find land from within existing agricultural areas. Model 1 predicts that the level of population density at which agricultural land would actually decline is 350, a level that was exceeded in only one parish.

Other important variables in the change in agricultural land share regressions were the 1960 share of agricultural land and the distance to a tarmac road. The coefficient on the 1960 share of agricultural land was negative and very strong; this is expected because at higher share levels, the potential for additional expansion is less and the value of the resources in nonagricultural land may rise sufficiently to warrant some regulation or protection. Distance to a tarmac road was positively and significantly related to increased agricultural land share in all cases, indicating that greater agricultural expansion during the 1960–95 period was taking place away from major roads. This is likely due to the simple fact that land near main roads was heavily populated and already converted in response to market opportunities before 1960 and possibly to lower wage rates away from roads, which increases the returns to conversion.

Tables 6.6 and 6.7 show the results from the tree cover change regression on agricultural and nonagricultural land, respectively. The models for agricultural land explained a large share of observed variation, between 70 and 73 percent. The models for nonagricultural land did not show such a strong fit but nevertheless explained a respectable 52 percent of variation in tree cover change. In what follows, we discuss the results from the two tables together.

Among tenure variables, the main effect found was that tree cover change on agricultural land was positively related to *mailo* tenure (compared with public land). There were no observed differences between "more exclusive" and "more open" *mailo* land, but positive tree cover change seems somewhat stronger in *mailo* land dominated by resident owners. These results support our hypothesis that individual rights to land and trees are stronger in *mailo* land than in public land, especially where owners are resident. There were, however, no significant differences in tree cover between *mailo* land area and customary land area, even though land rights are weaker in the latter (see Table 6.9). This result may be taken to imply that land rights are strengthened after tree planting under customary land tenure systems, which provides sufficiently strong incentives to plant trees, as was demonstrated by the empirical model developed in Chapter 1.

TABLE 6.6 Determinants of change in tree cover on agricultural land: 2SLS regressions

Variable	2SLS Model 1	2SLS Model 2	2SLS Model 3
Constant	.523*	.534*	.489*
	(2.21)	(2.18)	(2.07)
Share of customary tenure	.047		.042
	(0.69)		(0.62)
Exclusive customary tenure[a]		.049	
		(0.66)	
Open customary tenure[a]		.090	
		(1.01)	
Share of *mailo* tenure	.187*		
	(1.91)		
Exclusive *mailo* tenure[a]		.173	
		(1.68)	
Open *mailo* tenure[a]		.213*	
		(1.98)	
Resident *mailo* tenure[a]			.201*
			(2.06)
Absentee *mailo* tenure[a]			.149
			(1.46)
1960 population density	.00035	.0005	.0002
	(0.32)	(0.43)	(0.15)
1960 population density squared	.0000003	.0000003	.0000003
	(0.29)	(0.28)	(0.27)
Predicted population growth	−.0127	−.0141	−.0095
	(−0.65)	(−0.70)	(−0.49)
Number of dry days	.00001	−.0001	.0002
	(0.01)	(−0.08)	(0.17)
Sandy soil	−.129**	−.129**	−.120**
	(−2.85)	(−2.72)	(−2.64)
Distance to tarmac road	−.0028**	−.0032**	−.0027**
	(−2.64)	(−2.46)	(−2.58)
Distance to Kampala	.0002	.0003	.0001
	(0.43)	(0.60)	(0.33)
1960 share of agriculture land	−.362**	−.402**	−.357**
	(−3.26)	(−3.15)	(−3.24)
1960 agricultural tree cover	−.971**	−.956**	−.978**
	(−6.41)	(−6.11)	(−6.51)
1960 nonagricultural tree cover	−.076	−.073	−.073
	(−0.76)	(−0.69)	(−0.74)
Coffee important crop	.063	.076	.068
	(1.45)	(1.60)	(1.57)
Adjusted R-squared	.72	.71	.73

NOTE: $N = 42$. Figures in parentheses are t-values.

[a]Interaction terms: tenure category × exclusivity of land right; *mailo* tenure × residence status of *mailo* owners.

*.05 level.

**.01 level.

TABLE 6.7 Determinants of change in tree cover on nonagricultural land: 2SLS regressions

Variable	2SLS Model 1	2SLS Model 2	2SLS Model 3
Constant	−.837**	−.885**	−.882**
	(−3.12)	(−3.24)	(−3.26)
Share of customary tenure	−.052		−.054
	(−1.00)		(−1.03)
Exclusive customary tenure[a]		−.084	
		(−1.44)	
Open customary tenure[a]		.019	
		(0.26)	
Share of *mailo* tenure	−.0105		
	(−0.27)		
Exclusive *mailo* tenure[a]		.006	
		(0.12)	
Open *mailo* tenure[a]		−.019	
		(−0.42)	
Resident *mailo* tenure[a]			.026
			(0.51)
Absentee *mailo* tenure[a]			−.033
			(−0.75)
1960 population density	.0010	.0012	.0009
	(0.88)	(1.02)	(0.80)
1960 population density squared	−.000003**	−.000003**	−.000003**
	(−2.49)	(−2.58)	(−2.57)
Predicted population growth	.065**	.067**	.069**
	(2.79)	(2.86)	(2.93)
Number of dry days	.0055**	.0057**	.0057**
	(3.76)	(3.83)	(3.85)
Sandy soil	.181**	.192**	.189**
	(3.40)	(3.51)	(3.53)
Distance to tarmac road	.0028*	.0029*	.0028*
	(2.29)	(2.21)	(2.32)
Distance to Kampala	−.0004	−.0004	−.0004
	(−1.20)	(−0.97)	(−1.19)
1960 share of agriculture land	.356**	.364**	.361**
	(2.90)	(2.81)	(2.94)
1960 agricultural tree cover	−.291	−.298	−.296
	(−1.93)	(−1.97)	(−1.97)
1960 nonagricultural tree cover	−.520**	−.504**	−.521**
	(−5.29)	(−5.08)	(−5.31)
Adjusted *R*-squared	.52	.52	.53

NOTE: $N = 67$. Figures in parentheses are *t*-values.

[a]Interaction terms: tenure category × exclusivity of land right; *mailo* tenure × residence status of *mailo* owners.

*.05 level.

**.01 level.

No other tenure variables were statistically significant, including those in the nonagricultural land regression. This indicates, among other things, that individual land rights on nonagricultural land are weak and relatively invariant under any tenure system and that community management of trees is not well developed across our sites.

Population density and population growth had much less impact on tree cover change than on land use change. The exception was the positive and statistically significant relationship between predicted population growth and tree cover in nonagricultural land (as well as a significant coefficient on the squared 1960 population density variable in Table 6.7). The reason for this is not apparent, but the variable may be picking up the effect of the 1980–86 war, which may have simultaneously ravaged vegetation cover and lowered population growth in these sites.[4] To summarize the effect of population pressure in the three models, increased population unambiguously leads to conversion of land to agriculture; the effect of population on tree cover or its change on agricultural or nonagricultural land is ambiguous. This is further demonstrated in Table 6.2, where tree cover on agricultural land increased, along with population, during the 1960–95 period. It is unlikely that the resiliency of aggregate tree cover over time, close to roads or otherwise, was linked to decreasing demand for tree products. Data show that the percentage of cooking energy from tree products remains very high today at 94 percent and 89 percent among rural and urban households, respectively (World Bank 1996).

Other noteworthy findings include the importance of market access, soil type, and climate. Distance from a tarmac road was negatively related to the change in agricultural tree cover change. This is the expected effect if market access leads to more favorable prices for outputs and induces adoption of tree planting for coffee/shade, fruit, and wood products. Table 6.7 also indicates that proximity to tarmac roads has adversely affected tree cover in nonagricultural lands. Both results together suggest that in areas near tarmac roads incentives for exploiting trees are greater, but only in agricultural land, where tenure is privatized, has this led to improved long-term tree management. Better soil quality had a positive effect on tree cover change on agricultural land and a negative effect on tree cover change on nonagricultural land. The result for agricultural land, that farmers plant and protect trees where they are likely to grow better, is expected. The coffee variable in Table 6.6 was not significant, showing that tree cover change did not depend exclusively on increased coffee plantings, though these certainly did contribute to improved tree cover.[5]

---

4. Indeed, the effect disappears when a dummy variable for parishes strongly affected by the war is included. The war dummy itself was not significantly related to land use or tree cover change when included.

5. Our data indicate that tree cover change was greater in parishes where coffee was important than in those where it was not. However, these same parishes have favorable climate and infrastructure that also promote the adoption of noncoffee tree species. Last, as mentioned earlier, a great deal of coffee is intercropped with other trees in agroforestry systems.

Last, it is worth noting the significance of the 1960 tree cover and agricultural land share variables. The strong negative signs on the 1960 tree cover variables indicate that individuals and communities do react to the increasing scarcity value of trees by planting and protecting tree resources. This is especially true in the case of agricultural land, as evidenced by the high coefficient estimate. When we control for initial tree cover, the initial share of agricultural land had a positive effect on tree cover change on nonagricultural areas but a negative effect on tree cover change on agricultural land. The positive effect on nonagricultural land would be expected if some tree products in nonagricultural land cannot be substituted for in agricultural land, thus leading to a rise in their value with greater land conversion. For agricultural land, the variable could be capturing a comparative advantage for cereal cultivation through tree clearing or perhaps a lack of access to tree germplasm, due to few natural wooded areas nearby.

Summary and Conclusions from Extensive Study

In this analysis we obtained strong statistical evidence, based on parish-level data in Uganda, that population pressure, market access, and land tenure are important factors affecting land use and tree resource management. Specifically, it is found that three variables representing population pressure significantly affect the conversion of woodland and grazing land to agricultural fields. While agricultural land expansion was positively related to population growth, our evidence shows that the rate of area expansion declines with increases in population density. Distance to tarmac road was also strongly and positively linked to expansion of agricultural land. Our survey data indicate that most lands near main roads had already been converted to agriculture before the study period.

Customary land tenure institutions in Uganda provide strong private rights in agricultural land but are relatively weak in collective management of other resources. These appear to have promoted, or at least not retarded, the pace of land conversion. Whether private ownership systems per se are conducive to the preservation of woodland and grazing land or whether the tenancy regulations retard the conversion to agricultural land, however, is not clear from our data.

With respect to tree cover change, population pressure did not have a major impact, aside from its indirect effect through land use change. Proximity to tarmac road had a positive effect on tree cover on agricultural land but a negative impact on nonagricultural land. Another important finding of this study is the increased tree density in agricultural land, especially in response to lower initial density. Thus, tree planting and conservation have been taking place at the same time as the conversion of woody areas to agricultural land, and "deforestation" is neither ubiquitous nor inevitable if one considers all tree resources. Our data show a more or less stable tree cover over time, with the contribution of agricultural land to overall tree resources (measured by canopy cover) rising from 35 to 58 percent over the study period.

Intensive Study

Defining Hypotheses

Following the theoretical model of tree planting developed in Chapter 1, we postulate empirically testable hypotheses on the impacts of land tenure on the management of land and trees in this section. This model assumes that the household will compare the present value (PV) of agroforestry development to other alternatives such as a fallow/cropping system. In doing so, the farmer must take into consideration several factors. According to the model, the value of tree planting is determined by its direct effect on profits on the one hand and its indirect effect on expected profits through the reduction in the probability of losing land rights on the other. The direct profit effect is determined by market access and prices. Because coffee is a globally traded commodity, its marketing has not been of major concern, other than normal price fluctuations. For other tree products, markets are thinner and prices are more reflective of local supply factors—the greater the scarcity of trees, the greater will be the profits from tree planting.

Tree planting may enhance tenure security under customary land tenure institutions, because work effort of planting trees is rewarded by strong individual land rights (for example, Shepherd 1991). We developed the regression model in Chapter 1 to verify the significance of this effect on tree planting. Whether management effort affects land rights is not empirically known. In our study sites, there are also specific reasons to hypothesize that some types of investment will enhance tenure security in the *mailo* and public tenure systems as well. First is the case of *mailo* long-term tenants. Their tenure security rests on the decision of the landlord not to evict them (which the law allows them to do). Eviction requires landlords to compensate tenants for investments, and thus the establishment of highly valued investments helps to reduce the likelihood of eviction. Coffee is one such investment that pays in a relatively short time and is easily valued. Other types of trees may not serve this role as well, and in fact, as will be discussed in detail in relation to Table 6.9, there appears to be some informal agreement that the proceeds from a few valuable timber trees would go to the landlord. On public lands occupied by landholders who operated under a de facto customary system for many years, tree planting will enhance individual tenure security, as in the case of customary lands. Furthermore, growing trees will help prevent squatting on this type of land.[6] Given these effects, observed tree planting under customary land tenure may be on par with farmers of higher security owing to the indirect security effect of tree planting. Conversely, if tree planting cannot affect tenure security, the optimal

---

6. It does not, on the other hand, change the likelihood of losing land rights to a traditional or formal authority, but this possibility is remote throughout the study area.

level of tree planting increases with the original level of tenure security. This is likely to be the case for investments in planting of a few fruit or firewood trees, because these trees are much less important than coffee. Community agreement to enhance individual land rights through the planting of these less valuable trees has not been established.

Unlike tree-planting efforts, effort involved in managing trees is not directly observable and is thus less valuable as evidence that an investment in land is being made. Moreover, once trees have been planted, the probability of losing rights may become close to zero. Then the choice of management effort may be independent of initial tenure insecurity.

The fallow/crop strategy would have nearly the opposite effect. Fallowing will not decrease the probability of losing land rights and in fact may increase it under customary land tenure rules. This is not the case under *mailo* ownership. It is therefore obvious that the incidence of fallowing will be less for lower levels of tenure security.

These outcomes lead to the following hypotheses:

1. Long-term investment in coffee may not differ significantly between tenure systems with different levels of tenure security because of the security-enhancing effect of planting coffee.
2. Plot-level profits from coffee will tend to be similar across tenure systems with different levels of tenure security because tenure may not affect management effort. In the case of annual crops, profits will not be different, because tenure security does not affect short-term decisions.
3. Planting of noncoffee trees is affected not only by tenure factors but also by price factors, which in turn depend on scarcity of trees in the local area.
4. Incidence of fallowing will be greater in areas where tenure security is higher, since otherwise fallowing may lead to loss of individual land rights. Therefore, we expect more fallowing in *mailo*-owner land and less in customary land.

Description of Data

GENERAL CHARACTERISTICS OF HOUSEHOLDS AND PARCELS. Table 6.8 shows some descriptive data pertaining to sampled households and parcels. Most households are headed by males, but female heads are fairly common in Nabalanga (22 percent). Age of household head was nearly identical in both sites, at around 47 years. Both farm sizes and family sizes differed across the study sites. Mean farm size was 4.7 hectares in Nabalanga and 2.5 hectares in Bupadengo.[7] Barrows and Kisamba-Mugerwa (1989) found similar-sized farms in their *mailo* study sites in Luwero and Masaka Districts. The farms are

---

7. These means exclude three very large farms that are clearly outliers. Because of this, the log of farm size is used in regression analysis rather than actual values.

TABLE 6.8 Household and parcel variables

Variable	Total	Nabalanga	Bupadengo
Female household heads (percentage)	14.0	22.0	5.0
Age of household head (mean)	47.5	48.3	46.6
Adult equivalents (mean)	2.9	2.5	3.5
Farm size (mean in ha)[a]	3.7	4.7	2.5
Good soil fertility (percentage of parcels)	61.6	47.2	74.6
Sloping land (percentage of parcels)	43.9	44.3	43.2
Years since parcel acquired (mean)	20.3	22.2	18.6
Number of household observations	97	47	50

SOURCE: Intensive survey.

[a]The mean is calculated after the exclusion of three extreme outliers.

large in *mailo* areas because (1) there remains some carryover of the maldistribution of farm sizes in *mailo* land from historical factors and (2) land sale and land rental markets are not effectively functioning owing partly to incomplete land rights and tenancy regulations. Conversely, family sizes were lower in Nabalanga than in Bupadengo, and there was on average one more adult equivalent in the latter. These observations mean that land-labor ratios are much greater in Nabalanga than in Bupadengo. Not surprisingly, much more hired labor is reported in the Nabalanga site. There was some variation in reported soil fertility and toposequence location of parcels. Just over 40 percent of parcels in each site were on sloping land, while significantly higher fertility assessments were reported by Bupadengo farmers.[8] Parcels were on average held for slightly longer periods in Nabalanga than Bupadengo (22.2 to 18.6 years).

LAND TENURE AND TENURE SECURITY. Table 6.9 shows the classification of parcels by tenure type for the entire sample. The most common tenure was a permanent occupant of customary land (that is, through inheritance or purchase), which includes nearly all of the parcels in Bupadengo. This is followed by long-term *mailo* tenants (17.3 percent), occupants on public land (13.5 percent), and *mailo* owners (12.5 percent). There were nine parcels acquired on a temporary basis (for example, renting or caretaking), two-thirds of which were found in Bupadengo.[9]

Table 6.9 also reports the relationship between tenure type and the ability to exercise various land rights. Despite the high proportion of parcels that had been acquired through purchase, the unfettered individual right of sale is relatively uncommon, with only about 20 percent of parcels reported to fit into this

---

8. Farmers classified the soil fertility of their fields as very good, good, fair, or poor.

9. These parcels were omitted from the regression analyses. First, none of the investments considered in the analyses were made on these parcels. Second, data were missing on outputs for some, meaning that the number of cases was too small to provide for reasonable analysis.

TABLE 6.9 Relationship between tenure system and land rights

Tenure System	Individual Right to Sale	Individual Right to Give	Individual Right to Plant Timber Trees	Has Title	Number of Parcel Observations
Mailo owner	28.6	71.4	78.6	64.3	14
Mailo long-term tenant	26.3	68.4	47.4	15.8	19
Public holder	28.6	64.3	92.9	14.3	14
Customary holder	12.5	26.8	57.1	14.3	56
Significance level of chi-square statistic	.13	.00	.00	.01	

SOURCE: Intensive survey.

category. Respondents claimed to enjoy no rights of sale for as many as 55.8 percent of parcels. A remaining quarter of the parcels could be sold, but only after notification or approval. This lack of certainty over sale rights permeates through all tenure types but is more pronounced among customary farmers.[10]

Other rights of transfer are more individualized, though clear distinctions are visible comparing the *mailo* tenure with customary tenure. The right to give without any notification or approval is claimed on approximately 70 percent of all *mailo* parcels in Nabalanga and slightly less on public land parcels. Conversely, fewer than 30.0 percent of customary parcels enjoy similar status. A similar pattern occurs for the right to choose heirs, except that the difference between *mailo* and customary parcels is even more pronounced. It is also important to note that the individualization of rights over public land parcels is noticeably greater than that on customary land except for the right to sell, which is relatively low in both cases.

Rights to plant trees follow an interesting pattern. Nearly three-fourths of all households claim the unfettered rights to plant trees, but fewer when only timber trees are considered. The reason for this difference is that it is widely known that one particular timber tree (*Chlorophora excelsa,* or *mvule* in the local language) is a protected species under forestry codes. This is subject to various interpretations, but one common result is that some farmers do not plant them (and other high-value trees), believing that only the forestry department or land owner can plant and manage this species. A second outcome is that *mailo* owners prohibit their tenants from planting them on their land fearing that this would lead to loss of land rights for the owner. Thus, Table 6.9 shows that in fact the rights to plant timber trees are clearly lower among *mailo* tenants, relatively low among customary farmers, and higher among *mailo* owners. *Mailo* tenants, on the other hand, perceive little difficulty in planting other types of trees.

As in many other countries in Africa, formal land registration and titling were never undertaken on a large scale by the government, but the machinery was put in place for farmers to register their parcels at their cost. Because this process requires investment in cash and time, most farmers do not decide to acquire title, unless the expected benefits are unusually large. In our sample, 14.3 percent of parcels acquired on a permanent basis in Bupadengo had been titled. There was a higher percentage of parcels under title in Nabalanga (31.1 percent), mainly because of the presence of *mailo* owners who often use title as security for credit (agriculture or nonagriculture).

AGRICULTURAL INVESTMENTS AND PRODUCTIVITY. When evaluating the impact of tenure on agricultural efficiency, it is important to look both at short-term and long-term considerations. In the short term, it is possible to

---

10. *Mailo* long-term tenants are able to sell their rights to land, which do not include ownership rights, to others. Often they are required to have approval from the *mailo* owner.

study the impact of tenure on measures of productivity or profit (annual crops). For long-term efficiency, panel data sets are normally not available or feasible to collect, and so instead one is interested in land investments such as tree planting and subsequent management that are hypothesized to increase future efficiency measures, ceteris paribus. Several types of indicators could be used to assess farmer investment in agriculture and resulting productivity. In our study sites, farmers report very few long-term investments or prolonged use of short-term investments. No land and water constructions, such as terracing or water harvesting, were reported on more than a handful of plots. Fewer than 5 percent of all plots had received manure, fertilizer, mulch, or crop residues in any of the past five years in both sites. The major reasons for this are the high costs of imports into Uganda (fertilizer), the relatively low number of cattle (manure), and the poor condition of extension services in Uganda (conservation and green organic systems).

What remains as potential investments are those that have overcome these constraints. This amounts to three types of investment: coffee planting (made available partly as a result of government involvement), noncommercial tree planting (farmers can access seed and wildings on their own), and fallowing (requires no inputs). To measure production efficiency, a profit function approach is used. Profits are defined as the value of production less the costs of all purchased inputs and less the imputed value of all family labor. This is then evaluated on a per hectare basis. A description of the crops evaluated follows.

Agricultural Investment and Productivity:
Econometric Results

COFFEE PLANTING.   Coffee is by far the major foreign exchange earner in Uganda. As such the government of Uganda has long had an interest in promoting its diffusion among farmers. Support has been in the form of research of new cultivars and in the promotion of nurseries to distribute planting material. There has not, however, been substantial involvement in the area of enhancing the use of fertilizers on coffee, unlike the cooperative program in Kenya.

A large majority of farmers in our study sites had planted some coffee. In Nabalanga, the percentage of farmers planting coffee was 89.2 percent, and in Bupadengo it was 81.4 percent. This provides general support to the first hypothesis, that coffee planting will be more or less the same across tenure systems. According to Table 6.10, the mean proportion of area devoted to coffee was 15 percent in both Nabalanga and in Bupadengo.[11] Since the mean farm size is higher in Nabalanga, the absolute area devoted to coffee per farm is generally higher in Nabalanga, and there is considerable variation in coffee area across farms in each site.

---

11. Barrows and Kisamba-Mugerwa (1989) found the proportion of land planted to coffee to vary between 13 and 34 percent in their study sites.

TABLE 6.10 Agricultural investment and productivity variables

Variable	Nabalanga	Bupadengo	Total
Tree planting and management			
Total planted per hectare (mean)	12.4	53.5	33.2
Fruits planted per hectare (mean)	2.4	14.4	8.5
Percentage of fuelwood from own farm	67.4	81.0	74.0
Fallowing			
Percentage of parcels fallowed	80	33	55
Percentage of noncoffee parcels fallowed	88	38	61
Percentage of parcel area under coffee	15	15	15
Profits per hectare (mean in Uganda shillings)	262,899	456,676	351,381
Labor days per hectare (mean)	165.0	187.3	175.2

SOURCE: Intensive survey.

Table 6.11 shows the results of a tobit regression to explain the proportion of parcel area under coffee.[12] Among the three tenure variables, only the result pertaining to *mailo* long-term tenants is significant. The positive result indicates that these farmers devote greater proportions of land to coffee than customary farmers. There may be relatively high planting of coffee among *mailo* tenants in order to reduce the likelihood of their eviction (since owners would have to compensate for this investment). It is worth emphasizing that coffee planting is no less active under customary tenure than *mailo* owners, despite weaker land rights. These results are largely supportive of hypothesis 1, suggesting that planting may be used to increase security of tenure.

Also important were farm size, the length of time since the parcel was acquired, and the soil fertility status. Farm size was negatively related, implying that factor markets are not efficient to allow larger farmers to rent out land or to hire labor in sufficient quantities (Hayami and Otsuka 1993). The years since acquisition had a positive effect on proportion of coffee area. This indicates that farmers make gradual investments in coffee, and given the insecurity and disruption of markets in Uganda's recent history, this is not surprising. More coffee was associated with soils of higher fertility. Since coffee is among the most profitable options for farmers, this reflects a profit-maximizing strategy by farmers.[13] No other variables were significantly related, including the family

---

12. We also specified the regression function in which explanatory variables include Bupadengo dummy and land right dummy as well as interaction terms between land right dummy and *mailo* owner, *mailo* tenant, or public holder dummy. In this specification, site-specific effects are controlled for by the site dummy, whereas the land tenure effects are supposed to be captured by the four land right variables. Qualitatively, the estimation results are not so different from those reported in Tables 6.11 to 6.13.

13. Although it could also be argued that farmers are more likely to apply fertilizers to cash crops such as coffee, it is well known that the use of fertilizers in Uganda is among the lowest in the world.

TABLE 6.11 Determinants of adoption of coffee and use of fallowing

	Dependent Variable	
Independent Variables	Percentage of Parcel Area under Coffee: Tobit Regression	Whether Field Had Been Fallowed in Past 10 Years: Probit Regression
Constant	−.0100	−.4888
	(−0.10)	(−0.99)
Mailo owner	.0239	1.5581**
	(0.29)	(3.70)
Mailo long-term tenant	.1534**	1.3755**
	(2.39)	(4.25)
Public land holder	.1122	2.1613**
	(1.45)	(4.92)
Log of farm size	−.0492	−.1319
	(−1.80)	(−0.92)
Years since parcel acquired	.0058**	−.0316**
	(2.72)	(−3.12)
Sloping land	−.0570	−.0222
	(−1.15)	(−0.10)
Good soil fertility	.0960*	.8923
	(1.94)	(0.38)
Female head of household	−.0180	−.0539
	(−0.25)	(−0.17)
Age of household head	−.0025	.0213*
	(−1.31)	(2.25)
Number of adult equivalents	.0222	.0187
	(1.40)	(0.25)
Log likelihood	−10.44	
Percentage of observations correctly predicted		75.7

NOTE: Figures in parentheses are *t*-values.

*.05 level.

**.01 level.

labor endowment. Given the result on farm size, the interpretation is that while labor markets are not perfect, they do function to some extent, allowing households with relatively small labor endowments to adopt proportions of coffee area similar to those in households with more labor.

FALLOWING.   Another investment that is practiced by a number of farmers is fallowing. Unlike other types of investment, fallowing does not require explicit work effort and hence does not enhance tenure security. On the contrary, tenure security tends to decline if land is not utilized under traditional tenure systems. The data indicate that 80 percent of fields and 88 percent of non-coffee fields in Nabalanga had been fallowed for at least one year during the past 10 years. The extent of fallowing is much less in Bupadengo, and only 33 percent of noncoffee fields had been fallowed over the same period.

Fallowing is not a viable option on fields planted exclusively to permanent crops such as coffee. Two regression models were made. The first retained all fields and included a dummy variable for the presence of coffee. A second excluded all coffee fields and contained no crop dummy variables. Because the results on the tenure and many other variables are consistent, only the latter analysis is presented, the one in which coffee fields are excluded.

Table 6.11 shows the results of a probit regression explaining the incidence of fallowing within the past 10 years by field. Several variables are statistically related to fallowing, and among them are three tenure variables. The set of tenure results show that fallowing is less common on customary land than on the other tenures, after controlling for the effects of farm size, soil fertility, and other variables. The likely explanation is that in customary tenure areas there may be greater motivation to keep all land occupied so as to prevent demand for land from relatives. This supports hypothesis 4. The frequency of fallowing was slightly higher in public land as opposed to *mailo* owner land, which is opposite what we had expected. The difference between them, however, is not significant.

Two other variables with significant effects on fallowing are age of household head and years since acquisition of parcel. Age is positively related to the likelihood of fallowing and may indicate a lack of need for continuous cultivation as well as an experience factor. Somewhat in opposition to this, the longer a parcel has been held, the less likely it is to be fallowed. One explanation might be that selected fields of newly acquired parcels are being converted to coffee fields or otherwise undergoing significant investment, which requires intensive use of labor, and other fields may tend to be left uncultivated. No other variable was found to be significantly related to the incidence of fallowing. Among these are the size of farm and family labor supply, which would be hypothesized to be positively and negatively correlated with fallowing, respectively.

TREE PLANTING AND MANAGEMENT.   All households reported having multipurpose trees (nontree crops and nonshrubs) on their farms, and all but 4.4 percent planted some. The average number of trees planted at the parcel level is 33.2 on a per hectare basis. The most common type of tree found or planted was fruit (mango, papaya, avocado, and jackfruit), and as many as 95.6 percent of households had at least one on their farm. Pole and timber trees were found on more than half of the farms, and the remaining trees comprised those used for shade, soil improvement, firewood, or boundary demarcation.

More trees were planted by farmers in the Bupadengo (customary) site than in Nabalanga. The difference is substantial, with an average of 53.5 per hectare versus 12.4 per hectare (Table 6.10). A similar disparity is observed for fruit trees. The comparative difference is consistent with the trends noted from an interpretation of aerial photographs in the two sites. Support for the differences in tree planting comes from an analysis of firewood sources. The average percentage of firewood coming from one's own farm is greater in Bupadengo (81 percent), where more tree planting has taken place than in Nabalanga (67 percent).

Table 6.12 shows the results from tobit regressions explaining the density of tree planting and fruit tree planting. Tenure variables were found to be important for both dependent variables. Lower plantings per hectare were found in *mailo* tenant and public land households than on customary farms. The result for *mailo* tenant households contrasts with the result for coffee. This could imply that higher-value permanent investments are preferred to reduce the risk of eviction or that *mailo* tenants already have sufficient security of tenure for investing in permanent crops. Finally, the result could also be related to the weak prevalence of rights to plant timber trees, as reported in Table 6.9. The result for public landholders may be related to the many changes in formal legal status and intended uses on the part of successive governments (see section on land tenure systems earlier in this chapter). Interestingly, *mailo* owners planted the same densities of trees as their counterparts in customary land. That *mailo* owners appear different from tenants and public land farmers is congruent with findings in the community-level study in this chapter.

The density of trees planted was lower on larger farms. This result is compatible with those found in other countries (for example, Burundi studied by Place [1995]). Tree-planting density was also positively related to the length of time the parcel had been held by the current occupant (this does not hold for fruit trees), which is the expected sign. Tree-planting density is also positively associated with good soil fertility and larger numbers of family members. Arguments could be found to support results in positive or negative directions for these variables. A positive finding on household size may indicate that tree planting is generally reflective of intensification strategies. Tree planting was independent of tree density at the time of parcel acquisition, except in the case of fruit trees. Having fruit trees upon acquisition led to further fruit tree planting, perhaps because of greater access to planting materials, which are rarely commercially traded in rural Uganda.

The final column of Table 6.12 shows the results from a household-level regression, with the percentage of firewood coming from the household's own farm as the dependent variable. In agreement with columns 1 and 2, the effect of tenure is strong, indicating a greater reliance on one's own farm in customary land than in *mailo* or public land. A study in a nearby district by Aluma et al. (1995) also found that many households in *mailo* areas collected firewood from off-farm sources, mainly on the larger *mailo*-owner farms (some with absentee owners). The availability of trees in such sources inhibits the investment in trees for firewood. Farm size effect is positive, which is the expected sign and indicates that the larger farms across all tenure systems can more easily provide for firewood needs. There is more own-farm collection in female-headed

TABLE 6.12 Determinants of tree planting

Independent Variables	Trees Planted per Hectare: Tobit Regression	Fruit Trees Planted per Hectare: Tobit Regression	Percentage of Fuelwood from Own Farm: OLS Regression
	Dependent Variable		
Constant	−2.0316	1.7698	68.0568**
	(−0.19)	(0.39)	(5.45)
Mailo owner	−7.0864	−6.1392	−29.7923**
	(−0.85)	(−1.67)	(−2.78)
Mailo long-term tenant	−11.478*	−11.722**	−31.3178**
	(−1.75)	(−3.76)	(−3.70)
Public land holder	−15.486*	−8.3455*	−13.6627
	(−1.95)	(−2.29)	(−1.44)
Log of farm size	−10.542**	−1.6668	7.3308*
	(−3.81)	(−1.37)	(2.14)
Years since parcel acquired	.6883**	.2415**	
	(3.32)	(2.60)	
Sloping land	−4.6412	.5501	
	(−0.91)	(0.24)	
Good soil fertility	10.440*	3.9759	
	(2.08)	(1.78)	
Trees per hectare at acquisition	−.0039	.8042**	
	(−0.05)	(5.96)	
Female head of household	−2.9913	3.0049	19.0454*
	(−0.41)	(0.92)	(2.05)
Age of household head	.0941	−0.360	.2793
	(0.50)	(−0.42)	(1.58)
Number of adult equivalents	3.484*	−.1015	−1.2578
	(2.15)	(−0.14)	(−0.62)
Log likelihood	−407.4	−289.4	
Adjusted *R*-squared			.28

NOTE: Figures in parentheses are *t*-values.
*.05 level.
**.01 level.

households. Rather than being reflective of differences in tree stocks, it may be more related to the preferred use of existing trees.

In relation to our hypothesis 3, it seems that tree planting has responded largely to availability of trees within and near the village. This is supported by greater self-reliance in firewood collection by households in Bupadengo. The results could also support the hypothesis that tree planting is used in the customary tenure system to help secure long-term individual rights. In other words, it seems clear that lower tenure security under customary land tenure institutions does not immediately imply lower incidence of tree planting owing to tenure security–enhancing effects of tree planting.

CROPPING EFFICIENCY.   A number of crops are found on fields at the sites. The most common were coffee, plantain, potato, sweet potato, maize, cassava, beans, and groundnut. Fields are equally devoted to monocultures and intercrops. Table 6.10 indicates that average profits were 351,381 Ugandan shillings per hectare of cropped fields (or about $351 in 1996–97). Although the absolute number of monocultures is low and thus statistical inference is difficult, the main crop contributing to profits is coffee. There are wide variations in profits after controlling for the presence of other types of crops, and no clear patterns emerge. Profits seem to be substantially higher in Bupadengo, although the difference is not statistically significant. Table 6.10 also shows that the average labor intensity was 175.2 days per hectare, with more in Bupadengo than in Nabalanga. Together, the results suggest that the lower profits in Nabalanga seem to be due to poor yields rather than excessive labor use. It should be noted that hired labor is much more common in Nabalanga than in Bupadengo, and this partially offsets the lower family input.

Table 6.13 shows ordinary least squares (OLS) regression results, with profits per hectare and family labor input per hectare as dependent variables. Because of significant diversity of crops and intercropping, one of the regressions retains all surveyed fields and uses crop dummies as explanatory variables. A second regression included only coffee plots. The latter involved a small number of fields, and because all but one result remained the same in the profit regression, only the first regression model is presented (the different results are noted in the text).

None of the tenure variables was significant in the profit regression; therefore, short-term profits were not affected by tenure. This supports hypothesis 2, that management effort is independent of land tenure institutions. A separate regression omitted the crop dummies (under the assumption that tenure may affect crop choice) and also found that tenure did not matter. It is not likely that farm-level profits are affected by tenure, either, since the proportion of area under coffee, the most profitable farming enterprise, was not highly related to tenure. Other regressions, not reported, found that the presence of individual rights to sell and give land and the presence of title were not statistically related to profits per hectare, again supporting the second hypothesis.

Ideally we should like to control for the impact of fallowing on soil fertility in the profit function estimation. It was, however, hard to obtain precise data on recent history of fallowing at the field level, as fields changed season after season. What is clear from Table 6.13 is that despite the shorter fallow cycle, the profitability under customary land tenure is not significantly lower.

Profits are strongly linked to the presence of coffee (against the base case of maize). While average profit is higher for coffee, its variance is also higher.

TABLE 6.13 Determinants of profits and family labor use per hectare

Independent Variables	Profits per Hectare: OLS Regression	Family Labor per Hectare: OLS Regression
	Dependent Variable	
Constant	125770.9	237.50**
	(0.60)	(4.58)
Mailo owner	−173524.1	29.28
	(−1.04)	(0.70)
Mailo long-term tenant	−132369.0	49.84
	(−1.04)	(1.57)
Public land holder	−100530.1	36.54
	(−0.61)	(0.89)
Log of farm size	−18947.7	−14.76
	(−0.35)	(−1.09)
Size of field (m^2)	−24.3**	−.01**
	(−3.29)	(−5.02)
Years since parcel acquired	−4096.4	0.21
	(−1.15)	(0.24)
Sloping land	27587.1	24.25
	(0.30)	(1.06)
Good soil fertility	41990.7	11.08
	(0.43)	(0.45)
Coffee on plot	656973.4**	6.92
	(6.67)	(0.28)
Plantain/banana on plot	426158.5**	−14.08
	(4.14)	(−0.55)
Potato on plot	472834.4**	68.98
	(3.21)	(1.89)
Bean/groundnut on plot	−29978.3	−19.13
	(−0.20)	(−0.52)
Cassava/sweet potato on plot	309494.5*	21.84
	(2.08)	(0.59)
Female head of household	−73014.5	−1.89
	(−0.60)	(−0.06)
Age of household head	1669.0	−1.12
	(0.50)	(−1.34)
Number of adult equivalents	24106.4	1.53
	(0.81)	(0.21)
Significance of *F* statistic	.000	.000
Adjusted *R*-squared	.24	.18
Number of observations	202	202

NOTE: Figures in parentheses are *t*-values.

*.05 level.

**.01 level.

Thus, higher profitability of coffee does not necessarily imply that farmers could improve efficiency by devoting more land to coffee. Also note that since coffee is a perennial crop, the rigorous comparison of the profitability requires the assessment of the present values of the different land uses. Similarly, profits from fields with plantains (a staple food), potato, or cassava were higher than those from fields with maize. The only other variable significantly related to profits per hectare was the size of the field, which has a negative sign. Profits could be higher on smaller parcels owing to higher payoffs from a greater intensity of labor effort (found in the second column).

In the family labor intensity regression, tenure is again found to be unimportant. The size of field is significantly and negatively related to labor intensity. This may be linked to management practices whereby farmers visit certain fields on a particular day, thus spending more time per hectare for smaller fields. It could also reflect recall errors. The other variable of statistical significance is the dummy for potato, which is positively related.

Summary and Conclusions from Intensive Study

It was postulated that incentives to plant and grow commercial trees, such as coffee, may not be thwarted by weak individual land rights under customary tenure institutions because of the land rights–enhancing effect of tree planting. We provided evidence to support this: namely, that both the incidence of planting coffee trees and its profitability are largely independent from land tenure institutions. These findings are consistent with the findings of Chapters 3 and 4. It will be fair to conclude that customary land tenure institutions do not impede the investment in trees and subsequent management activities.

This does not imply, however, that land tenure does not matter in agricultural decisionmaking. On the contrary, we found evidence that fallowing is less frequent under the customary tenure system, which indicates that land rights are significantly weaker under this institution. This is also consistent with the findings of the Ghana study (Chapter 3). Continuous use of land will be inefficient in the absence of fertilizer use and may lead to loss of soil fertility in the long run. Moreover, occupants of *mailo* and public lands relied to a much greater extent on collection of firewood outside their farms, implying that under the customary system there is a greater degree of conversion to agriculture, resulting in loss of tree cover at the community level (as found in the extensive study earlier in this chapter).

Larger farms, which tend to be related to the *mailo* tenure system, were found to be related to a smaller proportion of planted coffee areas and lower density of other trees planted. However, farm size was not related to profits per hectare, so that there is no indication that the tenure systems have a significant indirect impact on efficiency through effects on landholdings.

If factor markets worked, renting out land on a temporary basis or hiring in labor would remove such inefficiency. Labor contracts, however, are difficult to enforce effectively because of high policing costs. Thus, it is land rental markets that can significantly contribute to the efficient allocation of land and labor across farms in practice (Hayami and Otsuka 1993). In our study, however, we failed to identify why land rental markets do not work in the context of Uganda. It could be due to incomplete rights of land owners or tenancy regulations. How pervasive the inefficiency of large farm size is and what factors prevent land rental markets from working need to be investigated further.

Overall Summary and Policy Implicatuions

Our study has compared land and tree management and agricultural efficiency across different tenure systems in Uganda. By using econometric techniques, the effect of tenure could be quantified and isolated from the impacts of other variables. We found that conversion of land use from woodlands to agriculture was more rapid under the customary tenure system. Conversion was less under *mailo* and public tenure systems, in which more private or public controls were in place. Tree cover on agricultural land at the community level was found to be greater in the *mailo* tenure system, especially in sites where resident (as opposed to absentee) owners were more common. The extensive study of 64 parishes was not able to ascertain whether this reflected preservation of trees or planting of trees, though both have taken place to some extent. The household study, though only of two parishes, would indicate that such an outcome is more linked to preservation of trees than to planting of trees. One reason is that we found quite a bit of inequality in farm holdings in the *mailo* area, with a good number of relatively large farms. Another reason is that tree planting per se was considerably higher in our customary tenure site as opposed to the *mailo* tenure site. Therefore, although customary tenure appears to lead to reduced tree cover through greater land conversion, the system provides sufficient incentives for tree planting on the converted land. We found evidence to suggest that part of the reason for planting trees on customary land may in fact be linked to expected increase in tenure security. Conversely, investment in fallowing was much lower in customary land than in *mailo* land. Whereas investing in trees can enhance tenure security, investing in fallowing may have the opposite effect and lead to intrafamily demands for use of "idle" land. In terms of agricultural efficiency, as measured by profits per unit of land area, we did not find that any particular tenure system in Uganda was superior to others.

Given rapid population growth, as well as a lack of employment opportunities in nonagricultural sectors, the conversion of nonagricultural land to agricultural fields will continue to some degree. The new Ugandan Land Act should enable such processes to be negotiated and conducted with fewer uncertainties and conflicts than has occurred in the past. This is because the new act has rescinded previous state control over all the lands of Uganda and thus has harmonized legal and commonly held perceptions over land tenure rights. This will further help to clarify long-term rights over land and trees and may promote investments in resources. Given the increasing importance of agricultural land, in order to increase the tree resource base to meet basic wood product demands of the population, the feasible strategy is to support tree planting on agricultural land. This strategy is compatible with farmers' incentives, as long-term land use rights are for the most part well established on agricultural land or enhanced by tree planting (with the exception of some tree tenure rights among *mailo* tenants). Tree-planting programs would certainly be appropriate, and our analysis suggests that land tenure and infrastructure policy can also play a catalyzing role in changing the stock of tree resources on agricultural land. This result is notably different from evidence pertaining to virgin forest areas in the Amazon (Fujisaka et al. 1996). Conversely, we found that the maintenance of tree stocks on nonagricultural land, where tenure rights are less clear, is more difficult.

One of the reasons we were unable to identify much difference in agricultural productivity between tenure systems is that nearly all farmers employed low-input farming systems. The data from the extensive community survey show that the use of purchased inputs and long-term investments is very low, irrespective of geographical area or tenure system. While it could be that one of the reasons for such a lack of investment is ambiguities in the tenure systems (for example, overlapping rights of *mailo* owners and long-term tenants), we interpret such a finding as pointing to other constraints. Likely constraints include poor information (for example, awareness of options for investment), poor input markets, and absence of rural credit. Improvement in these areas appears to be the most critical first step in boosting agricultural productivity. If these constraints are removed, long-term investments in agricultural intensification will be stimulated, which will help strengthen individual land rights. The individualization of land rights, in turn, will promote not only investments but also a land rental market that would further improve efficiency of land use.

References

Aluma, J. R. W., J. Kigula, M. Owor, and F. Place. 1995. The role of land and tree tenure on the adoption of agroforestry technologies: The case of Uganda. International Centre for Research in Agroforestry. Mimeo.

Barrows, R., and W. Kisamba-Mugerwa. 1989. Land tenure, access to land, and agricultural development in Uganda. Land Tenure Center, University of Wisconsin, Madison.

Bazaara, N. 1992. Land policy and the evolving forms of land tenure in Masindi District, Uganda. Centre for Basic Research Working Paper 28, Kampala.

Besley, T. 1995. Property rights and investment incentives. *Journal of Political Economy* 103:913–937.

Boserup, E. 1965. *The conditions of agricultural growth: The economics of agrarian change under population pressure.* London: George Allen and Unwin.

Breyer, J. 1996. Land use cover change in Central Uganda. Report prepared for International Food Policy Research Institute and International Centre Research in Agroforestry, Nairobi, Kenya.

Bruce, J., and S. E. Migot-Adholla. 1994. Searching for land tenure security in Africa. Dubuque, Iowa: Kendall/Hunt Publishers.

Food and Agriculture Organization (FAO). 1984. *Agroclimatic data for Africa: Countries south of the equator.* Rome: FAO.

Fujisaka, S., W. Bell, N. Thomas, L. Hurtado, and E. Crawford. 1996. Slash and burn agriculture, conversion to pasture, and deforestation in two Brazilian Amazon colonies. *Agricultural Ecosystems and Environment* 59:115–130.

Hayami, Y., and K. Otsuka. 1993. *The economics of contract choice: An agrarian perspective.* Oxford: Clarendon Press.

Hosier, R. H. 1989. The economics of deforestation in Eastern Africa. *Economic Geography* 64:121–136.

Kisamba-Mugerwa, W. 1989. Land tenure and agricultural development in Uganda. Land Tenure Center, University of Wisconsin, Madison.

Langdale-Brown, I. 1960. The vegetation of Uganda. Ser. 2, No. 6. Research Division, Uganda Department of Agriculture.

Muhereza, E. F. 1992. Land tenure and peasant adaptations: Some reflections on agricultural production in Luwero District, Uganda. Centre for Basic Research Working Paper 27, Kampala.

Nielsen, F., Y. Guinand, and J. Okorio. 1995. *Farmer participatory diagnostic research: Lakeshore banana-coffee land use system of Uganda.* Kampala, Uganda: Forestry Research Institute of Uganda.

Ollier, C. D., C. J. Lawrance, P. H. Beckett, and R. Webster. 1969. Terrain classification and data storage: Land systems of Uganda. Military Engineering Experimental Establishment Report No. 959, Department of Agriculture, University of Oxford.

Place, F. 1995. The role of land tenure in the adoption of agroforestry in Burundi, Uganda, Zambia, and Malawi: A summary and synthesis. Land Tenure Center Report, Madison, Wisconsin.

Place, F., and K. Otsuka. 2001. Population pressure, land tenure, and tree resource management in Uganda. *Land Economics* 76 (2): 233–251.

Shepherd, G. 1991. The communal management of forests in the semi-arid and sub-humid regions of Africa: Past practice and prospects for the future. *Development Policy Review* 9:151–176.

Uganda Ministry of Finance and Economic Planning (MFEP). 1992. *The 1991 population and housing census (district summary series).* Entebbe, Uganda: MFEP.

Uganda Ministry of Planning and Economic Development (MPED). 1996. *National food strategy.* Kampala, Uganda: MPED.

World Bank. 1993. *Uganda: Agriculture.* World Bank Country Study. Washington, D.C.: World Bank.

———. 1994. *World development report.* New York: Oxford University Press.

———. 1996. *African development indicators.* Washington, D.C.: World Bank.

World Resources Institute, United Nations Environment Programme, United Nations Development Programme, and World Bank. 1998. *World resources 1998–99: A guide to the global environment.* Oxford: Oxford University Press.

7 Management of State Land and Privatization in Vietnam

TOWA TACHIBANA, TRUNG M. NGUYEN,
AND KEIJIRO OTSUKA

After Vietnam gained its independence from France in 1954, its government nationalized agricultural land and the large area of forestland. Cooperatives were then set up to serve as the basic management unit of agricultural production under a collective system. Collective farm work was organized under the leadership of cooperatives. After the end of the Vietnam War in 1975, the re-unified Vietnamese government attempted to extend the collective system to the south. The collectivization, however, led to food shortages in the whole region of reunified Vietnam beginning in the late 1970s (Pingali and Xuan 1992).

Henceforth, the government began to implement drastic tenure reforms, which abandoned the collective farming system in favor of a virtual privatization of arable land. Major reforms governing this transition are Directive 100 in 1981, Resolution 10 in 1988, and the Land Law of 1993 (Pingali and Xuan 1992; Hayami 1993; Kerkvliet and Porter 1995). Directive 100 introduced the production contract system under which farmers individually carried out crop care and management on land under lease from a cooperative for a specific period, even though land preparation, irrigation management, and input distribution were collectively carried out. Resolution 10 strengthened private use rights over arable land by officially assigning use rights to individual farm households on the basis of 15-year renewable leases and delegating the whole decision-making authority over farming to individual farmers. Furthermore, by Resolution 10, the monopolistic distribution system of farm inputs and outputs by cooperatives was abolished. The 1993 Land Law allows the transfer of private use rights over arable land under certain conditions.[1] These new policies pertaining to the agricultural sector have been supported by the Doi Moi policy, which the Vietnamese government commenced in 1986 to transform the centralized communist economy into a market economy. The economic reform has pro-

We are particularly grateful for constructive comments on an earlier version by Dao The Tuan, John Pender, and Yujiro Hayami. This chapter draws partly on Tachibana, Nguyen, and Otsuka (2001).

1. Under the current constitution, however, land and other natural resources in Vietnam are *owned* by all the people.

234

vided farmers with an enhanced incentive to engage in commercial agricultural production (Irvin 1995).

Vietnam has experienced significant deforestation during the socialist period. Forestland was lost at an annual rate of 2.3 percent between 1965 and 1989, which was the highest among low-income countries and much faster than the 1.3 percent deforestation rate in former and current socialist countries between 1980 and 1990 (World Bank 1992). As of 1987, 13 million hectares, or 40 percent of the whole area of the country, had been converted from dense forest to so-called bare hills.

In Vietnam, as in many other developing countries, the expansion of agricultural land, particularly that of shifting-cultivation area, into hitherto uncultivated land has been a principal cause of deforestation (Rowe, Sharma, and Browder 1992).[2] An official document argues that "shifting cultivation is a rational method of food cultivation in mountain areas where flat or slightly sloping land suitable for intensive agriculture is in extreme short supply" (Vietnam, Ministry of Forestry 1991:113). It is also argued that "food crop cultivation on forest land may bring an income of 4–5 times higher than from cultivation of forest tree crops" (Vu Hoai 1993:21). Recently, however, the pace of deforestation has declined and that of reforestation increased. Such observation suggests that various economic reforms implemented in recent years, particularly reforms to strengthen individual land rights, have been conducive to prevent deforestation and to promote reforestation.

A unique characteristic of the Vietnamese land tenure reform is the allocation of forestland to individual farmers, which even developed countries have not implemented historically (Hayami 1993).[3] As early as 1983, the Vietnamese government began to allocate some forestland to farm households (Sikor 1996). This process accelerated after 1993. Forestland, mainly the barren area, has been allocated to volunteer farm households on the basis of a 50-year lease under the condition that the recipients undertake reforestation by means of tree planting and regeneration.

This chapter assesses the impacts of various tenure reforms of both forest and agricultural lands on forest conditions in the northern hill region of Vietnam, where flat lowlands along rivers coexist with hilly upland areas of forest and agricultural land. In such geographical conditions, the choice between agricultural intensification in the flat lowland and extensification (that is, expansion of farmland) into the marginal forest area is highly relevant, as argued by classical economists (Ricardo 1821: chap. 2). Inadequate work and management incentives under the collective farming system might have led to low produc-

---

2. See Angelsen (1995) for a view opposing this dominant view. In our observation, however, his argument does not apply to the case of northern Vietnam.

3. According to the Land Laws of 1988 and 1993, forestland is defined as the area with slopes greater than 25 degrees.

tivity in lowland farming, which in turn may have stimulated the expansion of farmland into forest areas to produce sufficient food staples. Thus, in addition to land tenure reforms in upland forest areas, in which shifting cultivation is practiced, tenure reforms in the lowland can affect forest resource conditions through their effects on farmers' choice between agricultural intensification and extensification.

In the Appendix of this chapter, we develop a simple dynamic model of land use, which considers not only the choice between the intensification of lowland agriculture and the extensification into forestland but also the choice of fallow cycle under shifting cultivation in the upland area. By applying the model to commune-level data, we explore the impacts of various tenure reforms on forest conditions in the northern hill region of Vietnam. We also examine the impacts of forestland allocation to individual farmers on the use of such land using household data.

This chapter proceeds as follows. We provide a brief description of field sites in the next section. Then, using the extensive survey data, we present the results of regression analyses examining the effect of tenure reforms on lowland rice production per capita and upland cropping intensity in 1978, 1987, and 1994, as well as on the changes in denuded forest areas and in reforestation areas for the periods 1978–87 and 1987–94. We then summarize the results for the extensive study. Using the intensive household survey data, we analyze how individual farmers use newly acquired forestland for different purposes including tree planting. The policy implications are discussed in the final section.

Study Sites

The northern hill region, in which our study sites are located, has a large forest area, accounting for about 20 percent of the total forest area in Vietnam as of 1994 (Vietnam, Department of Agriculture, Forestry and Fishery 1996). The forest area was supposed to be protected and managed by cooperatives with a view to conserving the natural environment. The area, however, has experienced drastic deforestation since the late 1970s, which was faster than the national average (Sikor 1996). Two notable characteristics of the northern hill region—shifting cultivation and significant in-migration—are often referred to as the main causes of this drastic deforestation.

The majority of hill inhabitants have been ethnic minorities. Some of them, such as Thai and Tay, have mainly engaged in paddy cultivation; the others, such as Dao and San Chay, have traditionally practiced shifting cultivation. After independence from France in 1954, the area had accepted a huge influx of migrants from the lower Red River delta region under the government program, even though this area was a food deficit area (Cuc, Gillogly, and Rambo 1990; International Food Policy Research Institute 1996). Most of these migrants were Kinh, the major ethnic group in the country. When the nationwide food shortage occurred in the late 1970s and the early 1980s, farmers expanded shifting-cultivation areas by clearing forests, which were freely accessible by commune members.

By nature, deforestation is a dynamic process, and as such, data on forest conditions at different points in time are needed to analyze factors affecting deforestation. Fortunately, official data on forest areas are available at the commune level, which is the lowest local administration unit consisting of several hamlets, in 1978, 1987, 1991, and 1994. Since the 1991 forest data seem to have limited coverage of forest conditions, we use them only for the analysis of reforestation. Forest areas are classified on the basis of estimated tree volume density: for example, bare land, newly planted area, and rich, medium, poor, and renascent forests. These forest inventories and measurements were mainly based on visual inspection by local forestry officials, while aerial photographs were utilized in two out of seven districts of our sample in the 1980s.[4] Considering the difficulty of measuring the forest areas in the absence of aerial photographs, data on forest area by type are likely to be crude. The present study focuses on deforestation area, that is, the changes in bare land area, which is denuded as a result of complete clearance for shifting cultivation. In contrast, a forest is not totally denuded by logging because selective felling is generally practiced. Compared with the areas of forests classified by estimated tree volumes, the size of entire bare land is less likely to be subject to measurement errors. From the data on bare land, we obtained the deforestation rate for the periods 1978–87 and 1987–94. The former corresponds to the periods of food shortage, whereas the latter corresponds to the period of tenure and other reforms.

Because of several administrative changes and the inappropriate storage of official documents, data collection was far from simple for both forest inventory and agricultural production records at the commune level. We had to solicit the cooperation of a large number of local government officials. For the sake of collecting reliable and consistent data, we limited the survey areas to a manageable number of provinces and districts. We selected Bac Thai and Son La Provinces, where our collaborating institution, the Vietnam Agricultural Science Institute, had prior on-site projects and established its presence (see Figure 7.1). Both provinces share the typical geographical conditions in the northern hill region, particularly a limited area of lowland along rivers and between hills. Bac Thai Province is representative of the hilly northern midlands in terms of forest cover, whereas Son La Province is one of the most denuded areas in the northern mountainous region. We collected data from 62 randomly selected communes altogether. After dropping 6 communes that experienced

---

4. At the national level, there are three sets of aerial photos taken for forest inventory, those in 1975–79, 1985–87, and 1993–94. Because of several administrative changes, both the local and central government officers of forestry are not sure how these photos were utilized in generating the forest inventory data in our field sites.

FIGURE 7.1 Location of study sites in northern Vietnam

changes in administrative boundaries, we use data from 29 communes in Bac Thai Province (out of 65 in the three selected districts of Phu Luong, Dinh Hoa, and Cho Don) and 27 communes in Son La Province (out of 62 in the four selected districts of Yen Chau, Mai Son, Son La Town, and Thuan Chau). Thus, total sample size in the extensive community study is 56. All these selected communes are predominantly agriculture-based with very few nonfarm households. Most villages have some irrigated paddy fields in lowlands along rivers and streams, rainfed (nonirrigated) lowlands, and upland fields that are officially on sloped areas of less than 25 degrees. Average rainfall in Bac Thai Province is about 1,800 millimeters per year; that of Son La Province, 1,380 millimeters. The highest altitude in Bac Thai Province is 920 meters, which is lower than the highest peak of 1,270 meters in Son La Province. In general, communes in Son La have larger hilly areas than those in Bac Thai.

We have chosen the commune of Yen Do in the Phu Luong District of Bac Thai Province as the site for the intensive household survey. Yen Do is located approximately 150 kilometers north of Hanoi. Owing to the paved highway, it takes only three hours from Hanoi to reach this commune by car. Compared with other areas in the northern midlands, this commune is located at lower altitudes, the highest of which is 400 meters, and has relatively flat land that is used for paddy cultivation. Many small hills, which look like teacups placed upside down, are scattered in the midst of the lowland.

Since forestland allocation has not been implemented in Son La Province, Bac Thai is obviously more appropriate for the intensive survey, which is concerned with the effects of change in land tenure institutions. We have chosen Yen Do for two specific reasons. The first is that Yen Do is known to have many traditional private forests, which have been developed historically on small hills. In the hill and mountainous regions, the Vietnamese government did not implement the land collectivization program thoroughly, and as a result many small forests were left intact under private management. We are particularly interested in the comparison of the management of traditional private forests with that of newly allocated forests under the land privatization policy. The second reason is that Yen Do hosts several reforestation projects. Through the assistance of the cooperatives, the provincial government implemented tree planting projects in the 1980s. From 1990 to 1993, the World Food Programme implemented a reforestation project in Yen Do, which is popularly called PAM project. These projects promoted the planting of nonlocal tree species, such as eucalyptus and acacia, for pulp and timber production. We are interested in the comparison of investment behavior in tree planting between project-assisted cases and cases determined by farmers' own initiatives.

Out of 1,100 households in the commune of Yen Do, we have randomly selected 250 households that hold some farmlands. This site is predominantly an agricultural area, and fewer than 2 percent of households do not have any lowland farms. There are 17 villages in this commune, and 250 households were sampled in total with the proportion from each village corresponding to the proportion of village households to total commune households.

Extensive Study

Population Pressure and Deforestation

As shown in Table 7.1, population growth in both Bac Thai and Son La Provinces was fast in both the 1978–87 and 1987–94 periods, with acceleration from the former to the latter period. Such high population growth in these rural areas occurred partly because interregional migration from rural to urban areas was prohibited in Vietnam. In Son La, high population growth in the period 1987–94 took place mainly because the Kinh people formerly residing in the

TABLE 7.1 Changes in average population in selected communes

	Population			Population Growth Rate		Proportion of Kinh
	1978	1987	1994	1978–87	1987–94	1994
				(percentage/year)		(percentage)
Bac Thai	1,957	2,575	3,307	2.9	3.8	27.1
Son La	2,302	3,128	4,479	3.5	4.9	12.2

SOURCE: Extensive survey.

NOTE: Average of 29 communes in Bac Thai and 27 communes in Son La.

hydroelectric dam site of Hoa Binh Province were moved to Son La by the government. How the government allocated those migrants to various locations in mountainous regions is not clear. It is, however, questionable whether they were allocated to various communes primarily in accordance with the availability of unexploited forestland suitable for cultivation. The soil fertility, the size of paddy land, and a host of political considerations most likely affected the government decisions. Aside from this recent migration, the large-scale migration programs to the mountainous regions were implemented mostly before the 1980s.[5] The prohibition of voluntary out-migration and the implementation of involuntary immigration programs by the government suggest that the local population and its growth rate are fairly exogenous or largely unaffected by the rate of deforestation or the availability of unexploited forestland. The average size of population in communes and its average growth rate were higher in Son La Province, whereas the proportion of Kinh, which is the majority group in Vietnam, was larger in Bac Thai Province. On the other hand, between Bac Thai and Son La Provinces, there is no appreciable difference in average distance to the subdistrict capital from communes (18 kilometers for both provinces) and average slope, measured by the difference between the highest and the lowest altitudes (440 meters and 496 meters, respectively). The proportion of communes situated in fertile soil, which is defined to include reddish yellow humic soils, is higher in Son La (17 of 27 communes) than in Bac Thai (12 of 29 communes). This is consistent with the results of our interviews with commune leaders, which show that fallow periods of 6.4 and 3.3 years used to be required in the 1970s for the restoration of fertility of upland farms in Bac Thai and Son La, respectively. Although the reported fallow periods may seem very short, they are likely to reflect frequent cropping of nitrogen-fixing legumes. Fallow

5. Judging from the low correlation between the population growth rates and the population ratio of Kinh group in 1994, the in-migration of Kinh group from the Red River delta region seems to have taken place mainly before 1978, which is consistent with the results of our informal interviews.

periods were also short because the cultivators easily lose cultivation rights without frequent cropping in the absence of clear individual use rights. Fallow periods in recent periods became shorter, even though it was difficult to obtain the relevant data from the farmers, because the prohibition of shifting cultivation has been more strictly enforced.

Rapid population growth in the first period was associated with rapid deforestation (Table 7.2); bare land in forest areas increased from 1978 to 1987 by about 32 percent in Bac Thai and by 47 percent in Son La. As a result, the ratio of bare land to total forest area, which includes bare land, approached 55 percent in Bac Thai and reached 75 percent in Son La in 1987. Bare land area per capita, however, did not change much during this period in both provinces.

It is interesting to observe that the expansion of bare land slowed down considerably from the first period (1978–87) to the second period (1987–94), despite the accelerated trend of population growth. In fact, bare land per capita declined significantly from 1987 to 1994 (see numbers in parentheses in Table 7.2). It seems clear that a structural change in the management of forest areas took place between the two periods. Specifically we hypothesize that agricultural reforms, which include the establishment of the individualized farming system, the liberalization of market transactions, and the allocation of long-term use rights over forestland, led to intensification of lowland farming and reduced incentives to cultivate less fertile upland for production of food crops. One may also argue that increased employment opportunities in the nonfarm sector reduced incentives to engage in upland farming.

Deforestation was more pronounced in Son La than in Bac Thai Province in terms of the rate of bare land expansion, the ratio of bare land to forestland, and bare land per capita. One reason is higher fertility of upland soil in Son La,

TABLE 7.2 Average deforestation rate in selected communes

	Proportion of Bare Land to Total Forest Area[a]			Annual Increase in Bare Land Area per Commune		Average Forest Area
	1978	1987	1994	1978–87	1987–94	1994
	(percentage)			(hectares)		(hectares)
Bac Thai	41	54	58	32.7	4.8	2,235
	(0.52)[b]	(0.51)	(0.41)			
Son Lai	51	75	84	145.0	76.8	5,619
	(1.18)	(1.29)	(1.02)			

SOURCE: Extensive survey.

[a]Total forest area includes bare land area.

[b]Numbers in parentheses are bare land area per capita in hectares.

TABLE 7.3 Average lowland area and lowland rice production per capita in selected communes

	Lowland Area per Capita			Lowland Rice Production per Capita		
	1978	1987	1994	1978	1987	1994
	(hectares)			(kilograms)		
Bac Thai	0.098	0.077	0.066	276	250	242
Son La	0.038	0.028	0.021	129	111	114

SOURCE: Extensive survey.

which increases the profitability of shifting cultivation on upland areas. Another reason, which is likely to be more important, is the smaller endowment of lowland, particularly paddy fields, per capita in Son La Province (Table 7.3).

Farming Systems

Since lowland area suitable for intensive rice farming had been exhausted quite some time ago, there was no opportunity to expand lowland areas in our study sites in the 1980s and 1990s. Thus, lowland area per capita continued to decline with population growth, as demonstrated in Table 7.3.

In both Bac Thai and Son La Provinces, the majority of lowland area is accounted for by paddy fields, and less than one half of lowland area has been irrigated, in which case two crops of rice were generally grown. Lowland rice output per capita declined appreciably from 1978 to 1987 but stopped declining from 1978 to 1994, despite the declining lowland area per capita. In contrast, increases in paddy yield per unit of land accelerated. Yields of paddy per hectare during the main season increased from 2.3 tons in 1978 to 2.8 tons in 1987, and to 3.0 tons in 1994 in Bac Thai, whereas the corresponding figures were 2.5, 2.8, and 3.5 tons in Son La. Such increases in rice yields would have been made possible by the strengthened decisionmaking authority of individual farmers resulting from increased tenure security and by the improved marketing efficiency of agricultural inputs, including fertilizer, due to the dismantling of agricultural cooperatives and promotion of private-sector marketing (International Food Policy Research Institute 1996).

In Bac Thai, declining lowland rice output per capita from 1978 to 1987 was associated with increasing upland area planted to annual crops, particularly upland rice, to compensate for the declining availability of lowland rice distributed by the government. The rice market was liberalized later in the 1980s when rice production in mountainous region improved owing to tenure reform (International Food Policy Research Institute 1996). In Son La, upland cultivation area per capita was much larger, but the intensity of cultivation declined modestly for the same period (Table 7.4).[6] Upland cropping intensity, which is measured by the ratio of upland area planted to annual food crops to cultivable bare land area (that is, total bare land minus rocky area), declined appreciably from 1987 to 1994. Cultivated upland area also declined absolutely for the same period. Such a decline in upland cultivation, if continued, will lead to regeneration of forest areas, which, in fact, has been taking place widely according to our own observations. In other words, massive deforestation was followed by buoyant reforestation in northern hill region of Vietnam.

Two other interesting findings emerge from Table 7.4: an increase in commercial tree crop area and a decrease in yields of upland food crops represented by cassava, particularly in the latter period. In the shrinking upland cropping area, the proportion of perennial commercial crop area drastically increased from 1987 to 1994. The upland area planted to tea expanded in Bac Thai, while the area of mulberry, fruit trees, and coffee expanded in Son La. According to our interviews with village elders and other farmers, tree planting was carried out by many farmers (not particularly by wealthy farmers) when land rights on sloping upland were granted. Tree-planting projects were implemented in some villages in Bac Thai, but their coverage accounts for relatively small areas. During our field trips, we found a large number of young tree gardens.

Soils on sloping upland are not infertile at the time of conversion from virgin forests, but their fertility declines rapidly with frequent cropping. The yield of cassava, which usually grows well even on infertile soil, was low in both provinces and declined in Son La in 1994.[7] This observation supports the hypothesis that excessive shifting cultivation without technological change during the food shortage period degraded upland soil.[8]

Table 7.5 shows the indicators of implementation of Directive 100 and Resolution 10, in terms of the proportion of the area covered by these programs to total lowland fields. Since both Directive 100 and Resolution 10 were implemented almost completely in lowland areas, it may be difficult to detect statistically their impacts on intensification of lowland from our cross-sectional data. Table 7.5 also shows the proportion of communes to which forestland was officially distributed with use rights of 50 years by 1993 and 1994. According to these statistics, the forestland distribution was implemented faster in the communes in Bac Thai Province than in Son La Province.

---

6. Since cultivation in forest areas had been formally prohibited, the upland cropping area in official statistics would be grossly underestimated. We may safely assume, however, that the true area of upland farming was roughly proportional to the numbers reported in official statistics.

7. Cuc, Gillogly, and Rambo (1990:69) report that high yields of cassava from 15 to 18 tons per hectare were found on recently cleared land in another area of the northern midland.

8. There has been no major technological change in upland farming. Fertilizer and manure application is ineffective unless fields are terraced or bunded, for which investment is needed. There had been, however, few incentives to invest in land improvement until recently, when individual land rights were granted. Thus, there had not been high-input food cropping on upland areas. Green manure application started only in the 1990s, according to our observation.

TABLE 7.4 Upland farming in selected communes

	Upland Cropping Intensity[a]			Cassava Production per Hectare			Proportion of Perennial Tree Crops[b]			Average Upland Cultivation Area per Commune		
	1978	1987	1994	1978	1987	1994	1978	1987	1994	1978	1987	1994
	(percentage)			(tons)			(percentage)			(hectares)		
Bac Thai	3.9	8.6	5.3	9.3	10.9	10.5	5.4	11.4	40.1	33	69	52
Son La	23.1	21.3	16.2	13.3	11.4	9.8	1.8	1.9	11.8	358	423	374

SOURCE: Extensive survey.

[a]Proportion of upland area planted to annual crops to total cultivable bare land.

[b]Proportion of perennial commercial crop area to total upland area.

TABLE 7.5 Extent of tenure reform implementation in selected communes

	Directive 100 in 1987[a]	Resolution 10 in 1994[a]	Forest Land Distribution[b]	
			1993	1994
		(percentage)		
Bac Thai	77.3	78.6	41.3	62.1
Son La	94.8	97.2	0.0	22.2

SOURCE: Extensive survey.

[a]Proportion of area under the program to total lowland area.

[b]Proportion of communes in which the program was implemented.

Several explanations are possible for declining food-cropping intensity on upland areas in the recent period. First, increased production of lowland rice reduced incentives to grow upland crops, particularly upland rice. Second, strengthened use rights on forestland reduced incentives to grow food crops. Actually, in the past, forestland had been open access for commune members, and, hence, the cultivation rights could have been secured only by continuous cultivation.[9] Third, the establishment of long-term use rights on forestland induced planting of perennial crops, such as mulberry, coffee, tea, and fruit and timber trees, as well as farmers' efforts to regenerate natural forests for future sale of timber. The degraded upland soil also led farmers to plant perennial commercial crops rather than annual food crops. Fourth, improved access to market and improved marketing efficiency reduced the need to rely on locally produced foods and facilitated the sale of forest products for the purchase of rice and other food items produced in the Red River delta areas.

Theoretical Framework

In the tradition of economics, there have been two competing views on the interaction between the development of agricultural production and deforestation. Classical economists, among whom David Ricardo (1821: chap. 2) is representative, distinguished two ways to increase agricultural output: intensifying the use of the existing cultivated area and increasing the extensive margin, that is, the expansion of agricultural land. In this view, farmers compare the net return from the "intensification" of the existing farms with that from "extensification" of farm area (Hayami 1997). When farmers choose the latter, de-

---

9. In the field sites, Dao, Kho Mu, San Chay, and Xinh Mun ethnic groups were traditionally engaged in rotational shifting cultivation within specific areas of upland forests. In this system, each family owned generally secure use rights over the whole rotational area. In the period of food shortage, however, the expansion of upland cultivation by the other ethnic groups made traditional use rights less secure.

forestation takes place in the form of the loss of forest areas. Later, Boserup (1965) criticized the classical economists' view based on the observations that shifting cultivation is the common practice in primitive agriculture. In shifting cultivation, clear distinctions can hardly be drawn between existing and new farms. Boserup maintains that agricultural production systems evolve by adopting more intensive methods of land use, which is induced by population pressure and manifested in more frequent and prolonged cropping intervals. In this view, deforestation mainly takes place in the form of less tree cover in shifting-cultivation areas owing to shortened fallow periods.

Recent models of deforestation do not formalize the insights of both classical economists and Boserup. Without considering intensification as an alternative strategy, Ehui, Hertel, and Preckel (1990) and Barbier and Burgess (1997), for example, compare the benefit of preserving forest area with that of converting it into farmland. In their framework, an increase in the profitability of agriculture due to technological change leads to greater deforestation.[10] Such a framework has relevance for deforestation in areas in which the existing farm area and newly converted area are relatively homogeneous, so that there is no clear difference in the cost of intensification in both areas. A typical example of such an area may be relatively flat woodlands in Sub-Saharan Africa on which Ehui, Hertel, and Preckel (1990) and Barbier and Burgess (1997) seem to focus. Elnagheeb and Bromley (1994) provide empirical support to their view. Trade-offs between intensification and extensification arise, however, when the cost of intensification is vastly different between the existing and newly developed farms and intensification in the existing and more productive land requires additional resources, which otherwise would have been allocated to forest clearance.

We construct a model that explicitly incorporates geographical and historical features of our field sites discussed earlier in the chapter: namely, a clear distinction between lowland and upland, the prevalence of shifting cultivation in upland, an in-migration from other provinces, and various tenure reforms in lowland and forest areas. The model describes a dynamic optimization problem of the representative farm family in a commune. We adopt this analytical unit because the actual implementation of various tenure reforms has depended on the commune as the administrative unit. We may be able to capture the impacts of tenure reforms through the cross-sectional variation among sample communes, in addition to the change in trend over the sample periods.

The representative family is assumed to maximize the benefit from agricultural production over time given the total amount of work at each point in

---

10. Barbier and Burgess (1997) suggest that an increase in agricultural yield would reduce deforestation, as it implies more production from existing arable land. In their framework of deforestation comparing the benefit from agriculture with that from timber production, however, an increase in agricultural yield should increase the benefit of converting forest to agricultural area.

time.[11] The geographical conditions in the northern hill region render the agent three ways to expand the agricultural production: intensification in lowland, extensification of shifting-cultivation area, and *depriving* intensification (see the Appendix for the rationale behind this term) in the cleared upland area. The possibility of technological change for upland farming is ruled out, as it is practically infeasible to develop and disseminate new useful technology for upland farming on a large scale. Although the first and the last options accompany intensification, intensification in uplands is fundamentally different from that in lowlands. The depriving intensification in uplands takes the form of larger area of cultivation within the existing area of rotational shifting cultivation, which leads to shorter fallow periods and to degradation of upland soil. Unlike intensification in lowlands, depriving intensification is not accompanied by a technological and institutional improvement. Both extensification and depriving intensification of upland fields cause deforestation. The former reduces the forest area, and the latter deteriorates the tree cover in the rotational shifting-cultivation area (secondary forest). In reality, almost all farm households have practiced both lowland and upland farming with some exceptions in Bac Thai, which are endowed with larger lowland paddy areas per capita.

There are a couple of empirically important results from the solution of the dynamic model of forest and upland use developed in the Appendix. First, it is shown that an improvement in lowland production efficiency leads to a small upland cultivation area and a lower deforestation rate along the steady state. A critical assumption, which led to this conclusion, is the absence of labor market: increased labor demand for lowland farming diverts labor from upland because of the lack of opportunity to hire additional labor. Second, it is also established that an increase in endowment of family labor (associated with population growth) leads to expansion of upland areas at the expense of forest areas.

Determinants of Deforestation

EMPIRICAL SPECIFICATION.   We attempt to evaluate statistically the consequences of changes in various exogenous factors on deforestation and reforestation. Our main interest lies in quantifying the effect of tenure reforms implemented in the 1980s and the 1990s. Although we have developed the formal dynamic model, the specification of the estimation function is not different from equation (2) less formally developed in Chapter 2, which also relates changes in natural resource management with exogenous variables and initial

---

11. The family is assumed to place no value on leisure of its members up to a given level. This would not be an unrealistic assumption under the persistent food shortage in the 1970s and the 1980s. To account for the effects of significant number of in-migrants, we assume that the size of the representative family expands when migrants settle in the commune. This specification is not unrealistic because cooperatives in the socialist period continuously reallocated lowland area equally to new and incumbent members.

conditions. The dynamic model, however, theoretically predicts the effects of certain key variables.

The first-order conditions of the model indicate a recursive determination of endogenous variables. In other words, we can implement regression analysis first on lowland labor use (L_l) and upland cropping intensity (s) and then on deforestation rate (D) using the predicted values of L_l and s. As a first-order approximation, we assume that optimum L_l and s (given by equations [17] and [18] in the Appendix) can be explicitly solved in linear forms:

$$L_l = \alpha_0 + \alpha_1 T_\lambda + \alpha_2 E_l + \alpha_3 P + \alpha_4 T_u + \alpha_5 a + \alpha_6 c \qquad (1)$$

$$s = \beta_0 + \beta_1 T_l + \beta_2 E_l + \beta_3 P + \beta_4 T_u + \beta_5 a + \beta_6 c, \qquad (2)$$

where α_i and β_i are parameters; T_l is lowland farm area, which is fixed; E_l is lowland production efficiency, which would be affected by tenure policies; P represents the relative price of upland food crop to rice; T_u refers to the total upland area under rotational shifting cultivation; a stands for the unit cost of clearing forest; and c is the cost of protecting upland fields arising from the insecurity of tenure. Since the model does not provide any structural relation between L_l and s, these are simply reduced forms. Note that we use per capita T_l and T_u to normalize the effect of the size of population.[12] As another first-order approximation, we assume that the optimum deforestation area can be solved in linear form.[13]

$$D = \gamma_0 \gamma_1 \text{MI} + \gamma_2 L_l + \gamma_3 s + \gamma_4 P + \gamma_5 a + \gamma_6 c + \gamma_7 T_u, \qquad (3)$$

where MI represents the migration and population growth, and L_l and s are determined in equations (1) and (2). If we further assume that the system is already in steady state, equation (3) can be further simplified as:[14]

$$D = \gamma_0 \gamma_1 \text{MI} + \gamma_2 L_l + \gamma_3 s + \gamma_4 P + \gamma_5 a + \gamma_6 c. \qquad (4)$$

Note that lowland production efficiency (E_l) does not appear in equation (4). In the steady state, E_l indirectly affects D only through its effects on L_l and s. But the drastic reform of tenure system and other economic policies toward market economy may make the assumption of steady state unrealistic. Furthermore, all the tenure reforms, Directive 100, Resolution 10, and distribution of forest land, were implemented in the middle of our sample periods. Consider-

---

12. We deleted the time preference, because we expect that it does not vary much across the communes in our sample.

13. We assume that the saddle paths corresponding to various exogenous variables do not intersect. Formally it is desirable to implement comparative dynamics analysis along the saddle paths.

14. This is because sT_u can be deleted by substitution of equation (7) into (19) in the Appendix.

ing the potential importance of efficiency in lowland rice farming in the land use and supply of foods, we decided to include policy variables to capture the effects of E_l in regression equations of D.[15]

DATA. One practical problem in the empirical analysis is that we do not have data directly corresponding to labor input in lowland farming. We use lowland rice production per capita as a proxy for L_l per unit of land. To obtain a better approximation, several variables that are likely to affect lowland rice productivity are included in the empirical model, such as the proportion of irrigated land and a soil fertility indicator.

Distance from town, which is expected to be a good proxy for market access as villages are primarily connected by unpaved mountain paths, is included to represent the relative price (P). We expect that a greater distance will raise the relative price of the heavier and bulkier food commodities relative to rice. We do not necessarily expect that it has significant effect in the regressions, because most food crops were not marketed until the late 1980s. To study the effect of tenure reform, proportions of farm land covered by Directive 100 and Resolution 10 are included in the regression functions for the relevant periods. The ratio of bare land to total forest area is included to capture the cost of forest clearance (Table 7.2). If the remaining forest area is small and far from the villages, the cost of forest clearance would be high.

It is often argued that the minority ethnic groups who have traditionally engaged in shifting cultivation are responsible for deforestation. It is also argued that in-migration into mountainous areas aggravated deforestation. We include the proportion of Kinh people, who are the in-migrants in the area and have no tradition of shifting cultivation, in the regression equations, expecting that we may be able to obtain some information regarding the validity of the popular views. Unfortunately, however, we could only obtain the official data of ethnic population composition for 1994. Because it is highly correlated with the population growth rate in Son La during the period 1987–94, we cannot use the proportion of Kinh people in the regressions including population growth rate in that period.

REGRESSION RESULTS. Tables 7.6 to 7.9 report the estimation results. First, Table 7.6 displays the estimation results of the reduced-form function explaining per capita rice production for 1978, 1987, and 1994. As may be expected, the coefficients of lowland area per capita and irrigated land ratio have highly significant and positive coefficients throughout the three periods. Furthermore, the coefficients of lowland area per capita progressively increased over time, which indicates the positive effects of various reform measures affecting our sample sites uniformly, such as new liberal market policies, and the introduction of new technologies, such as high-yielding varieties of rice. Un-

---

15. Lowland area per capita (T_l) also does not appear in equations (3) and (8). Unlike E_l, however, population growth rates and rice production per capita capture the indirect effects of T_l.

TABLE 7.6 Reduced-form regressions of rice production per capita

	1978	1987	1994
Intercept	0.078	−0.005	−0.113
	(1.68)	(−0.10)	(−2.33)
Lowland area per capita	1.620**	2.603**	3.141**
	(4.84)	(6.41)	(8.45)
Irrigated lowland ratio	0.161**	0.145**	0.153**
	(4.19)	(4.36)	(6.55)
Cultivable bare land per capita	−0.009	0.002	−0.003
	(−0.74)	(0.18)	(−.022)
Directive 100	n.a.	−0.013	n.a.
		(−0.40)	
Resolution 10	n.a.	n.a.	0.111**
			(3.59)
Forest distribution by 1994	n.a.	n.a.	0.005
			(0.37)
Ratio of Kinh in 1994	−0.009	−0.004	−0.119
	(−0.18)	(−0.10)	(−0.33)
Fertile soil dummy	−0.030	−0.011	0.005
	(−1.74)	(−0.74)	(0.44)
Distance from town	−0.001	−0.000	−0.000
	(−0.71)	(−0.11)	(−0.56)
Son La dummy	−0.042	−0.001	−0.015
	(−1.54)	(−0.05)	(−0.75)
Adjusted R-squared	0.74	0.76	0.84

NOTE: Numbers in parentheses are t-statistics. "n.a." refers to "not applicable."
**.01 level

like the results of Pingali and Xuan (1992), our estimation for 1987 does not reveal the significant effect of the introduction of production contracting system on lowland rice cultivation through Directive 100. In contrast, the proportion of area covered by Resolution 10 is significant in the 1994 regression, which indicates the positive incentive effects on paddy yield of de facto privatization of lowland ownership. On the other hand, there is no indication of the effect of distribution of usufruct rights of forestland on paddy yield.

A close examination of the data on upland cropping intensity (s) over the sample communes suggests that the distribution of s is skewed to the right. Thus, we take the square root of each side of equation (2). The estimation results of reduced-form function for the square root of upland cropping intensity are displayed in Table 7.7. The factor that persistently and significantly affects cropping intensity negatively is cultivable bare land area per capita, which is reasonable because the large stock of cultivable bare land indicates abundant

TABLE 7.7 Reduced-form regressions of upland cropping intensity (s)

	1978	1987	1994
Intercept	0.323	0.513	0.213
	(3.37)	(2.99)	(1.16)
Lowland area per capita	−0.883	−1.501	0.081
	(−1.26)	(−1.18)	(0.06)
Irrigated lowland ratio	−0.048	−0.138	−0.069
	(−0.60)	(−1.33)	(−0.78)
Cultivable bare land per capita	−0.043*	−0.108**	−0.100*
	(−1.80)	(−2.74)	(−2.38)
Directive 100	n.a.	0.021	n.a.
		(0.20)	
Resolution 10	n.a.	n.a.	0.087
			(0.75)
Forest distribution by 1994	n.a.	n.a.	−0.030
			(−0.62)
Ratio of Kinh in 1994	−0.098	−0.396**	−0.021
	(−0.96)	(−2.91)	(−0.16)
Fertile soil dummy	0.108**	0.064	0.060
	(3.00)	(1.35)	(1.36)
Distance from town	−0.002	0.001	−0.002
	(−1.52)	(0.46)	(−1.14)
Son La dummy	0.217**	0.101	0.190**
	(3.75)	(1.23)	(2.56)
Adjusted R-squared	0.66	0.42	0.42

NOTE: Numbers in parentheses are t-statistics. "n.a." refers to "not applicable."

*.05 level

**.01 level

supply of upland area. None of the land tenure policy variables, however, is significant. There is some tendency that upland cropping intensity is higher in areas where soil is more fertile. The significantly negative coefficient of the proportion of Kinh people in the 1987 regression may indicate that people from the delta region did not practice shifting cultivation. Or it may be the case that the government sent the Kinh migrants from the dam site into the relatively land-abundant communes, whose residents, including the migrants, did not have to expand the upland fields.

Regarding changes in bare land area, we show estimation results of equation (4) under the assumption of the steady state in Table 7.8, whereas we exhibit estimates of equation (3) without assuming the steady state, which includes upland area under cultivation per capita as an explanatory variable, in Table 7.9. In both cases, we included the land policy variables in addition to the variables included in equations (3) and (4). For rice production per capita and

TABLE 7.8 Determinants of deforestation along assumed steady state

	1978–87		1987–94	
	OLS	2SLS	OLS	2SLS
Intercept	0.041	0.138*	0.009	0.028
	(1.12)	(2.40)	(0.26)	(0.65)
Population growth rate	0.014**	0.011*	0.003	0.003
	(3.12)	(1.99)	(0.95)	(0.96)
Rice production per capita[a]	−0.038	−0.225*	0.035	−0.038
	(−0.54)	(−1.90)	(0.48)	(−0.42)
Upland cropping intensity[a]	−0.142**	−0.389**	−0.037	−0.124
	(−3.10)	(−2.92)	(−1.20)	(−1.32)
Ratio of bare land to forest[a]	−0.087**	−0.084**	−0.100**	0.096**
	(−3.35)	(−2.64)	(−3.29)	(−3.11)
Directive 100	−0.016	−0.032	n.a.	n.a.
	(−0.67)	(−1.08)		
Resolution 10	n.a.	n.a.	0.042	0.046*
			(1.54)	(1.73)
Forest distribution in 1994	n.a.	n.a.	−0.004	−0.004
			(−0.38)	(−0.33)
Ratio of Kinh in 1994	−0.046	−0.061		
	(−1.44)	(−1.53)		
Distance from town	0.001*	0.000	0.000	−0.000
	(1.79)	(0.01)	(0.59)	(−0.38)
Son La dummy	0.067**	0.85**	0.036*	0.37*
	(3.72)	(2.71)	(1.89)	(1.68)
Adjusted R-squared	0.53	0.59	0.23	0.23
F-test statistics		5.14**		2.00

NOTE: Numbers in parentheses are t-statistics. "n.a." refers to "not applicable."
[a]Initial values, that is, value in 1978 for 1978–87 regression and value in 1987 for 1987–94 regression.
*.05 level
**.01 level

ratio of bare land to forestland, we used 1978 data for 1978–87 regressions and 1987 data for 1987–94 regressions. We implemented F-tests to determine the appropriateness of ordinary least squares (OLS) and two-stage least squares (2SLS) estimation methods for the estimation of our recursive model. The results of the F-tests indicate that 2SLS is more appropriate for the period 1978–87 with the assumption of the steady state; for the other period, it is indicated that OLS is more appropriate.

Several important findings can be observed in Table 7.8. First, the population growth rate has a positive and significant effect on the rate of deforestation in the early period (1978–87). This suggests that as population pressure on limited lowland areas increased, people chose to clear forestland for cultivation of additional food crops. This conclusion must be qualified, however, if the government had purposefully sent the migrants to those locations where uncultivated forestland amply existed. Yet this is not likely the case, because the rate of population growth in the early period was relatively low, suggesting that the population growth rate roughly corresponds to the natural rate of growth. If the endogeneity of the government migration program were important, the population growth variable should have had a significant effect in the second period but not in the first. Second, consistent with the above finding, lower rice production per capita led to clearance of forestland in the early period. This result is inconsistent with the predictions of the models of Ehui, Hertel, and Preckel (1990) and Barbier and Burgess (1997) that increased efficiency in farming leads to increased deforestation. Third, an increase in upland cropping intensity resulted in a lower rate of deforestation during the 1978–87 period, as more resources were allocated to upland production on already cleared fields. This observation suggests that if insecure property rights induce a large resource allocation to secure use rights in specific upland fields, it would have helped arrest the loss of forest area. One can also argue that high cropping intensity reflects largely limited remaining forest areas, as reported in Table 7.7. In short, the food shortage was a key driving factor behind increased resource allocation to uplands when upland was open access. Unlike the popular belief, shifting cultivation is not the root cause of deforestation.

It is worth emphasizing that the effects of these three factors lost significance during the reform period of 1987–94. These results suggest that there were structural changes in functional relations between the pre-reform and reform periods.[16] In particular, it appears that population pressure on lowland areas ceased to exert critical influence on the rate of deforestation during the reform period because of the enhanced attractiveness of intensification strategies.

Fourth, the ratio of bare land to total forestland affected deforestation negatively in both periods, which is reasonable, as a larger bare land ratio implies less remaining forest areas to be exploited. Fifth, lowland policy variables (that is, the implementation of Directive 100 in the 1978–87 regression and that of Resolution 10 in 1987–94 regression) are at best weakly significant when the proper estimation methods are applied. We expect, however, that the strongly positive effect of Resolution 10 on lowland rice production per capita in 1994 shown in Table 7.6 would further arrest deforestation through its effect on the choice of intensification over extensification. In general, Son La Province had a higher rate of deforestation throughout the sample periods.

---

16. We also estimated the deforestation function by the random effects model, while assuming the stability of coefficients over time. As might be expected from the structural changes, the fits of the panel estimation are less reasonable than the results shown in Tables 7.8 and 7.9.

TABLE 7.9 Determinants of deforestation along assumed nonsteady state

	1978–88		1987–94	
	OLS	2SLS	OLS	2SLS
Intercept	0.201	0.025	0.021	0.024
	(0.76)	(0.65)	(0.62)	(0.66)
Population growth rate	0.010**	0.009**	0.001	0.002
	(3.00)	(2.90)	(0.32)	(0.67)
Rice production per capita[a]	0.016	−0.014	0.062	0.013
	(0.31)	(−0.18)	(0.92)	(0.17)
Upland cropping intensity[a]	−0.057	0.017	−0.005	0.024
	(−1.58)	(0.17)	(−0.17)	(0.26)
Cultivated bare land area per capita[a]	0.038**	0.041**	0.025**	0.026**
	(6.45)	(5.60)	(3.03)	(3.12)
Ratio of bare land to forest[a]	−0.114**	−0.116	−0.109**	−0.108**
	(−3.86)	(−6.14)	(−3.86)	(−3.79)
Directive 100	−0.005	−0.004	n.a.	n.a.
	(−0.31)	(−0.23)		
Resolution 10	n.a.	n.a.	0.029	0.035
			(1.14)	(1.57)
Forest distribution in 1994	n.a.	n.a.	−0.006	−0.006
			(−0.61)	(−0.60)
Ratio of Kinh in 1994	−0.009	−0.008		
	(−0.37)	(−0.31)		
Distance from town	−0.000	−0.000	−0.001	−0.001
	(−0.44)	(−0.30)	(−1.09)	(−1.41)
Son La dummy	0.051**	0.314	0.033*	0.020
	(3.77)	(1.55)	(1.85)	(1.01)
Adjusted R-squared	0.75	0.74	0.34	0.33
F-test statistics		1.88		1.03

NOTE: Numbers in parentheses are t-statistics. "n.a." refers to "not applicable."

[a]Initial values, that is, value in 1978 for 1978–87 regression and value in 1987 for 1987–94 regression.

*.05 level

**.01 level

The estimation results are largely unchanged qualitatively when we assume nonsteady state and used bared land per capita as an additional explanatory variable (Table 7.9). Aside from the positive and significant effects of bared land area per capita on deforestation, however, there are two major exceptions. First, the effect of rice production per capita is no longer significantly negative in the 2SLS estimation for 1978–87. It seems that rice production per capita and bared land per capita are negatively associated, which led to the lower significance of the rice production effect on deforestation. Second, the negative effect of upland cropping intensity on deforestation rate becomes insignificant in the period 1978–87. This is not surprising, because by construction this variable is closely and negatively related to the amount of bare land per capita.

Determinants of Reforestation

The analysis of deforestation suggests that the structural changes took place as a result of the land tenure and other reforms. We found that lowland rice production affected deforestation through the choice of extensification and intensification in the early period of 1978–87. The tenure reforms in lowland can affect forest resource management through this channel. The most directly relevant reform pertaining to the management of forestland was, however, the distribution of use rights of upland to individual farmers for the maximum of 50 years. Because of this semiprivatization policy of land rights, forestland including already bared land ceased to be open access. In fact, those farmers who have acquired forestland began to undertake plantations of timber, fruit, and other trees of commercial value as well as protection of degraded forest areas for regeneration. This tenure reform seems to have resulted in increases in the so-called poor forest and renascent forest areas, which are considered to reflect regeneration of forest areas, and newly planted forest area in the early 1990s.[17]

In order to examine the effect of the land rights distribution policy on reforestation, we regressed changes in the sum of poor, renascent, and newly planted forest areas per capita from 1987 to 1994 and from 1991 to 1994. For the latter period, we have fairly reliable data on forest conditions, but not on agricultural production. Table 7.10 shows the estimation results of reduced-form regressions. Since the period of investigation ended in 1994, we use two alternative dummy variables of forest distribution: communes that received distributed forest area by 1993 and alternatively by 1994. There are two major findings. First, larger bare land area per capita promoted reforestation. This is reasonable because there is wider room for natural regeneration in larger areas. Second, and much more important, forest distribution policy resulted in significantly higher rates of reforestation when we used a forest distribution dummy in 1993. It is not unreasonable that the 1994 dummy is insignificant, as the new policy would affect reforestation with time lags. Since denuded forestlands were allocated to individual farmers on a voluntary basis, who are likely to grow trees, the significant effect of the 1993 dummy may not be surprising. This policy, however, was not necessarily implemented in areas most suitable for tree plantation; its implementation began in areas close to district towns. In

---

17. All mature trees are felled and burned before planting food crops under shifting cultivation, so that cleared forest and bush areas become bare land rather than poor and renascent forest areas.

TABLE 7.10 Determinants of changes in reforested area per capita

	1987–94		1991–94	
Intercept	0.007	0.012	0.018	0.024
	(0.41)	(0.67)	(0.62)	(0.76)
Population growth rate	−0.001	−0.001	0.001	0.001
	(−0.58)	(−0.58)	(0.79)	(0.60)
Lowland area per capita[a]	0.171	0.164	0.147	0.186
	(1.29)	(1.20)	(0.63)	(0.76)
Irrigated lowland ratio[a]	−0.012	−0.013	−0.014	−0.013
	(−1.14)	(−1.10)	(−0.88)	(−0.76)
Cultivable bare land area				
per capita[a]	0.009*	0.010*	0.018**	0.017**
	(2.33)	(2.31)	(2.76)	(2.55)
Resolution 10	−0.013	−0.017	−0.031	−0.037
	(−1.05)	(−1.33)	(−1.49)	(−1.76)
Forest distribution in 1993	0.015*		0.028**	
	(2.19)		(2.50)	
Forest distribution in 1994		0.007		0.012
		(1.36)		(1.33)
Fertile soil dummy	0.004	0.005	−0.007	−0.005
	(0.70)	(0.88)	(−0.79)	(−0.57)
Distance from town	−0.000	0.000	0.000	0.000
	(−0.77)	(−0.79)	(0.20)	(0.22)
Son La dummy	0.006	0.003	0.010	0.007
	(0.66)	(0.30)	(0.73)	(0.49)
Adjusted *R*-squared	0.23	0.19	0.28	0.22

NOTE: Numbers in parentheses are *t*-statistics.

[a]Initial values, that is, value in 1987 for 1987–94 regression and value in 1991 for 1991–94 regression.

*.05 level

**.01 level

other words, the places where the policy was implemented are not necessarily unrepresentative, so that the tenure effects are indeed real and replicable in other sites. Thus, there is no denying that such land tenure policy, which strengthens the land rights of individual households, is conducive to reforestation of highly degraded forest areas.

Summary of Findings for Extensive Study

The fundamental proposition of the extensive study is that the choice between intensification of existing agricultural land and extensification into hitherto uncultivated forestland, rather than fallow cycle intensification, is of critical importance to the proper understanding of deforestation processes in areas where flat lowland and sloped upland coexist.[18] If intensification is costly owing to low production efficiency of lowland farming, extensification tends to be chosen, leading to deforestation. Conversely, if extensification is costly owing to the establishment of individualized land rights in upland, deforestation will be deterred.

The experience of the northern hill region of Vietnam for the past few decades suggests that low productivity of collective farming under the commune system, coupled with unclear ownership rights of cultivable forestland, has been a significant cause of deforestation. In fact, we obtained evidence that increased rice production reduced deforestation. This finding does not support the conventional wisdom that improvement in agricultural productivity leads to deforestation in the hilly region, where the expansion of lowland agricultural fields is limited. We also found that allocation of forest use rights led to significant reforestation in communes where the forestland allocation policy was implemented. This seems to testify to the superior management of forests by individual farmers as compared with the state. It is also important to point out that population pressure on limited lowland areas is another important cause of deforestation, unless land rights in forestland are established. It is clear from our extensive study that the establishment of land rights on uplands had positive impacts on upland intensification and sustainable use of upland areas.

Intensive Study

Table 7.11 summarizes the major characteristics of the land use in the commune of Yen Do based on official statistics in 1994. Forestland with slopes greater than 25 degrees accounts for almost three-fourths of total area, whereas lowland farm area, mostly paddy land, accounts for 10.2 percent. A more important observation is that bare land occupies as much as 45.9 percent of forestland, indicating that substantial deforestation took place as a result of the expansion of shifting-cultivation areas. The proportion of bare land, however, is somewhat lower than the average in Bac Thai Province (see Table 7.2). Official statistics also show that 200 hectares of traditional forestland exists, accounting for 7.7 percent of forest area in the province.

Basic Characteristics of Sample Households

Selected households are nuclear, so that the average family size is 5.3, whereas the average number of working members, which is defined as those between 16 and 60 years of age, is merely 2.8.

---

18. Interestingly, Coxhead and Jaysuriya (1994) derive a qualitatively similar result in their model on upland soil erosion. For example, they demonstrate that productivity changes in lowland food agriculture could substantially reduce the rate of land degradation in uplands, whereas the upland technology improvement does not have clear effect. However, except for the explicit consideration of the interaction between lowland and upland farming, the structure of their model is quite different from ours.

TABLE 7.11 Land use patterns of Yen Do commune in 1994

	Area	Proportion
	(hectares)	(percentage)
Composition of total area		
Total	3,502	100.0
Forestland	2,601	74.3
Lowland farms	265	10.2
Composition of forestland		
Total	2,601	100.0
Bare land	1,195	45.9
Private forest	200	7.7

SOURCE: Intensive survey. Data provided by courtesy of the Phu Luong district office.

One of the most important determinants of land use in the northern hill region of Vietnam is ethnicity, as different ethnic groups traditionally engaged in different farming practices. Table 7.12 displays the ethnic composition of our sample households based on the ethnicity of households heads. Kinh is the dominant ethnic group in Vietnam but is not native in the northern hill region. After independence from France in 1954, the government promoted the migration of the Kinh from densely populated delta regions to the mountainous areas. They prefer to engage in lowland paddy farming, in which they have had a long experience. Since they are not natives, their land rights tend to be weaker than the native households. Because Yen Do is relatively close to the Red River delta, there are 98 Kinh households in our sample, accounting for 39 percent of all households. Forty-four out of 86 households whose heads migrated to their current villages are Kinh-headed households.

Tay is one of the largest minority ethnic groups in the northern hill region and has traditionally engaged in paddy cultivation on flat lowlands. The Tay constitute the second largest ethnic group in our sample. Dao and San Chay are ethnic minorities who have traditionally practiced shifting cultivation, whereby families move from one location to another, rotating between fallow and cultivation. Gradually they have settled in fixed locations, as cultivable land per household declined and they were required to be members of cooperatives to engage in collective farming with other ethnic groups. Nonetheless, there is some disposition among these minority ethnic groups toward shifting cultivation of upland.

Most of the lowland parcels were allocated from the cooperatives to individual households during the process of land tenure reforms in the 1980s. The allocation of use rights is basically egalitarian, even though migrants are discriminated against to some extent (Table 7.13). Out of 250 sample households,

TABLE 7.12 Ethnic composition of sample households

	Number of households	Proportion
		(percentage)
Kinh (migrants from delta)	98	39
Tay (wet rice cultivators)	96	38
Dao (shifting cultivators)	34	14
San Chay (shifting cultivators)	13	5
Others	9	4
Total	250	100

SOURCE: Intensive survey at commune of Yen D., Bac Thai Province.

237 households received some irrigated lowland, and 216 households received rainfed lowland. Most farmers had already obtained official use certificates over these lands by 1995. The average farm size per household is very small, consisting of 0.155 hectares of irrigated land and 0.097 hectares of rainfed land among native households, whereas the corresponding figures are somewhat smaller among migrant households, particularly irrigated land, which is far more productive than rainfed land. *Soi* soil land is an unproductive area commonly developed along riverbanks and represents the smallest area of farmland for both groups.

It is fair to say that compared with other communities, migrant households are treated favorably in Yen Do. In fact, we gathered that restitution of land ownership to the original owners was widely implemented in other communities, so that migrant households were excluded from the allocation of lowland. In such cases, they were forced to migrate to cities or to engage in shifting cultivation of upland fields. In Yen Do, however, most of the migrant households were considered as legitimate members of the commune, as they had moved to this area before the agricultural collectivization reform in the 1970s.

TABLE 7.13 Holdings of lowland farms by sample households by type of land

	Number of Households	Irrigated Lowland	Rainfed Lowland	*Soi* Soil Land[a]	Total
		(hectares)			
Natives	164	0.155	0.097	0.014	0.256
Migrants[b]	86	0.127	0.091	0.021	0.239
Average	250	0.145	0.095	0.016	0.256

SOURCE: Intensive survey.

[a]Farms located on riverbanks.

[b]Those households whose household heads have moved to the commune.

Despite the possession of the authorized and secure land titles over farmland, land and land rental markets are still inactive. Only seven households reported purchasing use rights of lowland parcels. Only one household rented in land from its neighbor. Furthermore, no sampled households reported any sale of land use rights in our survey.[19]

The average size of lowland per household is a mere 0.256 hectares, which is barely sufficient for subsistence living. The availability of such small lowland area would have led to increased clearing and shifting cultivation of upland areas, particularly when the food shortage took place. In the process of market-oriented economic reforms under the Doi Moi policy (Irvin 1995), however, many households began to initiate new businesses other than crop farming. Among our sample households, 29 began operating small stores in the villages. Many households reported expanding livestock production; 238 households raised at least a few pigs, among which 25 households raised more than five pigs. Two households started to raise cows for milk production. Fish raising in fishponds is another popular new business; 120 households were engaged in fish production, using an average fishpond area of 915 square meters. There is no question that these new business activities increased cash income of households as well as the opportunity cost of labor for cultivation of upland fields.

Use of Forestland

As was explained earlier, there are two types of forests in the commune of Yen Do. One is the traditional private forest (TPF) that has always been managed by individual households. This type of land has been inherited from earlier generations. Another type is newly allocated forest (NAF) land that originates from the cooperatives and is granted for 50 years of use on the basis of voluntary application by cooperative members. Farmers believe that their use rights will be renewed 50 years later, so they perceive that NAF lands essentially belong to them. The majority of NAF was bare land at the time of allocation. This is in sharp contrast to TPF, which has been well maintained almost without exception even during the time of food shortage in the early 1980s.

Table 7.14 reports the forestland holdings among our sample households by type of forests. There are 68 households that manage NAF alone, another 68 households that manage both NAF and TPF, and 85 households that manage only TPF.[20] We call them pure NAF owners, mixed owners, and pure TPF owners, respectively. The majority of forest patches are small and seldom exceed 1 hectare. The total holdings of NAF are on average 1.82 hectares among the

---

19. We suspect that the negligible number of reported land and land rental transactions may be due to underreporting by our respondents, who seem to be reluctant to disclose true information about these transactions.

20. We show the data of 221 households rather than full sample of 250 because we found a number of unreliable answers in the questionnaire.

TABLE 7.14 Holdings of forestland by sample households

	Pure Owners of New Forestland	Owners of Both New and Traditional Forestland	Pure Owners of Traditional Forestland
Number of households	68	68	85
New forestland			
Average size (ha)	1.82	1.32	—
Average number of plots	1.8	1.7	—
Average year of allocation	1990	1990	—
Percentage of plots with certificate	25.9	33.3	—
Traditional forestland			
Average size (ha)	—	0.81	1.69
Average number of plots	—	1.6	1.4
Percentage of plots with certificate	—	53.2	67.5

SOURCE: Intensive survey.

pure owners and 1.32 hectares among the mixed owners. The mixed owners also manage 0.81 hectare of TPF, which is smaller than the 1.69 hectares managed by the pure owners of TPF. It appears that those households that did not own much TPF lands obtained a relatively large amount of NAF.

Owing to tree planting-projects implemented since the late 1980s, the allocation of bare hills began relatively early in this commune. In fact, the average year of allocation is 1990, which precedes by three years the date when the Vietnamese government decided to accelerate the allocation of forestland to individual households. Yet the distribution of formal land use certificates has been implemented with much delay. As of December 1996, formal land use certificates had been issued to only 30 percent of the 224 NAF plots. An interesting observation is that the proportion of plots with the certificates is much higher for TPF, which indicates that private ownership of TPF has been well recognized by the local government office.

Before the formal allocation from the cooperatives, many beneficiaries used the allocated areas for shifting cultivation and firewood collection. This suggests that there was some agreement about the individual use rights of particular areas of communal forestland among cooperative members. This does not imply, however, that individual farmers had secure land use rights on the sloping upland plots that they cultivated. In fact, to our knowledge, no farmer has ever made major investments in communal land, such as tree planting and terracing, before the formal allocation. Therefore, the formal allocation has not only confirmed but considerably strengthened the individual use rights of upland plots.

TABLE 7.15 Tree planting on forestland by sample households

	Pure Owners of New Forestland	Owners of Both New and Traditional Forestland	Pure Owners of Traditional Forestland
Number of households	68	68	85
New forestland			
Percentage of households			
planting trees	75.0	72.1	—
(percentage with subsidy)[a]	(58.8)	(65.3)	
Percentage of areas planted			
to trees	40.5	43.4	—
(percentage with subsidy)[b]	(61.9)	(70.5)	
Traditional forestland			
Percentage of households			
planting trees	—	38.2	47.1
(percentage with subsidy)[a]		(11.5)	(20.0)
Percentage of areas planted			
to trees	—	12.4	9.9
(percentage with subsidy)[b]		(10.6)	(31.1)

SOURCE: Intensive survey.

[a]Proportion of households planting trees with subsidy provided by tree-planting projects.

[b]Proportion of areas planted to trees with subsidy provided by tree-planting projects.

We found that 20 households were still engaged in shifting cultivation on their NAF plots in 1997 despite its legal prohibition. They were, however, rather exceptional. As is demonstrated in Table 7.15, 75 percent of pure owners and 72.1 percent of mixed owners of NAF have planted some trees, including timber, tea, fruit, coffee, and cinnamon trees. As a result, 40.5 and 43.4 percent of NAF areas owned by pure NAF owners and mixed NAF and TPF owners, respectively, have been planted to trees. Tree planting is more intensive on NAF plots than on TPF plots; on the latter only 38.2 percent of mixed owner households and 47.1 percent of pure owner households planted trees, and planted areas amounted to only 10.9 percent of total TPF land on average.

The difference in tree-planting intensity between NAF and TPF lands is explained mainly by the difference in the original vegetation covers between them.[21] NAF land from the cooperative is mainly bare hills, whereas TPF land has generally been protected well and covered by densely grown trees, consisting of tall timber trees, shorter trees suitable for firewood, trees producing thatching material, bamboo, and others. Medicinal plants are also grown under the trees.

---

21. This was confirmed by the collected data on the tree-growing areas at the time of acquisition.

Unlike NAF plots supported by tree-planting projects, exotic tree species, such as acacia and eucalyptus, are seldom grown on TPF lands. According to interviews with owners of TPF, a major management activity of TPF is to replant trees so as to utilize sunlight to the maximum extent. Since the extracted forest resources are mostly used for home consumption, the farmers were unable to provide the market values of extracted resources. Because TPF lands are generally surrounded by roads and residential areas, protection is said to be relatively easy.

Another factor promoting active tree planting on NAF land is that this type of land has been allocated on the condition that the beneficiaries will undertake reforestation. It is therefore surprising that trees have yet to be planted on more than half of NAF areas.

Both NAF and TPF owners could apply to the PAM project for tree-planting assistance. Actually, much more than 50 percent of households owning NAF lands have received subsidies from the project, in the form of rice and free seedlings of mostly acacia or eucalyptus, to cover the opportunity cost of labor for tree planting and management. In contrast, relatively few TPF owners have received subsidies from the project. Such a difference can be explained by the preference of TPF owners not to grow exotic species. As is shown in Table 7.16, 19.4 percent of newly planted TPF land is planted to acacia and eucalyptus, whereas the corresponding figure is 63.4 percent on NAF lands. TPF owners actively planted tea on edges of hilly forest areas, which were sometimes partly degraded. Such sharp differences in the choice of tree species cast some doubts on the efficiency of the reforestation project, at least from the private point of view.

Policy Implications

As we have seen, massive deforestation in the 1980s was followed by buoyant reforestation in the 1990s in the mountainous regions of Vietnam. Such changes can be attributed largely to changes in policy environments. In particular, it will be fair to draw from the analyses of this chapter two major policy implications

TABLE 7.16 Composition of tree species planted in newly allocated forestland and traditional private forestland

	Acacia and Eucalyptus	Commercial Trees[a]	Other Trees[b]
		(percentage)	
New forestland	63.4	12.2	24.2
Traditional forestland	19.4	45.1	35.5

SOURCE: Intensive survey.

[a]Tea, cinnamon, coffee, and fruit trees.

[b]Mostly locally grown timber species.

to arrest excessive deforestation in hilly and mountainous regions. First, the effort to increase food production from lowland farming should be strengthened. It is likely that larger food production through the intensification of existing farming systems will reduce deforestation by affecting farmers' choice in favor of intensification over extensification, particularly where labor markets are underdeveloped and labor allocation is constrained by the endowment of family labor. We also expect that in the longer run, greater supply of foods from lowland areas will reduce food prices, which in turn will reduce incentives to expand upland areas at the expense of forest areas.

Second, private-property rights in forestland should be strengthened. Our empirical analysis indicates that population growth led to deforestation when forestland was practically open access. Since the beginning of the 1990s, however, tenure security of upland fields was strengthened. In this period, we did not observe any impact of population growth on deforestation. Furthermore, during this period, we observed that the establishment of individualized property rights in forestland resulted in significant reforestation from the extensive community survey data and in tree planting from the intensive household data. An important point is that the establishment of individualized land rights in degraded forestland has resulted in acceleration of reforestation, as well as deceleration of deforestation. Such a development is desirable not only from the individual farmers' viewpoint but also from a social point of view because of the positive environmental benefits of reforestation. Individualized land rights, however, should not be granted on the basis of cleared forest areas, which will lead to the socially undesirable, excessive race for land property rights. We conjecture that the distribution of land rights in degraded forestland to individual farmers on a voluntary basis in Vietnam, which is historically unprecedented in our knowledge, will make a significant contribution to reversing the trend of deforestation toward reforestation.

A final remark is in order regarding the use of allocated forestland by individual farmers. Although we did not mention it in the text, many small-scale communal irrigation systems are managed by a small number of households in our sites, utilizing water from small streams coming from nearby mountains. Collective farmwork has also been organized for a long period under the leadership of cooperatives. Thus, our sites have a tradition of collective work. None of the communities, however, organized the collective management of NAFs, even though they certainly could if they wanted. That farmers have decided to manage forestlands individually rather than collectively strongly suggests that it is more efficient to do so. In the next two chapters, we further consider under what conditions community management of forests under the common property system works well for the benefit of local people. It is important to consider why, unlike the experience of the hill region of Nepal examined in Chapter 8, community management of forest did not spontaneously develop in Vietnam.

Appendix: A Dynamic Model of Land Use

The purposes of this appendix are to construct and to sketch the solution of the dynamic optimization model of forest and upland use. Formally, the representative family is assumed to solve the following inter-temporal maximization problem:

$$\max U(\Pi) \, e^{-\rho\tau} \, d\tau, \tag{5}$$

where

$$\Pi = F(L_l, T_l, E_l) + PG(L - L_l, sT_u) - aD - c \, [1 - s]T_u, \tag{6}$$

subject to

$$\dot{T}_u = D - b(s) \, sT_u, \tag{7}$$

$$0 \leq s \leq 1 \tag{8}$$

$$T_u \leq W, \tag{9}$$

where U is an instantaneous utility function with $U' > 0$ and $U'' < 0$, which depends on household income (Π). The income consists of net revenue from paddy production (the first term in equation [6]), net revenue from upland agricultural production (second term), the cost of forest clearance (third term), and the cost of protecting rotational shifting-cultivation area (the last term). The cropping intensity in upland shifting-cultivation area, s, is bounded between zero and one, and the size of upland shifting-cultivation area T_u cannot exceed the size of initial forest area, W.

Income from lowland rice cultivation is given by a constant-returns-to-scale production function (F), which depends on labor input (L_l), lowland (irrigated) farm area (T_l), and index of production efficiency (E_l). Because of the hilly conditions in our study sites, there is no room for the expansion of lowland paddy fields. Thus, T_l is exogenous. E_l is intended to capture the effects of tenure reforms, since privatization of lowland farm is likely to enhance work incentives in the short run.[22] In the longer run, tenure reform may improve production efficiency by stimulating profitable investment. Market reform may also raise E_l by improving allocative efficiency of purchased inputs, which is not explicitly dealt with in the model. G is the production function of upland farming, which exhibits constant returns to scale in labor input and size of upland field under cultivation sT_u, where T_u is the total size of rotational shifting-

---

22. Intensification often entails farmers' capital investment in improving E_l. See Boserup (1965) and Clay, Reardon, and Kangasniemi (1998) for the various paths to intensification. In the case of Vietnam, however, the tenure reforms have been the most important events that resulted in major changes in production efficiency. Thus, we abstract from farmers' investment in the enhancement of E_l in this study.

cultivation area and s is the portion of T_u which is under current cultivation. L stands for predetermined level of total labor availability and, hence, $L - L_l$ corresponds to labor input for upland cultivation. P is the market price of upland products measured in terms of the price of lowland rice. The constant-returns-to-scale production function (F) is assumed to satisfy $F_1, F_2, F_3 > 0$; $F_{11}, F_{22} < 0$; $F_{12}, F_{13} > 0$; and $F_{11}F_{22} - (F_{12})^2 = 0$. Analogous conditions apply for G.

The cost of forest clearance is assumed to be linear in forest area to be cleared (D) with cost parameter a. This cost is not measured by the labor input for clearance but by the loss of income evaluated in terms of the price of lowland crop. This way of modeling will be more realistic than measuring the cost by labor input, because extensification into hill forests is usually carried out during the off-crop seasons. A natural interpretation is that aD captures the opportunity cost of off-farm work, which was negligible during the food shortage period and is likely to become higher during the period of the economic reforms. It also becomes higher as the bared land expands, because the farmers have to travel farther to clear new forests.

Insecure property rights in the sloped area impose another cost for a farm household. The upland area that is put into fallow, $[1 - s]T_u$, is subject to land grabbing from neighbors and strongmen in the village. Farmers expect to incur some cost to resolve land disputes, if they arise. A higher c therefore indicates the less secure property rights in the upland area. Since few upland areas had been *officially* allocated until 1993 in our field sites, we expect that significant structural change occurred after 1993. It is implicitly assumed in the current specification of the model that uncultivated forestland is open access, so that farm households clear the forest at will. Such an assumption, however, may not hold once use rights in forestland are granted to individual households.

Equation (7) describes how total shifting-cultivation area changes with time $(\dot{T}_u)$. An increase in D directly increases $\dot{T}_u$. A larger proportion of shifting-cultivation area under current production deteriorates the soil fertility of the cultivated area $s\dot{T}_u$ by shortening fallow periods, which is modeled as a decrease in the cultivable upland fields with a depreciation coefficient $b(s)$: $b'(s) > 0$ and $b''(s) > 0$.[23] This is why we refer to a higher s as *depriving* intensification.

In the model, a farmer chooses between lowland production (intensification in lowland) and upland production through the choice of L_p, between the current upland production and the future loss of upland soil productivity (depriving intensification) through s, and between the current loss of utility and the future increase in upland crop area (extensification) through D.

The current value Hamiltonian of equation (5) is:

---

23. This is a common formula in the literature of investment and capacity utilization (for example, Greenwood, Hercowitz, and Huffman 1988).

$$H = U(\Pi) + \lambda\{D - b(s)\,sT_u\} + w_1\,s + w_2\,\{1 - s\} + \mu\{W - T_u\}, \quad (10)$$

where λ is the multiplier that gives the marginal value of upland fields stock at t; w_1 and w_2 are the multipliers associated with the constraint on s; and μ is the multiplier associated with remaining forestland.

The first-order conditions for the maximization equation (5) are:

$$\partial H/\partial L_l = U'(.)\,\{F_1 - PG_1\} = 0, \quad (11)$$

$$\begin{aligned} \partial H/\partial s = U'(.)\,\{PG_2 T_u\} - \lambda\{b'(s)\,sT_u \\ + b(s)T_u - cT_u\} + w_1 + w_2 = 0 \end{aligned} \quad (12)$$

$$\partial H/\partial D = -aU'(.) + \lambda = 0 \quad (13)$$

$$\dot{\lambda} = [\rho + b(s)\,s + c\{1 - s\}]\,\lambda - U'(.)\,\{PG_2 s - c\,[1 - s]\} + \mu \quad (14)$$

$$\lim_{t \to \infty} T_u(t)\,\lambda(t)\,e^{-\rho t} = 0. \quad (15)$$

The bounded control on s implies

$$U'(.)\,\{PG_2 T_u\} - \lambda\{b'(s)\,sT_u + b(s)\,T_u - cT_u\} \begin{pmatrix} < \\ = \\ > \end{pmatrix} 0, \quad \begin{pmatrix} s = 0 \\ 0 < s < 1 \\ s = 1 \end{pmatrix}. \quad (16)$$

Let us show the results of interior solutions ($0 < s < 1$ and $T_u < W$), which correspond to what are actually observed in our field sites. A salient feature of this model is a recursive structure in its optimal conditions that assures tractability of the analysis, while maintaining a realistic description of farmer's choice (Greenwood et al. 1988). Equations (17) and (18), derived from the first-order conditions with respect to L_p, s, and D, simultaneously determine L_l and s:

$$F_1 - P\,G_1 = 0 \quad (17)$$

$$P\,G_2 + c - a\,\{b'(s)s + b(s)\} = 0. \quad (18)$$

Then given the choice of L_l and s determined above, transition equation (7) and equation (19) simultaneously determine how the optimal upland area changes:

$$\dot{T}_u = D - b(s)\,sT_u, \quad (7)$$

$$\dot{\lambda} = U'(.)[a\,\{\rho + b(s)s\} - \{PG_2 s - c[1 - s]\}], \quad (19)$$

where λ is the shadow price of upland area.

Table 7.17 summarizes the results of comparative statics at the steady state, where $\dot{\lambda} = \dot{T}_u = 0$ hold. Figure 7.2 presents the phase diagram on T_u and D plane. An increase in E_l shifts the $\dot{\lambda} = 0$ locus to the left and reduces the slope

TABLE 7.17 Theoretical relationships among variables: Results of comparative statics

Increase in	Lowland Labor (L_l)	Upland Cropping Intensity (s)	Upland Cultivation Area (T_u)	Cleared Forest Area (D^*)
Lowland production efficiency (E_l)	+	−	−	−
Lowland farm area (T_l)	+	−	−	−
Price of upland products (P)	−	+	+	+
Unit cost of forest clearance (a)	+	−	(?)	−
Tenure insecurity parameter (c)	−	+	−	(?)

NOTE: (?) indicates ambiguous.

of the $\dot{T}_u = 0$ locus. Thus, an improvement in lowland production efficiency (E_l) leads to a smaller upland shifting-cultivation area and a lower deforestation rate at the steady state. These results are consistent with our intuition.

An interesting result is the effect of changes in the security of property rights in upland (c). A deterioration of tenure security represented by an in-

FIGURE 7.2 The saddle path leading to the steady-state shifting-cultivation area

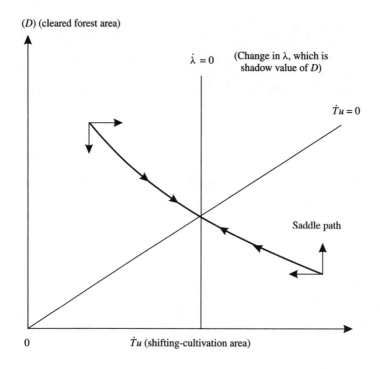

(D) (cleared forest area)

$\dot{\lambda} = 0$ (Change in λ, which is shadow value of D)

$\dot{T}u = 0$

Saddle path

0    $\dot{T}u$ (shifting-cultivation area)

crease in c lowers the upland area at the steady state. This is because farmers cultivate the existing upland more intensively (represented by higher s) to secure the right to cultivate. This result is generated from the assumption that is opposite the usual assumption that presumes the establishment of secure land rights in cleared land (Anderson and Hill 1990). The effect of change in c on the steady-state deforestation rate, however, is ambiguous.

References

Anderson, Terry L., and Peter J. Hill. 1990. The race for property rights. *Journal of Law and Economics* 33 (2): 177–197.

Angelsen, Arild. 1995. Shifting cultivation and deforestation: A study from Indonesia. *World Development* 23 (10): 1713–1729.

Barbier, Edward B., and Joanne C. Burgess. 1997. The economics of tropical forest land use options. *Land Economics* 73 (2): 174–195.

Boserup, Ester. 1965. *The conditions of agricultural growth.* London: George Allen and Unwin.

Clay, Daniel, Thomas Reardon, and Jaako Kangasniemi. 1998. Sustainable intensification in the highland tropics: Rwandan farmers' investment in land conservation and soil fertility. *Economic Development and Cultural Change* 46 (2): 351–377.

Coxhead, Ian, and Sisira Jayasuriya. 1994. Technical change in agriculture and land degradation in developing countries: A general equilibrium analysis. *Land Economics* 70 (1): 20–37.

Cuc, Le Trong, Kathleen Gillogly, and A. Terry Rambo, eds. 1990. Agroecosystems of the midlands of Northern Vietnam. Occasional Paper No.12. Environment and Policy Institute, East-West Center, Hawaii.

Ehui, Simeon K., Thomas W. Hertel, and Paul V. Preckel. 1990. Forest resource depletion, soil dynamics, and agricultural productivity in the tropics. *Journal of Environmental Economics and Management* 18 (2): 136–154.

Elnagheeb, Abdelmoneim H., and Daniel W. Bromley. 1994. Extensification of agriculture and deforestation: Empirical evidence from Sudan. *Agricultural Economics* 10 (2): 193–200.

Greenwood, Jeremy, Zvi Hercowitz, and Gregory W. Huffman. 1988. Investment, capacity utilization, and real business cycles. *American Economic Review* 78 (3): 402–417.

Hayami, Yujiro. 1993. Strategy for the reform of land property relations in Vietnam. Food and Agriculture Organization (FAO) Vietnam Mission Report (TCP/VIE/2252).

———. 1997. Development economics: From the poverty to the wealth of nations. Oxford: Clarendon Press.

International Food Policy Research Institute. 1996. *Rice market monitoring and policy options study.* Washington, D.C.: IFPRI.

Irvin, George. 1995. Vietnam: Assessing the achievements of *Doi Moi. Journal of Development Studies* 31 (5): 725–750.

Kerkvliet, B. J. T., and Doug J. Porter, eds. 1995. *Vietnam's rural transformation.* Boulder, Colo.: Westview Press.

Pingali, Prabhu L., and Vo-Tong Xuan. 1992. Vietnam: Decollectivization and rice productivity growth. *Economic Development and Cultural Change* 40 (4): 697–718.

Ricardo, David. 1821. *Principles of political economy and taxation.* 3d ed. Cambridge: Cambridge University Press.

Rowe, Raymond, Narendra Sharma, and John Browder. 1992. Deforestation: Problems, causes, and concerns. In *Managing the world's forests,* ed. Narendra Sharma. Dubuque, Iowa: Kendall/Hunt.

Sikor, Thomas. 1996. Forest policy reform in Vietnam: From state to household forestry. University of California, Berkeley. Mimeo.

Tachibana, Towa, Trung M. Nguyen, and Keijiro Otsuka. 2001. Agricultural intensification versus extensification: A case study of deforestation in the northern hill region of Vietnam. *Journal of Environmental Economics and Management.* 41 (1): 44–69.

Vietnam, Department of Agriculture, Forestry and Fishery. 1996. *Statistical data of agriculture, forestry, and fishery.* Hanoi: Statistical Publication House.

Vietnam, Ministry of Forestry. 1991. Forestry sector review: Tropical forestry action programme, main report. Hanoi.

Vu Hoai, Minh. 1993. *Economic realities to consider in developing strategies for forest land use.* Hanoi: Ministry of Forestry.

World Bank. 1992. *World development report 1992.* New York: Oxford University Press.

PART IV

Common Property Management

8 Common Property Forest Management in the Hill Region of Nepal

TOWA TACHIBANA, HARI K. UPADHYAYA,
RIDISH POKHAREL, SANTOSH RAYAMAJHI,
AND KEIJIRO OTSUKA

Physically, Nepal is an extremely diverse country. It includes the flat plains of the Tarai in the south and the sloping terrain of the middle hills and the snowy peaks of the mountains in the north. The climatic environments also vary greatly, ranging from warm tropical in the south to cold temperate in the north. It has a total land area of about 14 million hectares, of which 23, 42, and 35 percent fall in the Tarai, hill, and mountain regions, respectively. Less than 20 percent of the total land area is cultivated, with a major portion (56 percent) located in the Tarai. The hill and mountain regions account for only 37 percent and 7 percent of the cultivated area, respectively. Although all of the Tarai is generally accessible, many parts of the hills and most of the mountains are inaccessible by roads. Because of relatively greater accessibility and better prospects for agriculture in the Tarai, a large number of people from the hilly areas have migrated to this region, especially since the eradication of malaria in the 1960s. As a result, the Tarai population has grown rapidly to reach almost half of the country's total population of 22 million at present.

With a per capita income of about $225, Nepal is one of the poorest countries of the world. Nearly one-half of the population falls below the national poverty line, and two-thirds of the people fail to earn $1 per day. Poverty is particularly serious in more remote parts of the hills and the mountains. Overall, the infrastructure is underdeveloped, but its development varies significantly across regions. Accordingly, regional disparities in income and employment opportunities are large and persistent, with the hilly and mountainous areas having poor access to such opportunities.

More than 85 percent of the Nepalese people live in rural areas, where agriculture and its related sectors dominate economic activities. Although the share of agriculture in the GDP has fallen significantly, from 72 percent in 1975 to 40 percent in 1997, a vast majority of the rural people, in particular women,

We thank Bob Allen and Yujiro Hayami. We are also grateful to Rabindra M. Tamrakar, who analyzed aerial photographs. This research was partly supported by a grant from the Japan Economic Research Foundation.

still depend heavily on this sector for income and employment opportunities. In fact, agriculture employs more than 80 percent of the total labor force, compared with a meager 4 percent employed by the manufacturing sector. Thus the overall well-being of the Nepali people is greatly influenced by agriculture, which has remained largely traditional and subsistence-oriented.

Forests influence Nepali life and agriculture in several important ways. Besides contributing to natural watershed conservation and environmental balance, forests supply timber, fuelwood, fodder, grasses, leaf litter, and many other minor forest products, which are necessary for daily household use and agricultural production. They also provide raw materials to wood-based industries and promote tourism, which is an important source of foreign exchange earning of Nepal (Nepal, National Planning Commission 1997).

Fuelwood, which is supplied by the forests, is the most important source of energy for cooking in Nepal. The cooking energy supplied by fuelwood is nearly 68 percent for the entire country and more than 90 percent for the hill and the mountain regions. More than three-quarters of the households in Nepal and 90 percent of the households in its hilly regions use fuelwood for cooking. About 84 percent of the households collect fuelwood in Nepal, whereas almost all of the households do so in the hilly regions (Nepal, Central Bureau of Statistics 1996). More than two-thirds of the households collect fuelwood from public forests, whereas nearly one-fifth collect it from their own private land. National fuelwood demand has been estimated at nearly 15 million tons per year, of which agricultural land supplies about 3 million tons. The rest has to be supplied by the forests. Almost all the hilly districts have a shortage of fuelwood.

Livestock raising is an integral part of the farming system in Nepal, particularly in the higher altitudes, and is more common among the poorer households, that is, the small and marginal farmers and landless households. It contributes about 31 percent to agricultural GDP, of which 62 percent comes from the hilly regions. Nearly three-quarters of the total Nepali households keep cattle, and half of them keep buffaloes, goats, or poultry. The average livestock herd contains 3.3 cattle, 2.2 buffaloes, 4.1 goats/sheep, 1.7 pigs, and 7.3 poultry (Nepal, National Planning Commission and Asian Development Bank 1995). Crop residue contributes 47 percent to the livestock feed; the rest of the feeding requirements are met from forests, shrublands, and grazing lands. The total fodder requirement is estimated at nearly 8 million tons per year. As many as 65 percent of the districts in the country experience severe fodder shortages, and most of these districts are in the hill and the mountain regions.

The frequency and level of chemical fertilizer application to crops in Nepal are among the lowest in the world. Use of chemical fertilizer is most common in rice and wheat. However, fewer than half of the farming households apply fertilizer to rice, and only about one-third do so to wheat. A major source of fertilization is compost, which is made from animals' dung and leaf litter used as bedding materials for animals. Traditionally, fodder, grasses, and leaf litter were mostly obtained from the forests. In recent years, however, the availability of such materials from the forests has been greatly reduced.

Despite the importance of forests for subsistence farming and largely self-sufficient life, Nepal's forest area has declined from 45 percent of land area in 1964 to 29 percent in 1998. Such decline took place primarily in the Tarai, where timber production is particularly important. In the hills, forest area did not decline, but the quality of forest has deteriorated considerably owing mainly to excessive extraction of firewood and overgrazing (Metz 1991; Soussan, Shrestha, and Uprety 1995). How to maintain and improve forest conditions is therefore an urgent and critical issue in Nepal. We seek to analyze the effectiveness of community management of copse forests in the hills in this chapter and timber forests in the inner Tarai in the next chapter in comparison with the experience of timber forest management during postwar Japan.

The organization of this chapter is as follows. The major analytical issues of community or common property forest management and our hypotheses are discussed in the next section, which is followed by a brief review of historical changes in forest management systems in the hill region of Nepal. We then discuss the sampling strategies used in the extensive study of forest management and the intensive study of the management of firewood collection along with a description of the conditions and management rules of sample forests. The discussion of the extensive study is divided into subsections on the analyses of the determinants of the emergence of forest user groups and their consequences on forest management. The discussion of the intensive study includes subsections on a theoretical framework, empirical specification, and estimation results. Finally, the policy implications synthesized from both studies are summarized in the last section.

Issues and Hypotheses

Community management of local natural resources, such as forest, water, and rangeland, has been receiving increasing attention in the development literature as a potentially effective institutional arrangement to regulate the use of these resources (Bardhan 1993; Baland and Platteau 1996; Hayami 1997). Having perceived the failures of the central government's ownership and control, international donor agencies and the governments of many developing countries began to adopt the participatory community approach, in which the local resource users are entrusted to manage natural resources (FAO 1989; World Bank 1996). The promotion of this new policy has been supported by the new development in economic theory, particularly in the game theoretic fields, that suggests the possibility of avoiding the tragedy of the commons under a variety of conditions (Pearce 1992). Further, several authors argue that community management is potentially an effective institutional arrangement to attain efficient use of local natural resources, particularly if it is granted formal and assured land rights (Runge 1981; Ostrom 1990; McGranahan 1991; Bromley 1992; Ostrom and Gardener 1993; Baland and Platteau 1996).

Under the private ownership system every owner must exert effort to protect his or her property. In the case of forest resource management, we expect that the cost of protection will be particularly high if the resources are minor forest products grown in areas away from residential areas. This is because it is highly costly to identify the property from which these minor products are extracted. Tiny private forests are developed near farmers' residence in some places, and fodder trees are often planted on edges of private fields in the hill region of Nepal, because it is easy to oversee such forests and plantations. As will be seen in Chapter 9, the cost of protection tends to be lower and the importance of silvicultural operation higher in the case of timber forests, so that individualized arrangements compatible with work incentives are more important. The cost of protecting minor forest products, however, may be economized by organizing collective action in patrolling and guarding community resources under a common property regime (Grafton 2000).[1] It is also argued that community management will be efficient in traditional communities where people know one another and are tied by kinship and other enduring personal relationships (for example, Hayami 1997). In such circumstances, transaction costs of formulating management rules over community resources and enforcing them may not be too high, and hence the use of resources may be effectively regulated. A recent theoretical study based on evolutionary game theory demonstrates that whether forest resources are depleted under a common property regime depends on the cost of sanctions that maintain cooperative behavior among its members (Sethi and Somanathan 1996). Further, Aoki (2000) argues that to the extent that the threat of social ostracism is credible, cooperation in the commons game can become the norm of behavior in the village community.

In contrast to the development in theoretical studies, there have been relatively few empirical studies exploring the efficiency and effectiveness of local community management of natural resources.[2] Given the various outcomes predicted by theoretical analyses, it is clearly an empirical question whether community management of natural resources is effective in conserving and protecting common property resources. This study attempts to assess the feasibility and the effectiveness of forest resource management under the community management system based on a case study of community forests in the hill re-

---

1. *Community ownership* or *common property system* is defined as a system in which resources are subtractable like private goods and are owned and used jointly by a group of people. It is generally presumed that the exclusion of users is costly to a varying extent. See Ostrom (1990), who proposes to call resources with imperfect excludability common-pool resources.

2. See Wade (1988); Stevenson (1991); Fujita, Hayami, and Kikuchi (1999); Bardhan (2000); and Chapter 9 in this volume, among others. See also Arnold (2001) for a recent survey of the literature on the community forest management.

gion of Nepal. First, we attempt to identify factors facilitating or impeding the formation of community management systems. Second, we explore the consequences of different types of community forest management on forest conditions. Third, we assess the effectiveness of forest management rules under different institutions through an analysis of firewood collection behavior by individual forest users.

Specifically we postulate the existence of a U-shaped curve to describe changes in forest resources over time, in which deforestation is followed by reforestation (see Figure 1.3 in Chapter 1). The deforestation phase can be explained by open access to forest resources coupled with increased population pressure, whereas the reforestation phase can be explained by the emergence of effective community management. This hypothesis maintains that organizing community members, introducing management rules, and enforcing them are costly, and hence community management is introduced only when the benefit of initiating such management exceeds the cost. In other words, we argue that the benefit of initiating community management exceeds the cost of setting up such a system only when forest resources have become sufficiently scarce and valuable. We further hypothesize that community forest management, particularly the formal user group system, which has received official use rights of forests and support for management from the forestry department, is effective in reducing the overexploitation of forest resources.

Historical Changes in Forest Management

The hill region lies over the altitudes from 700 to 2,000 meters (Figure 8.1). Because of its rugged geographical conditions, the majority of inhabitants in the hill region of Nepal have unfavorable access to urban markets. Even now it is not exceptional to walk over hilly trails for a few days to reach one's village from the nearest market town. As a result, the main economic activity has been subsistence farming with minimum dependence on purchased inputs, such as chemical fertilizer, and the main source of household energy has been almost exclusively firewood. Furthermore, farmers depend on low value ("minor") forest products such as leaf fodder and grasses to feed livestock for milking, plowing, and making composts. Compost application is indispensable to maintain the soil fertility of terraced fields located on steep slopes. Even leaf litter collected from the forest is used as bedding material for livestock in order to collect nutrients contained in urine.

Historically under the feudal Rana regime, from 1846 to 1950, local government officials had controlled harvesting of timber trees in the forests. Such control was particularly strict in areas near the Tarai and main roads, which had favorable access to timber markets in India. Even in remote areas where market access was unfavorable, permission was required to fell timber trees for own

FIGURE 8.1 Location of sample forests in the midhills of Nepal

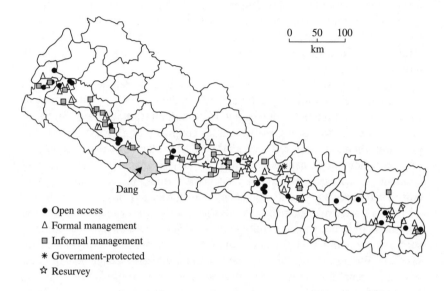

use, such as the construction of houses.[3] In contrast, the collection of minor forest products was usually unregulated, which would reflect the abundance of such resources at that time.

The feudal system, however, collapsed in 1950 and was followed by political upheaval and accelerated population growth. It is alleged that massive deforestation, highlighted by rampant felling of timber trees, began in the 1950s with the gradual collapse of the feudal forest management system (Gilmour and Fisher 1991). In order to arrest deforestation, forest areas were nationalized in 1957. With a limited number of forestry officers, however, the government could not implement the nationalization policy effectively except in the Tarai and the areas near district headquarters in the hill region (Bromley and Chapagain 1984; Graner 1997). According to our interviews with village elders, most forest users did not perceive that their forests were nationalized until cadastral surveys were conducted one or two decades later. Other factors, such as population pressure, would also have been responsible for deforestation (Gilmour and Fisher 1991).

---

3. It is not clear how strictly the regulation on timber harvesting was applied to the remote hill regions. Graner (1997: chap. 2) suggests that the Rana regime attached great importance to the forests even in the hill region. Gilmour and Fisher (1991: chap. 1) argue, however, that the central government of Rana promoted forest clearance in most areas of the hill region and protected limited forest areas as a source of fuel for manufacturing arms. In our field interviews, many older respondents recalled that, with required payment, it was not too difficult for them to obtain permission for timber harvesting during the Rana regime.

While the loss of forest area has been the major form of deforestation in most developing countries (see, for example, Deacon 1994), degradation of forest conditions has been the major concern in the hill region of Nepal. Indeed, based on aerial photographs taken in 1964–65 and 1978–79, it is reported that the loss of forest area had been negligible (Metz 1991; Soussan, Shrestha, and Uprety 1995). This is because most of the cultivable land had already been converted to farmland in the hill region by the first half of the twentieth century. According to our own estimates based on aerial photographs taken in 1978 and 1992–96, the average proportion of forest area in village development councils (VDCs),[4] which are local administrative units, changed only slightly, from 35.2 percent to 35.7 percent.

However, as will be seen, crown cover declined in many sample forests for the same period, indicating that the quality of forests has generally deteriorated. In the forests near main roads, timber extraction for market sale by villagers as well as outsiders has been a serious problem. In the more remote areas, however, timber trees were cut primarily for the construction of houses and cremations in the villages. Other direct causes for declining crown cover were grazing and the collection of firewood and leaf fodder for own consumption. Grazing is a major threat to forest regrowth, as cattle eat and step on seedlings and coppices. Although collection of dead and dry branches does not deteriorate the forest condition, cutting live branches for firewood and fodder results in major damages. As population increased, the intensity of grazing and the extraction of firewood and fodder increased, resulting in degradation of forest conditions.

The shortage of forest resources led to the reduction in the number of livestock and increased time allocation for the collection of forest resources from distant forests, which had traditionally been used by different communities or hamlets (Kumar and Hotchkiss 1988; Cooke 1998). This invasion of other forests has often created conflicts among people from different communities. Responding to continued deforestation and increasing conflicts, some communities spontaneously began to form informal forest user groups (IFUGs) to manage forests, even though the government possessed the legal ownership titles. It should be noted that such IFUGs were formed based on customary access rights to forest, but not on residence within political boundaries. Thus, it is not uncommon to find cases in which several hamlets from different VDCs form an IFUG.[5] These IFUGs began to exclude outsiders from the use of their own

---

4. The local administrative hierarchy in Nepal consists of (in order from large to small units) development region, district, VDC, and ward. Usually there are several hamlets in each ward.

5. Hamlet (*tol* in Nepali language) is not the geographically minimum unit for the membership of a forest user group. Although not so common, we encountered a case in which some households are members of a forest user group and others are those of another user group even within the same hamlet.

forests and to regulate the extraction of timber and other forest products by the user group members.[6] Gilmour (1989), Messerschmidt (1990), Gilmour and Fisher (1991), and Fox (1993), among others, indicate the burgeoning success of such indigenous forest management systems based on the results of several case studies in the early stages of their evolution.

Having observed favorable effects of forest user group management on forest conditions, the Government of Nepal has officially promoted the community management of forests since the late 1980s (Nepal, Ministry of Forests and Soil Conservation 1988). The policy of handing over formal usufruct rights to the user groups or the people who actually used forests was legalized in the amended Forest Act of 1987. The new legislation requires those communities that wish to obtain use rights of forests to form a formal forest user group (FFUG). The submission of a constitution and a management plan, in accordance with the guidelines prepared by the Ministry of Forestry, are required, and these must specify the rules of forest management agreed on by all community members. The ultimate ownership of forestland, however, still remains with the government. FFUGs established under the Forest Act include traditional and recently formed IFUGs.

The legal status of FFUGs has been further strengthened by the New Forest Act of 1993, following which (1) handing over is decided at the District Forest Office (DFO) level, (2) FFUGs can use the revenue from community forestry for purposes other than forest protection and management, and (3) FFUGs have the freedom to make changes in the management plans submitted earlier to the DFO (Karki et al. 1994).

Sample Forests, Forest Users, and Management Rules

Sample Forests

Nepal consists of five development regions: eastern, central, western, midwestern, and far western. Initially, we randomly sampled 100 forests from the whole hill region in proportion to the relative importance of forest area in each region compared with the total hill area.[7] A minimum forest size of 10 hectares was imposed in order to apply aerial photo analysis with sufficient accuracy.

---

6. Although the organizational structures of the IFUGs are diverse, it is common to select committee members in a general meeting. These committee members are entrusted with forest management activities, such as the selection of deformed and densely growing trees that are allowed to be felled by members of user group without deteriorating the overall forest conditions. There are also cases in which the leaders of the local administration are chosen to be the leaders of informal community forest management. In contrast, the formal user groups must select committee members by election.

7. By chance, we happened to select a few forests from the lower hills called Siwalik Mountains with altitudes of 300 to 700 meters.

Fifty forests were chosen from the nonremote areas and another 50 from remote areas; remoteness is defined by a distance of more than 10 kilometers from the main road as well as more than 15 kilometers from district capitals. Roughly speaking, nonremote forests can be reached within half a day's walk from the main road. Because of the inconsistency and the unreliability of some data, this study focuses on 74 sample forests.[8]

As is shown in Table 8.1, nonremote forests are located substantially closer to local markets and offices of forest rangers, who are in charge of local forest management. The average size of community forests in nonremote areas is about 70 percent of those in remote areas. In contrast, the number of user households is much larger in nonremote areas. As a result, the average forest area per user household in nonremote area is nearly one-half of that in remote areas. Therefore, population pressure on forest resources tends to be higher in nonremote areas. Such areas, however, have better access to alternative sources of energy for firewood, such as kerosene and biogas, and to chemical fertilizer, which is a major substitute for compost. Although population pressure will stimulate the emergence of spontaneous community forest management, favorable access to markets may hinder it.

According to Table 8.1, the proportion of sample forests managed by user groups, either formally or informally, is much higher in nonremote forests.[9] This may be explained by the deteriorated forest conditions in nonremote areas due to severe population pressure that led to the formation of forest user groups. As a matter of fact, the average crown cover in 1978 was 39 percent and 49 percent in nonremote and remote sample forests, respectively. According to the results of our group interviews, shortage of forest resources was the single most important reason to initiate the user group management in 70 percent of forest user groups.

Another important factor affecting the formation of user group management may be the direct intervention by the DFO. IFUGs are voluntary organizations that manage forests owned officially by the government. Since no formal use rights are granted, the IFUG may face difficulties in excluding outsiders and internal violators. Once the forest is handed over to the user group, secure use rights are granted, unless the user group grossly violates government regulations, such as felling mature timber trees without permission. The proportion of registered forests managed by FFUGs is definitely higher in nonremote areas (Table 8.1). This seems to reflect the fact that because of budget and per-

---

8. In certain areas, our survey teams had difficulty in locating sample forests chosen by the use of aerial photos. In this study, we have omitted those 26 sample forests that might not have been investigated by our survey teams by mistake with positive probabilities.

9. Actually several IFUGs are inactive, as evidenced by the absence of management rules and activities. Based on the results of our interview, we treated these cases as no user group management.

TABLE 8.1 Basic characteristics of sample forests

	Nonremote Forests	Remote Forests
Number of forests	38	36
Traveling time to (hours)		
Nearest local market	1.04	1.29
Nearest ranger office	6.24	5.90
Size of forest (ha)	86.1	117.8
Number of user households	187.9	132.8
Average forest area per household (ha)	0.46	0.89
Proportion of user group management (percentage)	92.1	50.0
Proportion of formal user groups (percentage)	74.3	33.3

SOURCE: Extensive forest survey.

sonnel constraints, DFOs have assisted primarily those user groups that are easily accessible.

Local DFO staffs also provide technical support for forest management, including the provision of seedlings for rehabilitation of degraded forests. The DFOs occasionally visit the formally managed forests to check forest conditions and user group activities. If they detect violations of management rules, they are expected to assist user group committees to implement punishment. In fact, users of the registered forests generally perceive that the enforcement of the rules of community forest management has become more effective since the forests were registered. Another major role of DFOs is to detect any serious conflicts over management rules among forest users proposed by IFUGs. The DFOs refuse to hand over forests to user groups if conflicts are found. As pointed out by Aoki (2000) and Baland and Platteau (1996), it is clear that the introduction of the third party, that is, DFO, has changed the nature of community management strategies.

As is shown in Table 8.2, relatively few IFUGs were formed before the mid-1980s. Since the change in government policy in favor of community user group management in 1987, not only has the number of IFUGs increased, but a sizable number of FFUGs were also established. The initiation of some user group management may have been inspired by the opportunity to acquire forest use rights. In fact, several user groups were set up as FFUGs from the beginning with the direct assistance of the DFO, even though the majority of FFUGs had formerly been active IFUGs.

Forest Conditions and Management Rules

If there are no regulations on the extraction of forest resources, the tragedy of the commons will inevitably take place, resulting in overexploitation and dete-

TABLE 8.2 Number of user groups initiating informal and formal management by period

	Informal User Group	Formal User Group
1966–70	4	
1971–75	1	
1976–80	4	
1981–85	3	
1986–90	20	1
1991–97	21	31
Total	53	32

SOURCE: Extensive forest survey.

rioration of forest conditions over time (Hardin 1968). In the standard economic model of common property management (for example, Dasgupta and Heal 1979), the crux of the management issue is how to prevent socially excessive exploitation of resources arising from the failure of coordination among resource users. In the reality of Nepal, overexploitation has already taken place, and forests have been seriously degraded. At present, the more important management issue is how to regenerate forest resources rather than simply protecting them. Thus, the extraction of scarce forest resources is not only regulated but also often prohibited by the user groups in the short run.

One of the critical questions is whether and to what extent the policy of handing over forest use rights to the community is effective in enhancing the efficiency of forest user group management. In practice, IFUGs often perceive that the local forests, which they have used for many years, belong to them. Based on such a perception, they *voluntarily* undertook forest management. Thus, some researchers argue that IFUGs have been successful in protecting forests in a sustainable manner, even though they do not possess official use rights (for example, Fisher 1989; Fox 1993). Others, however, disagree (for example, Gilmour, King, and Hobley 1989). According to our field interviews, management rules are more effectively enforced under FFUG management than their informal counterparts, primarily because the enforcement of management rules is supported, implicitly or explicitly, by the authority of the DFO.

We conducted an analysis of aerial photos taken in 1978 and 1992–96, in order to obtain information on general forest conditions and their changes over time. The most important indicator of forest conditions generated by the aerial photo analysis is the proportion of crown cover. The results, however, were not wholly satisfactory, primarily because it is difficult to distinguish between the canopies of big trees and short bushy trees generated by coppices of felled trees. As a result, relatively small differences and changes were found in crown cover across forests under no management, IFUG and FFUG management, and over

TABLE 8.3 Forest conditions in 1978, 1992–96, and 1997 by management regime in 1997

	No User Group	Informal User Group	Formal User Group
Number of forests	21	21	32
Crown cover (percentage)			
1978	42.4	31.4	31.9*
1992–96	38.6	33.3	28.1*
Biomass per hectare in 1997 (ton/ha)	143	135	131
Number of regenerated trees			
per 100 square meters in 1997	31.0	33.0	47.4*

SOURCE: Extensive forest survey.

NOTE: Statistical test is performed on difference in the mean values between no user group management and user group management.

*.05 level

time (see Table 8.3). A closer examination suggests, however, that forest conditions in the absence of user group management deteriorated more rapidly, even though they were more favorable than those under IFUG and FFUG management in both 1978 and recent years. These observations are consistent with our hypothesis that deforestation is followed by reforestation as a result of the formation of user group management. On the other hand, there is no clear indication that forest conditions were improved under FFUG management. Recall, however, that FFUG management was initiated mostly in the 1990s, so that the impact of FFUG management on changes in crown cover from 1978 to 1992–96 may not yet have emerged. This is another limitation of the use of aerial photos for our analysis.

In the hill region of Nepal, the most important forest resources for local users are not timber but minor forest products, such as firewood, leaf fodder, and leaf litter. It is therefore appropriate to use the biomass of all trees, rather than timber volume, for the analysis of management of forest resources in this region. Thus, we conducted a forest inventory assessment in which we directly measured the density and distribution of various tree species of different sizes in sample forests. We also measured the rate of regeneration of young trees (that is, shorter than breast height). Given that user group management was initiated relatively recently and that the major means to restore forest conditions is to generate coppices by strict protection, the rate of regeneration seems to be a more appropriate indicator of the effects of user group management than biomass.

It must be pointed out that the measurement of density and distribution of various trees in community forests in the hill region of Nepal is not an easy task, so we applied a sampling formula for the selection of sample plots. We anticipate that some measurement errors are inevitable, particularly when forests are large and their conditions are not uniform (see Rayamajhi and Pokharel 1998 for details of forest measurement).

It is interesting to find that the average biomass per hectare was greatest in the absence of user group management in 1997 (Table 8.3). In terms of the regeneration of trees, however, FFUG management seems to perform best. It is likely that the regeneration rate was low under IFUG management essentially because forests were so degraded that recovery required both time and strict protection. On the other hand, regeneration was poor without user group management despite the large stock of biomass, which is likely to reflect the absence of management. In contrast, the regeneration rate is high under the FFUG management despite meager endowment of biomass. Such differences can be explained by the effect of FFUG management on the regeneration of young trees. Overall, the above observations seem consistent with the hypothesis of U-shaped changes in forest conditions over time, in which forest conditions deteriorate when forest resources are abundant and improve after initiation of user group management, particularly that of FFUGs.

The restrictions on cutting timber trees by user groups have been effectively enforced, as they are bulky resources, and hence the cost of their protection is relatively low. Major management rules on the extraction of minor forest products are either the restriction on the number of days on which members of the user group are allowed to collect forest resources or the total prohibition of harvesting for a given period of time to facilitate regeneration. Slightly less than one-half of user groups employ watchers or adopt rotational patrolling, and mutual supervision is attempted by all user groups. Although the restriction on the collection of dead and dry branches is important to prevent the excessive collection of firewood, more important regulations for regeneration and recovery of forest conditions are the restrictions on cutting green branches and grazing of livestock. Cutting green branches and young trees except for deformed ones, very low branches, and those in dense patches must be strictly controlled for successful regeneration of trees.

Table 8.4 summarizes the regulations on the extraction of minor forest products implemented by IFUGs and FFUGs. The numbers simply indicate whether the user groups adopt some regulations or not, as it is difficult to assess the severity or intensity of regulations. For example, we cannot always assume that the total prohibition of resource extraction is stricter than regulated extraction of the resources as a management rule, because it is often desirable to remove some trees that are densely grown as well as low-lying branches to improve forest conditions.

Several important observations can be made from this table. First, as is expected, no management rules are adopted in the forests without a user group. This indicates that forest is open access, at least for community members, unless user group management is introduced. Second, it is clear that all the FFUGs, as well as almost all the IFUGs, adopt some regulations on the extrac-

TABLE 8.4 Frequency of sample forests adopting regulations on forest resource extraction/use, by management regime, in 1997

	No User Group	Informal User Group	Formal User Group
Number of sample forests	21	21	32
Number of forests with regulations on			
Green firewood collection	0	19	32
Dead firewood collection	0	3	14
Grazing	0	8	12

SOURCE: Extensive forest survey.

tion of green firewood, which include prohibitions and regulated extractions.[10] Since such regulations are of critical importance for protection of forests, not only FFUGs but also IFUGs implement some regulations. Thus, we cannot distinguish between the two management regimes in terms of the frequency of regulations of green firewood extraction. Third, the regulation of the collection of dead branches is less strict than that of green firewood, as it does not affect the forest conditions in the future. Fourth, the collection of dead branches is seldom regulated in informally managed forests, whereas it is regulated in nearly one-half of the formally managed forests. Thus, it seems reasonable to hypothesize that FFUGs manage forests more strictly than IFUGs by adopting stricter management rules, even though both manage forests to some extent, unlike the case of no user group management.[11]

Grazing is sometimes prohibited or allowed only in areas where trees are mature under user group management. Even if grazing is not explicitly prohibited, grazing is not feasible if the forests are "closed," as will be explained shortly. While regulations of grazing have become stricter over time, regulations of firewood collection have remained largely the same.

---

10. We gathered that young trees are not allowed to be cut for firewood even in those two IFUGs that do not have explicit rules on the extraction of green firewood. In these user groups, the users can enter their forests only with their neighbor households, usually four to five, for mutual supervision. Furthermore, their forests can be easily seen from their village residential areas.

11. To corroborate this hypothesis statistically, we attempted to estimate a simultaneous equation system in which the selected dummy variable for the presence of regulation (that is, for the collection of green firewood and dead and dry branches) is regressed on management regimes, among others, in the first-stage probit regression and the regeneration rate of young trees is regressed on the predicted management-rule dummy in the second-stage regression. This formulation, however, is not workable, because the management regime dummies used as regressors in the first-stage probit regression almost fully "explain" the dependent variable. In other words, the difficulty in estimation arises from the facts that no management rule is adopted without user groups and that either almost all FFUGs and IFUGs adopt some regulations, as in the case of green firewood extraction, or only a very few IFUGs adopt some regulations, as in the case of dead firewood extraction. See Greene (1997:892) on this point.

There are several ways to regulate forest resource extraction. Generally, prohibition implies that nobody is allowed to enter the forest except for management purposes organized by the user group committee, rather than simply prohibiting the cutting of trees and green branches. Similarly, rules of regulated use specify "open days" during which specific groups of user households are allowed to collect resources under the supervision of forest user group committee members. Potentially these regulations can be effectively enforced, as those who enter the forest on "closed days" are in principle immediately caught (see, for example, Chhetri and Pandey 1992).[12] The extraction of forest resources by a group of people on the same day facilitates mutual supervision. Furthermore, the extracted resources are usually piled up in one location at the end of the open day and are shared equally among the participating households in most cases. This practice reduces incentives to extract forest resources excessively.[13] The same regulations were widely employed in community forest management in prewar Japan (see, for example, McKean 1992; Chapter 9 in this volume).

Punishment rules differ from community to community. In general, for first-time offenses of illegal extraction of firewood a fine may be imposed that is equivalent to the value of the extracted firewood. The second and third offenses are subject to escalated punishments, which are stated in the management rules in the case of the FFUGs. In practice, repeated offenses seldom take place, and even if they do, the escalated clauses with severe punishments may not be applied to fellow community members. According to field interviews with the committee members of several user groups, illegal activities have been reduced after handing over, because such activities are more likely punished strictly because of the involvement of local DFO staff in the forest management. In general, the use of watchers is less common and the punishment less strict in the case of informal forest management.

Although concrete evidence is hard to come by, we believe that community norms play a significant role in the enforcement of community management rules. Since villages are geographically isolated in the hill region of Nepal, social interactions among villagers are intense. Farmers collectively participate not only in the management of forests but also in the management of local schools, irrigation and drinking water systems, festivals, funerals, and religious ceremonies. As Aoki argues (2000), linking management "games" with social activities generating social surplus may lead to a situation whereby cooperative behaviors become the community norm. Yet, in practice, cooperation in forest

---

12. We found an interesting regulation in which one tree is allocated to each household each year without specifying open and closed days. A household can cut its tree at any time, but only under the supervision of the committee members.

13. However, other sharing rules seem to have been increasingly adopted, such as the sharing based simply on one's collection of firewood on open days.

management seldom overlaps with cooperation in irrigation and drinking water management or other spheres, such as management of schools. This is because the relevant groups for management of forest and water resources are generally different; whereas forest management tends to be carried out jointly by a certain number of wards or villages, other social activities are often carried out by a ward or even hamlets within a ward. It seems that although such linkages are likely to play a role in reducing noncooperative behavior in forest management, it is difficult to identify the specific social activities that are closely linked with forest management.

Sample Forest Users

We conducted a survey of forest users by randomly selecting five households in each sample forest. Approximately 70 percent of our sample households reported some positive extraction of firewood from our sample forests. Other important forest resources include timber, leaf fodder, grasses, and leaf litter. Since the felling of timber trees without permission is prohibited and large fallen trees are infrequently harvested, their extraction is hardly amenable to statistical analysis based on household data for a single year. The extraction of other minor forest resources is less common and less frequent than firewood. Excluding 16 forests in which no user households collected firewood from the sample forests, this study focuses on the remaining 84 forests and 349 households that collected some firewood from the sample forests by allocating family labor.[14] We must point out that the data obtained from the sample households are subject to errors considering that sample farmers had difficulties in reporting the exact quantities and values of extracted firewood and accurate labor time allocated to firewood collection.

Major characteristics of sample forests used for the intensive analysis of firewood collection are shown in Table 8.5. While 44 percent of sample forests were managed by FFUGs, the rest were divided equally into the cases of IFUG and no user group management. On the average, all three types of our sample forests are located in areas within 1.5 to 3 hours walking distance from the nearest market towns. Size of forest is largest in the case of forests managed by FFUGs and smallest in the case managed by IFUGs. Corresponding to the difference in the size of forests, the average number of user households was largest in the formal user forest and smallest in the informal user forest. In fact, there is a relatively small difference in the average area of community forest

---

14. A major reason for not extracting firewood from the sample forests is the availability of kerosene, which is a cheaper source of energy in locations with favorable access to urban markets. In fact, the dummy variable representing the availability of kerosene is highly significant in the probit regression of whether households collected any firewood from the sample forests. The selection bias does not seem important in our statistical analysis, as indicated by the insignificance of the inverse Mill's ratio in the two-step analysis of the regression estimation following the Heckman formula.

TABLE 8.5   Characteristics of sample forests by type of management regime

	No User Group	Informal User Group	Formal User Group
Number of sample forests	23	23	38
Travel time to the nearest market (hours)	2.5	1.8	2.1
Average forest area (ha)	120	84	163
Average number of user households	141	112	207
Average biomass per household (ton)	164	120	146
Regulation on dead and dry branches			
Percentage of open-day restriction[a]	0	4	54
Regulation on green branches			
Percentage of complete prohibition	0	32	65
Percentage of restricted use	0	32	29
Percentage with forest watchers	14[b]	71	89

SOURCE: Extensive forest survey.

[a]Proportion of community forests regulating the number of open days during which collection of dead and dry branches is allowed.

[b]Proportion is non-zero in no user group category, because there are four forests to which district forest offices sent watchers.

per user household among the three forest management regimes. As in Table 8.4, the average biomass per household, however, was largest in the case of open-access or no-user group forests and smallest in the case of forests managed by IFUGs.

In our observation, the most effective management rule is the "open-day" rule, which restricts the exact days during which member households are allowed to collect dead and dried branches for firewood. This policy is effective because trespassing and the hauling of firewood collected from the forest on closed days can easily be detected. A little more than a half of FFUGs adopt some type of the open-day restriction, in which forests are open generally for a few days around the end of the dry season. However, only 1 out of 24 IFUGs adopts this system. It appears that the implementation of the open-day restriction and the imposition of penalties for the violation of the rules are infeasible without obtaining the legal use right status and receiving support from the local DFO. The important question is whether and to what extent the open-day restriction effectively reduces the extraction of firewood from the sample forests.

The felling of live trees is prohibited by the national forest policy, and the cutting of green branches tends to be strictly regulated except for those approved by the user group committee. Cutting green branches is completely prohibited in 65 percent of FFUGs, 32 percent of IFUGs, and in almost no forests in the absence of user groups. Only deformed trees and selected branches are allowed to be cut in approximately 30 percent of both FFUGs and IFUGs (Table 8.5). As was indicated earlier, the difference between the complete prohibition and the restrictive use is subtle and generally marginal.

Basic characteristics of sampled households are displayed in Table 8.6. It is clear that there was no appreciable difference in the average number of household members, economically active members of 16 to 60 years of age, and literate members, as well as total size of owned land, across the different forest management regimes. It is interesting to observe, however, that there were distinct differences in family labor hours allocated to firewood collection in the sample forests, the longest of which was in the formal user group forest, followed by the informal user group forest, and shortest in the no user group forest. The question is whether these observations imply that FFUG members allocate an excessive amount of time for firewood collection, despite the stricter regulations. It is also important to point out that despite having allocated the most time for firewood collection and having a fairly large biomass per user household, the amount of firewood collection was smallest in the case of FFUG management. As a result, the average labor productivity is approximately 25 percent lower than that in IFUG and no user group management. We postulate that these differences in labor productivity arose from the fact that forest user groups, particularly FFUGs, restrict cutting green branches and short trees and days and places of collecting dead branches. We also expect that such restrictions will be more effectively implemented when the open-day restriction is imposed. In other words, the management without the open-day restriction is likely to be less effective and more destructive of forest conditions over time.

The smaller amount of firewood collection from the community forests among FFUG households seems to be compensated for by the extraction of firewood from own trees, judging from the much larger number of trees grown on the edges of terraced private farms and sometimes on own private forests by those FFUG users. Planting and growing trees, particularly fodder trees, on private land is an important coping strategy of hill farmers against the deterioration of forest conditions, including decreasing availability of leaf fodder from community forests (Metz 1991; Fox 1993).[15] The larger the stock of private trees, the smaller will be the demand for firewood extracted from the community forests.

Table 8.6 examines the potential association between caste status and the forest management regime. No clear-cut relation emerged from the simple analysis. Yet from the equity point of view it will be important to explore later on whether there is any relationship between social status and the amount of resources collected from the community forests.

---

15. There are at least two important reasons for growing private trees. First, farmers grow trees for firewood in response to increasing scarcity of trees in the forest. Second, since entry to community forests is restricted under the open-day rule, the daily need for leaf fodder must be satisfied from sources other than the community forests. Leftover sticks, after feeding leaves, are used as firewood.

TABLE 8.6 Characteristics of selected user households by type of management regime

	No User Group	Informal User Group	Formal User Group
Number of selected user households	106	97	146
Average size of household members	7.4	7.9	7.3
Percentage of active members[a]	41	44	43
Percentage of literate members	44	51	54
Size of owned land (ha)	0.99	0.93	0.98
Average labor hours of firewood collection per household per year	204	238	253
Average firewood collection per household per year (kg)	2,168	2,437	1,977
Number of trees grown on private land	49	61	110
Proportion of high caste (percentage)[b]	47	47	65
Proportion of low caste (percentage)[c]	10	0	1

SOURCE: Extensive forest user survey.

[a]Active members refer to those between 16 and 60 years of age.

[b]High-caste class includes Brahman and Chhetri households.

[c]Low-caste class includes occupational caste groups such as ironsmith and tailor.

As will be discussed in more detail later, if a community forest is open access and there is a large number of forest users, labor will be allocated up to the point where the value of social average product is equated with the opportunity wage rate, in equilibrium. In this case, the factor share of labor becomes 100 percent, which implies that the value of output is equal to labor cost. If the extraction of forest resources is restricted, the factor share of labor will become less than 100 percent.

Table 8.7 compares factor share of labor, which is defined by the ratio of total labor cost to the value of collected firewood, by management regime. We

TABLE 8.7 Wage rate, firewood price, and factor share of labor in firewood collection

	No User Group	Informal User Group	Formal User Group
Number of selected sample households	56	67	80
Daily female wage rate (rupees/day)[a]	51	56	53
Firewood price (rupees/kg)	1.29	1.72	1.54
Factor share of labor (percentage)	65	59	53

SOURCE: Extensive forest user survey.

[a]Female daily wage rate for compost application.

use the female daily wage rate of compost application as an appropriate opportunity wage rate, because compost application is made at the end of the dry season, which coincides with the peak time of firewood extraction, and because firewood collection is primarily a woman's task (Kumar and Hotchkiss 1988; Amacher, Hyde, and Joshee 1993). Compared with the firewood price, this wage rate is relatively similar across wide areas.[16] The data on the prevailing wage rate of compost application were easily collected everywhere, but it was much more difficult to obtain data on the price or potential value of a bundle of firewood, because it is seldom sold or bought among community members. It is not sold to market, either, unless the community is located close to towns. In consequence, we were able to obtain the data on firewood prices from 203 households. Table 8.7 uses this subsample.

Although the price of firewood is lowest in the no user group forest case, the estimated factor share of labor is largest, which suggests that the serious overextraction of firewood takes place in this open-access forest. Yet labor share is far below unity even in this type of forest. It seems that the firewood price tends to be overestimated because firewood prices are often quoted prices in nearby towns. It is also important to note that the firewood price was substantially higher in forests managed by IFUGs. This would reflect the larger scarcity of trees in these areas where forests were most degraded (reflected in the lower biomass per user household), and farmers only recently began to grow trees on their private farms.

Extensive Study on Forest Management

Determinants of the Emergence of User Group Management

In order to identify the determinants of the emergence of user group management, we employed the two methods of empirical estimation. First, we estimated a probit function in which the dependent variable assumes unity when any types of forest user groups were set up. We did not distinguish between IFUG and FFUG management in this estimation, because we suspect that the initiation of FFUG management was affected critically by the intention of DFOs, which may be considered exogenous for user groups. Second, we estimated an ordered-probit function in which the dependent variable is rank-order dummies: one for IFUG and two for FFUG management. This method attempts to identify factors affecting not only the formation of IFUGs but also their conversion to FFUGs. The same set of explanatory variables are used, which include the following: the number of user households; the size of forest per user

---

16. Despite the underdeveloped transportation network, wage rates are generally similar across wide areas owing to active interregional migration, both seasonally and permanently (Upadhyaya, Otsuka, and David 1990).

household; homogeneity of social groups represented by ethnic composition; the proportion of households participating in other social activities; the number of local administration units encompassed by a single user group; crown cover in 1978; the ratio of forest area in VDCs in 1978 in which our sample forests are located;[17] and traveling time to the nearest ranger office.

The number of user households, for which we took logarithm in actual estimation, is supposed to capture the transaction costs of organizing collective forest management, which is related with the cost of reaching agreement. If the fixed-cost component of setting up user group management is high, a large forest area may have a positive effect on the initiation of user group management, partly because the total benefit of forest management will be larger and partly because scale advantages may exist in protection activities. In order to take into account the effect of forest area in addition to the effect of the size of user households, we added the logarithm of forest area per user household. If the transaction costs of community forest management increase with the size of user group and forest area, we expect to have negative effects of these two variables. We observed, however, that large community forests were sometimes divided into smaller units and were managed separately by different groups of people.[18] To the extent that such division of forest area is effective in reducing transaction costs, both the number of households and the forest area per household may not exert negative and significant influence on the formation of user groups. It must also be pointed out that the data on the number of user households suffer from measurement errors, particularly in forests under no user group management or open access, because anyone can freely use resources of open-access forests.[19] Also note that owing to data limitations, we had to use current-period variables for the size of user groups and a few other variables to explain changes in forest management institutions in the past.

The transaction costs of user group management would be affected not only by the size of the group and forest area but also by the group's ethnic homogeneity as well as the homogeneity of administrative units. We used the proportion of the dominant ethnic group to total population to represent the effect of ethnic homogeneity among the users. It is usually presumed that collective

17. When we calculated the ratio of forest area to total VDC area, we included the shrub area because this area also produces minor forest products.

18. In our observation, the number of community forests dividing the forest area into smaller units managed by the smaller groups of people is increasing. To what extent such division will continue toward the direction of management by a few or even private management will be an important issue.

19. In the survey of the open-access forests, we asked villagers residing near the forest the names of hamlets from which residents come to the forest. Then we visited each hamlet and asked for the number of households. This method may lead to underestimation because of the possible omission of hamlets and to overestimation because some households in hamlets are not users of the forest under investigation. According to Graner (1997), there are also cases in which user group management excluded socially and economically disadvantaged users.

action can be more easily organized among homogeneous members. In fact, leaders of 85 percent of user groups stated that the user groups were formed by the decisions of users at large rather than by initiatives of selected leaders. Group homogeneity, however, may imply the lack of leadership. We also considered the number of wards (the lowest local administrative unit in Nepal) from which the users come to the forest as an indicator of the group heterogeneity. Since a ward is an administrative unit, which roughly corresponds to a village in other societies, transaction costs within a ward tend to be low. Thus, we expect that the fewer the number of wards, the lower would be the cost of collective management.

We considered two variables to represent the forest conditions and access to forest resources in the earlier period. One is crown cover in 1978 obtained from aerial photo analysis. Although this indicator is not very sensitive to changes and differences in forest conditions, it seems to capture major changes and differences. We hypothesize that lower crown cover in 1978 would lead to greater probability of inducing the initiation of user group management. Another variable is the proportion of land area under forest in 1978 for each VDC in which the sample forest is located. The larger the proportion of forest area, the lower would have been the population pressure on forest resources in the sample forests. This is because, even if the sample forest was degraded, users might have easily gone to other forests in nearby locations, if the proportion of forest area in the VDC was high. Thus, we expect that a higher forest cover leads to a lower incidence of user group management.

We used the proportion of households participating in other social activities (that is, management of irrigation and drinking water systems and local schools) to capture the effects of possible linkages of forest management to other social activities. Finally, we included traveling time to the ranger office as a variable representing the influence of DFOs. If the formation of user group management is truly voluntary, this variable will be insignificant. To the extent that user groups were set up with the expectation of receiving official use rights or by the direct assistance from the DFO, this variable would have a negative effect on the formation of user groups.

The estimation results of probit and ordered-probit regressions are shown in the first two columns and the last column of Table 8.8, respectively. It should be pointed out that the estimated coefficients in the probit estimation are converted into marginal effects computed at the means of regressors but those in the ordered-probit estimation are not. Thus, the estimation results by probit and ordered-probit regressions are not directly comparable. The marginal effects of regressors on predicted probabilities of ordered-probit estimation are summarized in Table 8.9. It is found that the number of user households has only a weakly significant effect if we apply a two-tailed t-test, whereas forest area per user household is insignificant. It appears that the size of user group per se,

TABLE 8.8 Determinants of the emergence of forest user group management: Probit and ordered-probit regressions

	Probit[a]	Probit[a]	Ordered-Probit[b]
Intercept	.235	.209	−.178
	(0.482)	(.428)	(−.132)
Ln (number of households)	.154	.146	.453
	(1.708)	(1.636)	(1.650)
Ln (forest area per household)	.050	.045	−.011
	(.689)	(.643)	(.043)
Number of wards	−.100*	−.100*	−.244*
	(−2.181)	(−2.166)	(−1.748)
Ratio of households in other community activities	−.096		
	(−.522)		
Proportion of largest ethnic group	.041	.019	.337
	(.135)	(.063)	(.391)
Traveling hours to ranger office	−.030*	−.029*	−.123**
	(−2.152)	(−2.100)	(−3.637)
Crown cover in 1978	−.129*	−.123*	−.193
	(−2.204)	(−2.146)	(−1.166)
Ratio of forestland in VDC[c] in 1978	−.209	−.231	−.048
	(−.550)	(−.609)	(−.040)
Log likelihood	−34.95	−35.08	−68.71
Percentage of correct prediction	73.0	73.0	54.0

NOTE: The numbers in parentheses are *t*-statistics.

[a]Dependent variable is unity where either informal or formal management has been introduced.

[b]Ranked choices of formal (= 2), informal (= 1), and no community management (= 0) are considered as dependent variable.

[c]VDC = village development council.

*.05 level

**.01 level

measured by the number of households and the forest area, does not decisively affect the cost of organizing collective action and enforcing management rules. It may well be that both scale advantages and disadvantages coexist in forest management.[20]

The number of wards has a negative and significant coefficient (Table 8.8), suggesting that the larger the administrative heterogeneity, the larger will be

---

20. Suspecting that scale economies dominate in the range of small-scale forest management operations, whereas scale diseconomies dominate in the range of large operations, we estimated regression functions that added square terms of either the number of forest users or forest areas. The estimated coefficients, however, are not significant.

TABLE 8.9 Marginal effects for ordered-probit regression

	No Management	Informal User Management	Formal User Management
Intercept	.055	.014	−.069
Ln (number of households)	−.141	−.036	.177
Ln (forest area per household)	.003	.001	−.004
Number of wards	.076	.019	−.096
Proportion of largest ethnic group	−.105	−.027	.132
Traveling hours to ranger office	.038	.010	−.048
Crown cover in 1978	.060	.015	−.075
Ratio of forestland in VDC in 1978[a]	.015	.004	−.019

[a]VDC = village development council.

the cost of organizing collective action.[21] On the other hand, the proportion of households participating in other social activities and the proportion of largest ethnic group are insignificant, indicating that the presence of other community activities and ethnic homogeneity in terms of dominant caste do not directly affect the initiation of the forest management. The former result was expected because, as was noted earlier, the sphere of community cooperation for such social activities as irrigation and school management is usually different from that for forest management.

Traveling hours to the ranger office is significant in the probit regression and highly significant in the ordered-probit regression. The former finding indicates that the nearer the ranger office to the forest, the more likely user group management was to be initiated. Furthermore, the higher significance in the ordered-probit regression suggests that the proximity to the ranger office was particularly conducive to the initiation of FFUG management. In fact, Table 8.9 shows that the marginal effect of traveling hours to the ranger office is small for the formation of an IFUG but negative and comparably large for the conversion from an IFUG to a FFUG. It seems clear that the influence of DFOs on the formation of FFUGs has been pervasive.

Crown cover in 1978 has a negative and significant coefficient in the probit regression, implying that forest user group management was more likely to be initiated in forests that were more degraded in 1978. This supports our hypothesis that deforestation leads to the formation of forest user groups. This is

---

21. It must be pointed out that the number of wards may partly capture the effects of forest size and geographical conditions. If the forest is large or lies on the top of a hill and ridges, usually multiple numbers of wards have access to it. For effective protection and management of such forest, it is necessary to organize all the wards around it, since it is difficult to protect the forest from one or few sides.

also consistent with a finding of Fujita, Hayami, and Kikuchi (2000) that collective irrigation management in the Philippines is more likely to be organized effectively where water supply is scarce. This variable, however, is insignificant in the ordered-probit regression. This insignificance and the negative sign of the marginal effect for FFUG management seem to suggest that crown cover in 1978 did not significantly affect the transformation of IFUGs into FFUGs.

The ratio of forest area to total land area in VDC in 1978 is not significant. It appears that it was not merely the proportion of forest area but the availability of forest resources that affected the formation of user group management.

Consequences of the Forest User Group Management

There are several difficulties in properly assessing the effects of forest user group management on forest conditions. First of all, the representative indicators of forest conditions (timber volume, biomass, and so on) are stock variables, which change slowly over time. Considering that user group management was initiated relatively recently, we believe that the rate of regeneration of young trees is a more appropriate indicator of the improvement of forest conditions. Second, management rules can be highly complex; there are a variety of management rules ranging from no regulation to complete prohibition of resource extraction, and they vary from one resource to another. It is therefore very difficult to construct a single indicator of regulation intensity. Third, management rules have often changed over time. Ideally we have to assess the effect of each management rule with due consideration of the periods during which such rule was implemented. Finally, there are potential estimation problems associated with the endogenous nature of the management rules and institutions. As we have seen in the previous section, the initiation of user group management was likely to be induced by scarcity of tree resources associated with deforestation. To the extent that degraded forest conditions deter regeneration of trees and foster the formation of user groups, the impact of user group management on regeneration of trees may appear negative in the regression analysis, even if it actually contributed to the rehabilitation of forests. In order to avoid this, we have to control properly for the effects of the forest conditions. The forest conditions, however, are also endogenous. In actual estimation, we used the ratio of forest area to total VDC area in 1992 to 1996 as a variable representing the pressure on forest conditions in the neighborhood of our sample community forest. The other estimation difficulty caused by the problem of endogeneity is that there is a possibility that the more effective IFUGs tend to become FFUGs. In that case, even if FFUG management is found to be more effective than IFUG management, it may be due to the self-selection effect rather than the effect of receiving the legal use rights from the government with the support from the DFO for the community management. Since DFOs do not accept applications for handing over if there are conflicts among the users, this self-selection problem is likely to be pervasive.

In this study, as a first step to cope with the complexities in management rules, we used dummy variables for informal and formal management in regression analyses. As was indicated in the previous section, the current management system reflects the effects of the intervention of the DFO, forest conditions, and other factors. In the estimation of the effects of management systems on forest conditions, we include the proportion of forest area in VDC in 1992 to 1996, logarithm of average altitude, and pine forest dummy, in addition to dummy variables for management system. The last two variables are included to control for the effects of the ecological conditions; the regeneration of trees is slower in the higher altitude, and the presence of pine trees deters regeneration.

In the first two columns of Table 8.10, we report the results of ordinary least squares (OLS) and weighted least squares (WLS) estimation, in which the dependent variable is the logarithm of the number of regenerated trees per hectare. The number of regenerated trees is a weighted average with weights in proportion to the height of regenerated trees. In the weighted least squares regression, we used the number of sample plots in the forest inventory as weights. Since R^2 is not a proper indicator of the goodness of fit in weighted regressions, we report the correlation coefficients between the actual and estimated dependent variables in the table.

The fits of these regressions are not very high, which is likely to reflect the measurement errors of the regeneration rates, or specifically of enumerating young trees. Except for the proportion of forest area, however, all the independent variables have the expected signs. The two ecological variables have generally significant effects on regeneration. The most important finding is that the coefficient of the FFUG dummy is positive and highly significant, while that of the IFUG dummy is positive but only marginally significant according to a one-tailed t-test. Furthermore, the former coefficients are numerically larger than the latter coefficients; the estimated coefficients of around .6 for FFUG management and around .3 for IFUG management indicate that the formal and informal management systems increase the rate of regeneration of young trees by approximately 80 percent and 35 percent, respectively.[22] These results support the hypothesis that FFUG management is more efficient than IFUG management in improving forest conditions.

As pointed out above, one may question that the significant effect of FFUG is due to self-selection of effective user groups. In order to check this self-selection bias of FFUGs, we have tried the two-step estimation known as treatment effects model (Greene 1997:981). Based on the assumption that the self-selection occurs only for the formation of FFUGs, we used the probit esti-

---

22. Since the logarithm is taken for the dependent variable, the exponential of estimated dummy coefficients must be taken to assess the quantitative impacts of the formal and informal management institutions.

TABLE 8.10 Determinants of regeneration per hectare in 1997

	Model 1		Model 2[a]	
	OLS	WLS[b]	OLS	WLS[b]
Constant	12.809	10.772	11.909	9.675
	(7.156)	(6.249)	(5.590)	(4.549)
IFUG dummy	0.264	.360	0.428	.545*
	(1.191)	(1.657)	(1.357)	(1.784)
FFUG dummy	.571**	.651**	.839*	.936**
	(2.746)	(3.289)	(2.003)	(2.395)
Proportion of forest area in VDC in 1992–96[c]	−.484	−.339	−.471	−.409
	(−.916)	(−.691)	(−.918)	(−.845)
Ln (average altitude)	−.640**	−.374	−.538*	−.241
	(−2.534)	(−1.534)	(−1.905)	(−.844)
Pine forest dummy	−.364**	−.356*	−.357*	−.347*
	(−2.131)	(−2.166)	(−2.149)	(−2.162)
R-squared	.323	.301	.310	.280
Correlation coefficients	.571	.559	.562	.534

NOTE: Dependent variable is ln (regeneration per hectare). The numbers in parentheses are *t*-statistics.

[a]Predicted values are used for formal forest user (FFU) dummy.

[b]Weighted least squares regression with weight being the number of sample plots in forest measurement.

[c]VDC = village development council.

*.01 level

**.05 level

mation for formal management as a first-step estimation. The explanatory variables are the same as those in Table 8.8. The predicted dummy variable for FFUG management is then used as an instrument in the second-stage estimation for the rate of regeneration. The results are reported in the third and fourth columns of Table 8.10. The two-step estimation does not result in much difference in the qualitative results compared with those from the simple OLS and WLS estimation. That is, the effect of FFUG dummy is positive and significant even after removing the possible self-selection bias.

Conclusions of Extensive Study

The extensive study of forest management attempted to explore the causes and the consequences of forest user group management. Despite the difficulty in measuring the conditions of forests, their changes over time, and the number of user group members, we obtained some useful empirical evidence. First, we found that the formation of user groups was induced by the shortage of forest resources. This finding suggests that when forest resources are abundant, user group management is less likely to be practiced, which leads to deforestation and the shortages of forest resources. The degraded forest conditions, in turn, stimulate the formation of user groups, because it is costly to sustain livelihood and subsistence farming without a sufficient supply of forest resources in the hill region of Nepal.

Second, there is no indication that the size of forest and the number of user group members hindered the initiation and the effectiveness of user group management. Unlike the usual presumption, the size of the management unit does not seem to increase the transaction cost of user group management significantly. It may well be that not only scale disadvantages but also scale advantages exist in the protection of forests, as a small number of people can enforce protection of large forest areas. We believe, however, that scale advantages should exist, if the community forest is divided more or less equally among the forest user group members, so that the size of forest becomes very small.

Third and most important, we found that management of community forests by FFUGs seems more effective in regenerating trees than management by IFUGs, not to mention the case of no management. It seems clear that the formation of FFUGs, which are granted official use rights of forests and are supported by the local forestry department, is critically important for the effective management of community forests. In fact, our field surveys strongly indicate that handing over can be an effective policy instrument only if it is supplemented by the supporting activities of the local forestry department. In other words, community initiatives and government supporting activities are complements but not substitutes. This point is explored further in this chapter by the analysis of firewood collection using the data of individual forest users.

Intensive Study on Firewood Collection

Conceptual Framework

Following the theoretical framework developed in Chapter 1, in this section we attempt to specify the firewood extraction, labor share, and family labor allocation functions based on the theory of common property resource management and a simple model of household utility maximization. We use the volume of firewood extraction, factor share of family labor, and total hours of the extraction work per household as dependent variables in the regression analysis. Unlike Bluffstone's (1995) comprehensive model of farm household behaviors under the setting of open-access community forest in the hill region of Nepal, our model focuses explicitly on the role of forest user group management.

We expect that diverse forces will be at work in the determination of the volume of firewood collection and the amount of family labor supply. Broadly they can be classified into the following categories: (1) forest conditions that determine the potential supply of firewood; (2) household characteristics that determine the household demand for firewood and supply of family labor for firewood collection; and (3) management rules and their effectiveness, which affect the extent of divergence between the individual noncooperative optimum and the actual outcome. In what follows, we provide a theoretical framework with a view to specifying the properties of the estimation functions.

We assume that a well-behaved aggregate firewood extraction function, analogous to the conventional production function, exists, in which the quantity of output (Q) is a function of aggregate labor input in the community (L) and the biomass of tree resources in the forest (R):

$$Q = F(L, R), \tag{1}$$

where the marginal products of labor and the stock of biomass are assumed to be positive ($F_1, F_2 > 0$) and diminishing ($F_{11}, F_{22} < 0$). Since the firewood extraction is a simple task performed by adult women and men, and even children, labor inputs of individual members are assumed to be perfect substitutes, so that $L = \sum_i l_i$ holds, where l_i is labor input of ith member household. Following Dasgupta and Heal (1979:55–73), the amount of resources collected by ith member household (y_i) is expressed as

$$y_i = [l_i/L]F(L, R). \tag{2}$$

Note that the private marginal product of labor, which is defined as $\partial y_i/\partial l_i$, can be different from the social marginal product of labor, that is, F_1, because individual members may not care about the negative external effect of their activity on the productivity of other members. If the total number of households (n) is sufficiently large, it can be shown that the private marginal product of labor approaches the social average product under the assumption of Nash behavior (Weitzman 1974; Dasgupta and Heal 1979; Sethi and Somanathan 1996). Such an assumption would approximately hold if the forest is open access with no regulations on the extraction of firewood. Thus, the optimum labor input determined by individual user households will be greater than the socially optimum level, leading to the overextraction of firewood under the open-access regime without user group regulations.

The role of user group management is to restrict the extraction of forest resources by setting up rules, enforcing them, and punishing those who violate them. In these ways, y_i and l_i, actually chosen by user households may be reduced to the levels lower than those achieved under the open-access regime. In fact, the major purpose of an open-day restriction is precisely to reduce y_i (or Q) by controlling l_i. On the other hand, prohibition of cutting green branches and similar restrictions, which aim to achieve sustainable management of forest resources, will affect labor productivity directly by restricting the behavior of user group members. If the policy to prohibit cutting trees is more effectively implemented when the open-day policy is also implemented, the latter may also affect y_i directly rather than through its effect on l_i alone.

For simplicity, we assume that members of the user group are identical and that the production function is subject to constant return to scale. The latter assumption is reasonable as there is practically no scope for team production or the division of labor leading to the scale economy in the firewood extraction. Then, using the symmetric equilibrium condition ($l_i/L = 1/n$), equation (2) can be rewritten as[23]

$$y_i = F(l_i, R/n, M), \tag{3}$$

where M stands for management rules. Since labor input is endogenous in equation (3), we apply the two-stage squares estimation method. We used biomass per user household as a variable representing (R/n).[24]

We assume that each household maximizes its utility by choosing family labor allocated to community forest to extract firewood, given forest conditions, management rules, households characteristics, and other location specific factors, such as wages. We assume that management rules adopted by forest user group are exogenously given to each individual household, because a single household can have but negligible influence on collectively determined management rules.

We expect that since firewood is a necessity, its demand is highly inelastic with respect to the cost of firewood extraction. Although it may be presumed that the demand is largely determined in proportion to the number of household members, that may not always be the case, since firewood is a "semipublic good" within a household. Although the total demand for firewood may be largely determined by the above considerations, the demand for firewood extracted from the community forest will be conditioned by the availability of firewood from own trees. Thus, we consider the number of private trees as a factor reducing labor time allocated to the community forest and the amount of firewood collected from there.

We also considered factors affecting the supply of labor for collecting firewood, such as the endowment of economically active household members. Since the size of household is included as an important demand side variable,

---

23. Considering the possibility that forest user households are highly heterogeneous, we used the estimate of (l_i/L) in equation (3) instead of ($1/n$) in the earlier statistical analysis. The results, however, were largely the same.

24. In the earlier regression runs, we specified the two separate variables, namely, the average forest area per user household and biomass density per hectare. It turns out, however, that the estimated coefficients of the two variables were almost the same, so we decided to employ only biomass per household as a variable representing the forest condition.

we included the proportions of economically active members to represent the supply side effect. We also considered the wealth effect by incorporating the owned farm area.

To capture the effect of the opportunity cost of labor, we included the daily female wage rate of compost application, the access to nonagricultural labor markets measured by walking time to the nearest market, and proportion of literate household members. In order to capture the effect of the availability of kerosene, which is an important alternative source of energy, we included a dummy for close access to market towns where kerosene is available, so that its use is common among villagers.

We postulate that the most common and potentially most effective management rule to restrict the extraction of firewood is the designation of open days during which member households are allowed to collect firewood. In order to test this hypothesis, we construct a variable representing the proportion of "closed" days in a year, during which a user household is not allowed to collect firewood. This variable is zero, if no restriction is imposed, that is, an open-access situation. If this variable has a negative and significant effect on family labor allocation, the hypothesis that the management rule of closing forests actually reduces the overexploitation of firewood is supported. Since only one IFUG adopted this policy, its effect can be attributed largely to the management policy of FFUG. It is, however, possible that effective IFUGs tend to become FFUGs, so the estimated effect may partly capture such self-selection effect.

The implementation of the rule of closed days may not be effective if the enforcement cost is high. Thus, we inserted an interaction term between the proportion of closed days and the size of forest, which is expected to capture the enforcement cost in spatially wide forest areas. The size of forest is chosen rather than the number of user households, because we expect that while the number of user group members affects the cost of reaching agreement on the rules, the size of forest directly affects the ease of enforcing them.

Aside from the closed-day restriction, potentially important rules include the prohibition of felling trees and cutting green branches. Unlike the case of the closed-day restriction, this policy is widely adopted by both FFUGs and IFUGs. Thus, we use the two intercept dummies (that is, dummies for prohibition by FFUGs and IFUGs) to examine the effectiveness of this policy in the regression analysis. We will examine whether there is a significant difference between the coefficients of these two variables, in order to test if forest management is more effective under the FFUG than the IFUG regime. For comparison, we alternatively use FFUG and IFUG dummies to explore the effects of nonquantifiable difference between FFUG and IFUG management.

Empirical Specification

Based on the considerations discussed above, we specify the following functional relationship for the labor allocation function:

$\ln l_i = a_0 + a_1$ (percentage closed days) $+ a_2$ (percentage closed
    days × forest area) $+ a_3$ FFUG $+ a_4$ IFUG $+ a_5 \ln$ (biomass per
    household) $+ a_6$ (a vector of household characteristics)
    $+ a_7 \ln$ (walking time to market town) $+ a_8 \ln$ (wage rate),   (4)

where (percentage closed days) refers to the proportion of closed days, and
FFUG and IFUG stand for dummies for prohibition of cutting green branches
by FFUGs and IFUGs in the first specification and dummies for FFUGs and
IFUGs in the second specification, respectively. In actual estimation, we took
the logarithm of all continuous variables and included four regional dummies
to control for unobservable region-specific factors.

   We assume that the production function can be characterized by a translog
form. Thus, the production function can be specified as (Griliches and Ringstad
1971)

$\ln y_i = b_0 + b_1 \ln l_i + b_2 \ln (R/n) + b_3 [\ln (nl_i/R)]^2 + b_4$ FFUG
    $+ b_5$ IFUG $+ b_6$ (percentage closed days)
    $+ b_7$ (percentage closed days × forest area),   (5)

where b_i $(i = 0, \ldots, 7)$ are parameters. If constant returns to scale prevail, $b_1 +$
$b_2 = 1$ holds. If coefficient b_3 is not significantly different from zero, the Cobb-
Douglas form of the production function cannot be rejected. While coefficients
b_4 and b_5 may be negative when the restriction on cutting green branches is effective, coefficient b_6 may not be significantly different from zero if the role of
closing forests is solely to reduce labor allocation to forest. Coefficient b_7 is
supposed to assess whether the effectiveness of a closed-day rule decreases
with increases in forest area.

   If the use of common property is effectively regulated by collective action,
equality of the social marginal product of labor and the real wage rate holds.
This implies equality of the production elasticity of labor with its factor share
(s_i):

$$s_i = wl_i/y_i = (\ln y_i/\ln l_i) = b_1 + 2b_3[\ln (nl_i/R)].   (6)$$

   If the forest resource is extracted excessively, the wage rate should exceed
the marginal product of labor, which amounts to the excess of labor share over
the production elasticity of labor. In order to test whether and to what extent
overextraction of firewood takes place, we estimate the following labor share
function:

$$s_i = c_0 + c_1 [\ln (nl_i/R)] + d_1 \text{ FFUG} + d_2 \text{ IFUG}$$
$$+ d_3 \text{ (percentage closed days)} + d_4 \text{ (percentage closed}$$
$$\text{days × forest area)},   (7)$$

where c_i and d_i $(i = 1, 2, 3)$ are parameters, FFUG and IFUG are dummies for
user group regimes. If the social optimum is achieved, $b_1 = c_0$, $2b_3 = c_1$, and

$d_i = 0$ $(i = 1, \ldots, 4)$ hold. Such optimal solution, however, will not be achieved in the presence of transaction costs.[25] If the enforcement of prohibition of cutting green branch es is effective, we expect that d_1 and d_2 are negative. Similarly, if the enforcement of the closed-day rule effectively reduces labor allocation from private optimum with no social coercion, d_3 will be negative.

Estimation Results

The estimation results of the labor allocation function are shown in Table 8.11. Model 1 uses the dummies for restriction of cutting green branches by FFUGs and IFUGs, respectively, whereas Model 2 includes dummies for FFUG and IFUG management.

The estimation results indicate that the closed-day restriction, implemented primarily by FFUGs, effectively reduced labor time allocated to community forest, but its effectiveness tended to decrease with an increase in forest area. On the other hand, the restriction of cutting green branches does not seem to have any influence on labor allocation. The coefficients of the FFUG and IFUG dummies in Model 2 are positive, and the latter is highly significant. It appears that given the limited availability of private trees and the absence of closed-day restriction, in addition to the degraded forest conditions, members of IFUGs compete to extract forest resources by allocating more labor to resource extraction activities in the community forest. It seems clear that the mere formation of user groups does not significantly reduce labor allocation to community forests.

Biomass per user household is not significant, either, which seems to indicate that while the greater availability of trees increases the amount of firewood collection, the demand for labor did not increase owing to the enhanced efficiency of firewood collection. It is also found that a larger number of private trees substantially reduced the labor allocation to community forest, as it reduces the demand for firewood from the forest. This finding is consistent with the generally held view that farmers planted trees on private land in response to the reduced availability of trees in community forests.

There is no evidence that other household characteristics affected the amount of labor allocated to community forests, except for positive effects of walking time to forest and low caste status. The former result is expected, as labor time includes time spent walking between the residence and the forest. The weakly positive effect of low caste status and insignificant effect of high caste status indicate that there is no discrimination for higher-caste people or against lower-caste people in access to community forests. The wealth of households, measured by the ownership of land and proportion of literate members, did not affect the labor allocation. These findings may be taken to imply that user households have more or less equal access to community forests regardless of

---

25. We do not pursue this issue statistically because sample sizes for estimating the two equations are different.

TABLE 8.11 Determinants of labor allocation for firewood collection

	Model 1	Model 2
Intercept	2.80	2.69
	(3.07)	(2.97)
Percentage of closed days	−1.54*	−1.38*
	(−2.32)	(−2.13)
Percentage of closed days × ln (forest area)	.32*	.27*
	(2.14)	(1.87)
Dummy for restriction of cutting by FFUG	.11	—
	(.78)	
Dummy for restriction of cutting by IFUG	.22	—
	(1.51)	
FFUG dummy	—	.25
		(1.57)
IFUG dummy	—	.38**
		(2.61)
Ln (biomass per household)	.05	.06
	(1.22)	(1.45)
Ln (number of private trees)	−.12**	−.13**
	(−3.56)	(−3.84)
Ln (size of owned land)	.02	.05
	(.29)	(.60)
Ln (size of household members)	.13	.10
	(.84)	(.68)
Proportion of active members	.04	.06
	(.14)	(.23)
Proportion of literate members	.26	.24
	(1.22)	(1.11)
Ln (daily wage)	.20	.18
	(.98)	(.89)
Ln (walking time to market town)	.06	.07
	(1.62)	(1.90)
Ln (walking time to forest)	.14*	.15*
	(1.97)	(2.17)
Market area dummy	.03	−.002
	(.14)	(−.008)
High-caste dummy	−.14	−.13
	(−1.18)	(−1.04)
Low-caste dummy	.53	.61*
	(1.61)	(1.82)
R-squared	.317	.327

NOTE: Numbers in parentheses are *t*-statistics. For simplicity, we omitted the coefficients of four regional dummies.

*.05 level

**.01 level

wealth, education level, and social status. In other words, management of community forest is basically egalitarian, as in the Indian and Japanese cases (Jodha 1986; McKean 1992).

Using the estimates of the labor allocation function shown in Table 8.11 as the first-stage regression, Table 8.12 displays the estimation results of the second-stage firewood collection function. As may be expected, the coefficients of labor and biomass per household are positive and highly significant. Moreover, the sum of their coefficients, that is, 0.84, is not significantly smaller than unity, which does not refute the hypothesis of constant returns to scale. The coefficient of squared aggregate labor-biomass ratio, $[\ln (nl_i/R)]^2$, is insignificant. Thus, the Cobb-Douglas form of production function cannot be denied.

It is worth emphasizing that neither proportion of closed days nor its interaction term with forest area is significant. These results indicate that the purpose of the closed-day restriction is solely to reduce the amount of labor allocation to community forest, which is subsumed under the labor term and the squared aggregate labor-biomass ratio in the firewood collection function. In contrast, the coefficient of the dummy variable for restriction of cutting green branches by FFUG, as well as that of the FFUG dummy, is negative and significant. These findings suggest that the regulations of firewood extraction by FFUGs, in general, and the restriction of cutting green branches, in particular, resulted in reduced amount of firewood collection, controlling for labor allocation and the stock of biomass. The coefficients of two dummy variables pertaining to IFUG management are not significant. It seems that management of IFUG is ineffective in reducing the firewood collection, even though informal groups collect less firewood than formal groups (see Table 8.6). It is possible that in areas where IFUG management is adopted, people depend crucially on firewood from the forest, so that restriction of firewood collection is particularly difficult.

Finally, let us examine the estimation results of the labor share function shown in Table 8.13. Since the sample households used for the estimation of labor share function are the subset of the whole sample, it is hazardous to compare the estimates in Tables 8.12 and 8.13. Nonetheless, it is instructive to find that the estimates of production elasticity of labor (which is 0.71 if we disregard the insignificant coefficient of square term of aggregate labor-biomass ratio shown in Table 8.12) are close to the estimate of the intercept term in the labor share function (which is .67 to .68). This is reasonable if the factor share of labor is critically affected by its production elasticity (see equations [6] and [7]). Yet the coefficient of aggregate labor-biomass ratio is positive and highly significant, which is incompatible with the determination of the labor share by its production elasticity because the square term of this variable is insignificant in the estimation of firewood collection function. This indicates that the labor share is not simply determined by the production elasticity of labor, which is achieved only under the socially optimum solution.

TABLE 8.12 Determinants of firewood collection: 2SLS regression

	Model 1	Model 2
Intercept	3.11	3.17
	(7.87)	(8.42)
Ln (labor)	.71**	.71**
	(6.84)	(6.89)
Ln (biomass per household)	.13**	.13**
	(3.38)	(3.17)
$[\ln (nl_i/R)]^2$	$5.57 \times e^{-8}$	$4.61 \times e^{-8}$
	(1.23)	(1.00)
Percentage of closed days	.21	.29
	(.41)	(.58)
Percentage of closed days × ln (forest area)	−.11	−.11
	(−1.08)	(−1.14)
Dummy for restriction of cutting by FFUG	−.16*	—
	(−2.14)	
Dummy for restriction of cutting by IFUG	.04	—
	(0.56)	
FFUG dummy	—	−.22**
		(−2.76)
IFUG dummy	—	.05
		(.67)
Eastern region dummy	.16	.13
	(1.81)	(1.50)
Western region dummy	.28**	.26**
	(2.99)	(2.77)
Midwestern region dummy	.62**	.60**
	(5.72)	(5.72)
Far-western region dummy	−.45	−.44
	(−4.39)	(−4.54)
R-squared	.856	.860

NOTE: Numbers in parentheses are *t*-statistics.

*.05 level

**.01 level

Literally, the positive effect of the aggregate labor-biomass ratio suggests that the greater the pressure on forest resources, the greater the extent of over-exploitation of firewood.

The proportion of closed days is negative and highly significant, whereas its interaction term with forest area is positive and highly significant, indicating that the extraction of firewood is critically affected by the closed-day restriction and the extent of its enforcement. These results reinforce the earlier findings from the estimation of labor allocation function: although the closed-

TABLE 8.13 Determinants of labor share in firewood collection: 2SLS regression

	Model 1	Model 2
Intercept	.67**	.68**
	(20.06)	(19.60)
[ln (nl$_i$/R)]	.05**	.06**
	(4.97)	(5.48)
Percentage of closed days	−.81**	−.84**
	(−4.43)	(−4.80)
Percentage of closed days × ln (forest area)	.22**	.22**
	(4.60)	(4.79)
Dummy for restriction of cutting by FFUG	.00	—
	(0.07)	
Dummy for restriction of cutting by IFUG	−.03	—
	(−.69)	
FFUG dummy	—	−.02
		(−.02)
IFUG dummy	—	−.09*
		(−1.98)
Eastern region dummy	−.09*	−.07
	(−1.98)	(−1.61)
Western region dummy	−.29**	−.27**
	(−7.45)	(−6.60)
Far-western region dummy	.05	.08
	(0.74)	(1.07)
R-squared	.382	.394

NOTE: Numbers in parentheses are *t*-statistics.
*.05 level
**.01 level

day rule is effective in reducing the labor allocated to collection of firewood and its amount, its effectiveness tends to decrease with forest area. The effectiveness tends to decrease presumably because the cost of enforcing the closed-day rule increases with forest area.

Somewhat unexpectedly, neither the coefficient for restriction of cutting green branches by FFUG nor that of IFUG is significant, because these dummy variables have positive and significant effects on the amount of firewood collection but do not have significant effects on labor allocation. It appears that the major way by which labor allocation is regulated by FFUGs is the closure of forests for designated days. The negative and significant effect of the IFUG dummy is also counterintuitive, as it suggests that IFUG is effective in reducing labor allocation by means other than regulating closed days. The most plausible explanation for this anomalous result is that since tree resources are highly scarce in IFUG areas, firewood prices are also high, which tends to suppress the measured factor share of labor.[26]

Conclusion of Intensive Study

The intensive study of forest users assesses *quantitatively* the efficiency of management of common property forests by user groups. A few conclusions emerged from our analysis. First, the closed-day restriction is the effective rule to reduce overextraction of firewood from community forests by regulating users' time allocated to firewood extraction. This is particularly the case where forest areas are small. IFUGs, however, seldom adopt this rule, and hence their management is generally ineffective. Second, restrictions on cutting green branches are effective in reducing the amount of firewood collection only under FFUG management. These findings strongly suggest that it is the management of FFUGs, not IFUGs, that has significantly reduced the amount of firewood extraction. We must admit, however, that this can be partly due to the result of self-selection of user groups in which effective IFUGs have chosen to become FFUGs. Yet this conclusion is consistent with the major finding of the extensive study of forest management that FFUGs effectively promoted the recovery of forest conditions in recent years.

It is likely that other forest resources are also overextracted under IFUG management, as well as under no user group management, judging from the fact that IFUGs seldom adopt the closed-day rule and fail to implement the rule to restrict cutting green branches effectively. It is clear that the transfer of use rights over forestland to user groups, coupled with support from the local forest office, is a necessary condition for sustainable management of forest resources.

Policy Implications

As far as the management of minor forest resources is concerned, there seems to be no doubt that common property or community forest management is *potentially* an effective organization in protecting and promoting the recovery of those resources. As is discussed in the next chapter, however, community management is not necessarily an effective system to manage timber forests. We emphasize the potential of community forest management because it seems that voluntarily formed user groups without official use rights of forests fail to manage forest resources effectively.

The transfer of use rights to user groups is necessary for effective forest management because it enhances the incentives to manage community forests, thereby facilitating the adoption of closed-day and other effective management rules. Yet such transfer alone does not seem sufficient. According to the forest

---

26. This argument suggests that the coefficient of IFUG is biased downward because of its effect on firewood prices.

users, support from the local forest office for user group management, particularly the punishment of violators of management rules, is also necessary for the effective management.

Thus, community management will not function well without governmental supports. Therefore, a major policy implication is that the government should continue its handing-over policy of forests to the community and strengthen its support activities.

In all likelihood, however, even with such supports the user group management will not function well where forest resources are not scarce. The abundance of forest resources implies weak incentives for organizing collective action, and hence, unless truly strong support measures are provided by the government, community management of forest resources will not be effective in the protection of forest resources. Herein lies a dilemma of forest management policy: in order to prevent deforestation in its initial stages, the government needs to become seriously involved and allocate large amount of resources for community forest management. If that is not feasible, deforestation necessarily proceeds before reforestation begins.

Thus, we must seek other factors that facilitate and strengthen the effective management of community forests by user groups. One policy recommendation is to promote management by smaller user groups, which are more effective in reducing the overexploitation of forest resources according to our analysis of firewood collection. Another recommendation is to introduce profitable nontimber resources, such as medicinal plants and plants useful for high-quality papers. Increased profitability of forest management is likely to stimulate the formation of user groups and induce effective user group management. Further research in this direction is needed to formulate more comprehensive policy framework for forest management in the hill region of Nepal.

References

Ahuja, V. 1998. Land degradation, agricultural productivity, and common property: Evidence from Cote d'Ivoire. *Environment and Development Economics* 3 (1): 7–34.

Amacher, G. S., W. J. Hyde, and B. R. Joshee. 1993. Joint production and consumption in traditional households: Fuel wood and crop residues in two districts in Nepal. *Journal of Development* Studies 30:206–225.

Aoki, M. 2000. Norms and other governance structure. In *Community and market in economic development,* ed. Y. Hayami and M. Aoki. Oxford: Clarendon Press.

Arnold, J. E. Michael. 2001. Devolution of control of common pool resources to local communities: Experiences in forestry. In *Access to land, rural poverty, and public action,* ed. A. de Janvry, G. Gordillo, J.-P. Platteau, and E. Sadoulet. Oxford: Oxford University Press.

Baland, J.-M., and J.-P. Platteau. 1996. *Halting degradation of natural resources: Is there a role of rural communities?* Oxford: Clarendon Press.

Bardhan, P. K. 1993. Symposium on management of local commons. *Journal of Economic Perspectives* 7:87–92.

———. 2000. Water community: An empirical analysis of cooperation on irrigation in South India. In *Community and market in economic development,* ed. Y. Hayami and M. Aoki. Oxford: Clarendon Press.

Bluffstone, R. A. 1995. The effect of labor market performance on deforestation in developing countries under open access: An example from Nepal. *Journal of Environmental Economics and Management* 29:42–63.

Bromley, D. W. 1992. The commons, property, and common-property regimes. In *Making the Commons Work,* ed. D. W. Bromley. San Francisco: ICS Press.

Bromley, D. W., and D. P. Chapagain. 1984. The village against the center: Resource depletion in South Asia. *American Journal of Agricultural Economics* 66 (5): 868–873.

Chhetri, R. B., and T. R. Pandey. 1992. *User group forestry in the Far-Western Region of Nepal.* Kathmandu: International Centre for Integrated Mountain Development.

Cooke, P. A. 1998. Intrahousehold labor allocation responses to environmental good scarcity: A case study from the hills of Nepal. *Economic Development and Cultural Change* 46 (4): 807–830.

Dasgupta, P. S., and G. M. Heal. 1979. *Economic theory and exhaustible resources.* Cambridge: Cambridge University Press.

Deacon, R. T. 1994. Deforestation and the rule of law in a cross-section of countries. *Land Economics* 70:414–430.

De Meza, D., and J. R. Gould. 1992. The social efficiency of private decisions to enforce property rights. *Journal of Political Economy* 100:561–580.

Demsetz, H. 1967. Toward a theory of property rights. *American Economic Review* 57:347–359.

Fisher, R. J. 1989. Indigenous systems of common property forest management in Nepal. EAPI Working Paper No. 18, Environment and Policy Institute. Hawaii: East-West Center.

Food and Agriculture Organization of the United Nations (FAO). 1989. *Community forestry.* Rome: FAO.

Fox, J. 1993. Forest resources in a Nepali village in 1980 and 1990: The positive influence of population growth. *Mountain Research and Development* 18:89–98.

Fujita, M., Y. Hayami, and M. Kikuchi. 2000. The conditions of farmer participation in irrigation management: A cross-section analysis for the Philippines. In *Community and market in economic development,* ed. Y. Hayami and M. Aoki. Oxford: Clarendon Press.

Gilmour, D. A. 1989. Forest resources and indigenous management in Nepal. EAPI Working Paper No. 17, Environmental and Policy Institute. Hawaii: East-West Center.

Gilmour, D. A., and R. J. Fisher. 1991. *Villagers, forests, and foresters.* Kathmandu: Sahayogi Press.

Gilmour, D. A., G. C. King, and M. Hobley. 1989. Management of forests for local use in the hills of Nepal: Part 1, changing forest management paradigm. *Journal of World Forest Resource Management* 4:93–110.

Grafton, R. Q. 2000. Governance of the commons. *Land Economics* 76 (4): 504–517.

Graner, E. 1997. *The political ecology of community forestry in Nepal.* Saarbrucken: Verlag fur Entwicklungspolitik.

Greene, W. H. 1997. *Econometric analysis.* 3d ed. Upper Saddle River, N.J.: Prentice-Hall.

Griliches, Z., and V. Ringstad. 1971. *Economies of scale and the form of production function: An econometric study of Norwegian manufacturing establishment data.* Amsterdam: North-Holland.

Hardin, G. 1968. The tragedy of the commons. *Science* 162:1243–1248.

Hayami, Y. 1997. *Development economics: From the poverty to the wealth of nations.* Oxford: Clarendon Press.

Jodha, N. S. 1986. Common property resources and rural poor in dry regions of India. *Economic and Political Weekly* 21:1169–1181.

Karki, M., J. B. S. Karki, and N. Karki. 1994. *Sustainable management of common forest resources: An evaluation of selected forest user groups in western Nepal.* Kathmandu: International Centre for Integrated Mountain Development.

Kumar, S. K., and D. Hotchkiss. 1988. *Consequences of deforestation for women's time allocation, agricultural production, and nutrition in hill areas of Nepal.* IFPRI Research Report No. 69. Washington, D.C.: International Food Policy Research Institute.

McGranahan, G. 1991. Fuelwood, subsistence foraging, and the decline of common property. *World Development* 19:1275–1287.

McKean, M. A. 1992. Management of traditional common lands (*Iriaichi*) in Japan. In *Making the commons work,* ed. D. W. Bromley. San Francisco: ICS Press.

Messerschmidt, D. A. 1990. Indigenous environmental management and adaptation: An introduction to four case studies from Nepal. *Mountain Research and Development* 10:3–4.

Metz, J. J. 1991. A reassessment of the causes and severity of Nepal's environmental crisis. *World Development* 19:805–820.

Nepal, Central Bureau of Statistics. 1996. *Nepal living standard survey report, 1996.* Kathmandu: NPC Secretariat.

Nepal, Ministry of Forests and Soil Conservation. 1988. *Master plan for the forestry sector.* Kathmandu: Ministry of Forests and Soil Conservation.

Nepal, National Planning Commission. 1997. *Ninth plan, 1997–2002.* Kathmandu: NPC Secretariat.

Nepal, National Planning Commission and Asian Development Bank. 1995. *Nepal agriculture perspective Plan: Final report.* Kathmandu: NPC Secretariat.

Ostrom, E. 1990. *Governing the commons: The evolution of institutions for collective action.* Cambridge: Cambridge University Press.

Ostrom, E., and R. Gardner 1993. Coping with asymmetries in the commons: Self-governing irrigation system can work. *Journal of Economic Perspectives* 7:93–112.

Pearce, D. G. 1992. Repeated games: Cooperation and rationality. In *Advances in economic theory,* ed. J.-J. Laffont. Cambridge: Cambridge University Press.

Rayamajhi, S., and R. Pokharel. 1998. From deforestation to reforestation: Common-property forest management in the hill region of Nepal. Report submitted to the Environment and Production Technology Division, International Food Policy Research Institute, Washington, D.C.

Runge, C. F. 1981. Common property externalities: Isolation, assurance, and resource depletion in a traditional grazing context. *American Journal of Agricultural Economics* 63:595–606.

Sethi, R., and E. Somanathan. 1996. The evolution of social norms in common property resource use. *American Economic Review* 86:766–788.

Soussan, J., B. K. Shrestha, and L. A. Uprety. 1995. *The social dynamics of deforestation: A case study from Nepal.* New York: Parthenon Publishing Group.

Stevenson, G. G. 1991. *Common property economics: A general theory and land use applications.* Cambridge: Cambridge University Press.

Upadhyaya, H. K., K. Otsuka, and C. C. David. 1990. Differential adoption of modern rice technology and regional wage differential in Nepal. *Journal of Development Studies* 20:450–468.

Wade, R. 1988. *Village republics: Economic conditions for collective action in South India.* Cambridge: Cambridge University Press.

Weitzman, M. 1974. Free access vs. private ownership as alternative systems for managing common property. *Journal of Economic Theory* 8:225–234.

World Bank. 1996. *World Bank participation source book.* Washington, D.C.: World Bank.

9 Timber Forest Management in Nepal and Japan

TAKESHI SAKURAI, YOKO KIJIMA, RIDISH POKHAREL,
SANTOSH RAYAMAJHI, AND KEIJIRO OTSUKA

Whether common property management of natural resources is a viable and efficient institutional arrangement has been widely debated in the literature. Earlier it was believed that private ownership is more efficient, as it was thought to internalize the externality whereby resource extraction by individuals reduces the amount of resources available to others, which otherwise would arise from self-interested behaviors of community members in extraction of community-owned resources (Gordon 1954; Scott 1955; Demsetz 1967; Weitzman 1974). In the past, this confusion followed erroneously from comparisons of private property with open-access systems. Common property regimes, however, can be different from open-access systems and can function as a superior alternative to private-property regimes in which people have the capacity to regulate the use of common resources (Bromley 1992). They can also emerge as superior once the cost of protecting private resources is considered (de Meza and Gould 1992).

The heart of the controversy lies in whether the transaction cost of a common property regime is higher than that of a private-property regime (Cheung 1970, 1987; Dahlman 1980; Runge 1981). As such, it must be resolved empirically. Yet empirical research in the area of common property management is deplorably weak.[1] One of the cases often referred to as successful community management of forest is *iriaichi* in prewar Japan, where strict management rules were formulated informally by community members and enforced effectively by rotational patrolling and severe punishment schemes (McKean 1992; McKean and Ostrom 1995). Similarly, effective indigenous community management of forests is widely observed in the hill region of Nepal, even though the evidence is generally qualitative (Arnold 2001). Our econometric studies in Chapter 8 demonstrated that collective community management effectively

---

We are grateful for useful comments on an earlier draft by Ganesh Thapa and Govind Koirala. We are also grateful to Mr. Ranbindra M. Tamrakar, who analyzed aerial photographs. This chapter partly draws on Kijima, Sakurai, and Otsuka (2000).

1. There are, however, a few exceptions. For example, see Stevenson (1991).

prevents overexploitation of minor forest products, such as firewood and leaf fodder, so as to improve forest conditions.

This chapter is concerned with the management efficiency of timber forests and plantations. The central question is whether participatory or collective community forest management is more efficient in timber production than other management schemes, such as private and centralized community management. Collective management user group committees, whose members are supposed to be elected, stipulate and enforce communal regulations of livestock grazing and forest resource extraction activities and organize collective work for management of trees. This system was found in both timber plantations and natural timber forests in our sites: in the inner Tarai region of Nepal's Dang District (see Figure 8.1) and in timber forests in Japan's Gunma Prefecture, located 150 to 200 kilometers north of Tokyo. In the Nepal site, other management systems coexist, namely, private timber plantations managed by individual farmers and centralized community management of natural timber forests, in which community members provide labor for protection of forests but hired labor is used for management of trees under the centralized decisionmaking system. In the Japan site, individual management is also practiced after dividing the forestland into smaller pieces and allocating the exclusive use rights to individual forest user group members. Taking advantage of the coexistence of various management systems, we undertake comparative studies of the management efficiency of timber forests and plantations. We address the efficiency in terms of the cost of protection, the quality of timber forests, and the overall profitability.

We argue that, unlike the management of copse forests observed in the hill region of Nepal at present and in prewar Japan, management systems that provide stronger individual work incentives are likely to be more efficient for management of timber forests and plantations. This is because, compared with minor forest products, it is easier to protect timber trees, as it is difficult for anyone to fell big trees illegally, haul them from the forest, and process them without being noticed by community members. It is also important to emphasize that in order to grow valuable timber trees, various silvicultural operations are required, for which work incentives ought to play a critical role. Thus, we hypothesize that although collective management may be superior to individual management for protection of timber trees because of the scale advantages, private and centralized management with clearer profit incentives is more efficient for management of trees. If so, management systems that can apply both principles will be the most profitable.

The organization of this chapter is as follows. First, we briefly review community forest management in the inner Tarai of Nepal and postwar Japan. We then report the results of case studies of Nepal and Japan in separate sections. We discuss the policy implications of our empirical findings in the final section.

Community Forestry in Nepal And Japan

The Case of the Inner Tarai in Nepal

As was discussed in Chapter 8, formal and informal user group management co-exist in Nepal, even though both are called community forestry. Although some empirical studies report that informal forest user groups (IFUGs) have been able to protect and manage forests for a sustainable supply of forest resources (for example, Fisher 1991), others call into question their ability to carry out sustainable management of forests in view of their weak financial basis (for example, Dahal 1994). These discussions pertain to copse forests in the hills, where nontimber products are major forest resources. An important point for our analysis is that once user groups become formal and natural forests are handed over, they may be allowed to harvest timber for sale to markets. Needless to say, harvesting has been freely allowed if trees have been planted by the community or individual farmers. Many hill forests, which have been studied more extensively in the literature (see Chapter 8), are generally too remote for significant sales of forest products, particularly timber. Our study is concerned with the inner Tarai, which has distinctively more favorable access to roads and markets.

The policy of handing over official use rights of forests to communities has been applied primarily to hill forests but not to natural forests in the Tarai (Chakraborty et al. 1997), which is characterized by flat topography. The major tree species in natural forests is sal (*Shorea robusta*), which has a strong capacity to coppice and is a valuable timber tree. The natural forests in the Tarai, which have been managed by the government up to now, have deteriorated significantly as a result of illegal logging and encroachment by migrants over time. On the other hand, timber production on formerly marginal crop fields by private farmers is becoming common in the Tarai, which indicates the rising value of timber because of its increasing scarcity in natural forests.

The inner Tarai is located in the valley surrounded by the Siwalik mountain range and the Mahabharat mountain range. Consisting of both hilly or mountainous areas where copse forests exist and flat Tarai-like areas where sal forests exist, this area has characteristics of both hill and Tarai. Interestingly, the Government of Nepal has applied the policy of handing over forest use rights not only on the copse forests but also on the natural timber forests in the inner Tarai. In particular, this policy has been most actively followed in Dang District, according to our brief visits to most inner Tarai districts. Furthermore, the most liberal policy regarding the sale of timber trees to markets has been adopted in this district, owing to the liberal decisions of the District Forest Office (DFO).

Another interesting feature of this district is the coexistence of timber plantations managed by individual farmers and those managed by communities under social forestry projects, which advocate collective management and equal benefit-sharing rules analogous to the management systems in the community forestry in the hills. Management of timber plantations and natural timber forests is active in Dang, primarily because of the favorable access to roads and markets. Thus, this district provides the rare opportunity to assess the relative management efficiency of collective management vis-à-vis private or centralized management.

The Case of Japan

Community forest, called *iriaichi,* used to supply indispensable inputs for farming and for rural life in isolated and largely self-sufficient communities located in mountainous areas in Japan before the war (Sakurai 1997).[2] Grasses were extracted to produce green manure and compost for paddy fields and to feed horses, which were used for plowing. Firewood was widely used as a major source of energy at home. In order to prevent overexploitation of these forest resources, strict management rules were implemented, such as the designation of date, time, place, and amount of specific resources allowed to be extracted each year. Collected firewood is usually divided equally at the end of the day and distributed equally to participating members, as in the contemporary management of hill forests in Nepal. This practice discourages the excessive extraction of firewood. The use of tools, such as saws, was also strictly regulated. In addition, collective work was organized, particularly for burning portions of forests to facilitate the regrowth of feeding grasses. The similarity of management rules between copse forests in prewar Japan and contemporary hill forests in Nepal is striking.

As mountainous villages became integrated into the market economy, charcoal production for sale to urban markets emerged during the winter months when farm jobs were limited. For charcoal production, sites growing mature trees were chosen and delineated, and all the trees were completely felled. Those trees were miscellaneous broad-leaf trees, which had the ability to coppice and to regrow naturally without much human care. Casual evidence indicates that such community management systems were successful in sustainable management of forest resources (for example, McKean 1992).

Views of *iriaichi* changed dramatically after the war. Demand for grasses sharply declined as cheap chemical fertilizer and hand tractors became available. Similarly, demand for firewood and charcoal diminished with the increased availability of and increased consumers' preference for kerosene, gas, and electricity. In contrast, reflecting the shortages of houses, demand for timber increased appreciably with the recovery of the economy. Consequently, the

---

2. There are numerous documents on traditional *iriaichi,* but all of them are written in Japanese except McKean (1992). For example, see Furushima (1955), Kondo (1959), and Kasai (1964).

FIGURE 9.1 Changes in price of cedar board relative to that of wood for charcoal and firewood

Index (1960 = 100)

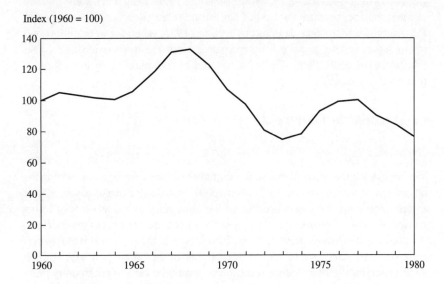

price of timber relative to that of wood for firewood and charcoal also increased until the end of the 1960s (see Figure 9.1).[3]

The government initiated the Tree Plantation Expansion Program in 1956, which provided subsidies for the plantation of timber trees. As a result, expected returns to planting timber trees became high enough to warrant massive tree planting (Kitabatake 1992; Hagino 1996). Based on recall data from leaders of community forests relating to management and harvesting around 1960, Kijima (1998) computed internal rates of return to timber tree plantation and regrowth of miscellaneous trees for firewood and charcoal while assuming no change in the real product prices. They are found to be about 9 percent and 2 percent for timber and firewood/charcoal, respectively, which supports the view that investment in the conversion to timber forest had a reasonably high payoff.

The average proportion of forest area planted with timber trees increased from about 15 percent in 1955 to nearly 50 percent in 1975 in our sample forests. Thus, timber has become a major forest product in postwar Japan, similar to the inner Tarai in Nepal in recent years. Because of declining timber prices thereafter due to massive imports of cheap timber facilitated by the ap-

---

3. We used the price of cedar board, which is representative of timber prices in Japan, and the price of logs of miscellaneous trees for firewood and charcoal, both of which are obtained from Japan, Ministry of Agriculture, Forestry, and Fishery (1970–90).

preciation of the Japanese yen (see Figure 9.1), however, tree planting has seldom been carried out since the mid-1970s. Furthermore, we found that timber trees had rarely been harvested in the 1980s and 1990s even when some of them became mature, because the cost of harvesting often exceeded the revenue. In this study, we focus on tree planting between 1955, when the agricultural sector in Japan is said to have fully recovered from the devastation of the war (Hayami et al. 1991), and 1980, when voluntary tree planting by communities practically ceased.

Case Study of the Inner Tarai

Hypotheses

We begin with the premise that scale economies or scale advantages exist in the protection of forests and trees (Grafton 2000). Patrolling consists essentially of information collection, and because of the nonrivalry characteristics of information, the cost of protection can be reduced by the use of selected watchers under community management systems. In contrast, in the case of private ownership systems, each owner has to protect his or her own property. Mutual supervision may further reduce protection costs in the case of community management. With respect to the implementation of the silvicultural operations, such as pruning, weeding, thinning, singling, and harvesting, we postulate that work and management incentives play a decisive role, such that private management or centralized management under the strong leadership of user group committees is more efficient than collective management. In fact, collective management, which assigns community members to share equally in labor inputs and benefits, would suffer from the same incentive problems facing collective management of farms, such as communes in China (Lin 1988). In this system, the marginal return to labor for each member is only a small fraction of the value of marginal product of labor because of the benefit-sharing arrangement.

Based on these considerations, we postulate the following four testable hypotheses regarding the relative efficiency of different management systems.

Hypothesis 1: Collective community management is less costly than private management for the protection of timber tree plantations. Livestock grazing is the major factor degrading tree plantations, especially in the early stage of tree growth. Unless seedlings are protected from grazing, survival rates and crown cover will be low. In community plantations, all users participate in patrolling and supervision, and penalties are imposed for violations. On the other hand, in the case of private plantations, owners may have to rely on fencing and private employment of watchers, in addition to their own efforts, to protect seedlings. Thus, private management is expected to be more costly than community management to protect trees per unit of plantation area.

We test this hypothesis by comparing the protection costs of private and community management. The protection cost is measured by the labor involved in and material costs of setting up fences and their maintenance and the cost of hiring watchers. The protection cost can be considered as an appropriate measure of the efficiency of protection if the effectiveness of protection does not differ between the two systems. Thus, we examine the effectiveness of protection by comparing the survival rate of planted seedlings after the first year and crown cover. It is difficult to assess a priori which measure is a better indicator for protection activities, as both of them would be affected by protection as well as care of young seedlings. It must also be pointed out that minor forest products, such as medicinal plants, are seldom grown in tree plantations, so the protection of such products assumes no major significance.

Hypothesis 2: A larger amount of labor is allocated to the management of planted trees under private management than under collective community management. In order to produce high-quality timber trees, silvicultural operations are required. It is reasonable to assume that private owners have proper incentives to carry out such operations for their own benefits, leading to efficient management. On the other hand, collective community management is likely to be less efficient in silvicultural operations, because it has to organize and enforce collective work. Conflicts can easily arise among community members as to the appropriate collective work and the fulfillment of individual work obligations. Thus, the question is whether a smaller amount of labor is allocated to the management of trees under collective than private management.

We test this hypothesis first by comparing labor inputs for silvicultural operations (weeding, pruning, and thinning) in private and community plantations. We consider that community management fails to coordinate collective actions if the amount of labor allocated for silvicultural operations is less than under the private system. We argue that less labor for management is inefficient because inappropriate incentive systems will lead to an undersupply of management labor, whereas less labor for protection is efficient because ineffective protection systems will require more labor for protection. Also note that property rights on privately owned land have been well established, so unlike the case of customary land areas of Asia and Africa, the act of tree planting does not strengthen private land rights (see Chapters 3–6).

Hypothesis 3: Formal user groups are more efficient than informal user groups for protection of natural forests. This hypothesis attempts to examine the validity of the often held view that informal community management does not work because of the lack of clear community rights in forestland and resources. In fact, IFUGs do not have the rights to harvest timber trees, so this group may have weaker incentives to protect forests. We tested the same hypothesis in Chapter 8 by using the data from the hill region.

Since all our sample forests were selected from the list of formal forest user groups (FFUGs), we test this hypothesis by examining the extent of improvement of natural forest conditions after handing over. We expect that the longer the period for which a formal user group has protected the forest, the greater will be the improvement of forest conditions. We also expect that the larger and more heterogeneous user groups are, the less efficient the protection of forests will be because of the higher costs of reaching communal agreements and enforcing them.

Hypothesis 4: Centralized management is more efficient than collective management in the management of natural timber forests. After handing over, FFUGs are allowed to harvest timber trees, and consequently they potentially have incentives to manage timber trees to increase profit. If they adopt a participatory collective approach, however, they will face incentive problems because each member is motivated to free-ride. Under the centralized management system, a user group committee employs wage laborers, or alternatively what forest user committees call *contractors,* for silvicultural operations. Because performance of timber harvesting, as well as most other activities (for example, weeding), can be monitored relatively easily, the enforcement of the hired workers is likely to be effective.[4] Therefore, we expect that centralized management is more efficient than collective management in the management of timber forests. We test this hypothesis by comparing the profits from the extraction of tree resources under collective and centralized community management.

Sample Forests

Since Dang District is one of the pioneer districts in community forestry in Nepal, as much as 16,273 hectares of national forestlands have been handed over to 153 forest user groups as of 1997. These forests are classified as either community natural forests or community plantations. According to our own analysis of aerial photos taken in 1978 and 1996, the average crown cover changed from 33 percent to 48 percent for the 18-year period. Private plantation of timber trees on abandoned crop fields has also been increasing, and 73 private plantations have been registered to the DFO as of 1997. Also increasing are community plantations on degraded community forests. Both community and private plantations have developed in response to increasing scarcity of timber. The expansion of community plantations, however, is limited to highly degraded areas of community forests.

From the list of registered plantations and natural forests provided courtesy of the DFO, we randomly selected 25 private plantations, 25 community plantations, and 52 community natural forests. For all the sample community forests, we conducted a forest management survey by means of group interview in the presence of the chairman or secretary of the FFUG committee and a

---

4. Only three forest user committees employ contractors or piece-rate workers. The prevalence of daily wage employment indicates that the enforcement of work effort is not too costly. See Hayami and Otsuka (1993) on this point.

forest/tree inventory survey by carrying out actual measurement of tree conditions.[5] In the case of private plantations, we interviewed their owners. In addition, we identified the forest conditions of all the selected natural forests using aerial photos taken in 1978 and 1996. We adopted a conventional survey method, rather than participatory methods widely used in the study of Nepal's forest sector (Hobley 1996; Chambers 1997; Richards et al. 1999), simply because the quantitative data collected by the conventional approach are necessary for our hypothesis testing.

The basic characteristics of those three types of forests are shown in Table 9.1.The average size of community natural forests is by far the largest, and most of them are partially planted. Since sal trees have the ability to coppice, regeneration is the common method of improving natural forest conditions. The community plantations include four large forests partially planted to timber trees. If we exclude them, average plantation size becomes 13.3 hectares, rather than 64.7 hectares, and average plantation rate becomes 100 percent in this category. The size of private plantations is much smaller. Community plantations began earlier than private plantations, whereas the handing over of community forests and registration of planted forests occurred more recently. The latter observation indicates that it is premature to assess the full impact of handing over on the growth of timber trees. In general, both natural forests and timber plantations are located close to residential areas.

Private versus Community Plantations

Now we test hypotheses 1 and 2. Table 9.2 compares selected characteristics of private and community plantations. Private plantations were mostly established on previously marginal agricultural fields, while community plantations were established predominantly on degraded community forestlands for which natural regeneration of forest could hardly be expected. Consequently, there is a significant difference in the previous use of plantation areas between them. We consider that private and community plantations coexist because each system has its own weaknesses and advantages as postulated in the two hypotheses.

Soil type is significantly different only in the proportion of gravel soil. Sisso is a fast-growing, multipurpose species and more prevalent on private plantations than on community plantations. Other characteristics, such as tree-planting density and the first-year survival rate of seedlings, are not significantly different in the two types of management systems.

Planted trees at the early stage need to be protected from grazing by fences and the use of watchers. We compare the costs of protection of trees in private and community plantations. As is shown in Table 9.3, 80 percent of private plantations and 28 percent of community plantations are protected by fences.

---

5. See Rayamajhi and Pokharel (1998) for details of methods of sampling patches and measured outcome.

TABLE 9.1 Comparison of three types of forests in inner Tarai

	Private Plantation	Community Plantation	Community Natural Forest
Total forest/plantation size (ha)	0.72	64.7	166.2
Size of planted area (ha)	0.72	15.4	16.3
Plantation rate (percentage)	100	81.8	15.7
Number of users per forest/ plantation (mean)	1	130.4	304.0
Forest/plantation area per household (ha)	0.72	0.35	0.86
Years since plantation (mean)	7.4	8.6	5.9
Years since handing over (mean)	5.6[a]	4.0	2.9
Walking time to forest/ plantation (minutes)	13.7	14.8	15.4
Percentage of Brahmin households	36.0	12.5	13.8
Number of samples	25	25	52

[a]Years since registration.

TABLE 9.2 Characteristics of private and community plantations in inner Tarai

	Private Plantation	Community Plantation	Chi-Square and *t*-Statistics[a]
Previous use of land (percentage)			
Agriculture	80	8[b]	26.30**
Grazing land	20	68	11.68**
No use or barren land	0	36	10.98**
Soil type (percentage)[c]			
Gravel	20	52	5.56*
Sandy loam	4	40	0.00
Loam	32	32	0.00
Clayey loam	20	36	1.59
Proportion of sisso species	91.4 (11.3)	77.5 (17.7)	3.32**
Planting density (number per ha)	3,093 (1,520)	3,035 (3,261)	0.08
Seedling first-year survival rate (percentage)	80.3 (16.1)	73.4 (15.7)	1.53
Number of samples	25	25	

NOTE: Standard deviations are in parentheses.

[a]Pearson's chi-square test statistics for the first seven comparisons and *t*-statistics for the last three.

[b]Used as agricultural land because of encroachment.

[c]Total becomes more than 100 percent because some plantations have more than one soil type.

*.05 level

**.01 level

TABLE 9.3   Comparison of protection cost between private and community plantations in inner Tarai

	Private Plantation	Community Plantation	*t*-Statistics
Use of fences (percentage)	80.0	28.0	13.61**[a]
Labor cost to build fences (rupees/ha)[b]	3,642 (4,358)	6.27 (31.37)	4.17**
Material cost for fences (rupees/ha)	2,081 (9,055)	0 (0)	1.15
Maintenance cost (rupees/ha/year)	806 (1399)	30.5 (90.8)	2.77*
Use of watchers (percentage)	72	100	6.94**[a]
Number of watchers per hectare	2.08 (2.62)	0.25 (0.28)	3.47**
Watcher cost (rupees/ha/year)[b]	13,885 (24,642)	1,818 (2,036)	2.44*
Number of samples	25	25	

NOTE: Standard deviations are in parentheses.
[a]Pearson's chi-square test.
[b]Both family labor and users' participatory labor are included.
*.05 level
**.01 level

In general, the whole area is fenced in the case of private plantations, whereas small portions are protected by fences in the case of community plantations. Since building fences requires labor and material, private plantations have significantly larger costs for fencing, even if the cost of "free" participatory labor in community plantations is imputed by using the prevailing agricultural wage rates. Note that because all fences are made of bush trees (live hedge) in community plantations, there is practically no material cost. On the other hand, purchased materials, such as barbed wire, poles, and bamboo, are used in some private plantations. All community plantations employ watchers; some private plantations do not. Owners of private plantations may be able to watch their trees while they work in the field, or their plantations may be too small to employ watchers, who usually work full time. The average number of watchers employed and the cost of watchers per hectare per year, however, are significantly higher in private than community plantations. It is clear from these observations that the larger cost of protection is incurred by private rather than community plantations.

In order to examine the effect of the difference in management systems on the cost of protection more rigorously, we estimate regression functions in which fence cost and the number of watchers per hectare are dependent variables. Explanatory variables include a dummy for private plantations, variables related to the cost of plantation management (that is, total plantation area per household and walking time to plantation), timing of plantation establishment, and soil type dummies. We included soil type dummies, because they critically affect the growth of timber trees, which in turn may affect incentives to protect them. We also assess the effects of building fences and employing watchers on the condition of plantations by means of two-stage estimation models, in which the first-year survival rate of planted trees is a dependent variable in the second-stage regression.

Table 9.4 shows the regression results. As would be expected, fence cost and the number of watchers per hectare are significantly higher in private plantations, judged from the significant coefficients of the dummy variable for private plantations. We also applied the two-stage estimation procedure to the first-year survival rate in which the predicted fence cost or the number of watchers is used as an explanatory variable (see the last two columns of Table 9.4).[6] Both the cost of fences and the number of watchers have a significantly positive effect, while the dummy for private plantations has no significant effect in those two-stage estimations, which implies that there is no significant difference in the survival rate between private and community plantations, after controlling for the effect of the cost of fences or the number of watchers. Thus, private plantations seem to invest more in protection, which leads to a higher first-year survival rate. Therefore, although community plantations incur less cost of tree protection than private plantations, we cannot conclude that the community management is less costly to achieve the same level of protection, as far as the first-year survival rate is an appropriate measure of protection. In consequence, hypothesis 1 is not strongly supported by the analysis of the survival rate.[7]

We also assess the difference in management performance between private and community plantations in terms of labor inputs, excluding those specifically used for patrolling and watching, and the proportion of good-shaped trees.[8] Table 9.5 summarizes labor inputs for management of plantations. Although both private and community plantations use hired labor, the latter hire significantly less labor than the former. Since trees in timber plantations are still young, thinning is not carried out widely. Labor inputs for weeding and pruning per hectare per year are higher in private plantations than community

---

6. Since there is no strong a priori reason to assume direct effect of timing of plantation establishment (years since tree plantation) on the first-year survival rate of seedlings, we omitted it from the second-stage regressions. Rainfall variable is not used in the analyses of this study simply because our sample forests are located in relatively small areas, so that variations in rainfall are relatively small.

7. This result, however, is consistent with the observation of Chakraborty et al. (1997:91) that "historical experience has shown that forest protection is not feasible without the cooperation of the local communities."

8. Information about crown cover and good-shaped trees was collected in the forest inventory survey by professional foresters. Crown cover is the measure of stocking density of forest, whereas proportion of good-shaped trees is the measure of the quality of young timber trees judged by the foresters.

TABLE 9.4 Determinants of protection and its effect on first-year survival rate in inner Tarai

	Fence Cost (1,000 rupees/ha): Tobit Model		Number of Watchers per Hectare: OLS Model		First-Year Survival Rate: 2SLS Model		First-Year Survival Rate: 2SLS model	
Intercept	−21.40	(−2.22)	2.89	(2.97)	64.40	(6.62)	57.40	(5.95)
Dummy for private plantation	21.20	(3.99)**	1.90	(3.30)**	9.23	(1.40)	9.55	(1.41)
Total plantation area per household (ha)	1.13	(0.69)	−0.82	(−2.42)**	−6.70	(−1.63)	0.01	(0.10)
Years since plantation	−0.74	(−1.25)	−0.24	(−2.39)*	n.a.		n.a.	
Walking time to plantation (minutes)	0.23	(3.45)**	−0.01	(−0.76)	−0.14	(−0.94)	−1.50	(−0.37)
Soil type dummy (gravel)	−5.14	(−0.87)	−0.76	(−1.39)	15.80	(2.61)**	18.00	(2.35)*
Soil type dummy (sandy loam)	9.25	(1.95)	0.14	(0.26)	0.79	(0.20)	1.64	(0.24)
Soil type dummy (loam)	6.39	(1.57)	−0.03	(−0.04)	8.59	(1.98)	12.10	(1.74)
Soil type dummy (clayey loam)	6.92	(1.68)	−0.63	(−1.13)	5.16	(0.74)	5.13	(0.72)
Fence cost (1,000 rupees/ha)	n.a.		n.a.		1.19	(2.25)*	n.a.	
Number of watchers per hectare	n.a.		n.a.		n.a.		3.81	(2.68)**
R-squared	n.a.		0.41		0.11		0.14	
Number of samples	49		45		49		45	

NOTE: t-Statistics are in parentheses. "n.a." refers to "not applicable."

* .05 level

** .01 level

TABLE 9.5 Comparison of labor input between private and community plantations in inner Tarai

	Private Plantation	Community Plantation	*t*-Statistics
Percentage of hired labor in total labor input	54.2 (45.7)	11.8 (32.1)	3.53**
Weeding labor (person-days/ha/year)	11.0 (11.0)	6.0 (9.6)	1.60
Pruning labor (person-days/ha/year)	7.2 (7.6)	0.9 (2.0)	3.98**
Thinning labor (person-days/ha/year)	0.2 (0.6)	0.04 (0.2)	1.03
Total labor input (person-days/ha/year)	18.3 (16.6)	6.9 (10.3)	2.84**
Number of samples	25	25	

NOTE: Standard deviations are in parentheses.
**.01 level

plantations, even though the significance level is low for weeding. Total labor input is significantly higher in private plantations.

The regression results, which control for the effects of various factors, such as years since tree plantation, its square term, and the number of trees by size class based on diameter at breast height (DBH), confirm that total labor input is significantly higher in private plantations (Table 9.6). Moreover, the estimation of reduced-form ordinary least squares (OLS) equations demonstrates that crown cover does not differ between the two types of plantations. If crown cover is an appropriate measure of protection efforts, this finding, coupled with the earlier finding that the cost of protection is higher for private plantations, supports hypothesis 1, that collective management is less costly than private management for protection. It is also found that the conditions of tree plantations measured by the percentage of good-shaped trees are better in private plantations than in community plantations. Note that this percentage would reflect the intensity of the management of trees but not the intensity of protection. Thus, this result indicates that a private management regime has a noticeable effect on the management of trees, which is consistent with hypothesis 2.

Effects of Handing Over

In order to test hypothesis 3 regarding the effect of handing over from the state to formal user groups, we analyze whether the condition of communally managed natural forests has improved after handing over. All our sampled natural forests had already been handed over to forest user groups in recent years. The average years passed since handing over were 2.9 as of 1997, as shown in Table 9.1.

Table 9.7 displays current regulations on community natural forests. Grazing and the cutting of live branches are totally prohibited in most forests, while collection of grass and dead firewood is permitted with some restrictions in most cases. It is also noteworthy that timber harvesting is not totally prohibited

TABLE 9.6 Determinants of labor input and its effect on forest quality in inner Tarai

	Total Labor Input[a] (person-days/ha/year): OLS model	Crown Cover (percentage): OLS model	Good-Shaped Trees (percentage): OLS model
Intercept	5.37 (0.33)	3.90 (0.16)	75.7 (3.28)
Dummy for private plantation	11.3 (2.26)*	6.79 (0.81)	23.4 (2.44)**
Years since plantation	2.20 (0.50)	10.30 (1.43)	−3.02 (0.48)
Years since plantation squared	−0.08 (0.33)	−0.55 (1.38)	−0.04 (0.12)
Total forest area per household (ha)	−4.33 (1.77)	0.94 (0.27)	1.60 (0.85)
Walking time to forest (minutes)	−0.05 (0.07)	−0.28 (1.69)	−0.18 (1.81)*
Number of trees per hectare, DBH = 5–10 centimeters[b]	0.00 (0.34)	0.02 (2.29)*	−0.00 (0.43)
Number of trees per hectare, DBH = 10–15 centimeters	−0.01 (3.01)**	0.02 (1.82)*	0.01 (0.57)
Number of trees per hectare, DBH = 15–20 centimeters	−0.02 (1.53)	0.03 (1.04)	0.05 (1.62)
Number of trees per hectare, DBH = 20–25 centimeters	−0.11 (2.89)**	−0.01 (0.06)	0.12 (1.19)
Number of trees per hectare, DBH = 25–30 centimeters	0.12 (3.06)**	−0.01 (0.06)	0.00 (0.06)
Soil type dummy (gravel)	n.a.	9.32 (1.12)	20.0 (1.97)*
Soil type dummy (sandy loam)	n.a.	1.98 (0.22)	14.0 (1.59)
Soil type dummy (loam)	n.a.	0.41 (0.05)	4.23 (0.62)
Soil type dummy (clayey loam)	n.a.	−13.3 (1.26)	18.6 (1.55)
R-squared	0.44	0.64	0.50
Number of samples	44	44	44

NOTE: *t*-Statistics are in parentheses. "n.a." refers to "not applicable."

[a]Total labor input includes family, users' participatory, and hired labor for weeding, pruning, and thinning.

[b]DBH stands for diameter at breast height (1.37 meters).

* .05 level

** .01 level

TABLE 9.7 Regulations on resource extraction in community natural forests after handing over in inner Tarai

	Current Regulations			Changes in Regulations after Handing Over		
	Totally Prohibited	Regulated/ Controlled	No Regulation	More Restricted	No Change	More Relaxed
			(percentage)			
Collection of						
Grass	7.7	69.2	23.1	64.0	34.0	2.0
Dead firewood	5.8	84.6	9.6	75.5	18.4	6.1
Green firewood	78.8	21.1	0	38.0	48.0	14.0
Grazing	61.5	34.6	3.8	74.0	26.0	0
Timber harvest	23.5	74.5	2.0	42.0	22.0	36.0

TABLE 9.8 Use of watchers before and after handing over in inner Tarai

	Before Handing Over	After Handing Over	*t*-Statistics
Average number of watchers per FUG[a]	1.45	1.74	2.00*
Use of rotation system (percentage)	8.3	0	1.77*
In-kind payment (percentage)	23.3	3.3	2.95**

[a]FUG stands for forest users group. Forest area did not change after handing over.

*.05 level

**.01 level

in the majority of cases. As shown in Table 9.7, regulations have become stricter after handing over, especially for grass and dead firewood collection and grazing. In contrast, it is interesting to observe that regulations on timber harvesting have been relaxed after handing over in more than one-third of the sample forests. This is because before handing over, IFUGs were not allowed to harvest timber. This observation is consistent with the fact that the New Forest Act of 1993 allowed FFUGs to harvest timber for sales.[9] Thus, we expect that user groups have a stronger incentive to manage their forests after handing over.

The average number of watchers has increased after handing over (Table 9.8). In addition, forest user groups abolished the rotation system of patrolling by their members and in-kind payment to the hired watchers after handing over. These changes seem to imply that because FFUGs now receive sale revenues, they are willing to and can afford to pay monetary rewards for watchers to protect forests.

In order to test hypothesis 3, we estimated a probit regression to examine whether the improvement of forest condition can be explained by "years since handing over." The dummy variable for the improvement was constructed based on the interpretation of aerial photos taken in 1978 and 1996: if the crown cover improved from 1978 to 1996, then the dummy variable assumes one.[10] Out of 52 forests, crown cover improved in 25 forests, whereas deterioration occurred in 4 forests. As shown in the second row in Table 9.9, the variable "years since handing over" (YSH) has no significant effect on the improvement of forest condition. This may be explained by the fact that the period after handing over is generally too short to exert significant effect on crown cover.

---

9. Out of 52 sample forests, 34 sold timber in 1997, and among them only 3 sold timbers to external markets, as mature trees were still scarce.

10. Crown cover was estimated by five categories, ranging from 0–20 percent class to 80–100 percent class. Improvement refers to change from one category to the next upper category in the majority of cases. Also note that we used only 44 samples, rather than the full sample of 52, because of the lack of certain variables in eight forests.

TABLE 9.9 Determinants of improvement of natural community forests in inner Tarai

	Crown Cover Improvement: Probit Model	Crown Cover Improvement: Probit Model	Crown Cover Improvement: Probit Model
Intercept	−2.72 (2.40)	−2.49 (2.14)	−1.83 (1.35)
Years since handing over (YSH)	−0.19 (1.07)	−0.22 (1.20)	−0.63 (1.82)*
Centralized management dummy (CMD)	n.a.	−0.50 (0.95)	−2.49 (1.83)*
YSH × CMD	n.a.	n.a.	0.76 (1.58)
Forest area (ha)	−0.004 (2.07)*	−0.004 (2.08)*	−0.003 (1.77)*
Percentage of forest area located on slopes	0.01 (1.42)	0.01 (1.46)	0.01 (1.46)
Walking time to forest (minutes)	0.04 (1.37)	0.04 (1.37)	0.05 (1.30)
Traveling time to market (minutes)	0.001 (0.23)	−0.000 (0.12)	−0.001 (0.37)
Number of users	0.001 (0.82)	0.001 (0.89)	0.002 (0.98)
Number of Brahman households	0.01 (0.99)	0.02 (1.23)	0.02 (0.94)
Soil type dummy (gravel)	0.61 (1.13)	0.63 (1.15)	0.54 (0.86)
Soil type dummy (sandy loam)	1.82 (2.73)**	1.86 (2.81)**	1.92 (2.67)*
Soil type dummy (loam)	1.17 (1.66)	1.24 (1.71)	1.44 (1.72)
Soil type dummy (clayey loam)	2.21 (2.53)*	2.32 (2.64)*	2.53 (2.45)*
Fraction of correct predictions	0.77	0.80	0.84
Number of improved forests	22	22	22
Number of samples	44	44	44

NOTE: The improvement of crown cover is represented by a dummy variable (unity for improvement), whose judgment is based on aerial photos taken in 1978 and 1996. *t*-Statistics are in parentheses. "n.a." refers to "not applicable."

*.05 level

**.01 level

We also considered the effect of centralized community management and its interaction effect with years since handing over.[11] While there are no significant independent effects of years since handing over and centralized management (third column in Table 9.9), their significance levels improve when we added the interaction term between them (fourth column). Even in the last case, however, the tests of joint effects reject the significant effect of any of these variables. Thus, there is no evidence that handing over and centralized management significantly affected changes in crown cover.[12]

---

11. The hypothesis regarding centralized management is tested in the next section, where we describe the features of the centralized management system.

12. Considering the possibility that the choice of centralized management system is endogenous, we also applied the bivariate probit model to estimate the determinants of crown cover improvement and the presence of centralized management simultaneously. As in the results of probit estimates shown in Table 9.10, we did not find a significant effect of centralized management on the improvement of crown cover.

Forest size has negative effect, as it will increase the cost of enforcing collective agreements on the use of forests. The number of user households, however, is not significant, as are the percentage of forest area on hill slopes, walking time to forest, traveling time to market towns, and the proportion of Brahman households. On the other hand, two of the soil type dummies have significant coefficients.

To sum up, although data in Tables 9.7 and 9.8 strongly indicate that the establishment of formal user groups strengthened the protection and management efforts of forests after handing over, the regression results failed to confirm the significant effects of changes in management systems on the forest conditions. We may conjecture that the period after handing over is too short to observe a positive and significant effect of the increased protection on forest conditions.

Centralized Management versus Collective Management

We now compare the efficiency of centralized management with collective management of community forests, in order to test hypothesis 4. Among 52 natural forests sampled in this study, 24 forests adopt the centralized management system, and the other 28 forests adopt the traditional collective system. Under the centralized system, forest user committees, whose members are elected by members of the forest user group, have the absolute authority to make management decisions, including the employment of wage workers for forest management operations. Such a management system was introduced recently when the forests were handed over to take care of timber trees with a view to selling high-valued timber trees to markets in the future. Under the collective management system, the decisionmaking authority of user group committee is comparably more restricted, and all members of forest user group are supposed to participate in the whole range of forest management operations. We expect that the centralized management system manages forest more effectively.

The basic characteristics of these two types of timber-harvesting forests are compared in Table 9.10. Regarding the characteristics and the conditions of forests, there is not much difference between collective and centralized management. As for the village characteristics, it can be seen that communities that manage forests centrally tend to be located significantly closer to markets and have a significantly higher percentage of Brahman households. There is, however, no significant difference in the number of user households and growth rate of households for the past 18 years.[13]

Revenues and expenditures of forest user groups are also summarized in Table 9.10. There is no significant difference in total revenue (sale of timber or firewood and membership fee) between centralized and collective management

---

13. In general, there is no major difference in the characteristics of agriculture between the two management systems, such as the ratio of households using chemical fertilizer, the proportion of irrigated paddy fields, and the rate of reduction in the size of livestock.

TABLE 9.10 Characteristics of centrally and collectively managed community forests in inner Tarai

	Centralized Management	Collective Management	t-Statistics
Forest characteristics			
Total forest area (ha)	173 (151)	160 (146)	0.31
Forest area located on slopes (percentage)	66.7 (36.8)	60.4 (41.4)	0.57
Land use in 1978 (1 for forest)[a]	0.71 (0.46)	0.79 (0.42)	0.63
Walking time to forest (minutes)	14.8 (9.22)	16.0 (10.4)	0.42
Years since handing over	2.63 (1.61)	3.04 (1.73)	0.88
Forest conditions			
Percentage of good-shaped trees	69.1 (23.2)	59.2 (25.4)	1.46
Regeneration rate (100 plants/ha)	63.0 (51.5)	41.1 (47.7)	1.59
Village characteristics			
Number of user households	363 (452)	253 (256)	1.10
Growth rate of household (percentage)	33.1 (24.9)	56.5 (102)	1.07
Traveling time to market (minutes)	68.7 (60.1)	107 (75.2)	1.94
Percentage of Brahman households	19.5 (20.6)	8.84 (841)	2.37*
Cash flow of forest management in 1996			
Total revenue (1,000 rupees)	53.8 (56.9)	43.2 (87.6)	0.51
Total expenditure (1,000 rupees)	26.2 (23.6)	13.9 (9.4)	2.41*
Gross profit (1,000 rupees)[b]	27.6 (43.0)	29.4 (84.7)	0.91
Gross profit per hectare (1,000 rupees)	0.29 (0.65)	0.12 (0.34)	1.32
Gross profit per user (1,000 rupees)	0.17 (0.34)	0.07 (0.18)	1.38
Number of samples	24	28	

NOTE: Standard deviations are in parentheses.

[a]If the current community forest area used to be covered by forest in 1978, this land use variable is unity, and otherwise it is zero. This dummy variable is constructed based on the interpretation of aerial photographs.

[b]Gross profit is defined as total revenue minus expenditures for forest management and protection.

*.05 level

systems in 1996. But total expenditures (including those for forest management and protection but excluding investment in tree planting, nursery, and community development) are significantly higher in centrally managed community forests than collective ones. This is partly because users' participatory labor in collectively managed forest is not included in the expenditure data owing to the difficulty in obtaining reasonable estimates of aggregate labor inputs from the interview with user group committee members. Thus, expenditure is underestimated for the collective management system. Gross profit, which is defined as the difference between the total revenue (sale of timber and firewood and collection of membership fees) and the total expenditures (including those for forest management and protection but excluding investment in tree planting, nursery, and community development), is not significantly different; neither is gross profit per unit of forest area or per user group member. The absence of significant difference in the gross profit may be partly explained by the underestimation of the expenditure under the collective management system.

We estimated the profit functions to examine the effect of centralized management on the gross profit after controlling for the effects of other variables (see Table 9.11). In order to take into account the endogenous choice of the management systems, we applied the switching regression procedure in which whether centralized management is adopted is determined in the first-stage probit regression (see the second column). The incidence of centralized management is affected positively by the proportion of Brahman households and negatively by traveling time to the nearest market town. These results indicate that the centralized management system was introduced in those forests that have favorable access to markets and that the leadership of Brahman households is conductive to the centralized management.

Using the results of probit regression, we obtained the predicted probability of the adoption of centralized management and the predicted probability density and estimated the switching regression model to explain gross profit per forest user. We added the interaction term between the predicted probability of the adoption of centralized management and years since handing over because the management incentives under centralized management system would have been changed by the handing over of forest use rights. It is found that centralized management has a positive and significant coefficient in the second-stage regression. Although its interaction term with years since handing over is negative and highly significant, the total effect is found to be significantly positive, which renders support for our hypothesis 4, that centralized management is more efficient than collective management.[14] In addition, the total effect of

---

14. On a priori ground we expected a positive interaction between centralized management and years since handing over. A close examination of the data suggests, however, that centralized management makes particularly large profits immediately after handing over by selling mature natural trees.

TABLE 9.11 Determinants of profitability and regeneration rate of timber harvesting forests in inner Tarai

	Dummy for Centralized Management: Probit Model	Gross Profit per Forest User (rupees/user): Switching Regression Model	Regeneration Rate (100 plants/hectare): Switching Regression Model
Intercept	0.67 (0.52)	−3,590 (1.95)	847 (1.54)
Years since handing over (YSH)	−0.23 (1.28)	376 (4.14)**	7.23 (0.27)
Predicted probability of CM (Φ)	n.a.	3,810 (2.58)***	−283 (0.64)
YSH × Φ	n.a.	−517 (3.90)**	31.1 (0.78)
Forest area per household (ha)	−0.23 (0.91)	50.7 (2.00)*	−7.70 (1.01)
Percentage of forest area located on slopes	−0.02 (0.08)	0.19 (0.22)	−0.56 (2.07)*
Walking time to forest (minutes)	0.00 (0.02)	−5.81 (1.85)*	−1.44 (1.53)
Traveling time to market (minutes)	−0.01 (1.71)*	1.75 (2.22)*	0.53 (2.25)*
Percentage of Brahman households	0.05 (1.81)*	2.46 (0.55)	−2.29 (1.71)
Land use in 1978 (1 = forest)	0.25 (0.44)	−81.9 (1.30)	−32.5 (1.72)
Soil type dummy (gravel)	0.11 (0.22)	−46.9 (0.84)	10.4 (0.62)
Soil type dummy (sandy loam)	0.78 (1.27)	−56.1 (0.15)	−14.0 (0.48)
Soil type dummy (loam)	0.50 (0.70)	−13.0 (0.76)	17.7 (0.67)
Soil type dummy (clayey loam)	1.42 (1.68)	−122 (0.76)	−54.4 (1.14)
Probability density of CM	n.a.	2,930 (1.12)	−1,650 (2.09)*
Fraction of correct predictions	0.74	n.a.	n.a.
R-squared	n.a.	0.60	0.49
Number of samples	44	44	44

NOTE: t-Statistics are in parentheses. "n.a." refers to "not applicable."

[a]CM stands for centralized management.

* .05 level

** .01 level

years since handing over, which takes into account the effect of its interaction term with centralized management, is significantly positive, indicating that years since handing over do have significant influence on the observed efficiency of forest management measured by profitability.[15] This finding supports our hypothesis 3.

Finally, we examine the effect of centralized management on forest condition in terms of the number of regenerated trees per hectare, which are shorter than breast height. This can be used as a proxy for the short-run measure of the improvement of forest conditions because regeneration takes place soon after the protection begins. The estimation result of switching regression is exhibited in the last column of Table 9.11. It is found that regeneration does not depend on years since handing over, the probability of centralized management, and their interaction effect.[16] The absence of the significant effect of centralized management implies that both centralized and collective management systems protected the forests equally well, so that there is no difference in the number of regenerated trees. In other words, the management systems affect silvicultural operations but not protection.

Thus, we may conclude that forest user groups adopting a centralized management system are more efficient for the management of timber forests, rendering clear support for hypothesis 4. In terms of the protection of natural forests, both types are equally efficient, which is also consistent with hypothesis 2.

Summary of Findings

Regarding the efficiency of private and collective community tree plantations, our study demonstrated that neither private management nor community systems completely dominate. Private management is more efficient for the management of trees, where collective community management tends to be more efficient for protection of trees, though the statistical evidence for this is not definitive.

The effect of handing over on the conditions of natural community forests was not clearly identified in this study. Since we observed a distinct increase in protection levels after handing over, however, it is expected that there will be a positive effect of strengthened community land rights on forest conditions in the longer run.

The most important finding of this study is the demonstration of superior management efficiency of a centralized user group management system, in which a user group committee organizes participation of community members

---

15. This result is in contrast to no significant effect of handing over on the improvement of crown cover as shown in Table 9.9.

16. While no significant effect of the predicted probability of centralized management is found, the coefficient for the predicted probability density of centralized management is estimated to be significantly negative. These results imply that between centralized and collective management systems there is some difference in the regeneration of plants that cannot be explained by the exogenous variables used in the first-stage probit regression.

for protection of trees and hires laborers for management of trees. As was indicated by the comparative study of timber plantations, collective community management works better than private or individualized management for protection of trees. Thus, centralized management relies on community labor for protection. Unlike collective management, however, centralized management employs hired labor for management activities of trees, such as weeding, singling, pruning, thinning, and harvesting. Since a part of timber revenue will accrue to user group committee members, as well as to members of the community at large (for example, in the form of investment in village infrastructure), there are clearer incentives to manage forests under this system than that of collective management, in which benefits are shared more or less equally. When both the advantages and disadvantages of collective and private management are considered conceptually and empirically, it seems clear that the centralized management system is highly efficient in the management of timber forests compared with the other existing forest management systems. Therefore, we expect that a centralized management system will be adopted more widely in timber growing areas of Nepal.

Case Study of Postwar Japan

Hypotheses

In the case of postwar Japan, there has been practically no demand for firewood, nor has there been any need for grazing. Thus, protection of timber forests has not been much of a problem. For management of trees, work incentives matter. We hypothesize that individualized management is more efficient than collective management, as the former provides stronger work incentives than the latter, which shares the revenue, in principle, equally among forest user group members. One may wonder why complete privatization did not take place if individual management is more efficient. Actually it took place in a non-negligible number of cases throughout Japan (Sakurai 1997). Complete privatization, however, was infeasible in many cases. Although shares of community ownership rights were officially granted to individual members in some community forests in the late nineteenth century by the land titling program (when the land tax system was introduced), the inheritance of those rights was not registered in many cases, and some offspring of original owners had left their villages. Without consent of all the official owners, joint community ownership could not have been officially resolved into truly private ownership. Many other forests were claimed to be government land at the time of the introduction of land tax system.[17] The communities were, however, allowed to purchase back

---

17. When the land tax system was introduced in 1873, many community forests were nationalized, even though they were used by communities. Responding to repeated requests of communities, the government sold the forestland to communities in the decade 1910–20 (Kasai 1964).

their forests under the names of villagers from the government at nominal prices during the second decade of the twentieth century. Yet the transfer of owner-ship rights was often unregistered thereafter. Another problem was that the fair division of forest area into individual parcels was not easy because of the lack of measurement of forest area and its geographical heterogeneity, both of which made it difficult to partition the forestland equally to community members, who possessed equal rights.

Specifically, we postulate the following hypotheses:

Hypothesis 1: Timber trees are more actively planted under individual man-agement than collective management. Since reliable official data on areas planted with trees ("tree-planted areas") at the forest level are available in Japan, we as-sess the validity of this hypothesis using the data of selected sample forests.

Hypothesis 2: Thinning is more actively carried out under individual man-agement than collective management. Because of the superior work incentives, we expect that trees were more actively planted, in terms of both planting area and density, and more carefully managed under the individual system than un-der the collective system. In consequence, the number of young trees thinned out would be larger under the individual system. We used aerial photos taken at two points in time to measure the amount of thinning at the parcel level within se-lected community forests. As suggested earlier, significant transaction costs had to be incurred to transform collective management into individual management with clear individual use rights. Thus, we postulate the following hypothesis:

Hypothesis 3: The larger the forest area, the greater would be the likeli-hood that the individual management of community forests was introduced, partly because of the greater costs of community forest management under the collective system and partly because of the larger expected benefits of the change in management systems. While the homogeneity of community forest users would also affect the choice of forest management institutions, the direc-tion of its effect is uncertain. This is because the more homogeneous the forest user group members, the lower the transaction costs of both maintaining col-lective management and introducing the new individual management system. In Japan there was no appreciable heterogeneity in ethnicity and social status. In our observation, the major factor affecting the differences in the interests of community members in the management of community forests was the owner-ship of private forests. It seems that those who owned large private forests did not have strong interests in the management of community forests. Thus, we pay particular attention to the ownership structure of private forests in the en-suing statistical analysis.

Sample Forests

We randomly selected 61 community forests in the northern, mountainous ar-eas of Gunma Prefecture based on the Shinrin-Bo (forestry account books) of the early 1990s, which are unpublished internal statistics compiled by the prefectural government based on the analysis of aerial photography and actual surveys conducted every five years with rotation of covered areas. Our sampling was restricted to those forests larger than 5 hectares managed by more than 10 households, as it was presumed that the smaller forests are similar to private forests in terms of management policies and practices. The forestry account books contain detailed information about location, area, altitude, slope, tree species, and age of trees by parcel distinguished by growth of natural and planted trees.[18] Harvesting was almost never carried out in the postwar period, because timber prices dropped unexpectedly in the 1980s and 1990s, when timber trees planted in the 1950s gradually became mature 30 to 40 years later. We traced out the history of tree planting from 1955 to 1980 using the data on ages of trees and areas of parcels collected in the early 1990s.

We also conducted interviews with the leaders of community forests to inquire into the historical process of establishing a community forest management system, management rules and their changes, changes in the use of forestland, and the location of forests. We used a map with the scale of 1:25,000 to estimate the average distance between the center of the residential area and the forest and to ascertain the land use changes over time.

Out of 61 forests, we found that 45 were collectively managed under the leadership of core members, whereas individualized management was practiced in all or part of 16 forests. Among these 16 forests, 12 had adopted some degree of individualized management since the prewar period (many of which pertained to the collection of grasses). Another 3 did so when the government measured the community forest areas for the land inventory survey in the early 1950s.[19] These historical facts indicate that the decision of individualization had been made before 1955, when the communities actively began to plant trees. This does not imply, however, that other communities did not attempt to introduce the individualized management system during the postwar period. We gathered that many did but failed because of the insurmountable difficulties in reaching agreement. There were also community forests whose members did not express any interest in dividing the use rights because collective management worked well, according to the interviews with the leaders.

Table 9.12 exhibits the basic statistics of sample community forests and characteristics of communities by management system. Individually managed land accounts for 56 percent of forestland under individualized management. Consistent with our hypothesis, the area planted to timber trees per member

---

18. A parcel is called *fude,* which is the unit of area distinguishable from other areas in terms of land use.

19. We failed to determine a clear reason for the individualization in one case because it took place before the turn of the century, and we found only one case in which community members clearly demanded the change to the individualized system in the early postwar period.

TABLE 9.12 Characteristics of community forests and communities by management system in Japan

	Collective Management	Individualized Management	*t*-Statistics
Proportion of forest area under	0	0.56	6.10**
individualized management	(0)	(0.37)	
Tree-planted area per member	0.16	0.47	2.67*
household (ha)	(0.18)	(0.44)	
Forest area (ha)	53.8	107.8	1.90
	(57.8)	(108.3)	
Number of member households	67	66	0.07
	(56)	(62)	
Percentage of share system	56	81	2.05*
	(50)	(40)	
Percentage of tree-planted area in 1955	16.4	12.4	0.96
	(22.8)	(10.0)	
Altitude (m)	640	673	0.55
	(196)	(222)	
Slope (degree)	24.2	24.5	0.13
	(8.1)	(8.2)	
Distance from residential area (km)	2.03	1.95	0.19
	(1.62)	(1.11)	
Average paddy field area per	0.20	0.20	0.03
household (ha, 1970)	(0.10)	(0.11)	
Average private forest area per	1.67	1.36	1.26
households (ha, 1970)	(0.91)	(0.68)	
Gini coefficient of private forest	0.71	0.65	1.72
ownership (1970)	(0.08)	(0.18)	
Number of samples	45	16	

NOTE: Standard deviations are in parentheses.

*.05 level

**.01 level

household under individualized management was about three times as large as under collective management between 1955 and 1980, even though the total forest area of the former was also twice as large as the latter on average. The number of member households was almost the same between the two management systems. The number of member households has generally been fixed over time, particularly in those cases in which individual households owned shares of ownership rights, which were distributed when forestlands were purchased from the government between 1910 and 1920. In those cases in which shares were not held, it is not clear whether newly established households and newcomers were entitled to use forestland, in which case incentives to manage timber forests for incumbent members would have been lower. This possibility is rather remote because the number of households did not increase significantly and in some cases even decreased during the postwar period in most communities.

The larger area of tree planting per household under individualized management does not seem to be explained by the innate advantage of those individually managed forests for tree planting over those managed collectively. First, the proportion of tree-planted areas was smaller under individualized management in 1955; if the forests managed by individualized systems were particularly suitable for timber tree planting, the proportion of tree-planted areas in 1955, which included areas planted to timber trees before the war, would have been larger. Second, in terms of average altitude, slope, and distance from the village settlement to the forest, there is no noticeable difference between the two. Thus, we hypothesize that the more active tree planting under individualized management was attributable to its superior incentive system.

Using the agricultural census (Japan, Ministry of Agriculture, Forestry, and Fishery 1995), we collected baseline (1970) information about communities that managed our sample forests.[20] Specifically we obtained data on paddy field area and private forest area per household and computed the Gini coefficient of private forest ownership.[21] The first two variables are assumed to reflect the average level of wealth of member households. Since the selected communities were highly dependent on rice production, the paddy area is supposed to represent the wealth level relatively accurately. Average paddy field area per household can be legitimately considered exogenous, as paddy fields were redistributed by the postwar land reform, and their transaction was severely restricted by law. We expect that the larger the paddy and private forest areas, the smaller will be the timber tree plantation on community forest because of the negative wealth effect on incentives to perform community labor. The private forest ownership, however, may capture other effects aside from the wealth effect. First, management of private forests during the off-farm season may compete with that of community forests. Because of this, the larger ownership of private forests may lead to a lower incidence of tree planting on community forests. Second, management experience and know-how of private forests may have a positive effect on management of community forests, which will lead to the larger area of timber tree plantation. Third, the larger the ownership of private forest area, the smaller would be the demand for the use of

---

20. The year 1970 was the earliest year for which data on communities (*shuraku*) could be obtained. *Shuraku* has the origin of a natural village and is smaller than the smallest administrative unit (village, town, or city, depending on the population). We believe that the relative magnitudes of the community-specific variables we used for the regression analysis have been largely unchanged for many years.

21. Among our sample communities, about 60 percent of households owned private forests, which are generally located in flatter areas near residences. Private forests used for timber were generally used for grassland before the war.

forestland. According to our interviews, households that owned private forests had higher priorities for the management of private forests than that of community forests. Although this may indicate the superior incentive system of private ownership, it may be due to advantageous location and generally more fertile soil of private forests.

Table 9.12 indicates that there was no significant difference in average area of paddy ownership between the two types of systems, whereas there is an indication that individualization of forest management took place more often in areas endowed with smaller private forests.

The size and heterogeneity of community would affect the transaction costs of community forest management. We expect that the total forest area will be related to the cost of enforcing community agreements, whereas the total number of member households will be related to the cost of reaching agreements. That forest areas were generally much larger for those forests managed individually suggests that the individualization took place in order to save the higher cost of enforcing the collective agreements. We measured the heterogeneity of interests in management of community forests by the Gini coefficient of private forest ownership.[22] It is generally believed in the literature that the larger the heterogeneity of interests, the greater the cost of reaching agreements, so that the community management system does not function well (Wade 1988). Table 9.12 indicates that *iriaichi* tended to be managed by individual members in areas where the inequality of private forest ownership was smaller.

In order to examine the effect of individualization on the management of timber forests, we selected eight individualized community forests that operated both collectively managed and individually managed parcels. Then, from the list of parcels of each community forest we randomly sampled four parcels managed collectively and another four managed individually. For ease of comparison, we selected parcels planted to cedar, which is the most popular tree in our sites.[23] Using aerial photographs taken in 1973 and 1986 or in 1979 and 1989, we identified all the selected parcels and counted the number of cedar trees per hectare.[24] We assume that the reduction in the number of trees was caused mainly by thinning operations. This assumption is reasonable because neither the encroachment of noncedar trees, which is caused by the lack of thin-

---

22. Since private forest was not subject to the land redistribution program of the land reform, the inequality of private forest ownership would not have changed significantly before and after World War II. On the other hand, the inequality of the ownership of paddy fields must have changed substantially as a result of the land reform.

23. Although we tried to select 4 parcels from each parcel group (8 community forests and 2 management systems make 16 parcel groups in total), we could select only 3 cedar-planted parcels suitable for the analysis from two groups. Hence, we additionally selected 1 parcel from two other groups, so that we have 32 collectively managed parcels and 32 individualized parcels.

24. The analysis of aerial photographs was conducted by specialists at Japan Forest Technical Association, Tokyo.

ning and weeding, nor total denudation of certain portions of forest, which takes place as a result of harvesting, was observed in the analysis of aerial photos. Thinning is a necessary operation to produce high-quality timber and is normally carried out repeatedly after the age of 10. In this chapter we use the reduction in the number of planted trees per hectare per year as the measure of the management intensity of timber forest.

Table 9.13 indicates that the number of trees per hectare declined more sharply on individualized parcels than on collectively managed parcels, whose difference is statistically significant at the 5 percent level. However, trees are younger on average on individualized parcels, and partly because of this, the number of trees per hectare in the base year might have been higher on individualized parcels. Parcel area is significantly different in that the average area of collectively managed parcels is larger. Parcel area per household under collective management, however, is substantially smaller. Among other variables, altitude, slope, and distance to road are not different between the two types of parcels.

TABLE 9.13 Characteristics of cedar-planted parcels by management system in Japan

	Collective Management	Individualized Management	*t*-Statistics
Number of trees per hectare in the base year	2,260 (820)	2,580 (820)	1.57
Number of trees per hectare after 10–13 years	1,660 (710)	1,770 (670)	0.65
Reduction of number of trees per hectare per year	−51 (28)	−70 (43)	2.06*
Age of trees in the base year	23 (12)	18 (7.6)	2.17*
Altitude (m)	760 (440)	810 (400)	0.51
Slope (degree)	23 (9.0)	23 (7.6)	0.06
Area of parcel (ha)	1.83 (3.23)	0.41 (0.27)	2.36*
Area of parcel per household (ha)	0.02 (0.04)	0.41 (0.27)	8.05**
Distance from nearby road to the center of parcel (m)	120 (92)	140 (140)	0.72
Number of samples	29	32	

NOTE: Standard deviations are in parentheses.

*.05 level

**.01 level

Econometric Analysis of Tree Planting

We now estimate the timber tree–planting function using the tree-planted areas per household from 1955 to 1980 as a dependent variable. Independent variables include the proportion of forest area under individualized management, as well as other variables shown in Table 9.12, which are considered exogenous. Although we believe that the individualization of forest management took place exogenously during the prewar period, the possibility of endogenous self-selection cannot be ruled out a priori. Thus, in addition to the OLS estimation of a tree-planting function in which the proportion of individualized forest area is assumed to be exogenous, we estimated a recursive system of equations in which a predicted proportion of individualized forest area is used in the second-stage estimation (see Appendix to this chapter for further details of estimation method).

The results are shown in Table 9.14. The first two columns show the estimation results of a probit model explaining the individualization and those of a corresponding tobit model explaining the proportion of forest area under individualization. The percentage of tree-planted area in 1955 is not included in the probit and tobit models because it might have been affected by individualization. Both results are very similar and confirm several important results. First, large forests in which enforcement of a collective agreement will be costly tend toward individualized management. This supports hypothesis 3. Second, the larger the average size of private forest in a community, the less frequently individualized management was adopted. Naturally, demand for an individual plot inside a community forest is lower if community members own large areas of private forest. Third, greater community heterogeneity, as measured by the Gini coefficient of private forest ownership, decreases individualization. This may be explained by the high transaction cost to reach an agreement to divide a community forest among heterogeneous community members. Fourth, community forests located closer to residential areas tend to be individualized.

The last three columns demonstrate the estimation results from tree-planting area regressions by OLS and recursive systems, respectively. The estimated coefficients of the two recursive systems are the same, but different methods to compute standard errors are applied: the first one is heteroskedastic-consistent, and as a result significance levels are a little better, while the second one uses the standard Gauss algorithm. The three results are very similar not only in coefficients but also in the significance levels. The following points are particularly worth emphasizing.

First, and most important, it is found that the variable for the proportion of forest area under individualized management has positive and significant coefficients. This finding supports hypothesis 1, which states that the individualized management system provides more appropriate incentives to plant timber trees than does collective management. Second, it is found that forest

TABLE 9.14 Determinants of tree planting per household and choice of individualized management in Japan

	Choice of Individualized Management (Probit)	Proportion of Individualized Area (Tobit)	Tree Planting per Household (OLS)	Tree Planting per Household (Second-Stage)[a]	Tree Planting per Household (Second-Stage)[b]
Intercept	3.03	1.27	-0.24	-0.24	-0.24
	(1.49)	(1.95)	(0.80)	(-1.09)	(-0.85)
Forest area	0.01**	0.03*	0.002**	0.002**	0.002**
	(2.65)	(1.94)	(4.17)	(4.73)	(4.52)
Number of households	-0.001	-0.0008	-0.0006	-0.0006	-0.0006
	(-0.29)	(-0.33)	(-1.15)	(-1.45)	(-0.89)
Shareholding dummy	0.43	0.39	0.11*	0.11*	0.11
	(0.96)	(1.24)	(2.03)	(2.30)	(1.33)
Distance	-0.29	-0.18*	0.03*	0.03**	0.03
	(-1.62)	(-1.67)	(2.24)	(2.52)	(1.37)
Altitude	-0.0007	-0.0004	-0.0002	-0.0002*	-0.0002
	(-0.77)	(-0.55)	(-1.60)	(-1.80)	(-1.29)
Slope	0.008	0.002	0.002	0.002	0.002
	(0.28)	(0.11)	(0.45)	(0.54)	(0.52)
Paddy area per household	1.21	1.10	-0.58*	-0.58**	-0.58*
	(0.58)	(0.85)	(-2.32)	(-2.61)	(-1.79)

Private forest area per household	−0.44*	−0.19	0.03	0.03	0.03
	(−1.82)	(−1.24)	(0.99)	(1.14)	(0.86)
Gini of private forest	−4.52*	−2.02**	0.50*	0.50**	0.50
	(−1.89)	(−2.55)	(2.02)	(2.72)	(1.59)
Percentage of tree-planted area in 1955	n.a.	n.a.	−0.001	−0.001	−0.001
			(−1.32)	(−1.58)	(−0.76)
Proportion of individualized area	n.a.	n.a.	0.36	0.32*	0.32**
			(1.53)	(1.71)	(2.78)
Adjusted R-squared	n.a.	n.a.	0.42	0.42	0.42
Pseudo R-squared	0.21	n.a.	n.a.	n.a.	n.a.
Percentage of correct prediction	0.75	n.a.	n.a.	n.a.	n.a.
Log likelihood	−29.41	−35.91	8.32	8.65	8.65
Number of samples	61	61	61	61	61

NOTE: t-Statistics are in parentheses. "n.a." refers to "not applicable."

[a]Standard errors computed from heteroskedastic-consistent matrix (Robust-White).

[b]Standard errors from quadratic form of analytic first derivatives (Gauss).

*.05 level

**.01 level

area has a positive and significant coefficient. If we assess the elasticity at the mean values, it is about 0.5, implying that a 1 percent increase in forest area is associated with a 0.5 percent increase in tree-planted area. Third, the coefficient of the share system dummy is positive and generally significant, which supports our hypothesis that incentives to plant trees were larger in forests where ownership rights were clearer. This seems to imply that incentives to manage forests have an important effect on the investment in tree planting. Fourth, distance to forest tends to be positively related to tree planting. Although it is difficult to interpret this finding, it indicates that the cost of protecting planted timber trees does not increase sharply with an increase in distance to forest from residential area. Fifth, the coefficient of ownership of paddy area indicates that the wealth effect tends to reduce the timber tree–planted area.[25] Sixth, despite the suggested negative effect of wealth, ownership of private forest does not seem to have deterred tree planting. There might have been economies of scale or scope in planting trees on private and community forests, which might partially offset the negative wealth effect. Seventh, although heterogeneous communities, reflected in the low Gini ratio of private forest ownership, tended to choose collective management, such communities planted more timber trees per member. It may well be that strong leadership existed in heterogeneous communities.

To sum up, our econometric analysis strongly indicates that not only clear ownership rights of community forest, as reflected in the shareholding system, but also individualized management system is conducive to timber tree planting, which was considered more profitable than growing miscellaneous trees.[26]

Econometric Analysis of Thinning

As discussed earlier, we use the performance of the thinning operation as the measure of the efficiency of timber plantation management. Here we estimate the thinning operation function by the OLS estimation technique by using the reduction in the number of planted trees per hectare per year as a dependent variable. A dummy variable for individualized parcel is used as an independent variable, which is considered exogenous in this estimation because individualization had been determined before tree planting and was given when the decision to conduct thinning was made.

---

25. This is different from the finding of Patel, Pinckney, and Jaeger (1995) that trees were planted more actively by wealthier people in East Africa.

26. This point was commonly and widely recognized by those who are concerned with the community forest management and policies in Japan. Based on this common recognition, the Forestry Agency of Japan has implemented the "modernization of *iriaichi*" program (Iriai Kindai-ka Jigyo) since 1967 to reorganize *iriaichi* toward the individualized ownership system or cooperative ownership system in which clear ownership rights are established formally. See Takei et al. (1989).

We estimated two models. One is to use seven community forest dummies to control for unobservable variables pertaining to each community forest, such as soil type, heterogeneity of the community, distance to the timber market, and nonfarm income opportunities. The other was an estimation without the community forest dummies. Because the first thinning operation is normally carried out 10 years after tree planting, we dropped three parcels whose trees were younger than 10 years of age in the base year. Thus, the number of samples for this estimation is 61 rather than 64. In the estimated thinning functions, the larger positive number of dependent variable corresponds to the greater thinning activity.

Table 9.15 shows the estimation results. Both models give very similar estimates except for the effect of the altitude of parcels. The effect of the dummy for individualization is significantly positive in both models consistently, which suggests that the thinning operation was more intensively carried out on individualized parcels than on collectively managed parcels. This finding strongly supports our hypothesis 2, that the individualized management system is more efficient than the collective management system for management of timber trees. The effect of tree age is negative, but its absolute magnitude declines with age. Parcel area per household has a negative effect, implying that the larger parcels are, the less thinning per hectare is carried out, owing probably to the larger cost of organizing thinning activity.

Summary of Findings

Our basic argument is that it is the demand for minor forest products that leads to the development of common-pool resource management. Timber is likely not common pool in any setting, and hence the protection of privately owned timber trees does not require much cost, except for occasional inspection in postwar Japan. The cost of protection will be particularly small in tightly structured local communities where people know one another and, explicitly or implicitly, agree to undertake mutual protection of their properties. Based on these considerations, we hypothesize that the individual management system, which provides stronger work incentives than collective management, leads to greater tree planting and thinning activities.

These hypotheses are clearly supported by the estimation results of tree-planting and thinning functions that larger forest areas were planted to timber trees and a larger amount of thinning was carried out under individual management. Also important for tree planting was the shareholding system, which clearly defines the holders of ownership of and use rights over community forests. All these findings point to the importance of land rights institutions in the appropriate use and management of forestland. We also found evidence that individualized management was more frequently introduced in areas where forest area was large so that the cost of organizing collective management was likely to be high. There is also indication that homogeneity of community members tends to lead to the adoption of individualized management system.

TABLE 9.15 Determinants of thinning per hectare per year in Japan

	Without Dummies for Community Forests (OLS Model)	With Dummies for Community Forest (OLS Model)
Dummy for individualized parcels	29.8**	22.7*
	(2.45)	(2.08)
Age of trees in the base year	−3.16**	−3.88**
	(−2.56)	(−3.01)
Age of trees in the base year squared	0.04**	0.05**
	(2.50)	(3.05)
Altitude (1,000 m)	70.1**	−32.8
	(2.57)	(−0.80)
Slope (degree)	−0.27	−1.11
	(−0.40)	(−1.28)
Area of parcel per household (0.01 ha)	−0.39*	−0.29*
	(−2.31)	(−1.70)
Distance from nearby road to the center of parcel (m)	−0.02	0.03
	(−0.56)	(0.67)
Constant	64.7**	198**
	(3.20)	(3.36)
Dummy for community forest 1	n.a.	−54.0
		(−1.44)
Dummy for community forest 2	n.a.	−78.4*
		(−2.19)
Dummy for community forest 3	n.a.	−70.4*
		(−1.94)
Dummy for community forest 4	n.a.	−46.5
		(−1.43)
Dummy for community forest 5	n.a.	−96.9**
		(−2.55)
Dummy for community forest 6	n.a.	−3.91
		(−0.16)
Dummy for community forest 7	n.a.	−33.2
		(−1.21)
Adjusted R-squared	0.24	0.33
Number of samples	61	61

NOTE: t-Statistics are in parentheses. "n.a." refers to "not applicable."

*.05 level

**.01 level

Policy Implications

In Nepal as elsewhere, forests were degraded before community actions were organized to rehabilitate them. At present, the need to rehabilitate degraded forests in developing countries is enormous. Tree planting, therefore, is increasingly a critical component of forest management. In the past, however, social science research on forest resource management exclusively focused on protection of forest or prevention of overexploitation of forest resources. Thus, the issue of the relative efficiency of private and collective forest management amounts to that of relative cost of protection of forest resources under different land property rights regimes. This approach is inadequate to identify the efficient management systems of timber forests, which require such management activities as planting, weeding, pruning, and thinning. We argued that an individualized management system or centralized management system with clear profit motives is more efficient than a collective management system because of the superior management incentives. This point explains why social forestry projects that attempt to share the benefits from forest management equally among community members have generally failed to grow valuable timber trees. A recent study by Gebremedhin, Pender, and Tesfaye (2000) also finds that trees are more actively planted under private management than collective management in Ethiopia.

We do not imply that individualized management systems are always more efficient than collective management systems, because collective management has an advantage over individualized management in the protection of forest resources. In postwar Japan, the demand for firewood and charcoal was nil, and hence the need to protect immature trees was minimal. Not only in Nepal but also in many other developing countries, however, there is ample demand for firewood and charcoal, which suggests that the protection of tree resources, both mature and immature ones, is costly and critically important. How to protect forests from the damage of cattle grazing is another important issue in forest management in many developing countries. Thus, in designing the most efficient system, the merits and demerits of individualized and collective management in the protection of forest and management of trees need to be considered. Specifically, we propose that the combination of the two systems, in which the protection of forest is carried out collectively and the management of timber trees is undertaken individually or centrally, will best serve the interests of community members.

One may argue, however, that individualized or centralized management is likely to lead to inequitable access to community forest and inequitable distribution of benefits obtained from forest management. We must note that we did not find any evidence supporting the scale economies in timber forest management in this study. Thus, efficiency should not be sacrificed by egalitarian distribution of land use rights. In conclusion, we would like to emphasize that a forest or plantation system in which tree rights or use rights of land planted with trees are granted to individual members on an egalitarian basis and the protection is carried out collectively is likely to serve both efficiency and equity most effectively in the developing world.

Appendix: Estimation Procedures of Recursive System

Let us briefly explain how we estimated the recursive system of equations in which the proportion of individualized forest area is determined in the first stage and the proportion of tree-planted area is determined in the second stage. We assume that the proportion of individualized forest area (PD_i) is determined by the following equation (Maddala 1983):

$$E(PD_i) = Pr(PD_i > 0) * E(PD_i \mid PD_i > 0) + Pr(PD_i = 0) * E(PD_i \mid PD_i = 0)$$

$$= \Phi_i \left(\alpha' X_i + \sigma \frac{\phi_i}{\Phi_i} \right) + 0$$

$$= \alpha' \Phi_i X_i + \sigma \phi_i \tag{1}$$

$$GPL_i = \beta' X_i + \gamma E(PD_i) \tag{2}$$

where E is the expectation operator; $Pr(PD_i > 0)$ is the probability of incidence of individualization; $Pr(PD_i = 0)$ is the probability of no individualization; Φ and ϕ are, respectively, the probability density function and the cumulative distribution function of the standard normal; and X_i is the vector of exogenous variables. To obtain $E(PD_i)$, first Φ_i and ϕ_i are estimated in a probit model that explains the choice of individualization by exogenous variables. Then, predicted Φ_i and ϕ_i obtained from the probit model are used to estimate α and σ in equation (1) by OLS. This OLS regression gives the predicted proportion of individualized area, which is then used in the second-stage estimation of tree-planting function given by equation (2), where GPL_i is tree-planted area per member household from 1955 to 1980. Note that after estimating equation (2) by OLS, standard errors are corrected by using the original PD_i.

References

Arnold, J. E. Michael. 2001. Devolution of control of common pool resources to local communities: Experiences in forestry. In *Access to land, rural poverty, and public action,* ed. Alain de Janvry, Gustavo Gordillo, Jean-Philippe Platteau, and Elizabeth Sadoulet. Oxford: Clarendon Press.

Baland, Jean-Marie, and Jean-Phillippe Platteau. 1996. *Halting degradation of natural resources: Is there a role for rural communities?* Oxford: Clarendon Press.

Bromley, Daniel W. 1992. The commons, property, and common-property regimes. In *Making the commons work,* ed. Daniel W. Bromley. San Francisco: ICS Press.

Chakraborty, R. N., I. Freier, F. Kegel, and M. Mascher. 1997. Community forestry in the Terai region of Nepal: Policy issues, experience, and potential. German Development Institute, Berlin. Mimeo.

Chambers, R. 1997. *Whose reality counts? Putting the first last.* London: Intermediate Technology Publication.

Cheung, Steven N. S. 1970. The structure of a contract and the theory of a non-exclusive resource. *Journal of Law and Economics* 13 (1): 49–70.

———. 1987. Common property rights. In *The new palgrave: A dictionary of economics,* Vol. 1, ed. John Eatwell, Murray Milgate, and Peter Newman. London: Macmillan.

Dahal, D. R. 1994. *A review of forest user groups: Case studies from Eastern Nepal.* Kathmandu: International Centre for Integrated Mountain Development.

Dahlman, Carl. 1980. *The open field system and beyond: A property rights analysis of an economic institution.* Cambridge: Cambridge University Press.

De Meza, David, and J. R. Gould. 1992. The social efficiency of private decisions to enforce property rights. *Journal of Political Economy* 100 (3): 561–580.

Demsetz, H. 1967. Toward a theory of property rights. *American Economic Review* 57 (2): 347–359.

Fisher, R. J. 1989. Indigenous systems of common property forest management in Nepal. EAPI Working Paper No. 18, Environment and Policy Institute, East-West Center, Honolulu.

———. 1991. Studying indigenous forest management systems in Nepal: Toward a more systematic approach. EAPI Working Paper No. 30, Environment and Policy Institute, East-West Center, Honolulu.

Furushima, Toshio, ed. 1955. *Nihon ringyo seido no kenkyu* (A study on forestry institutions in Japan). Tokyo: Todai Shuppan Kai.

Gebremedhin, B., J. Pender, and G. Tesfaye. 2000. Community natural resource management: The case of woodlots in northern Ethiopia. EPTD Discussion Paper No. 60. Washington, D.C.: International Food Policy Research Institute.

Gilmour, D. A., and R. J. Fisher. 1991. *Villagers, forests, and foresters.* Kathmandu: Sahayogi Press.

Gordon, H. Scott. 1954. The economic theory of a common-property resources: The fishery. *Journal of Political Economy* 62 (2): 124–142.

Grafton, R. Q. 2000. Governance of the commons. *Land Economics* 76 (4): 504–517.

Hagino, Toshio. 1996. *Nihon gendai rinsei no sengo no katei: Sono 50 nen no jisho* (Process of modern forestry policies in Japan: Fifty years' experience). Tokyo: Nihon Ringyo Chosa Kai.

Hayami, Yujiro. 1997. *Development economics: From the poverty to the wealth of nations.* Oxford: Oxford University Press.

Hayami, Yujiro, and K. Otsuka. 1993. *The economics of contract choice: An agrarian perspective.* Oxford: Clarendon Press.

Hayami, Yujiro, and S. Yamada, with M. Akino et al. 1991. *The agricultural development of Japan.* Tokyo: University of Tokyo Press.

Hobley, M., ed. 1996. *Participatory forestry: The process of change in India and Nepal.* London: Overseas Development Institute.

Japan, Ministry of Agriculture, Forestry, and Fishery, Forestry Agency, eds. 1970–90. *Ringyo tokei yoran* (Statistical handbook of forestry). Tokyo: Rinya Kosai Kai.

Japan, Ministry of Agriculture, Forestry, and Fisheries, Statistics and Information Department. 1995. *Nogyo sensasu, nogyo shuraku kado (Agricultural census, agricultural community card*). Tokyo: Ministry of Agriculture, Forestry and Fisheries.

Karki, M., J. B. S. Karki, and N. Karki. *1994 Sustainable management of common forest resources: An evaluation of selected forest user groups in western Nepal.* Kathmandu: International Centre for Integrated Mountain Development.

Kasai, Kyoetsu. 1964. *Rinya seido no hatten to sanson keizai* (The development of forestry institutions and the economy of mountain villages). Tokyo: Ochanomizu Shobo.

Kijima, Yoko. 1998. Shinrin kanri no keizai kouritsu: Sengo Nihon no kyoyurin ni okeru jisho bunseki (Efficiency in management of community forests: An empirical analysis in post-war Japan). *Keizai to Keizaigaku* (Journal of the Faculty of Economics) 87:67–77. Tokyo Metropolitan University Faculty of Economics.

Kijima, Yoko, Takeshi Sakurai, and Keijiro Otsuka. 2000. *Iriaichi:* Collective vs. individualized management of community forests in post-war Japan. *Economic Development and Cultural Change* 48 (4): 867–886.

Kitabatake, Yoshifusa. 1992. What can be learned from domestic and international aspects of Japan's forest resource utilization? *Natural Resources Journal* 32 (4): 855–881.

Kondo, Yasuo, ed. 1959. *Bokuya no kenkyu* (A study on grass land). Tokyo: Todai Shuppan Kai.

Lin, J. Y. 1988. The household responsibility system in China's agricultural reform: A theoretical and empirical study. *Economic Development and Cultural Change* 36 (3): 199–224.

Maddala, G. S. 1983. *Limited-dependent and qualitative variables in econometrics.* Cambridge: Cambridge University Press.

McGranahan, Gordon. 1991. Fuelwood, subsistence foraging, and the decline of common property. *World Development* 19 (10): 1275–1287.

McKean, Margaret A. 1992. Management of traditional common lands (*Iriaichi*) in Japan. In *Making the commons work: Theory, practice, and policy,* ed. D. W. Bromley. San Francisco: ICS Press.

McKean, Margaret A., and E. Ostrom. 1995. Common property regimes in the forest: Just a relic from the past? *Unasylva* 46 (180): 3–15.

Metz, J. J. 1991 A reassessment of the causes and severity of Nepal's environmental crisis. *World Development* 19 (7): 805–820.

Oakley, P. 1991. *Projects with people: The practice of participation in rural development.* Albany, N.Y.: International Labor Office Publication Center.

Ostrom, Elinor, and Roy Gardner. 1993. Coping with asymmetries in the commons: Self-governing irrigation system can work. *Journal of Economic Perspectives* 7 (4): 93–112.

Patel, Sandeep H., Thomas C. Pinckney, and William K. Jaeger. 1995. Smallholder wood production and population pressure in East Africa: Evidence of an environmental Kuzunets curve? *Land Economics* 71 (4): 516–530.

Rayamajhi, S., and R. K. Pokharel. 1998. Status of community forests, community plantations, and private plantations in Dang district, Nepal. Institute of Forestry, Pokhara. Mimeo.

Richards, M., K. Kanel, M. Maharajan, and J. Davies. 1999. *Towards participatory economic analysis by forest user groups in Nepal.* London: Overseas Development Institute.

Runge, Carlisle F. 1981. Common property externalities: Isolation, assurance, and re-source depletion in a traditional grazing context. *American Journal of Agricultural Economics* 63 (4): 595–606.

Sakurai, Takeshi. 1997. Communal forest management in Japan: Its history and present situation. *Farming Japan* 31 (1): 48–51.

Scott, Anthony. 1955. The fishery: The objectives of sole ownership. *Journal of Political Economy* 63 (2): 116–124.

Sethi, Rajiv, and E. Somanathan. 1996. The evolution of social norms in common property resource use. *American Economic Review* 86 (4): 766–788.

Stevenson, Glenn G. 1991. *Common property economics: A general theory and land use applications.* Cambridge: Cambridge University Press.

Takei, Masaomi, Kaisaku Kumagai, Saburo Kuroki, and Hidetoshi Nakao, eds. 1989. *Rinya iriaiken: Sono seibi to kadai* (Common property rights: Their reorganization and problems). Tokyo: Ichiryu Sha.

Wade, Robert. 1988. *Village republics: Economic conditions for collective action in south India.* Cambridge: Cambridge University Press.

Weitzman, Martin L. 1974. Free access vs. private ownership as alternative systems for managing common property. *Journal of Economic Theory* 8 (2): 225–234.

PART V

Conclusion

10 Toward New Paradigms of Land and Tree Resource Management

KEIJIRO OTSUKA AND FRANK PLACE

Massive deforestation has been taking place in developing countries, resulting in deterioration of ecological environments and greater scarcity of forest resources, such as firewood, fodder, and timber. Cleared land is often used in low-input shifting cultivation, a system that cannot meet the needs of growing populations. Even though this scenario describes a substantial proportion of rural settings in developing countries, some positive natural resource trends are also occurring. For example, reforestation has followed deforestation in selected forests in the hill region of Nepal (Chapter 8) and northern Vietnam (Chapter 7). The use of agroforestry is significant and often growing, such as in the growing of commercial trees that are intercropped with annual crops when the trees are young. Examples include cocoa in Ghana (Chapter 3), coffee and other trees in Uganda (Chapter 6), and rubber and cinnamon in Sumatra (Chapter 4).

In this study we attempted to identify, systematically and quantitatively, the factors affecting the evolution of land tenure institutions; their effects on the use of land for forestry, agroforestry, and annual cropping; and their management efficiency at community and household levels. The objective was to draw generalizable conclusions through comparisons of Asia and Africa, where cultural, natural, and policy environments are vastly different. We confirmed that the use and allocation of forests, agroforest, and cropland are governed by a range of land tenure institutions. Broadly speaking, these include communal ownership of land, state ownership, common property, and private ownership. Further, we found that the conditions under which each of these institutions performs well and poorly in terms of promoting efficiency of natural resource management were consistent across the study sites.

This concluding chapter summarizes the major lessons of the seven country studies in order to draw out the major policy implications. The following major issues are summarized in this chapter. First, what are the more common types of property rights institutions? How, if at all, are they evolving, and to which factors are they most responsive? Second, how do land tenure institutions affect the pace of deforestation? Third, under what conditions are common property systems viable and efficient institutional arrangements? Fourth,

359

how do land tenure institutions affect investments in planting trees and their management efficiency? Fifth, how do land tenure institutions affect the efficiency of annual crop farming? Sixth, what effects do the different tenure systems have on equity and reduction of poverty? Policy implications arising from the answers to these six questions across the study sites are discussed in the final section.

Evolution of Property Rights Systems

In all the study sites operating under a communal tenure system, population pressure seems to be a driving force leading to the privatization of land rights on land converted and utilized for agriculture or agroforestry. Strong individual land rights are granted to cultivated land converted from forests and woodlands, even though such rights are weakened when the land is put into long fallow. Rights have been further individualized through long-term investment, most notably in tree planting. Transfer of land as a gift to wife and children in Ghana (Chapter 3) and the establishment of single family ownership from joint family ownership in Sumatra (Chapter 4) are clear examples of individualization after tree planting. There has also been evidence that land markets have developed during the process of individualization of land rights in nearly all our sites (see, for example, Figure 3.2 for Ghana). Such trends have caused traditional land acquisition methods to erode. This has been particularly true in the land inheritance systems of Malawi, Ghana, and Indonesia, where matrilineal customs have given way in part to patrilineal systems, gifts, or outright sales of land. More private-type farming systems, such as formal leasehold or freehold tenure, are increasing in some places (for example, Malawi) but generally remain a minute proportion of total farming area.

We have clear evidence that agroforestry systems desired by smallholder farmers in our sites are significantly more labor-intensive than shifting cultivation. Thus, the shift from the latter to the former with population growth is consistent with the prediction of the evolutionary view of farming systems proposed by Boserup (1965). Such a shift generally requires investment, but Boserup does not analyze how to provide appropriate investment incentives. The fact that investment in tree planting confers strong individual land rights implies that communal land tenure institutions have built-in rules to ensure the intensification of land use in areas where agroforestry has a comparative advantage. Whether similar incentive-enhancing rules exist in other farming areas, where investments in land improvement, such as irrigation and terracing, have high payoffs, is a critically important issue to be analyzed in future studies. Unless such rules exist, Boserupian theory will never be complete.

Much less institutional innovation has occurred within communal tenure systems with regard to forest and woodland management (for example, in

Ghana, Malawi, Uganda, and Indonesia). Our studies found that forests and woodlands continue to be managed as virtual open-access resources, with the exception of a few very small areas managed as common property (for example, the Village Forest Areas in Malawi). The reasons for lack of institutions to preserve and manage woodlands are diverse, ranging from heavy pressure for conversion by villagers, to low valuation of woodland resources, to greed on the part of some traditional authorities. On a more encouraging note, many state forests in Nepal, which used to be largely open access, have devolved to community management and are now thriving under common property management (Chapters 8 and 9). The reasons for these successes are detailed later in this chapter.

Land Tenure and Deforestation

Communal Ownership

In our observation, uncultivated forest area under communal tenure systems is generally open access, at least for members of the community. In Ghana, Uganda, Malawi, and Sumatra we repeatedly found that although the village chief is a custodian of the communal forests, he easily allows villagers to clear the forest for cultivation. In Ghana we even found some cases in which village members reported the clearance of communal forest to the chief *after* clearance was completed, in order to "register" their ownership. It appears that the major responsibilities of the village chief are to approve the clearance of forest and woodland and to record the land ownership so as to avoid possible land disputes in the future. Few woodlands or forests were conserved by traditional authorities largely because of demand for cropland from an increasing number of villagers. This demand arose partly as a result of poor markets for forest and food products, which meant that little income could be earned from forest products and those products that were harvested could not be easily traded for food.

Although it is difficult to prove rigorously that primary forest has been operating under open access over an extended period of time, there is no question that with population growth forest area has easily been cleared under communal ownership regimes. As shown in Table 10.1, in Uganda and Malawi the proportion of agricultural land increased substantially over the past few decades at the expense of forest and woodland, according to the analysis of aerial photographs at the community level (Chapters 5 and 6). Now, apart from the sparsely populated areas, only a small area of forest and woodland remains in these countries. Furthermore, through household analyses in Ghana and Indonesia, we found that cultivable primary forests have largely disappeared in recent years owing to clearance on a first-come basis. Evidence also suggests that remaining forests are largely concentrated in areas quite remote from roads and urban centers.

TABLE 10.1 Changes in land use in Uganda, Malawi, and Vietnam

Land Use	Uganda[a] 1960	Uganda[a] 1995	Malawi[b] 1971	Malawi[b] 1995	Vietnam[c] 1978	Vietnam[c] 1987	Vietnam[c] 1994
			(percentage)				
Agriculture	57	70	52	68	48	69	76
Forest and woodland	32	20	34	19	52	31	24
Others	11	10	14	14	—	—	—

[a]Average of 64 parishes in east-central region.

[b]Average of 57 enumeration areas throughout the country.

[c]Average of formerly forest areas with slope greater than 24 degrees in 56 communes in 2 northern provinces.

As indicated in Table 10.2, the significant factor accounting for the decrease in forests and woodland in Uganda and Malawi is population pressure, measured by population density and population growth. Similarly, from a household study in Sumatra, it is found that reduction in inherited land, due primarily to the increased number of family members relative to family-owned land, resulted in greater clearance of forestland.

In both Malawi and Uganda, we found that population pressure is not related to tree cover density within agricultural and nonagricultural lands. This provides support for the argument that deforestation is related principally to the demand for agricultural land rather than local energy demands, in which case one would have expected to find a thinning of tree cover in areas with high pop-

TABLE 10.2 Major determinants of conversion of land to agriculture

	Uganda	Malawi	Ghana	Sumatra	Vietnam
Population pressure	++	++	0	++[a]	++[b]
Land tenure institution	+[c]	+[d]	+[e]	0	++[f]
Distance to road or town	++	0	++	n.a.	+
Age of household head	n.a.	n.a.	++	+	n.a.

NOTE: ++ sign indicates highly significant and positive effect, + indicates significant and positive effect, and 0 denotes the absence of significant effect. "n.a." refers to "not applicable."

[a]Effects of reduction in inherited land area.

[b]Effects of population growth and rice production per capita during the prereform period (1978–87).

[c]Positive effect of communal ownership compared with private and state ownership.

[d]Positive effect of patrilineal inheritance compared with matrilineal inheritance.

[e]Positive effect of migrants, who are generally subject to patrilineal inheritance.

[f]Judged from the structural difference between strict state ownership and more privatized ownership systems.

ulation pressure. In the case of Uganda, because of relatively high tree planting and preservation on farms, tree cover densities are relatively similar in agricultural and nonagricultural land. Therefore, the conversion effect of population pressure had no major impact on overall tree cover. However, we wish to stress that the composition of tree species had changed considerably, and undoubtedly some of the functions provided by the forest trees have not been replaced by planted trees. Malawi is quite a different case, and conversion from woodland into agriculture entails a significant loss in aggregate tree cover because relatively few trees are found on agricultural land.

In Uganda, where patrilineal inheritance systems prevail, the speed of expansion of agricultural land was faster under communal ownership than private ownership, suggesting that protection of woodlands has been less strictly enforced under communal ownership (see Table 10.2 and Chapter 6). An important factor affecting deforestation is the conventional rule of communal land tenure honoring those who clear forestland with land ownership rights. There is also strong evidence from the case studies of Ghana and Sumatra (Chapters 3 and 4) that those who have cleared village forestland are granted strong individual rights. This accrual of strong individual land rights will explain, at least partly, why the conversion of woodland has been faster under communal than private ownership in Uganda.

To conclude, there is no built-in mechanism within communal ownership systems to protect forest area and forest resources. Thus, forests and woodlands have been converted to agricultural land to feed the growing number of household members. Halting this trend will not be simple. In the policy implications discussed later in the chapter, we suggest that a multifaceted strategy of institutional change, technology promotion, and market development is required.

Other Ownership Systems

Strictly speaking, woodland in Malawi, called *miombo* woodland, may be considered common property from which community members collect firewood, poles, and other nontimber products and graze cattle. According to our informal interviews with village chiefs, only dead and dry branches are allowed to be collected for use as firewood. No one may cut live trees and branches or sell firewood at the market under existing management rules. If only dead and dry branches are collected from communal woodland, its sustainable management is assured, so long as grazing is regulated, thus reducing damage to young seedlings and wildings. In practice, however, woodlands have rapidly degraded, and some have disappeared as a result of tree cutting for home use, sale in urban centers, and the use of trees for drying tobacco in the south and central regions of Malawi. One exception is the Village Forest Areas, which are formally demarcated and actively managed as common property; but to date they are few in number and very small in size, and management rules emphasize strict conservation over sustainable use.

Forests and woodlands are owned by the state in Vietnam and Nepal. The proportion of bare land or denuded forestland, which is used for shifting cultivation, increased by 21 percentage points from 1978 to 1987 in northern Vietnam mainly because of food shortages (Table 10.1). In our observation, forest area has essentially been open access with no regulation by the state. After long-term leases (50 years) were granted to individual farmers on a voluntary basis in the early 1990s, not only has the pace of deforestation declined, but farmers' initiatives (rather than government-sponsored projects) have led to the planting of timber and fruit trees and the regeneration of forests by protection. This has resulted in clear recovery of forest conditions in recent years (Chapter 7).

It is also important to observe that management of forests by user groups or under common property regimes did not spontaneously develop in Vietnam, even though Vietnamese communities have a long tradition of communal irrigation and other collective activities. As we argue, community management of forests is effective when the predominant forest products are minor products, such as firewood, grasses, and fodder. In our mountainous sites in Vietnam, these minor forest products are amply available, even though massive deforestation has taken place.

In Nepal, forests were nationalized in 1957, and deforestation followed. Whether deforestation would have been prevented significantly if forests had not been nationalized is a difficult question to answer. Yet it is true that deforestation was followed by reforestation with the recent establishment of forest user groups, particularly formal groups that received formal use rights of forests from the state (Chapters 8 and 9). However, few formal user groups changed their management rules when official use rights were granted. A more important factor was that among the long-established informal user groups, those that were active and effective tend to have been transformed into formal user groups as of now. Therefore, the significant effect of formal user group management is likely to reflect, at least in part, the self-selection effect rather than incentive-enhancing effect of establishing land use rights for forest user groups.

Unique to the case of the hill region of Nepal is the absence of expansion of agricultural land. In fact, deforestation primarily took the form of removing and thinning the density of forests. As is explained later, this would be due to the critical importance of minor forest products such as firewood, grasses, and leaf fodder for the livelihood of subsistence farmers. The value of these products is clearly perceived by the farming population, which prevented the encroachment on the forestland.

To sum up, our case studies demonstrate that forests are not well protected under the state ownership system. In fact, primary forests have largely disappeared in areas owned by the state. It must also be pointed out that common property regimes are not always viable for preserving forests and woodlands, judging from the experience of Malawi.

Management of Common Property Forests

Whether the management of forests and other natural resources under common property regimes is an efficient institutional arrangement has been widely debated in the literature. Yet empirical evidence is deplorably weak. The issue has very practical implications, as tree-planting projects supported by international organizations and aid agencies include social forestry or community forestry projects that follow the principles of equal participation and equal sharing of benefits. The same principles have been adopted by many voluntarily established community forest management institutions in the hill forests of Nepal (Chapter 8) and were found in community forests in prewar Japan (McKean 1992). In order to assess the management efficiency of common property forests, this study conducted an analysis of common property forests in the hill and inner Tarai regions of Nepal and mountainous parts of Japan, aside from the case of Malawi mentioned earlier.

Formal user group management of forests in Nepal has been successful in reducing the amount of extraction of dead and dry branches for firewood, preventing the cutting of green branches and felling of trees, and preventing cattle grazing (Chapter 8). On the other hand, informal user group management, which generally stipulates fewer rules and enforces them less strictly, has had no appreciable impact on forest conditions, even compared with the cases of no user group management or open access. This is partly due to the fact that informal user groups were newly formed with the main intention of fulfilling the government requirement to acquire the status of formal user group with official use rights.

Management rules have tended to strengthen as scarcity of forest and tree resources have increased over time (Chapter 8). It is certainly costly to organize collective action, set up management rules, and enforce them. Thus, forest user groups tend to be formed spontaneously when the scarcity of forest resources reaches a threshold level warranting the initiation of user group management. Evidence from Nepal suggests that once management rules are rigorously formulated, they tend to be obeyed by the user group members.

At least two fundamental factors explain the success of common property forest management in the hill region of Nepal. First, subsistence farming and livelihood critically depend on the availability of forest and tree resources, such as firewood, grasses, and leaf fodder. The transportation network is poorly developed, and access to markets that provide alternative sources of energy and soil nutrients is very poor in most communities in the hill region. Furthermore, the large and continuous application of compost is essential to sustain upland farming in terraced fields on steep slopes. Thus, the degradation of community forests immediately and significantly jeopardizes the livelihood of the farming population. This implies that there are potentially strong incentives for farmers to cooperate in the protection and management of forest resources.

In contrast, *miombo* woodlands in Malawi are located in relatively flat areas, and the access to markets is much more favorable. This seems to explain partly why the management of *miombo* woodland has been much less successful. In fact, the management of common property forest has not been successful in flat areas of contemporary Nepal or in prewar Japan. Hilly and mountainous topography also tends to favor the development of common property resources in that it gives rise to natural externalities (for example, movements of soil and water).

Second, it is important to recognize that the types of forest resources successfully protected by communities are minor forest products, products that are of relatively low value, whose value responds very little to improved management, and whose cost of protection would be extremely high if they were owned individually. It will be less costly to protect those resources communally by hiring a selected number of guards or adopting a rotational system of patrolling among community members than by hiring guards individually. In other words, we argue that the advantage of community management rests on the economies of scale in protection activities, for which supportive evidence is presented in the case of the hill region of Nepal (Chapter 8).

The cost of protection of forest resources by private owners is much larger than under community management if minor forest products prevail, because, unlike timber, it is easy to cut small trees and branches and haul them from forests without being identified by village people. There is, therefore, no question that it is less costly to protect timber than such minor forest products as firewood and grasses. It is also important to realize that timber production, to be successful, requires silvicultural activities such as weeding, pruning, thinning, and singling. Like the case of collective farming in socialist economies, each farmer has little incentive to carry out these activities so long as benefits are shared more or less equally among community members.

These considerations led us to examine the case of community forest management in postwar Japan, where forests have been converted from those with miscellaneous broad-leaf trees to timber forests. We found that timber trees have been more actively planted and managed on individually managed portions of community forests than those managed collectively (Chapter 9). The emerging conclusion is that the individualized management system is more efficient than the community management system in the case of timber forests in Japan.

This conclusion, however, does not necessarily hold in developing countries, where, unlike postwar Japan, there are competing uses of land areas such that overgrazing of livestock and excessive collection of firewood are major threats to the sustainable management of forests. In fact, one of the reasons for the higher cost of protecting timber plantations under private ownership in the inner Tarai is the cost of building fences and employing private watchers. For example, cattle and goats eat and trample young seedlings. In order to protect a timber forest, collective management with regulated use of forest resources and mutual supervision will be more cost-effective. In order to carry out management activities, however, the individualized system is more efficient. In our view, the best management system, therefore, is a combination of the two in which protection is carried out by participation of all community members and management activities are carried out under individualized management incentives. Such cases are found in the inner Tarai region, in which management of trees is carried out by labor hired by a central management committee. In this system, the community members agree to follow regulations on grazing and firewood collection and receive the privilege of purchasing firewood and timber at prices much lower than market prices. The proceeds of forest management are used partly for infrastructure development for the benefits of community members at large and allocated partly to the members of user group committee. This system proved to be superior to the conventional collective management in the case of timber forests (Chapter 9). It is also important to point out that the possibility of selling harvested timber to markets is the prerequisite for the efficient management of timber forests, as it enhances profit incentives.

A potential problem of such centralized management systems lies in the strong power of the user group committee, which can result in inequitable distribution of benefits obtained from forest resources between user group committee members and other community members. Since there is no reason to assume the existence of large-scale economies in the management activities of timber forests, other than protection, more equitable distribution of benefits can be achieved without sacrificing efficiency by granting tree ownership rights equally to individual community members.

We conclude that common property forest management can work when the predominant forest products are minor forest products for which exclusion of use is difficult. When products are valuable and depend on management, such as timber, the private tenure system is best in the absence of pressure on the resource from other users; otherwise the combination of collective management for protection and individualized or centralized management for management of trees is most efficient.

Communal Land Tenure and Development of Agroforestry

As we have argued, the single major cause for deforestation in our study sites is the expansion of farm areas for growing food and other crops. Those cultivators belong mainly to the poorest segment of society, and large forest areas have already been cleared and occupied by them. Such land is often marginal for agriculture, and some may be highly sloping. Unless decent work opportunities are made available, it is practically impossible to relocate these cultivators to restore forest conditions. It will be more socially desirable to promote agroforestry systems to mimic many of the forest ecological functions and to provide income-earning opportunities for the rural population. Many of the trees farmers plant, such as commercial trees, pole trees, fruits, and nitrogen-fixing trees, provide positive environmental externalities such as carbon sequestration and increased flora biodiversity. In marginal areas tree farming is usually more sustainable and can be more efficient than pure food crop enterprises.

It is widely believed, however, that because of weak individual land rights or tenure insecurity, trees are not planted and well managed under communal ownership in which the extended family often has influence over use rights in cultivated land (for example, Johnson 1972; Besley 1995). If this is indeed the case, it will be difficult to disseminate agroforestry in marginal areas even though agroforestry has a comparative advantage over food production under shifting cultivation. If the communal tenure institutions provide sufficient incentives to plant and manage trees, however, the enhanced efficiency of land use can reduce the incidence of poverty in marginal areas. Furthermore, the establishment of agroforesty on sloping land will help reduce soil erosion and contribute to the partial restoration of tree biomass and biodiversity. This is reported to be the case in coffee and shade tree systems in our Uganda sites, cocoa fields with big shade trees in Ghana (Gockowski, Nkamleu, and Wendt 2001), and in the so-called jungle rubber forest mixed with nonrubber trees in Indonesia (Tomich et al. 2001).

In matrilineal communities of Sumatra, cultivated land was traditionally owned by lineage members consisting typically of three generations descended from the same grandmother. Gradually, joint ownership by sisters became common. As is shown in Table 10.3, however, agroforestry plots are more likely to be bequeathed from mother to individual families of daughters and even to those of sons at present (Chapter 4). Private ownership acquired through land market transactions and forest clearance is also common. An important observation is that individual land rights are stronger under the single-family ownership than the collective ownership. Inheritance by sons increases their incentives to carry out forest clearance and tree planting. In this way, the inheritance system in Sumatra has been evolving toward a more egalitarian system in terms of gender differentiation. The stronger land rights under the single family ownership also promoted land market transactions.

In indigenous villages in Ghana, uterine matrilineal inheritance has been practiced whereby land is bequeathed from the deceased man to his nephew. Although those who clear forests are granted strong land rights, the cleared land eventually becomes the property of the extended family and may be temporarily allocated to those family members in need of land or bequeathed in accordance with the traditional rule. As is demonstrated in Table 10.4, individual land rights on these family-owned plots in indigenous villages are very weak. The individual rights of inherited land in migrant villages are much stronger;

TABLE 10.3 Distribution of area under different land tenure institutions and the index of land rights on agroforestry plots in Sumatra

	Lineage Ownership	Joint Family Ownership	Single Family Ownership	Private Ownership	
				Purchase	Forest Clearance
Distribution of area (percentage)					
High region	3	5	42	10	37
Middle region	5	2	62	14	19
Low region	0	3	46	12	39
Index of land rights[a]					
High region	0.0	0.6	1.6–2.0[b]	3.1	
Middle region	0.8	0.9	1.9–2.9	3.8	
Low region	0.0	1.0	1.9–2.8	3.8	

[a]The following four rights are considered: rights to rent out under share tenancy, rent out under leasehold tenancy, pawn, and sell. Numbers refer to the average number of rights without obtaining approval of family and/or lineage members.

[b]The first number refers to the case of single family ownership of daughters, whereas the second number corresponds to the case of single family ownership of daughters and sons.

TABLE 10.4 Distribution of area under different land tenure institutions and the index of land rights on cocoa plots in western Ghana

	Temporarily Allocated Family Land	Inherited Family Land	Acquired Village Forest Land	Gift	Others
Distribution of area (percentage)					
Indigenous villages	22	13	19	33	13
Migrant villages	9	18	22	26	26
Index of land rights[a]					
Indigenous villages	0.3	1.1[b]	3.0	4.9	—
Migrant villages	0.2	3.3[c]	3.9	5.3	—

[a]The following six rights are considered: the rights to plant trees; rent out; pawn; bequeath; give; and sell. Numbers refer to the average number of rights without obtaining approval of family members or village chief.

[b]The number pertains to the practice among matrilineal Akan people.

[c]The number pertains to the practice among patrilineal non-Akan people.

since patrilineal inheritance has been practiced in these villages, individualization was facilitated by the fact that only a small number of family members (typically a father and his sons) are involved in the inheritance decision. It is important to observe that the share of allocated and inherited land is relatively low now. Instead, plots planted with trees are often transferred to spouse and children as inter vivos gifts with the permission of members of the extended family (Chapter 3). The transfer to spouse and children represents a reward to their work effort to plant and manage cocoa trees. Although the proportion of women's land accounts for 20 percent or so in indigenous villages as of now, the inheritance system has been evolving spontaneously in favor of wives and daughters in western Ghana.

As is summarized in Table 10.5, we did not obtain any strong evidence to support the validity of popular arguments that customary land tenure systems in Uganda, Ghana, and Sumatra hinder investment: commercial trees have been planted under communal ownership systems as widely and actively as under private ownership systems (Chapters 3, 4, and 6). We observed this in part because land rights have become highly individualized owing to investment in trees and continuous cultivation by farmers driven by high population pressure. Even where land rights are relatively weak, the effort to plant trees is rewarded by strengthened individual land rights.

Given the positive and significant effect of tree planting on individual land rights, it is no wonder that sufficiently strong incentives to plant commercial

TABLE 10.5 Effects of land tenure institutions, farm size, and gender composition of family members on the intensity of tree planting and profit of agroforestry

	Tree Planting			Profit per Hectare		
	Land Tenure[a]	Farm Size	Gender Composition	Land Tenure	Farm Size	Gender Composition
Uganda	0	–	n.a.	0	0	n.a.
Malawi[b]	+	0	0	n.a.	n.a.	n.a.
Ghana	0[c]	n.a.	0	0	n.a.	0
Sumatra	0	0	+[d]	0	0	0

SOURCE: Intensive household survey data.

NOTE: + indicates significant and positive effect, 0 denotes the absence of significant effect, and – indicates significant and negative effect. "n.a." refers to either "not applicable" or "not analyzed." Data refer to commercial tree planting except in Malawi.

[a]+ indicates that greater tenure security leads to the greater incidence of tree planting and profit.

[b]Tree planting refers to timber and fruit trees, but profits of tree systems were not analyzed.

[c]There are a few significant variables.

[d]Male and female members have positive and negative effects, respectively.

trees exist under the communal ownership system. Once trees are planted, the land ownership system is converted to de facto private ownership within a community. Thus, as verified by our profit function results, the management efficiency of commercial tree fields under the communal system is generally comparable to other ownership systems. In other words, communal systems evolve toward individualized systems and do not impede the development of agroforestry.

It is important to point out that the institutional rule to grant strong individual land rights on fields planted with trees has been established in communities where agroforestry is more profitable than other cropping systems. Since most areas of Malawi are characterized by flat topography and adequate rainfall for food production, traditionally known agroforestry does not have an inherent comparative advantage compared with maize and tobacco production. Adding to this the effect of government policies that raised the profits of cereals over forest products, we observed that no institutional rule has emerged that grants strong individual land rights in return for tree planting. As a result, current land rights affect the decision to plant trees in crop fields in Malawi, as is shown in Table 10.5 (see also Chapter 5).

In sum, communal land tenure institutions in no way deter the development of profitable agroforestry, irrespective of the levels of tenure security in these systems, because of the expected increase in land rights after tree planting. Furthermore, incentives for establishing and managing agroforestry systems are strong in more marginal areas and on fragile hillsides, where the benefits of alternative cropping systems are low (for example, with low external inputs) or highly risky (for example, with high external inputs).

Land Tenure and Cropland Management

Land tenure rules affect expected future benefits accruing to those who invest in land improvement, including tree planting. Therefore, these rules affect long-term but not short-term management incentives. In support of this, we found that land tenure institutions did not have any impact on production efficiency of food crop fields in Ghana (Chapter 3) and paddy fields in Sumatra (Chapter 4), neither of which require much investment. The same point applies to the farming of maize in Malawi, for which we did not observe any difference in management efficiency between patrilineal and matrilineal inheritance systems, despite greater security of tenure for male household heads under the former (Chapter 5).

We observed, however, some differences in management efficiency of annual crop production under different land tenure institutions. First, farmers subject to patrilineal inheritance have introduced more profitable burley tobacco farming more quickly and more widely than those subject to matrilineal inheritance, after abolishment of the policy to prohibit burley tobacco production by smallholders in Malawi. Because it was a new crop, investment in the acquisition of relevant new farming knowledge was required for tobacco production. However, the adoption of new technology does not confer strong individual land rights, and hence those who are subject to tenure insecurity under the matrilineal inheritance tend to adopt the new crop less actively.

Second, we found that cropland owned by the extended family that was temporarily allocated under the communal ownership is less frequently fallowed than inherited land and other land tenure categories with stronger individual rights in Ghana (Chapter 3). Similarly, cropland in customary areas is less frequently fallowed than in areas with stronger individual land rights in Uganda (Chapter 6). Land use rights are fairly well established under communal ownership so long as land is continuously used for cultivation. Once it is put into fallow, however, individual rights are substantially weakened. Thus, the less frequent fallow under the communal ownership can be explained by the weaker tenure security, which forces farmers to continue to cultivate the land to secure use rights.

Thus, although customary land tenure institutions are not significantly inefficient for the management of tree-based farm enterprises, they are likely to be inefficient in the management of crop fields under shifting cultivation. According to the accumulated empirical evidence from Sub-Saharan Africa, however, land tenure institutions do not seem to affect significantly the productivity of sedentary farming, in which organic and inorganic fertilizers have more effectively substituted for fallowing (Place and Hazell 1993). A plausible hypothesis seems to be that like tree planting, investment in land improvement, such as terracing and destumping, as well as continuous cultivation strengthen one's land rights when such investments are highly profitable.

Property Rights Institutions and Equity

Several different aspects of equity are important to consider. The first is the contribution of property rights institutions to equity in land asset distribution across households within a village. We found that generally communal tenure systems distributed land fairly equitably across households. In land-abundant situations, this was accomplished primarily through land clearing and inheritance acquisition methods. As forestland and woodland become scarce, however, inequity in the distribution of land may emerge. Inequitable distribution can be exacerbated by the "market" transaction of land, which is made possible by the individualization of land rights. Thus, the wealthy members of the community tend to accumulate land by the purchase of cultivable land and the acquisition of forestland, as in the case of Sumatra. Interestingly, however, the development of land rental markets through the privatization of communal systems has led to significantly greater equity, counteracting the trend of inequitable land distribution under communal ownership. Renting of land is done mainly by households with poor access to inherited land and by migrants in both Ghana and Sumatra.

We encountered a large private tenure system in Malawi (Chapter 5) and the *mailo* tenure system in Uganda (Chapter 6), which because of inappropriate and conflicting state intervention are characterized by large maldistribution of land. Because of the absence of scale economies in most production systems, the maldistribution of land generally leads to inefficiencies in production and inequality in welfare.

Under effective common property management systems in Nepal and Japan, households typically enjoy equal opportunity to contribute to and benefit from the management of resources. There are normally effective rules over resource uses that prevent the wealthier households from benefiting disproportionately. In contrast, forest and woodland resources have been open access under communal and state tenure systems. Such systems could also improve equity if the opportunity costs of the wealthy are high enough to discourage them from extracting resources. On the other hand, there are no effective rules to prevent wealthy individuals from excessive harvesting of valuable products, such as timber and pole trees (for example, the extraction of trees for drying tobacco in Malawi).

A second type of equity to consider, which is on a more regional scale, is equity between access to land by different communities. In this context, communal tenure systems have performed quite well, at least in our study sites; migrants from land-scarce communities have been accommodated in the relatively land-abundant areas. In the case of Ghana, this is often through purchase of land and formal sharecropping contracts, which may later be converted into ownership. In Malawi, it is mainly through allocation of land by a chief. In Uganda, the major acquisition mechanism for migrants has been through outright purchase from a local family.

Finally, and most important, agroforestry systems, promoted in the private and communal tenure institutions, have a positive indirect effect on equity. This is because agroforestry is more favorable and profitable in marginal areas where there are relatively high levels of poverty, so that systems that encourage their development also make a contribution to reducing the welfare gap between the relatively wealthy and poor rural population.

Policy Implications

In this section we highlight the key policy implications from our studies for improving the efficiency of natural resource management while at the same time recognizing the importance of equity. This section is divided into three parts, the first focusing on property rights arrangements for both agricultural and nonagricultural land, the second on the development and dissemination of agricultural and agroforestry technologies, and the last on market development and other issues. We feel that all three areas must be addressed to improve natural resource management efficiency.

Property Rights Institutions and Arrangements

AGRICULTURAL LAND.   Property rights institutions are largely favorable or moving in the right direction to provide proper incentives for efficient natural resource management. It is particularly encouraging that tree planting is facilitated in the different customary systems because with the reduction in forest and woodland, there is an increased need for tree products to be produced on agricultural land. There are a few noteworthy exceptions and areas for improvement, however. First, some traditional tenure arrangements, for example, customary tenure in Uganda and matrilineal land tenure in Malawi, appear to provide suboptimal incentives for some types of agricultural investment, though not for short-term inputs. However, these systems have been found to be evolving toward greater individualization, and we believe that indirect policies, such as the promotion of profitable agricultural opportunities and encouragement of more efficient markets, will be effective in hastening this evolution.

Second, we continue to observe that, despite some positive developments, women have inferior rights to resources while at the same time are expected to be the primary users and managers of the resources. Unfortunately, this study was neither designed nor able to address this issue clearly. Although it seems reasonable that improved management will take place when there is a closer match between those who control and those who use resources (for example, women may plant more trees for fuelwood than men), direct intervention in gender-based property rights policy has proved to be extremely difficult.

One final observation concerns the emergence of more formal private tenure systems. We found that in Uganda and Malawi, households are legally entitled to convert their tenure from customary systems to private through the acquisition of a leasehold with the state. To date, very few households in customary lands have opted for this, and those that have are generally the more elite. There is no doubt that the demand for leasehold is rather low. Nonetheless, one should expect that the twin forces of commercialization and individualization of land rights will lead to a more widespread demand for titling over time by smallholder farmers. Although many titling programs have failed largely owing to prematurity of implementation, they have been found to be popular and sustainable in areas of high market and property rights development such as central Kenya (Migot-Adholla, Place, and Oluoch-Kosura, 1993). We believe that land titling programs will become feasible once communal land tenure institutions have become sufficiently individualized. If land is collectively owned, land titling programs aiming at the establishment of private rights will create conflicts among family members, thereby leading to tenure insecurity rather than security.

FORESTS AND TREE PLANTATIONS.   In contrast to the case of agricultural land, there are ample opportunities for changes in property rights institutions to improve the efficiency of forest and woodland management. The most ineffective and often inappropriate land ownership system is state ownership. This is evidenced by enhanced forest management effort in Vietnam when the use rights of state forests have been transferred to individual farmers. Except for the protection of biodiversity or other uniquely national objectives, the ownership of forests by the state is highly questionable. Communal tenure systems in all the study sites have also largely been unable to prevent massive conversion and degradation of forest and woodland resources. Common property arrangements have been relatively more successful, and many examples are found in Nepal and Japan. To date, governments have invested relatively heavily in agricultural technology development to raise the profitability of agriculture while leaving much of the institutional development to nongovernmental organizations. Certainly, much more effort is needed in developing or strengthening local institutions to manage forest resources better.

It must be clearly recognized that a common property forest regime is effective when predominant forest resources are minor forest products, whereas high-value tree production is less amenable to community management. Thus, the incentive system under social forestry projects needs to be redesigned. In particular, the system of equal benefit sharing should be replaced by systems that provide appropriate incentives to individual farmers to manage timber trees and other valuable products, for example, granting complete tree ownership rights to individual community members. The element of community management, however, should be maintained for protection of trees. It is also important to provide profit incentives to grow and manage timber trees by promoting marketing of harvested trees.

Development and Dissemination of Agricultural and Agroforestry Technologies

A major policy implication is that given the existence of strong incentives to manage agroforestry plots on sloping lands under the communal ownership, it makes sense to develop and disseminate profitable agroforestry systems, through such means as the development of improved germplasm of commercial trees, improving techniques for propagating useful tree germplasm, improving the flow of information on these new technologies, and, finally, providing proper incentives for germplasm delivery systems to develop. To date, however, research and development on agroforestry technologies, particularly on commercial trees, have been grossly inadequate relative to more traditional annual crops.

In addition, there are wide areas of barren land, which used to be planted to coffee, cocoa, and other tree crops, for which research on sustainable tree management needs to be carried out. The establishment of profitable agroforestry systems will contribute significantly to the reduction of poverty by enhancing the efficiency of farming in poverty-stricken marginal areas. It will also contribute to the prevention of soil erosion and the creation of tree biomass. Moreover, profitable agroforestry can help to strengthen individual land rights where they are weak. Thus, the development of agroforestry is expected to be conducive to both efficiency and equity from both the private and social viewpoints.

To prevent excessive degradation of natural resources, however, it is also necessary to reduce the flow of migrants to marginal areas containing the remaining forests and woodlands. Focusing only on technologies for the marginal areas may attract more migrants. Thus, technology development and transfer need to be strengthened in the more favorable, but highly populated, source areas of migration. Specialized food production may well have a comparative advantage in these areas, and this could be facilitated by improved varieties coupled with access to credit and fertilizer inputs, as was realized in Asia during the Green Revolution (David and Otsuka 1994; Otsuka 2000).

The small areas of uncultivated but arable land that remain will continue to face strong pressure from rural populations seeking agricultural land. Where agriculture is the dominant land use, it will be called on to produce many of the basic forest and woodland products and services formerly obtained from outside the farm. The remaining forests and woodlands should therefore be used strategically for products and services that are demanded by villagers or society but that cannot be efficiently produced on agricultural land or be substituted for with purchases from the market. For example, it is wasteful for communities or governments to set aside land for the growing of building poles, which are more efficiently grown by farmers. Instead, forestry efforts may be concentrated on the production of public goods such as biodiversity.

Market Development and Other Policy Issues

Market development is critical to generate the degree of intensification required to enable rural people to uplift themselves from poverty without mining their surrounding resources. Increased expenditure for rural road construction is a key component of such development. This point is well understood by policymakers. It must be also clearly understood that although the development of roads may accelerate deforestation by enhancing the profitability of timber harvesting, it will also accelerate the development of agroforestry and timber plantations where primary forests have already been cleared. Further, product market development is found to foster factor market development and will increase the demand for individualization of land rights. Thus, we argue that this is a vital strategy in improving natural resource management.

Our findings also strongly show that reducing population growth rates would help to mitigate against deforestation. Most countries are working to reduce population growth rates through improved family planning. However, the effects of these will only be long term; one can still expect a large number of new families to demand land in the next few decades. As indicated earlier, in the short term, governments should work more closely to strengthen local institutions so that they can more effectively respond to increased population, especially where in-migration is significant. In the longer run, the effect of population growth on forest and woodland resources can be greatly alleviated by increasing employment opportunities in the nonagricultural sector.

According to the results from our study sites, there is much less reason to focus on other policy areas. For example, little deforestation was found to be linked to timber trade and logging, except in state-owned areas. Thus, changes in export regulations and exchange rates would not have made much difference (such policy changes may have affected tree cover on agricultural land, however). Similarly, we have not found that local rural demand for fuelwood and other wood products has played a key role in depleting the remaining woodlands, except in such land-scarce economies as Nepal. Therefore, energy policy reform is equally not likely to have a sizable impact on resource degradation in most of our study sites. However, in areas where urban demand for fuelwood and charcoal is unusually high, there may be scope for energy policy change, even though our study did not attempt to quantify the rural-urban links.

Summary of Policy Implications

The problems of deforestation and land management are intertwined with the problems of poverty and food security in rural areas. There is no single-faceted or uniform approach to policy that can successfully address this complex problem. Thus, solutions will similarly need to be multifaceted, involving efforts to raise the profitability of agriculturally based rural livelihoods through technology development and market improvement and to strengthen natural resource management institutions. This approach strives to optimize private efficiency and hence growth out of poverty, while at the same time providing a better environment for socially more desirable solutions.

References

Besley, Timothy. 1995. Property rights and investment incentives. *Journal of Political Economy* 103 (5): 903–937.

Boserup, Ester. 1965. *Conditions of agricultural change.* Chicago: Aldine.

David, Cristina C., and Keijiro Otsuka. 1994. *Modern rice technology and income distribution in Asia.* Boulder, Colo.: Lynne Rienner.

Gockowski, James, Blaise Nkamleu, and John Wendt. 2001. Implications of resource use intensification for the environment and sustainable technology systems in the central African rainforest. In *Tradeoffs or synergies? Agricultural intensification, economic development, and the environment,* ed. D. R. Lee and C. Barrett. Wallingford, U.K.: CAB International.

Johnson, O. E. G. 1972. Economic analysis, the legal framework, and land tenure systems. *Journal of Law and Economics* 15 (1): 259–276.

McKean, Margaret A. 1992. Management of traditional common lands (*Iriaichi*) in Japan. In *Making the commons work: Theory, practice, and policy,* ed. D. W. Bromley. San Francisco: ICS Press.

McKean, Margaret, and Elinor Ostrom. 1995. Common property regimes in the forest: Just a relic from the past? *Unasylva* 46 (180): 3–15.

Migot-Adholla, Shem E., Frank Place, and W. Oluoch-Kosura. 1994. Security of tenure and land productivity in Kenya. In *Searching for land tenure security in Africa,* ed. John W. Bruce and Shem E. Migot-Adholla. Dubuque, Iowa: Kendall/Hunt.

Otsuka, K. 2000. Role of agricultural research in poverty reduction: Lessons from Asian experience. *Food Policy* 25 (4): 447–462.

Place, Frank, and Peter Hazell. 1993. Productivity effects of indigenous land tenure in Sub-Saharan Africa. *American Journal of Agricultural Economics* 75 (1): 10–19.

Tomich, Thomas P., Meine van Noordwijk, Suseno Budidarsono, Andy Gillison, Trikurniati Kusumanto, Daniel Murdiyarso, Fred Stolle, and Ahmad M. Fagi. 2001. Agricultural intensification, deforestation, and the environment: Assessing tradeoffs in Sumatra, Indonesia. In *Tradeoffs or synergies? Agricultural intensification, economic development, and the environment,* ed. D. R. Lee and C. Barrett. Wallingford, U.K.: CAB International.

Contributors

J. B. Aidoo is a research fellow at the Institute of Land Management and Development, University of Science and Technology, Kumasi, Ghana, and a member of Parliament in Ghana, representing the Western Region.

Yoko Kijima, formerly a graduate student of economics at the Tokyo Metropolitan University, is now a graduate student of agricultural economics at Michigan State University, East Lansing.

Redge Masupayi is a research assistant at the Agricultural Policy Research Institute at Bunda College, Lilongwe, Malawi.

Trung M. Nguyen, formerly a research follow at the Vietnam Agricultural Science Institute, Hanoi, is now a government official at the Ministry of Agricultural and Rural Development, Hanoi.

Keijiro Otsuka, formerly a professor of economics at the Tokyo Metropolitan University, is a professorial fellow at the Foundation for Advanced Studies on International Development, Tokyo, and a visiting research fellow at the International Food Policy Research Institute, Washington, D.C.

Ellen Payongayong is a research analyst in the Food Consumption and Nutrition Division of the International Food Policy Research Institute, Washington, D.C.

Frank Place is an economist at the International Centre for Research in Agroforestry, Nairobi, Kenya.

Ridish Pokharel, formerly an associate professor of community forestry at the Institute of Forestry, Tribhuvan University, Nepal, is now a graduate student of agriculture and natural resources at Michigan State University, East Lansing.

379

Agnes Quisumbing is a senior research fellow at the International Food Policy Research Institute, Washington, D.C., and a visiting researcher at the School of Nutrition Science and Policy, Tufts University, Medford, Massachusetts.

Santosh Rayamajhi is an assistant professor of forestry at the Institute of Forestry, Tribhuvan University, Nepal, and was posted as sustainable development officer for UNDP-Nepal in the field of National Park and Protected Area Management during 1998–2000.

Takeshi Sakurai, formerly a senior economist at the National Research Institute of Agricultural Economics, Tokyo, is now a senior economist at the Japan International Research Center for Agricultural Sciences, Tsukuba, and currently posted at the West African Rice Development Association, Bouaké, Côte d'Ivoire.

Joe Ssenteza is an agricultural economist at the Forestry Research Institute, National Agricultural Research Organization, Kampala, Uganda.

S. Suyanto, formerly a dissertation Ph.D. fellow of economics at the Tokyo Metropolitan University, is now a postdoctoral fellow at the International Centre for Research in Agroforestry, Bogor, Indonesia.

Towa Tachibana, formerly a postdoctoral fellow at the International Food Policy Research Institute, Washington, D.C., is now an associate professor of economics at Hokkaido University, Sapporo, Japan.

Thomas P. Tomich is a principal economist at the International Centre for Research in Agroforestry (ICRAF) and Global Coordinator of the Alternatives to Slash-and-Burn Programme, based in Nairobi, Kenya. He led ICRAF's policy research from Bogor, Indonesia, during 1994–2000.

Hari K. Upadhyaya is an agricultural economist and the founder-chairman of the Center for Environmental and Agricultural Policy, Research, Extension, and Development (CEAPRED), Kathmandu, Nepal.

Index

Page numbers for entries occurring in figures are followed by an *f;* those for entries occurring in notes, by an *n;* and those for entries occurring in tables, by a *t.*